Families Count

This book is concerned with the question of how families matter in young people's development – a question of obvious interest and importance to a wide range of readers and a question with serious policy implications. A series of topics concerning families is examined by the top international scholars in the field, including the key risks affecting children; individual differences in children's resilience; links between families and children's peers; the connections between parental work and children's family lives; the impact of child care, divorce, and parental separation; grandparents; and new family forms such as lesbian- and surrogate-mother families. The latest research findings are brought together with discussion of policy issues raised.

Alison Clarke-Stewart is a psychologist whose work focuses on the effects of social environments on children's cognitive and emotional development. Since receiving her Ph.D. from Yale University in 1972, she has studied family interactions, child care, divorce and custody, and children's eyewitness testimony. She is currently a professor in the Department of Psychology and Social Behavior and Associate Dean for Research in the School of Social Ecology, University of California, Irvine. She is a Fellow of the American Psychological Association and the American Psychological Society, a member of the Society for Research in Child Development, and a Principal Investigator in the NICHD Study of Early Child Care and Youth Development. She has been a visiting scholar at the Center for Advanced Study in the Behavioral Sciences and at Wolfson College, Oxford University. She has written more than 100 articles for scholarly journals such as *Child Development* and the *American Psychologist*, and her recent books include *What We Know about Childcare* (2005) and *Divorce: Causes and Consequences* (2006).

Judy Dunn is a psychologist whose research is focused on children's social, emotional, and communicative development. She has studied children's family relationships (she pioneered research on siblings) and friendships, stepfamilies, and children's understanding of other people, with a particular interest in longitudinal naturalistic observation approaches. She began her research at Cambridge University, spent eight years in the United States, and is currently a professor at the Institute of Psychiatry in London. She is a Fellow of the British Academy and of the Academy of Medical Sciences. She has received the Society for Research in Child Development's Award for Distinguished Scientific Contribution and the American Psychological Association's G. Stanley Hall Award. She has been a visiting scholar at the Center for Advanced Study in the Behavioral Sciences at Stanford University, the Van Leer Foundation in Jerusalem, and universities in Italy. She has written scholarly articles and books, including *Children's Friendships: The Beginnings of Intimacy* (2004).

The Jacobs Foundation Series on Adolescence

Series Editor: Dieter Wolke

The Jacobs Foundation Series on Adolescence addresses the question of what can be done to promote healthy development around the world. The series views this important question from different disciplines in the social sciences. Economists and sociologists may consider how we can promote human capital over time, specifically, an individual's ability to become educated and to develop earning power; demographers and sociologists may analyze development patterns over generations; psychiatrists and psychologists may tackle the problem of how much change is possible in psychological health during the life course and over generations. Drawing from these different domains of inquiry into human development, the Jacobs Foundation Series on Adolescence examines the potential for change across generations and during the life course in three areas: (1) human capital, (2) partnership behavior, and (3) psychological health and the rearing of children. The purpose of the series is to further the goals of the Jacobs Foundation – to contribute to the welfare and social productivity of the current and future generations of young people.

Michael Rutter and Marta Tienda, eds., *Ethnicity and Causal Mechanisms*

P. Lindsey Chase-Lansdale, Kathleen Kiernan, and Ruth J. Friedman, eds., *Human Development Across Lives and Generations: The Potential for Change*

Anne-Nelly Perret-Clermont et al., eds., *Joining Society: Social Interaction and Learning in Adolescence and Youth*

Marta Tienda and William Julius Wilson, eds., *Youth in Cities: A Cross-National Perspective*

Roland Vanddenberghe and Michael Huberman, eds., *Understanding and Preventing Teacher Burnout: A Sourcebook of International Research and Practice*

Ruby Takanishi and David Hamburg, eds., *Preparing Adolescents for the Twenty-First Century*

Michael Rutter, ed., *Psycho Social Disturbances in Young People: Challenges for Prevention*

Albert Bandura, ed., *Self-Efficacy in Changing Societies*

Anne Petersen and Jeylan Mortimer, eds., *Youth Unemployment and Society*

Families Count

Effects on Child and Adolescent Development

Edited by

ALISON CLARKE-STEWART

University of California, Irvine

JUDY DUNN

Institute of Psychiatry, King's College, London

CAMBRIDGE UNIVERSITY PRESS
Cambridge, New York, Melbourne, Madrid, Cape Town, Singapore, São Paulo

Cambridge University Press
40 West 20th Street, New York, NY 10011-4211, USA

www.cambridge.org
Information on this title: www.cambridge.org/9780521847537

First published 2006

Printed in the United States of America

A catalog record for this publication is available from the British Library.

Library of Congress Cataloging in Publication Data

Families count : effects on child and adolescent development / edited by Alison
Clarke-Stewart, Judy Dunn.
    p.   cm. – (The Jacobs Foundation series on adolescence)
Includes bibliographical references and index.
ISBN-13: 978-0-521-84753-7 (hardback)
ISBN-10: 0-521-84753-2 (hardback)
ISBN-13: 978-0-521-61229-6 (pbk.)
ISBN-10: 0-521-61229-2 (pbk.)
1. Child psychology.   2. Adolescent psychology.   3. Family – Psychological aspects.
I. Clarke-Stewart, Alison, 1943–   II. Dunn, Judy, 1939–   III. Title.   IV. Series.
BF721.F355   2006
305.231–dc22   2005030035

ISBN-13   978-0-521-84753-7 hardback
ISBN-10   0-521-84753-2 hardback

ISBN-13   978-0-521-61229-6 paperback
ISBN-10   0-521-61229-2 paperback

Contents

Contributors

Paul R. Amato, Department of Sociology, Pennsylvania State University, U.S.

John E. Bates, Indiana University, U.S.

Katharina Beckh, Department of Education, Ludwig Maximilians University, Munich, Germany

Alison Clarke-Stewart, Department of Psychology and Social Behavior, University of California, U.S.

W. Andrew Collins, University of Minnesota, U.S.

Ann C. Crouter, The Pennsylvania State University, U.S.

Kenneth A. Dodge, Duke University, NC, U.S.

Judy Dunn, Social, Genetic and Developmental Psychiatry, Institute of Psychiatry, King's College London, U.K.

Emma Fergusson, University Department of Child and Adolescent Psychiatry, Oxford, U.K.

Susan Golombok, City University, London, U.K.

Jacqueline J. Goodnow, Macquarie University, Sydney, Australia

E. Mavis Hetherington, University of Virginia, U.S.

Robert A. Hinde, St. John's College, University of Cambridge, U.K.

Jennifer E. Lansford, Duke University, NC, U.S.

Kathleen McCartney, Harvard University, MA, U.S.

Patrick S. Malone, Duke University, NC, U.S.

Ann S. Masten, University of Minnesota, U.S.

Barbara Maughan, Social, Genetic and Developmental Psychiatry, Institute of Psychiatry, King's College London, U.K.

Shari Miller-Johnson, Duke University, NC, U.S.

Gregory S. Pettit, Auburn University, AL, U.S.

Glenn I. Roisman, University of Illinois, U.S.

Michael Rutter, Social, Genetic and Developmental Psychiatry, Institute of Psychiatry, King's College London, U.K.

Arnold Sameroff, Center for Human Growth and Development, University of Michigan, U.S.

Anne Shaffer, University of Minnesota, U.S.

Sabine Walper, Department of Education, Ludwig Maximilians University, Munich, Germany

Introduction

The Jacobs Foundation hosts a series of conferences on topics that concern the risks and protective factors affecting the development of children and young people, in which experts from around the world discuss recent research findings, approaches to the prevention of problems and intervention, and the efficacy of different policies. In 2003, the conference focused on the question of how families matter in young people's development – a question of obvious interest and importance to a wide range of readers, with serious policy implications.

Recently, there have been strong claims made that suggest that how children are reared in families is of little consequence, on the grounds that most of the supposed environmental effects are actually genetically mediated, or that the important environmental effects derive from the peer group rather than the family. In addition, there were earlier claims that many of the parenting-child behavior associations represented children's effects on their parents rather than the effects of socialization experiences. The purpose of this conference was to consider how much this rejection of environmentally mediated family influences is warranted and what can be concluded about such influences in relation to different aspects of psychosocial development.

The book that has resulted takes a series of current topics concerning families and presents lively consideration of the most recent research findings by the top international scholars in the field. These topics include the key risks in families that affect children and account for individual differences in their resilience, the links between the influences of families and peers (for protection or for problems), the connections between parental work and children's family lives and outcomes, the issue of the impact of child care on children's development, what we know about the impact of divorce and parental separation on children, the significance of grandparents for children's well-being, and the impact of new family forms such as lesbian- and surrogate-mother families. In one volume,

1

the book brings together the latest research findings on these key aspects of family influence, with discussions of the policy issues raised by the research. The lessons learned are succinctly and clearly presented, and the questions raised are important and sometimes controversial. The research is current and rigorous; the researchers, the most distinguished in their fields.

PART ONE

RISK AND RESILIENCE

1

How Families Matter in Child Development

Reflections from Research on Risk and Resilience

Ann S. Masten and Anne Shaffer

Throughout the history of child development, the family has played a ubiquitous role in theory, research, practice, and policy aimed at understanding and improving child welfare and development. From grand theories to heated controversies, family processes and roles have been invoked in numerous ways in developmental science over the past century to explain or debate whether and how families matter (Collins, Maccoby, Steinberg, Hetherington et al., 2000; Maccoby, 1992). Psychoanalytic theory (Freud, 1933/1964; Munroe, 1955), attachment theory (e.g., Bowlby, 1969, Carlson & Sroufe, 1995; Sroufe & Waters, 1977), ecological and developmental systems theory (e.g., Bronfenbrenner, 1979, Ford & Lerner, 1992; Sameroff, 2000), family systems theory (Davies & Cicchetti, 2004; Fiese, 2000; Fiese & Spagnola, in press), social learning and social cognitive theory (Bandura, 1977, 2001; Gewirtz, 1969), coercion theory (e.g., Patterson, 1982), parenting styles theory (Baumrind, 1967, 1973), and a variety of other influential frameworks have emphasized the family in diverse ways. Theories about the origins of competence and about the origins of psychopathology also have focused on family roles and processes (Cummings, Davies, & Campbell, 2000; Fiese, Wilder, & Bickham, 2000; Masten & Coatsworth, 1995; Masten, Burt, & Coatsworth, in press). Family-based adversity in many forms, including loss (Bowlby, 1980; Brown & Harris, 1978, Sandler, Wolchik, Davis, Haine et al., 2003), deprivation and institutional rearing (Rutter, Chapter 2 in this book; 1972; Zeanah et al., 2003, Zeanah, Smyke, & Settles, in press), divorce (Amato, Chapter 8 in this book; Hetherington, Chapter 9 in this book; Hetherington, Bridges, & Insabella, 1998; Walper, Chapter 10 in this book), interparental conflict or domestic violence (Cummings & Davies, 2002; Graham-Bermann & Edelson, 2001; Wolfe, Crooks, Lee, McIntyre-Smith et al., 2003), maltreatment (Belsky, 1984; Cicchetti & Carlson, 1989), and poverty (Brooks-Gunn & Duncan, 1997; Luthar, 1999; McLoyd, 1990), has been the focus of extensive study, often with the goal of learning how to prevent or ameliorate the impact of such adversity on children. Not surprisingly, families also have been the target of many kinds of interventions aimed at altering family interaction or parenting behavior in order to change the course of child development (Albee & Gullotta, 1997; Szapocznik & Williams, 2000; Cicchetti & Hinshaw, 2002; Masten et al., in press; Weissberg, Kumpfer, & Seligman, 2003).

As developmental psychopathology emerged over the past four decades, family functioning has played a central role in theory and research on competence, risk, and resilience, reflecting the salience of family-oriented concepts and intervention strategies in the disciplines from which developmental psychopathology evolved: child development, psychiatry, pediatrics, and related social sciences (Cicchetti, 1990; Cummings et al., 2000; Fiese & Spagnola, in press; Luthar, 2003, in press; Masten, 2001; Masten & Coatsworth, 1998; Masten et al., in press; Rutter, 1990; Sameroff & Chandler, 1975; Sroufe, Carlson, Levy, & Egeland, 1999). In developmental psychopathology, the role of family in development has been particularly salient in the study of risk and resilience. For this reason, and because developmental psychopathology is such a broad and integrative approach to understanding and attempting to redirect development, we believe the research focused on risk and resilience in developmental psychopathology can provide a useful lens through which to consider the broader mission of this volume to delineate the case for how "families count" for development in childhood and adolescence. Based on the studies of risk and resilience, we aim in this chapter to frame how one might think about the diverse ways families could matter in human development.

Basic Models of the Ways Families Matter

Perusing the evidence in studies of risk and resilience, it is clear that there are several key ways that families may matter, including the fundamental fact that parents pass their genes on to their biological children (cf. Grant, Compas, Stuhlmacher, Thrum et al., 2003; Luthar, 2003, in press; Masten, 2001; Masten et al., in press; Repetti, Taylor, & Seeman, 2002). In Figure 1.1, we illustrate some of the basic models of family effects on child behavior and development. These are described generally here, with elaboration and examples to follow in this chapter.

Families can function as direct influences on child behavior, in positive or negative ways (Figure 1.1A). When a direct family effect is positive on desired child outcomes, the family effect is described as *promotive* (see discussion by Sameroff, Chapter 3 in this book) or the feature of the family under observation is termed a *resource* or *asset* for children. On the other hand, if a family attribute predicts psychopathology or negative outcomes on a desired child behavior such as academic achievement, it could be described as a *risk factor*. Sometimes positive family effects are viewed as

A. Direct family effects

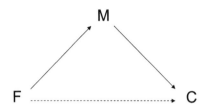

B. Mediated indirect family effects

C. Family as mediator

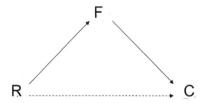

FIGURE 1.1. Basic models of family effects on child behavior [Note. R = Risk Factor; F = Family; C = Child behavior; M = Mediator (M_G = Geneticmediator; M_E = Environmental mediator).]

counterbalancing the effects of independent risk factors (R in Figure 1.1A), such as bad neighborhoods or deviant peer influences; in this case, the positive family effect is sometimes termed a *compensatory factor*. These are all relatively simple, additive models about how families matter, although the processes accounting for these influences could be very complex in nature. More complex variations of this model include more family factors or more additional risk factors. *Cumulative risk models*, for example, often include multiple features of the family or environment that are composited into a global index of overall riskiness for child behavior or development (see Sameroff, Chapter 3 in this book). Scores on composited risk indices of this kind typically indicate that child problems increase as a function of the number of risk factors, forming a *risk gradient*. Nonetheless, even cumulative risk models, which could reflect enormously complex processes, are variations on this basic model of direct influences.

D. Complex mediated family effects

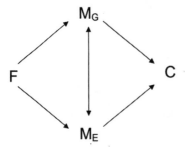

E. Family as moderator

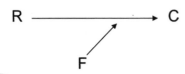

F. Transactional family-child effects

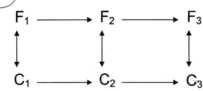

FIGURE 1.1. *continued*. Basic models of family effects on child behavior [Note. R = Risk Factor; F = Family; C = Child behavior; M = Mediator (M_G = Geneticmediator; M_E = Environmental mediator).]

The influences of families on child outcomes can also be indirect. Figure 1.1B illustrates a simple indirect effect of some family feature on a child outcome, where the effects of family on child are entirely mediated by some intervening factor and the processes the factor represents (which are often unknown). The mediator could be a feature of the child, the child's diet, the school, neighborhood, or health care system, or any other system that influences a child's behavior. A parent's income, for example, can influence where the family lives, which determines many features of a child's day-to-day context, including the quality of the school the child attends and how much violence the child observes in the surrounding environs. Families, of course, can influence many aspects of a child's life, at many levels. Thus, the same family could produce all kinds of risks, assets, and opportunities to the same child over the course of development, varying from genes to nice neighbors to actions resulting in tutors or college admission. Model D in Figure 1.1 illustrates a more complex variation on the indirect model, where family effects are mediated by both genes and environment and the interaction of those mediators.

Family can also function as the mediator of more distal conditions on children, as illustrated in Figure 1.1C. In this model, a risk factor alters family functioning (e.g., parenting) in some way, which in turn affects the child. Many models of distal risk factors such as social class or economic hardship are thought to be mediated by their effects on parents.

There are also models of family in a moderating role, where something about the family alters the impact of a risk factor on a child, as shown in Figure 1.1E. In this case of family as *moderator*, family alters the effect of another condition or factor on the child, in either a negative or a positive way. When the effect is positive, the family role is called a *protective factor*. Protective processes can be activated by adverse events, in much the way that an airbag is triggered by the impact of an automobile accident; analogously, parents may be spurred to protective action by perceived threats in the lives of their children. These moderating roles all imply some kind of interaction, where the influence of adversity depends on the family in some way. Families have been implicated in many studies as protective factors when child development is threatened by adversity of some kind (discussed further below and by Rutter, Chapter 2 in this book). Of course, families may also exacerbate negative effects, boosting the negative impact of a risk factor.

There are also models of more dynamic, complex interaction over time. A relatively simple example of a transactional model is illustrated in Figure 1.1F (adapted from the seminal work of Arnold Sameroff). In this model, ongoing interactions of child and family influence the family, the child, and their future interactions. Transactional models are based on systems theory, in which changes in one system (such as the family) can lead to changes in all other systems connected directly and indirectly to a family. There have been many elaborations on how this may work in development among systems theorists (Bronfenbrenner, 1979; Ford & Lerner, 1992; Sameroff, 2000; Thelen & Smith, 1998). All these models posit that many interactions among many systems at multiple levels (e.g., genes, central nervous system, peers, family, school, neighborhood, culture) give rise to child development, with bi-directional influences connecting multiple levels.

Intervention can also be conceptualized and modeled in relation to these basic models of family influence on children. If the family is the target of intervention, then the intervener must have a model of how the intervention will change the family (a theory of intervention) and how that in turn will change the child (a theory of family influence). As described later, a number of preventive interventions are designed to support positive parenting as a mediator in order to protect a child from the potentially deleterious effects of a risk factor such as divorce or poverty. In such cases, the intervention can be viewed as an effort to alter the mediator. Holmbeck (1997) illustrated such a model in his depiction of a moderated mediational model. In a family systems therapy model, in contrast, the intervention could be directed at the child, the parent, or their interaction, because changing any part of the system would theoretically change the other parties of interaction; in this case, the chosen target for change might be based on a theory about where in the family the intervener believes there is the greatest motivation or leverage for change.

In the following sections, we highlight examples of models of how families matter based on findings from the literature on risk and resilience. We focus particularly on models of families as adaptive systems for human development, as mediators and moderators of change, and as targets of intervention.

Families as Major Adaptive Systems for Human Development

In the risk and resilience literature, quality of parenting and the parent-child relationship have been implicated over and over again as correlates of positive development, both in normative situations and under adverse conditions, leading to the observation that families and parenting comprise a complex and fundamental system for human development, biologically and culturally evolved to promote and protect development (Masten, 2001; Fiese & Spagnola, in press). Effective parenting is pervasively associated with positive adjustment, in both normative and high-risk situations (Damon & Eisenberg, 1998; Fiese & Spagnola, in press; Luthar, in press; Maccoby, 1980; 1992; Masten & Coatsworth, 1998). In the resilience literature, relationships with competent and caring adults, who function in parenting or mentoring roles, top the list of the most widely observed correlates of good adaptation among children in risky or hazardous rearing environments or among children enduring or recovering from trauma (Luthar, 2003, in press; Masten & Powell, 2003; Masten & Reed, 2002; Wright & Masten, 2005). Moreover, moving a child from a context with poor caregiving to one with good caregiving, as happened with many Romanian orphans adopted around 1991 following the fall of the Ceausescu regime, has been followed in many cases by dramatic improvements in development (Rutter, Chapter 2; Rutter & the English and Romanian Adoptees (ERA) Study Team, 1998).

Families are charged by most societies with the job of socializing children to live in the society, and hence function as conduits of culture and standards of behavior. Other people, including teachers or mentors, certainly play important roles in a child's life, but parents typically have the primary role in child socialization, particularly early in development when children depend on adults for satisfying many needs and spend most of their time with family or designated surrogate caregivers. Some of the key debates and issues of the past few decades have focused on the importance of how well parents do this job or delegate it to others – whether or not, for example, day care or divorce is detrimental to child development. Parent-child relationships also are viewed as key regulators of child behavior, through such actions as soothing, monitoring, or providing security. Although the general aim of these regulatory functions to help children regulate their emotions and behavior may be similar over time, the actual behavior and function of families in this regard should change with development, as children grow up, because what is appropriate and effective for an infant, toddler, or adolescent may be vastly different and require very different kinds of parental behavior.

Attachment and Family Functions. Attachment relationships are fundamental to the role of the family as an adaptive system and to the development of emotion regulation as outlined earlier. The multiple functions of attachment relationships have been delineated by numerous scholars (Carlson & Sroufe, 1995; Sroufe & Waters, 1977; Cicchetti, 1990; Maccoby, 1980; Waters, Vaughn, Posada, & Kondo-Ikemura, 1995) since John Bowlby (1969) so eloquently described the nature of human attachment in terms of adaptive functions. In attachment theory, as in the empirical work supporting this theory, the special relationship initially formed between a child and primary caregiver can influence learning, reactions to threat, exploration, and many other behaviors associated with competence and maladaptation. Children who form insecure attachments or who do not have the opportunity to form such a relationship in early development because of severe privation or impaired functioning exhibit major developmental problems, and these findings have been replicated in studies of primates as well as humans (Cicchetti & Carlson, 1989; Hinde, 1974; Shonkoff & Phillips, 2000; Suomi, 2000; Zeanah, Smyke, & Settles, in press).

Family as Regulator. The attachment relationship and the larger family context serve regulatory functions of diverse kinds (Fiese & Spagnola, in press; Gunnar, in press; Sroufe, 1996). Arousal regulation is provided by the parent who soothes a fussing baby, comforts a frightened child, or encourages an adolescent to try something new. Under high threat conditions, separation from the attachment figure(s) is associated with high levels of distress in children, as observed long ago by Bowlby (1969), Spitz (1945) and others, and also, more recently, in systematic studies of children following traumatic life events, ranging from war and terrorism to hospitalization and natural disasters (Garmezy & Rutter, 1983; Pine, Costello, &

Masten, in press). Gradually, the parent's role in child regulation becomes less direct, and developmental theories have proposed for nearly a century that there are processes of *internalization* by which what is initially mother-child or family-based regulatory function gradually shifts to self-regulation, through various processes of learning, scaffolding, and assimilation (e.g., Breger, 1974). Recent studies of caregiver-offspring interactions are beginning to examine how such transfer from family to self-regulation occurs. Brain development research suggests that stress regulation provided by mothers (both animal and human) can alter the organization of the brain or gene expression so as to affect future behavior and development (Gunnar & Donzella, 2002; Pine et al., in press). Similarly, it has been argued that risky families may create or exacerbate vulnerabilities in their children, with lasting consequences on the child's regulatory capacity (Boyce, in press; Gunnar, in press; Gunnar & Donzella, 2002; Repetti et al., 2002; Shonkoff & Phillips, 2000). Such phenomena would represent biological embedding of context related to family function. In this new work, for example, stress regulation in parent-offspring interactions alters the stress-emotional response systems in the offspring, sometimes with lasting impact (Gunnar, in press).

Parent as Teacher, Socializer, Protector, and Cultural Conduit. In social development, parents have been accorded many roles as teachers, role modelers, and socializers who demonstrate, reward, punish, and otherwise shape behavior in children; reciprocally, parents are also shaped in turn by the behaviors of their children over the course of many interactions (Belsky, 1984; Bornstein, 1995; Collins, Maccoby, Steinberg, Hetherington et al., 2000; Fiese, 2000; Fiese & Spagnola, in press; Maccoby, 1992; Masten & Gewirtz, in press; Sameroff, Chapter 3 in this book). Parents also teach or expose children to cultural traditions that serve a regulatory function in human adaptation, including religious practices and ethnic traditions. Children may learn to pray or meditate, and to participate in culturally-specific rituals, such as a healing ceremony, to deal with loss or adversity (Crawford, Wright, & Masten, in press). Families also have their own internal culture and rituals that may serve many functions for children, such as imparting family values or life lessons (Fiese & Spagnola, in press). In these ways, parents play a major part in the establishment of children's social and cultural identity, both through direct education and the indirect provision of the child's earliest context for development.

Family as Provider, Broker or Purveyor of Resources and Opportunities. Parents also provide food, shelter, clothing, books, performing art lessons, sports team access, and many other resources and opportunities for children. Additionally, parent education, jobs, and choices often determine the nature of the neighborhood and school in which a child lives and learns; thus family can directly and indirectly influence many aspects of the daily context of a child's life, including the quality of education and the availability of social relationships, and recreational opportunities. (Collins et al., 2000; Sameroff, Chapter 3 in this book). Parents talk and read to children, and the degree to which they do so predicts vocabulary and school success (Hart & Risley, 1995). However, this relation could be confounded to some degree by shared verbal aptitude of parents and children that is, in part, genetically mediated, thus highlighting the complex interactions among family-related factors and their impact on child development.

Family as Source of Risks and Threat

In the risk literature, the family also can be the source of threats to development, in a number of different ways. Some are more *passive* in nature. At the biological level, for example, a parent may pass on the genes that convey risk for a specific disorder, such as schizophrenia (Gottesman & Hanson, 2005), or a biological disposition or temperament that may render the child more vulnerable to risky social environments. Families can also be risky social environments in and of themselves (Repetti et al. 2002). Although such actions may not be deliberate, family members may harm their children through neglect or incompetence. Parents who are impaired themselves, by mental or physical illness or disability, may not be able to provide normative levels of nutrition, security, or teaching for their children, or to see impending danger and take protective action, and thus place their child at risk for many negative outcomes. In fact, it is not surprising to find that a host of variables related to child competence and achievement are related to the socioeconomic status or functional competence of parents (Masten & Coatsworth, 1995; 1998; McLoyd, 1998; Repetti et al., 2002). There are a number of candidate processes that could explain the mechanisms by which parent competence or SES are linked to child outcomes; for example, less competent or less affluent parents may increase the exposure of the children to danger, toxins, deviant peers, or other bad influences in the environment due to their circumstances, choices, or behaviors (Collins et al., 2000; Masten & Gewirtz, in press). Very young children are particularly vulnerable to hazards posed by lack of attention or monitoring for safety (Masten & Gewirtz, in press).

In some cases, parent behavior or family functioning itself is the *active* source of threat. For example, child maltreatment perpetrated by a parent is a direct threat to children, and studies suggest that maltreatment by an attachment figure has greater effects on a child than maltreatment by a stranger (Masten & Wright, 1998). This is consistent with the idea of family as a key adaptive system for human development, such that disturbances to this system have particularly deleterious outcomes. Harsh, inconsistent parenting has also been consistently related to problems in child development (Repetti et al., 2002; Dodge, Malone, Lansford, Miller-Johnson et al., Chapter 5 in this book), most commonly being linked with later externalizing behavior problems. Finally, the relations of family conflict and aggressive behavior to child outcomes are not necessarily limited to those actions directed at the child. Observing domestic violence or interparental conflict may be highly disturbing to children, disrupting their sense of security; even toddlers react to observed conflict between strangers with distress (Cummings & Davies, 2002).

Cumulative Risk. Because of the multiple ways, both direct and indirect, that parents and families may play a role in the lives of children, studies that consider aggregate risk in the lives of children often consider multiple aspects of family attributes and function (see Sameroff, Chapter 3 in this book). These indices often include, for example, risk factors such as low parent education, low family income, parental unemployment, mental illness, incarceration, foster placement, large family size, child abuse, domestic violence, harsh or inconsistent parenting, divorce, and many other events and conditions that implicate family functioning. Cumulative risk indices and risk gradients that reflect the overall level of psychosocial risk in the lives of children often index family functioning in complex and diverse ways (Jessor, 1993; Masten & Gewirtz, in press; Rutter, 1979; 1983; Sameroff, Chapter 3 in this book; Sameroff & Fiese, 2000; Wyman, Sandler, Wolchik, & Nelson, 2000). Numerous studies have shown that the accumulation of risk factors is inversely related to a wide variety of indicators of positive adaptation, yet the processes underlying these effects may be obscured by the complexity of multiple risks when they are considered together. Paradoxically, aggregating risks may be more consistent with the reality of risks that interact and pile up in the lives of families and at the same time are so complex that the processes involved cannot be uncovered. Risk investigators have struggled with this dilemma in family research as well and developed creative strategies for detecting specific ways in which risk and protective factors operate in affecting children's lives or proximal causes that interact to influence developmental pathways.

Family as Proximal Mediator of Distal Events or Conditions

Ecological theory and systems theory have provided a great deal of guidance in the conceptualization of risk and resilience processes. In this view, child development is embedded in the family system, which is in turn embedded in other systems, including the parents' work, the community, and culture. Sometimes the family or particular individuals within the family become the proximal *mediators* of risks or protection arising outside the family system. Thus, for example, a father or mother can experience problems at work that affect his or her parenting and thereby the behavior of the child (see Crouter, Chapter 6 in this book). Economic situations at the national or regional level can also affect family life in many ways that then affect the children within those families. Many studies have examined the indirect effects of parent-related adversity on child adaptation via the deleterious impact on parental functioning (Grant et al., 2003). In a classic study of the Great Depression and development, Elder observed such effects among children and adolescents who were part of ongoing longitudinal studies of child development when this major historical event unfolded (Elder, 1974/1999). In recent years, Conger and colleagues have documented such effects in their important studies of farm families in Iowa, where economic conditions affected the parents and their relationship, which in turn affected the adolescents in the family (Conger, Ge, Elder, Lorenz et al., 1994; Elder & Conger, 2000).

Thus, research has examined how the processes of family adaptation unfold over time (Gest, Neemann, Hubbard, Masten et al., 1993), and analytic strategies that address these longitudinal relations enhance the possibility of empirically describing these theoretical processes of familial adaptation (e.g., Hinshaw, 2002; Kraemer, Stice, Kazdin, Offord et al., 2001). Through such research, it has become increasingly possible to demonstrate empirically the mediating role of parenting in understanding the negative yet indirect impact of many environmental stressors on child functioning, findings which are notably consistent with the theoretical models of family systems approaches.

Intervention strategies with foundations in systems theories have been developed explicitly to capitalize on parents' mediating role in the relations between risk factors and child outcomes. For example, Brody and colleagues have recently reported on a parenting intervention program implemented with African American families that specifically targeted improving regulated and communicative parenting behaviors in order to indirectly support and enhance protective factors for their children (Brody, Murry, Gerrard, Gibbons et al., 2004). This directed effort to "regulate the regulator" or moderate the mediator (as noted earlier) represents an important translation of theory and empirical research findings into applied efforts to intervene with families. Such intervention research has shown, quite promisingly, that the hypothesized mediating role of the parent in children's adaptation to risk and adversity is subject to change.

Parents as Mediators of Genetic Risk or Vulnerability

Parenting has also been shown to mediate the effects of genetic risks to adaptation in adverse circumstances. Specifically, in a recent study of genetic and environmental effects in the development of resilience among children living in poverty, results suggested that maternal warmth was associated with resilience, partly mediated by genetic processes and partly mediated by environmental processes (Kim-Cohen et al., 2004).

Family as Moderator of Risk and as Moderated by Other Influences

In the resilience literature, moderating effects of family on risk or vulnerability of children also have been posited, with growing corroborative evidence (Luthar, in press; Masten & Powell, 2003; Rutter, Chapter 2 in this book). In all the cases where a moderating effect is postulated, some kind of conditional or joint effect is proposed (indicating interactions among predictors). The quality of parenting is more important under certain conditions (presence or absence of a gene; good or poor neighborhood); other factors (such as deviant peers) vary in influence depending on the quality of family functioning; or there is a good versus poor fit of family (e.g., parenting style) with child (e.g., personality). In one kind of interaction, the family functions to buffer a child from the worst exposure to or impact of adversity. A family may provide an island of safety and security in a dangerous neighborhood (e.g., Richters & Martinez, 1993). In other instances, family factors may serve to exacerbate the effects of already negative contexts. For example, poor parenting may be particularly dangerous to children in bad neighborhoods because they are left unprotected or put at increased risk.

The quality of monitoring by parents in risky environments has been strongly implicated as a moderator (Dishion & McMahon, 1998; Fiese & Spagnola, in press; Repetti et al., 2002). Evidence also suggests that the influence of deviant peers depends on parenting (Galambos, Barker, & Almeida, 2003; Pettit, Bates, Dodge, & Meece, 1999). Deviant peers appear to be less influential in the context of positive parenting behavior and relationships. Families are also affected by the quality of neighborhood functioning (Sampson, Morenoff, & Earls, 1999).

Age and individual differences in children can also moderate family effects. In ways too numerous and complex to describe, parents change their perceptions and behavior in relation to developmental changes in their children and also according to how their children respond and how they expect their children to respond. Individual differences in child temperament and personality, for example, have been extensively investigated as moderators of parent behavior, and these ways of relating to the world change over the course of development (Caspi & Shiner, in press; Rothbart & Bates, 1998; Kochanska, 1995).

In all of the ways described that families may function to promote and
protect development, child qualities could moderate the effects of the parent or family (see Sameroff, Chapter 3 in this book). Gene-by-family interactions are also possible, as suggested by recent work on the joint effects of genes and context (see Rutter, Chapter 2 in this book). Caspi and colleagues (Caspi, McClay, Moffitt, Mill et al., 2002), for example, observed that variations in the genotype producing high versus low levels of monoamine oxidase A (MAOA) showed an interaction with serious maltreatment in predicting antisocial behavior problems. The combination of low MAOA

expression and maltreatment was associated with substantially higher risk for antisocial behavior.

The quality of parenting can also be moderated by the systems that regulate parent behavior, such as the marital relationship, the extended family, and the social systems of work, culture, or community. A supportive spouse or grandparent can serve as a protective factor for the children in a family during times of strain, adversity, or parental impairment, not only by direct actions toward the children, but also by regulating the arousal, affect, and behavior of the parent (Dunn, Fergusson & Maughan Chapter 12 in this book; Hetherington, Chapter 9 in this book; Sameroff, Chapter 3 in this book).

Ever More Complex Models of Family Influence

In addition to the effects described earlier, families vary in the degree to which they are affected by other systems or by negative life experiences, and a number of factors are likely to account for these individual differences in adaptation and functioning. Thus it is possible to imagine ways in which the mediating and moderating processes described might work together. For example, there are individual differences in the degree to which parenting itself is affected by adverse conditions. In some families, parenting is undermined by adversity, while in other families, parents take action to protect their parenting from the effects of adversity, by seeking social support or other kinds of assistance. In other words, there may be parents and families that are more resilient in the face of adversity in terms of how well they function to protect and care for children.

In considering the phenomenon of naturally occurring resilience, a child may appear to be more resilient under adversity, but a closer look reveals that the child's adaptation actually reflects the resilience of the parenting or family system; the child has simply not been exposed to the same level of risk as a child whose parenting has deteriorated in the face of adversity.

Interventions to Protect or Improve Family Functioning

In prevention science over the past two decades, there are many examples of interventions designed to help children through changing family interaction or parenting (Kumpfer & Alvarado, 2003; Luthar, in press; Masten et al., in press; Sameroff, Chapter 3 in this book; Sameroff & Fiese, 2000). Many interventions can be viewed as attempts to create moderating effects akin to the protective effects discussed above, in order to influence the course of development. In van den Boom's (1994, 1995) work with high-risk, irritable babies, mothers in the experimental group were trained to be more sensitive and tuned to their babies, in accordance with attachment theory (using strategies developed by van IJzendoorn, Juffer, & Duyvesteyn [1995]); experimental babies subsequently showed more secure attachment and also better competence. Investigators at the Oregon Social Learning Center have developed effective strategies for changing families (e.g., Forgatch & DeGarmo, 1999; Martinez & Forgatch, 2001). Forgatch and DeGarmo (1999), for example, demonstrated that parenting could be altered for families undergoing divorce, with the consequence of better outcomes for their children. Investigators at Arizona State University, in another experimental clinical trial with divorcing families, demonstrated significant effects on parenting and child outcomes in the experimental as compared with control families, with effects holding up for at least six years (Wolchik, Sandler, Millsap, Plummer et al., 2002). Successful efforts also have been made to improve mother-toddler interaction when mothers are depressed, as a preventive intervention for children (Cicchetti, Toth, & Rogosch, 1999). These interventions, as well as the intervention for African-American parents described earlier (Brody et al., 2004) illustrate successful interventions to alter parenting as a mediator of developmental risk factors such as divorce, maternal psychiatric illness, and poverty.

If one aims to alter family processes such as parenting, then an important step is to identify the influences on the nature and quality of parenting. Belsky (1984), in his article on the determinants of parenting, discussed a number of possible influences, including characteristics of the parent, social context, and child. Parenting itself has a developmental history, as Belsky observed, and thus may have long-term antecedents. At the same time, parenting may also be influenced by a host of more contemporary conditions, such as contextual challenges and supports. Social support in various forms was noted by Belsky and later by numerous others (e.g., Repetti et al., 2002) as a key empirically supported influence on parenting. Belsky also argued persuasively that because of its multiple determinants, the parenting system was buffered to some degree from harmful disruptions.

More complex models also have been used to capture the ongoing dynamics of family systems, both in interaction with other systems (e.g., schools, and peer groups) and in terms of the internal dynamics of interaction among subgroups of the family. Even in studies that focus on a single dyad, such as mother-child, it is not easy to model or study the ongoing complexities of relationships and their bi-directional effects on the people in the relationship (Fiese & Spagnola, in press). The role of transactional processes arising in the family for resilience have been noted (e.g., Egeland, Carlson, & Sroufe, 1993; Gest et al., 1993; Sameroff, Chapter 3 in this book) but rarely demonstrated in longitudinal designs with repeated measures over multiple points in time. As time goes on, there are more data sets with the kind of panel data that make it possible to investigate transactional effects over time involving family members (see Ge, Conger,

Lorenz, Shanahan et al., 1995, for example). Recent advances in growth curve and structural equation modeling provide powerful new tools for examining dynamic models of such bi-directional influences, and no doubt there will be more examples testing transactional models involving the family.

The Jacobs Conference

The 2003 Jacobs Conference brought together an exciting group of scholars to discuss the issues and evidence about how families matter. In the chapters that follow, these scholars highlight much of the best evidence for and against many of the processes delineated here, as well as the conceptual and methodological gaps and issues that will motivate future research. As often observed in the history of science, ideas and theories about important, complex topics tend to get ahead of the execution of the empirical research with the design and power to test the ideas. Numerous gaps remain in the database on how families matter for development. Nonetheless, promising signs abound in the pages of this volume that suggest we are on the horizon of a new era, in which dynamic, multilevel models about family processes in development, spanning genes to culture, will be put to the test in elegant, longitudinal studies.

References

Albee, G. W., & Gullotta, T. P. (1997). Primary prevention works. *Issues in children's and families' lives, Vol. 6* (pp. 3–22). Thousand Oaks, CA: Sage Publications.

Bandura, A. (1977). *Social learning theory.* New York: General Learning Press.

Bandura, A. (2001). Social cognitive theory: An agentive perspective. *Annual Review of Psychology, 52,* 1–26.

Baumrind, D. (1967). Child care practices anteceding three patterns of preschool behavior. *Genetic Psychology Monographs, 75,* 43–88.

Baumrind, D. (1973). The development of instrumental competence through socialization. In A. D. Pick (Ed.), *Minnesota Symposium on Child Psychology: Vol. 7* (pp. 3–46). Minneapolis: University of Minnesota Press.

Belsky, J. (1984). The determinants of parenting: A process model. *Child Development, 55,* 83–96.

Bornstein, M. H. (Ed.) (1995). *Handbook of parenting.* Mahwah, NJ: Erlbaum.

Bowlby, J. (1969). *Attachment and loss.* New York: Basic Books.

Bowlby, J. (1980). *Attachment and loss: Vol. 3 Loss: Sadness & depression.* New York: Basic Books.

Boyce, W. T. (in press). The biology of misfortune: Stress reactivity, social context, and the ontogeny of psychopathology in early life. In A. S. Masten (Ed.), *Developmental psychopathology: Integrating multiple levels of analysis. 33rd Minnesota Symposium on Child Psychology.* Minneapolis: University of Minnesota Press.

Breger, L. (1974). *From instinct to identity.* Englewood Cliffs, NJ: Prentice-Hall.

Brody, G. H., Murry, V. M., Gerrard, M., Gibbons, F. X., Molgaard, V., McNair, L. et al. (2004). The Strong African American Families Program: Translating research into prevention programming. *Child Development, 75,* 900–917.

Bronfenbrenner, U. (1979). *The ecology of human development: Experiments by nature and design.* Cambridge, MA: Harvard University Press.

Brooks-Gunn, J., & Duncan, J. (1997, Summer/Fall). The effects of poverty on children. *The future of childen, 7,* 55–71.

Brown, G. W., & Harris, T. (1978). *Social origins of depression.* London: Tavistock.

Carlson, E. A., & Sroufe, L. A. (1995). Contributions of attachment theory to developmental psychopathology. In D. Cicchetti & D. Cohen (Eds.), *Developmental Psychopathology: Vol. 1. Theory and methods* (pp. 581–617). New York: Wiley.

Caspi, A., McClay, J., Moffitt, T. E., Mill, J., Martin, J., Craig, J. W., Taylor, A., & Poulton, R. (2002). Role of genotype in the cycle of violence in maltreated children. *Science, 297,* 851–854.

Caspi, A., & Shiner, R. L. (in press). Personality development. In W. Damon & R. Lerner (Series Eds.) & N. Eisenberg (Vol. Ed.), *Handbook of child psychology: Vol. 3. Social, emotional, and personality development* (6th ed.). New York: Wiley.

Cicchetti, D. (1990). An historical perspective on the discipline of developmental psychopathology. In J. Rolf, A. S. Masten, D. Cicchetti, K. H. Nuechterlein, & S. Weintraub (Eds.), *Risk and protective factors in the development of psychopathology* (pp. 2–28). New York: Cambridge University Press.

Cicchetti, D., & Carlson, V. (1989). *Child maltreatment.* New York: Cambridge University Press.

Cicchetti, D., & Hinshaw, S. P. (2002). Editorial: Prevention and intervention science: Contributions to developmental theory. *Development and Psychopathology, 14,* 667–671.

Cicchetti, D., Toth, S. L., & Rogosch, F. A. (1999). The efficacy of toddler-parent psychotherapy to increase attachment security in offspring of depressed mothers. *Attachment and Human Development, 1,* 34–66.

Collins, W. A., Maccoby, E. E., Steinberg, L., Hetherington, E. M., & Bornstein, M. (2000). Contemporary research on parenting: The case for nature and nurture. *American Psychologist, 55,* 218–232.

Conger, R. D., Ge, X., Elder, G. H., Lorenz, F. O., & Simons, R. L. (1994). Economic stress, coercive family process, and developmental problems of adolescents. *Child Development, 65,* 541–561.

Crawford, E., Wright, M. O'D., Masten, A. S. (in press). Resilience and spirituality in youth. In P. L. Benson, E. C. Roehlkepartain, P. E. King, & L. Wagener (Eds.), *The handbook of spiritual development in childhood and adolescence.* Newbury Park, CA: Sage Publications.

Cummings, E. M., & Davies, P. T. (2002). Effects of marital conflict on children: Recent advances and emerging themes in process-oriented research. *Journal of Child Psychology and Psychiatry, 43,* 31–63.

Cummings, E. M., Davies, P. T., & Campbell, S. B. (2000). *Developmental psychopathology and family process.* New York: Guilford.

Damon, W. (Editor-in-Chief), & Eisenberg, N. (Vol. Ed.) (1998). *Handbook of child psychology: Vol. 3. Social, emotional, and personality development* (5th ed.). New York: Wiley.

Davies, P. T., & Cicchetti, D. (Eds.) (2004). Family systems and developmental psychopathology [Special issue], *Development and Psychopathology, 16,* 477–81.

Dishion, T. J., & McMahon, R. J. (1998). Parental monitoring and the prevention of child and adolescent problem behavior: A conceptual and empirical foundation. *Clinical Child and Family Psychology Review, 1*, 61–75.

Egeland, B., Carlson, E. A., & Sroufe, L. A. (1993). Resilience as process. *Development and Psychopathology, 5*, 517–528.

Elder, G. H. (1974/1999). *Children of the Great Depression*. Chicago: University of Chicago Press.

Elder, G. H., & Conger, R. D. (2000). *Children of the land: Adversity and success in rural America*. Chicago: University of Chicago Press.

Fiese, B. H. (2000). Family matters: A systems view of family effects on children's cognitive health. In R. J. Sternberg & E. L. Grigorenko (Eds.), *Environmental effects on cognitive abilities* (pp. 39–57). Mahwah, NJ: Erlbaum.

Fiese, B. H., & Spagnola, M. (in press). The interior life of the family: Looking from the inside out and outside in. In A. S. Masten, L. A. Sroufe, & B. Egeland (Eds.), *Developmental psychopathology: Integrating multiple levels of analysis. 33rd Minnesota Symposium on Child Psychology*. Minneapolis: University of Minnesota Press.

Fiese, B., Wilder, J., & Bickham, N. (2000). Family context in developmental psychopathology. In A. Sameroff, M. Lewis & S. Miller (Eds.), *Handbook of Developmental Psychopathology* (2nd ed., pp. 115–134). New York: Kluwer Academic / Plenum Publishers.

Ford, D. H., & Lerner, R. M. (1992). *Developmental systems theory: An integrative approach*. Newbury Park, CA: Sage Publications.

Forgatch, M. S., & DeGarmo, D. S. (1999). Parenting through change: An effective prevention program for single mothers. *Journal of Consulting and Clinical Psychology, 67*, 711–724.

Freud, S. (1933/1964). *New introductory lectures on psychoanalysis*. New York: W. W. Norton.

Galambos, N. L., Barker, E. T., & Almeida, D. M. (2003). Parents do matter: Trajectories of change in externalizing and internalizing problems in early adolescence. *Child Development, 74*, 578–594.

Garmezy, N., & Rutter, M. (1983). *Stress, coping, and development in children*. New York: McGraw-Hill.

Ge, X., Conger, R. D., Lorenz, F. O., Shanahan, M., & Elder, G. H. (1995). Mutual influences in parent and adolescent psychological distress. *Developmental Psychology, 31*, 406–419.

Gest, S. D., Neemann, J., Hubbard, J. J., Masten, A. S., & Tellegen, A. (1993). Parenting quality, adversity, and conduct problems in adolescence: Testing process-oriented models of resilience. *Development and Psychopathology, 5*, 663–682.

Gewirtz, J. R. (1969). Mechanisms of social learning: Some roles of stimulation and behavior in early human development. In D. A. Goslin (Ed.), *Handbook of socialization theory and research* (pp. 57–212). Chicago: Rand McNally.

Gottesman, I. I., & Hanson, D. R. (2005). Human development: Biological and genetic processes. *Annual Review of Psychology, 56*, 263–286.

Graham-Bermann, S. A., & Edelson, J. L. (2001). *Domestic violence in the lives of children: The future of research, intervention and social policy*. Washington, DC: American Psychological Association.

Grant, K. E., Compas, B. E., Stuhlmacher, A. F., Thrum, A. E., McMahon, S. D., & Halpert, J. A. (2003). Stressors and child and adolescent psychopathology: Moving from markers to mechanisms of risk. *Psychological Bulletin, 129*, 447–466.

Gunnar, M. R. (in press). Social regulation of stress in early child development. In K. McCartney & D. A. Phillips (Eds.), *Handbook of early child development*. New York: Blackwell.

Gunnar, M. R., & Donzella, B. (2002). Social regulation of the L-HPA axis in early human development. *Psychoneuroendocrinology, 27,* 199–220.

Hart, B., & Risley, T. R. (1995). *Meaningful differences in the everyday experiences of young American children.* Baltimore: Paul H. Brooks.

Hetherington, E. M., Bridges, M., & Insabella, G. M. (1998). What matters and what does not? Five perspectives on the association between marital transitions and children's adjustment. *American Psychologist, 53,* 167–184.

Hinde, R. A. (1974). *Biological bases of human social behaviour.* New York: McGraw-Hill Book Co.

Hinshaw, S. P. (2002). Process, mechanism, and explanation related to externalizing behavior in developmental psychopathology. *Journal of Abnormal Child Psychology, 30,* 431–446.

Jessor, R. (1993). Successful adolescent development among youth in high-risk settings. *American Psychologist, 48,* 117–126.

Kim-Cohen, J., Moffitt, T. E., Caspi, A., & Taylor, A. (2004). Genetic and environmental processes in young children's resilience and vulnerability to socioeconomic deprivation. *Child Development, 75,* 651–668.

Kochanska, G. (1995). Children's temperament, mothers' discipline, and security of attachment: Multiple pathways to emerging internalization. *Child Development, 66,* 597–615.

Kraemer, H. C., Stice, E., Kazdin, A., Offord, D., & Kupfer, D. (2001). How do risk factors work together? Mediators, moderators, and independent, overlapping, and proxy risk factors. *American Journal of Psychiatry, 158,* 848–856.

Kumpfer, K. L., & Alvarado, R. (2003). Family-strengthening approaches for the prevention of youth problem behaviors. *American Psychologist, 58,* 457–465.

Luthar, S. S. (1999). *Poverty and children's adjustment.* Newbury Park, CA: Sage Publications.

Luthar, S. S., Ed. (2003). *Resilience and vulnerability: Adaptation in the context of childhood adversities.* New York: Cambridge University Press.

Luthar, S. S. (in press). Resilience in development: A synthesis of research across five decades. In D. Cicchetti & D. J. Cohen (Eds.), *Developmental psychopathology: Risk disorder, and adaptation* (2nd ed.). New York: Wiley.

Maccoby, E. E. (1980). *Social development: Psychological growth and the parent-child relationship.* San Diego, CA: Harcourt Brace Jovanovich.

Maccoby, E. E. (1992). The role of parents in the socialization of children: An historical overview. *Developmental Psychology, 28,* 1006–1017.

Martinez, C. R., & Forgatch, M. S. (2001). Preventing problems with boys' noncompliance: Effects of a parent training intervention for divorcing mothers. *Journal of Consulting and Clinical Psychology, 69,* 416–428.

Masten, A. S. (2001). Ordinary magic: Resilience processes in development. *American Psychologist, 56,* 227–238.

Masten, A. S., Burt, K., & Coatsworth, J. D. (in press). Competence and psychopathology in development. In D. Cicchetti & D. Cohen (Eds.), *Handbook of developmental psychopathology* (2nd ed.) New York: Wiley.

Masten, A. S., & Coatsworth, J. D. (1995). Competence, resilience, and psychopathology. In D. Cicchetti & D. Cohen (Eds.), *Developmental psychopathology: Vol. 2. Risk, disorder, and adaptation* (pp. 715–752). New York: Wiley.

Masten, A. S., & Coatsworth, J. D. (1998). The development of competence in favorable and unfavorable environments: Lessons from research on successful children. *American Psychologist, 53,* 205–220.

Masten, A. S., & Gewirtz, A. H. (in press). Vulnerability and resilience in early childhood development. In K. McCartney & D. A. Phillips (Eds.), *Handbook of early childhood development*. New York: Blackwell.

Masten, A. S., & Powell, J. L. (2003). A resilience framework for research, policy, and practice. In S. S. Luthar (Ed.), *Resilience and vulnerability: Adaptation in the context of childhood adversities* (pp. 1–25). New York: Cambridge University Press.

Masten, A. S., & Reed, M-G J. (2002). Resilience in development. In C. R. Snyder & S. J. Lopez (Eds.), *Handbook of positive psychology* (pp. 74–88). London: Oxford University Press.

Masten, A. S., & Wright, M. O. (1998). Cumulative risk and protection models of child maltreatment. *Journal of Aggression, Maltreatment and Trauma, 2,* 7–30. Also published as a monograph, in B. B. R. Rossman & M. S. Rosenberg (Eds.), *Multiple victimization of children: Conceptual, developmental, research and treatment issues* (pp. 7–30). Binghamton, NY: Haworth.

McLoyd, V. C. (1990). The impact of economic hardship on black families and children: Psychological distress, parenting, and socioemotional development. *Child Development, 61,* 311–346.

McLoyd, V. C. (1998). Socioeconomic disadvantage and child development. *American Psychologist, 53,* 185–204.

Munroe, R. L. (1955). *Schools of analytic thought: An exposition, critique, and attempt at integration*. New York: Holt, Rinehart, & Winston.

Patterson, G. R. (1982). *Coercive family processes*. Eugene, OR: Castalia Press.

Pettit, G. S., Bates, J. E., Dodge, K. A., & Meece, D. W. (1999). The impact of after-school peer contact on early adolescent externalizing problems is moderated by parental monitoring, perceived neighborhood safety, and prior adjustment. *Child Development, 70,* 768–778.

Pine, D. S., Costello, J., & Masten, A. S. (in press). Trauma, proximity, and developmental psychopathology: The effects of war and terrorism on children. *Neuropsychopharmacology*.

Repetti, R. L., Taylor, S. E., & Seeman, T. E. (2002). Risky families: Family social environments and the mental and physical health of offspring. *Psychological Bulletin, 128,* 330–366.

Richters, J. E., & Martinez, P. (1993). The NIMH community violence project: I. Children as victims of and witnesses to violence. *Psychiatry, 56,* 7–21.

Rothbart, M. K., & Bates, J. E. (1998). Temperament. In N. Eisenberg (Ed.), *Handbook of child psychology: Vol. 4. Social, emotional, and personality development* (pp. 105–76). New York: Wiley.

Rutter, M. (1972). *Maternal Deprivation Reassessed*. Harmondsworth: Penguin.

Rutter, M. (1979). Protective factors in children's responses to stress and disadvantage. *Annals of the Academy of Medicine, Singapore, 8,* 324–338.

Rutter, M. (1983). Stress, coping, and development: Some issues and some questions. In N. Garmezy & M. Rutter (Eds.), *Stress, coping, and development in children* (pp. 1–42). New York: McGraw-Hill.

Rutter, M. (1990). Psychosocial resilience and protective mechanisms. In J. Rolf, A. S. Masten, D. Cicchetti, K. H. Nuechterlein, & S. Weintraub (Eds.), *Risk and protective factors in the development of psychopathology* (pp. 181–214). New York: Cambridge University Press.

Rutter, M., & the English and Romanian Adoptees (ERA) Study Team (1998). Developmental catch-up and deficit following adoption after severe global early privation. *Journal of Child Psychology and Psychiatry, 39,* 465–476.

Sameroff, A. J. (2000). Developmental systems and psychopathology. *Development and Psychopathology, 12,* 297–312.

Sameroff, A. J., & Chander, M. J. (1975). Reproductive risk and the continuum of caretaking casualty. *Review of Child Development Research, 4,* 187–244.

Sameroff, A. J., & Fiese, B. H. (2000). Transactional regulation: The developmental ecology of early intervention. In J. P. Shonkoff & S. J. Meisels (Eds.), *Handbook of early childhood intervention* (pp. 135–159). New York: Cambridge University Press.

Sampson, R. J., Morenoff, J., & Earls, F. (1999). Beyond social capital: Spatial dynamics of collective efficacy for children. *American Sociological Review, 64,* 633–660.

Sandler, I., Wolchik, S., Davis, C., Haine, R., & Ayers, T. (2003). Correlational and experimental study of resilience in children of divorce and parentally bereaved children. In S. Luthar (Ed.), *Resilience and vulnerability: Adaptation in the context of childhood adversities* (pp. 213–242). Cambridge: Cambridge University Press.

Shonkoff, J., & Phillips, D. A. (2000). Nurturing relationships. In *Neurons to neighborhoods: The science of early childhood development* (pp. 225–266). Washington, DC: National Academies Press.

Spitz, R. A. (1945). Hospitalism: An inquiry into the genesis of psychiatric conditions in early childhood. *Psychoanalytic Study of the Child, 1,* 53–74.

Sroufe, L. A. (1996). *Emotional development: The organization of the emotional life in the early years.* New York: Cambridge University Press.

Sroufe, L. A., Carlson, E. A., Levy, A. K., & Egeland, B. (1999). Implications of attachment theory for developmental psychopathology. *Development and Psychopathology, 11,* 1–13.

Sroufe, L. A., & Waters, E. (1977). Attachment as an organizational construct. *Child Development, 48,* 1184–1199.

Suomi, S. J. (2000). A biobehavioral perspective on developmental psychopathology: Excessive aggression and serotonergic dysfunction in monkeys. In A. Sameroff, M. Lewis, & S. M. Miller (Eds.), *Handbook of developmental psychopathology* (pp. 237–256). New York: Kluwer Academic Publishers.

Szapocznik, J., & Williams, R. A. (2000). Brief Strategic Family Therapy: Twenty-five years of interplay among theory, research and practice in adolescent behavior problems and drug abuse. *Clinical Child and Family Psychology Review, 3,* 117–134.

Thelen, E., & Smith, L. (1998). Dynamic systems theories. In R. M. Lerner (Ed.), *Handbook of Child Psychology: Vol. 1. Theoretical models of human development* (pp. 563–634). New York: Wiley.

van den Boom, D. C. (1994). The influence of temperament and mothering on attachment and exploration: An experimental manipulation of sensitive responsiveness among lower-class mothers with irritable infants. *Child Development, 65,* 1457–1477.

van den Boom, D. C. (1995). Do first-year intervention effects endure? Follow-up during toddlerhood of a sample of Dutch irritable infants. *Child Development, 66,* 1798–1816.

van IJzendoorn, M. H., Juffer, F., & Duyvesteyn, M. G. C. (1995). Breaking the intergenerational cycle of insecure attachment: A review of the effects of attachment-based interventions on maternal sensitivity and infant security. *Journal of Child Psychology & Psychiatry & Allied Disciplines, 36,* 225–248.

Waters, E., Vaughn, B. E., Posada, G., & Kondo-Ikemura, K. (1995). Caregiving, cultural, and cognitive perspectives on secure-base behavior and working models. *Monographs of the Society for Research in Child Development: Vol. 60.* Chicago: University of Chicago Press.

Weissberg, R. P., Kumpfer, K. L., & Seligman, M. E. P. (2003). Prevention that works for children and youth. *American Psychologist, 58,* 425–432.

Wolchik, S. A., Sandler, I. N., Millsap, R. E., Plummer, B. A., Greene, S. M., Anderson, E. R., et al. (2002). Six-year follow-up of preventive interventions for children of divorce. A randomized controlled trial. *JAMA: Journal of the American Medical Association, 288,* 1874–1881.

Wolfe, D. A., Crooks, C. V., Lee, V., McIntyre-Smith, A., & Jaffe, P. G. (2003). The effects of children's exposure to domestic violence: A meta-analysis and critique. *Clinical Child and Family Psychology Review, 6,* 171–187.

Wright, M. O'D., & Masten, A. S. (2005). Resilience processes in development: Fostering positive adaptation in the context of adversity. In S. Goldstein & R. Brooks (Eds.), *Handbook of resilience in children.* New York: Kluwer Academic/Plenum.

Wyman, P. A., Sandler, I., Wolchik, S., & Nelson, K. (2000). Resilience as cumulative competence promotion and stress protection: Theory and intervention. In D. Cicchetti, J. Rappaport, I. Sandler, & R. P. Weissberg (Eds.), *The promotion of wellness in children and adolescents* (pp. 133–184). Thousand Oaks, CA: Sage Publications.

Zeanah, C. H., Nelson, C. A., Fox, N. A., Smyke, A. T., Marshall, P., Parker, S. W., & Koga, S. (2003). Designing research to study the effects of institutionalization on brain and behavioral development: The Bucharest Early Intervention Project. *Development and Psychopathology, 15,* 885–907.

Zeanah, C. H., Smyke, A. T., & Settles, L. D. (in press). Orphanages as a developmental context for early childhood. In K. McCartney & D. A. Phillips (Eds.), *Handbook of early childhood development.* New York: Blackwell.

2

The Promotion of Resilience in the Face of Adversity

Michael Rutter

Resilience is a concept that suggests that some individuals have a relatively good psychological outcome despite suffering risk experiences that would be expected to bring about serious sequelae. In other words, resilience implies relative resistance to environmental risk experiences, or the overcoming of stress or adversity. It is not strictly social competence or positive mental health. Essentially, it is an interactive concept that involves the combination of serious risk experiences and a relatively positive psychological outcome despite those experiences (Cicchetti, Rogosch, Lynch, & Holt, 1993; Luthar, 2003; Masten, Best, Garmezy, 1990; Masten, 2001; Rutter, 1985; Rutter, 1987; Rutter, 1990; Rutter, 1999; Rutter, 2000a; Rutter, 2003; Werner & Smith, 1982; 1992).

RESILIENCE AND CONCEPTS OF RISK AND PROTECTION

Extensive research has been conducted into risk and protection factors as they operate in relation to the development of psychopathology (see Sameroff, Chapter 3 in this book). The findings show that, although the risk effects of most individual experiences are quite small, their cumulative effect may be great. To a considerable extent, adverse outcomes can be predicted on the basis of the overall number of risk factors (Fergusson, Horwood & Lynskey, 1994; Rutter, 1978; Williams, Anderson, McFie & Silva, 1990). It is therefore necessary to ask whether the concept of resilience is just a fancy way of reinventing the old and well-established concepts of risk and protection. Clearly, this is not the case. Risk and protection notions start with a focus on variables and move to outcomes, with the implicit assumption that the impact of risk and protective factors will be broadly similar in everyone. The implication is that outcomes will, therefore, be wholly dependent on the balance between risk and protective influences.

In sharp contrast, the notion of resilience starts with the recognition of the huge individual variation in people's responses to the same experiences, and assumes that outcomes are based on the mechanisms underlying that variation. Because understanding those mechanisms will cast light on the causal processes for psychopathology, it is expected that findings concerning resilience will have implications for intervention strategies with respect to both prevention and treatment.

The notion of resilience carries with it at least four implications. First, the focus on individual differences in response to risk experiences means that a feature that is protective in relation to risk may not operate protectively in nonrisk circumstances. The most obvious psychological example is provided by adoption. For children from abusive or neglectful families, adoption clearly brings protection through the provision of a much more positive rearing environment (Duyme, Arseneault, & Dumaret, 2004). However, it is unlikely to improve the outcomes of children from well-functioning families. Indeed, the psychological challenges that are inherent in adoption may even carry slight risks (Cohen, 2002). Internal medicine provides other even more striking examples. Sickle cell disease for example, is a major killer but carriers of the sickle cell genetic trait experience substantial protection against malaria (Rotter & Diamond, 1987). These examples demonstrate how the same variable may both carry risk and provide protection according to circumstances and underscore the importance of understanding causal mechanisms underlying individual differences in functioning.

Second, the inclusion of recovery in the concept of resilience means that experiences long after the initial risk effect brought about adverse psychopathology sequelae may influence the life course. Thus, there is replicated evidence that a supportive marriage greatly increases the likelihood that young people who exhibited persistent antisocial behavior in adolescence desist from crime and achieve good social functioning in adult life (Laub, Nagin & Sampson, 1998; Zoccolillo, Pickles, Quinton & Rutter, 1992). (In relation to this point, it should be added that although a supportive marriage exerts a major beneficial turning point effect in antisocial individuals, a lack of marital support is not a significant risk factor for the initiation of antisocial activities in adult life.)

Third, the focus on individual differences in response to risk experiences means that attention must be paid to how people process their experiences and to how they cope with the hazards they face. Experiences do not impinge on a passive organism; even very young children think about what happens to them, conceptualizing what the experiences mean with respect to their own self-concept and concept of the world about them. Equally, it matters what people do about their predicaments; human agency constitutes a crucial part of the developmental process. Biology has equipped human beings with the ability to contemplate both the past and the future and to plan out action in ways that change outcomes (Dennett, 2003). Laub and Sampson's (2003) long-term follow-up of the

Gluecks' sample of seriously delinquent boys clearly illustrates the point. Some boys claimed that they were turned off crime by their experiences in the custodial institutions for delinquents, whereas others felt that the experience was so negative that it reinforced their antisocial rejection of society's norms and expectations. Their experiences were essentially the same, because they were in the same institution at roughly the same time, but what these two groups of boys made of those experiences was quite different. Of course, their interactions with individual staff members may have differed in important ways, but such interactions were shaped in part by what the boys brought to the dyadic interchanges and how they responded to the other person.

Fourth, resilience research gains from the combination of quantitative and qualitative research approaches, as in the case of the Laub and Sampson (2003) follow-up study. The combination of the two approaches, if well planned and well conducted, can do much to cast light on why and how resilience occurs. For example, it might have been assumed that the beneficial turning point effect of a supportive marriage was derived from having a secure attachment relationship. Probably that was part of the mechanism, but the interview data suggested that benefits also stemmed from the extended kin network and friendship group that marriage brought, providing hitherto absent positive role models. The spouses frequently exerted informal control as well as support. Marital obligations often cut off the antisocial individual from his delinquent peer group; and marriage brought expectations of providing financial support (so that regular employment also provided social control). A focus on the meaning of key experiences forced an appreciation that a supposedly "narrow" variable such as a harmonious marriage entailed a much broader set of psychological and social influences.

It is obvious that resilience concepts and findings do not negate the value of risk and protective factor research. On the contrary, resilience builds on what has been learned from the study of risk and protective factors; the two approaches are complementary and mutually supportive. We need to gain an understanding of why and how particular experiences are usual, risky, or protective for most people, and why and how there is so much individual variations in people's responses to their experiences.

INDIVIDUAL DIFFERENCES IN RESPONSE TO ADVERSITY

The essential background for the concept of resilience lies in the universal finding of huge individual differences in people's responses to all kinds of environmental hazard. This applies to physical hazards such as malnutrition, infections, or irradiation, just as much as it does to adverse psychosocial experiences. The other background feature concerns the evidence of "steeling" effects in which successful coping with stress or adversity can lead to *improved* functioning and *increased* resistance to stress or adversity.

The first phenomenon can be studied most effectively in experimental studies, because individuals can be exposed to comparable risks and other circumstances can be controlled. In addition, it may be possible to determine the basis for individual differences in response (Petitto & Evans, 1999). For example, Cohen et al. (1991) inoculated volunteers with a cold virus and found substantial individual variation in response; moreover, psychosocial stress preceding inoculation was associated with an increased rate of infection among the inoculated subjects. Similarly, Stone et al. (1992) found that inoculation with the cold virus was more likely to lead to cold symptoms in volunteers if there had been recent stress. Wüst et al. (2004) used an experimental psychosocial stress procedure to examine cortisol responses (as measured in saliva). It was found that particular allelic variants of the glucocorticoid receptor gene were associated with differences in both the size and the timing of the cortisol increase following stress (despite a lack of difference in the baseline cortisol levels before the stress). Hinde and McGinnis (1977) showed individual differences in the response of infant rhesus monkeys to separation from their mothers, with disturbance most likely in those that had shown a tense and difficult mother-infant relationship before the separation. More than 30 years ago, Rutter (1972), reviewing the evidence on maternal deprivation, emphasized the importance of major individual differences in response to stress and adversity, and highlighted the phenomenon as one that particularly required research investment.

Individual differences are evident even in the physical consequences of environmental hazards. Thus, only a minority of babies exposed to alcohol from heavy maternal consumption during pregnancy develop the congenital abnormalities associated with fetal alcohol exposure (Kosofsky, 1999). The variation in psychosocial adaptation is also associated with differences in the postnatal rearing environment (Streissguth et al., 1997).

It might be anticipated that the extent of individual differences would be much diminished if the psychological deprivation of stress was exceptionally severe and prolonged, but the evidence indicates that this is not the case, as shown by the cognitive and social findings in the children who spent their first few years in extremely depriving Romanian institutions and who were then adopted into generally well functioning British adoptive families (Rutter, in press c; Rutter, Kreppner, O'Connor, & the English and Romanian Adoptees (ERA) Study Team, 2001a; Rutter, O'Connor, & the English and Romanian Adoptees Research Team, 2003). The average developmental quotient at the time the children left the institutions was in the retarded range but 2 years later it was nearly up to U.K. norms. Even among the children who had spent at least 2 years in appalling institutional conditions, the IQ recovery was remarkable, but there was huge individual variation. Among those who had spent the longest time in the institution, the IQ at 11 years varied from severely retarded level to highly superior, with the majority of children functioning in the average range. The same marked heterogeneity applied to children's social outcomes.

STEELING EFFECTS

The research literature on steeling effects is rather sparse but empirically-based examples do exist (Rutter, 1981). For example, experimental stress in rodents has been shown to lead to structural and functional effects on the neuroendocrine system associated with greater resistance to later stress (Hennessey & Levine, 1979). Similarly, repeated parachute jumping by humans leads to physiological adaptation associated with both a change in the timing and nature of the anticipatory physiological response and also reduced subjective feeling of stress (see Rutter, 1981). It is well known that exposure to infections (either by natural exposure or through vaccination or immunization) leads to relative immunity to later exposure to the same infectious agents. The experience of happy separations in early childhood may also lead to a better later adaptation to hospital admission (Stacey, Dearden, Pill, & Robinson, 1970). Older children's experience of coping successfully with family poverty seemed, in studies conducted in California, to lead to greater psychological strengths (Elder, 1974).

What leads to these steeling effects? We do not, as yet, have an entirely satisfactory answer to that question but it seems likely that the key feature is successful coping with the challenge, stress, or hazard. It is likely that this leads to a range of different consequences, all of which play a role in the steeling phenomenon. Thus, there is physiological adaptation, psychological habituation, the achievement of a sense of self-efficacy, the acquisition of effective coping strategies, and also a cognitive redefinition of the experience. The relative importance of each of these remains unknown but it may be anticipated that each plays a role, with the relative importance probably differing according to the different types of environmental hazard and the different types of outcomes.

HOW CAN WE BE SURE THAT THE RESILIENCE IS REAL?

Before turning to a more detailed consideration of resilience, it is necessary to recognize that there are several ways in which the observed individual differences in response to adversity (which constitutes the core of the resilience concept) may be seriously misleading with respect to resilience. For there to be true meaningful resilience, it is essential that the supposed risk experience is truly risky and that the risk is environmentally mediated. Also it is essential that the measures of outcome cover the range of likely possibilities. This is because the supposed good outcome could mean nothing more than that maladaptive consequences are not being assessed adequately by the measures used in the study.

To reiterate, the range of methodological issues is wide but three issues stand out as particularly important. First, there is the question of whether or not there has been a true risk experience that involved, environmental mediation second; there is the question of whether the apparent resilience was simply a function of variations in risk exposure; and third, there is the question of whether the supposed resilience was nothing more than a result of measuring too narrow a range of outcomes.

Testing For a True Risk Effect

With respect to testing for a true risk experience effect, this needs to be done in relation to particular risk variables as they occur in the general population, and testing needs to be done in the sample being studied for resilience.[1] Four main alternatives need to be considered; genetic rather than environmental mediation; person effects on the environment; social selection, and third variable effects (Rutter, in press a).

Environmental Mediation. There are several different types of natural experiment that can be used to test for environmental mediation (Rutter, in press a; Rutter et al., 2001b). These include effects within monozygotic twin pairs (so that a difference in risk experience between the twins is being assessed in pairs that have the same genes); the effects of adoptive family characteristics on psychological outcomes (so that the effects arise in families in which there is no genetic link between the parents and the children); and the effects of a radical change in environment (so that the alterations over time in the functioning of individuals can be assessed in relation to the major change in environment). The findings from such studies clearly demonstrate environmentally mediated risk effects from adverse experiences that involve family influences of various kinds including parental negativity, abuse, neglect, and amount of conversation and play (Rutter, in press b). Moreover, the environmentally mediated risks include variations with the normal range as well as extreme environments (although, for obvious reasons, the effects of the latter are greater).

Person Effects on the Environment. Person effects on the environment can be separated from environmental effects on the person through the use of longitudinal data (see Caspi 2004, Caspi et al., 2004; Thorpe, Rutter & Greenwood, 2003). In essence, the effects of particular individual

---

[1] Similar considerations apply with respect to resilience in relation to genetic risks, but are not considered here.

characteristics at time 1 on specific environments at time 2 can be contrasted with the effects of those environments at time 1 on the individual characteristics at time 2. The findings are consistent in showing both person effects and environmental effects; accordingly, both need to be considered in any study of resilience.

Social Selection. Social selection, meaning selection into risk circumstances, can readily give rise to spurious statistical associations between risk experiences and adverse outcomes. The remedy lies in always pitting the alternative of social selection against the alternative of social causation (see Borge, Rutter, Côté, & Tremblay, 2003). For example, before studying the effects of nonmaternal care, Borge et al. (2003) determined the differences between families using child-minding group day care and those in which the mother remained at home to look after the child. Major differences were found. These meant that because the families using nonmaternal care were so different, this had to be taken into account in assessing the effects of such care on the children.

Third Variable Effects. Third variable effects mean that the risk association actually derives from the association of both risk and outcome with some other variable. The research challenges inherent in these alternatives are considerable, and must be met but, when they are, the findings do show important environmentally mediated risk effects associated with the family environment (Rutter, 2000b).

Variations In Risk Exposure

The second challenge in resistance research is to consider the possibility that apparent resilience is simply a function of variations in risk exposure. That is to say, that variations in outcome are due to nothing more than the fact that some children have suffered more severe risk experiences than others. It is not that they have been in any way protected, but just that they have not suffered the same risk exposure. This is a real possibility, in view of the substantial evidence that the main risks derive from the cumulative effect of many negative experiences, rather than the major effects of just one (see Sameroff, Chapter 3 in this book). Studies of resilience have to take seriously the crucial need to assess the overall extent of risk exposure.

Range of Outcomes

The third challenge is to consider the possibility that apparent resilience results from measuring a range of outcomes that is too narrow. That is, that young people who seem to have escaped adversity have not really escaped; it is just that their problems have not been measured. Misspecification of risk, similarly, means that there is a risk effect but it is, in reality, brought on by some environmental feature other than the one identified (see later discussion).

For example, in the study of children experiencing profound deprivation in Romanian institutions, we studied seven major domains on both the 6-year-old and 11-year-old follow-up functioning (Rutter, in press c; Rutter, Kreppner, O'Connor, & the English and Romanian Adoptees (ERA) Study Team 2001a). Normal functioning was derived in terms of an absence of problems in all of these domains – a harsh criterion. Nevertheless, among the children experiencing the longest duration of institutional deprivation, about a fifth were free of problems.

If risk experiences are conceptualized in broad ways, it is inevitable that there will have been some misidentification of risk. For example, "broken homes" or parent-child separation were once conceptualized as major psychosocial risks. Numerous studies have now shown that, although family separations can be stressful, the main risk derives from the family discord or conflict that led to the break up of the family or the stressful nature of the particular features of the separation (Rutter, 1971). Fergusson, Horwood, and Lynskey (1992), using the Christchurch longitudinal study data, showed that family change and disruptions were not associated with any increase in delinquency after family discord had been taken into account. In contrast, family discord was associated with a marked increase in the rate of offense irrespective of whether discord involved family separations or break up. Alternatively, the risks may derive from the problems in parenting that sometimes follow family break up. Harris et al. (1986), for example, showed that parental loss was not a risk factor for adult depression if the loss did not lead to poor parental care. On the other hand, poor parental care did constitute a risk factor for adult depression even if it was not associated with parental loss. Numerous other examples could be given but the key point is that the study of resilience can only be valid if there is an accurate identification of the valid risk experiences that do actually substantially increase the risk of adverse psychological outcomes.

Much the same point arises in relation to the need to assess a broad range of psychological outcomes. Very few risk experiences are diagnosis-specific in their outcomes and, hence, outcome measures need to cover a broad range of possibilities encompassing emotional disturbance, disruptive behavior, and drug or alcohol problems.

VARIATIONS IN VULNERABILITY TO STRESS AND ADVERSITY

We also need to consider the influences that may be concerned with variations in young people's vulnerability to psychosocial stresses and adversities. At least four rather different features need to be considered: (1) genetic susceptibilities, (2) the consequences of prior experiences, (3) social context, and (4) the processing of experiences and coping with them.

Genetic Influences on Susceptibility to Environmental Risks

There is growing evidence in the fields of medicine and biology of the importance of gene-environment interactions. Comparable evidence is beginning to accrue in the field of psychosocial adversity (Rutter, 2003; Rutter & Silberg, 2002). For example, Kendler and his colleagues (1995) examined the risk of onset of an episode of major depression in a sample of monozygotic and dizygotic twins according to the presence or absence of a severe life event. The findings showed quite strikingly that the risk that a new episode of major depression would follow a severe life event was highest in individuals with the greatest genetic liability and lowest in those with the least genetic liability. In other words, the genetic effects were operating, in part, through their role in moderating the effects of an adverse environmental experience. Jaffee et al. (in press) have shown the same thing in relation to parental maltreatment and the development of conduct problems in the children.

In both of these studies, genetic liability had to be inferred from twin zygosity, but molecular genetic findings allow genetic risk to be assessed directly. Caspi et al. (2002) showed that the effects of maltreatment in childhood as a predisposing factor for antisocial behavior were strongly influenced by whether or not the child had a particular gene that influenced monoamine oxidase A (MAOA) activity. Similarly, they found that another gene influencing serotonin functioning had a major effect on whether or not people developed depression following either childhood maltreatment or, later, acutely negative life events (Caspi, Sugden, Moffitt, Taylor et al. 2003). Again, the implication from both of these findings is that the genes are operating not as a direct risk factor for a negative psychological outcome but rather as a moderating feature creating an influence through effects on susceptibility to stress experiences. There was no effect of the gene in the absence of the environmental adversities, but there was a major genetic influence in response to environmental risks.

PRIOR EXPERIENCES

Prior psychosocial experiences may also be influential. For example, an early study by David Quinton and myself (Quinton & Rutter, 1976) showed that multiple hospital admissions had a minor risk effect in relation to later emotional disturbance, when the children came from a background that did not include psychosocial disadvantage. By contrast, the risk was greater when children came from a socially disadvantaged background. It seemed that the experience of chronic adversity had rendered children more susceptible to the effects of acute stress.

SOCIAL CONTEXT

The social context operating at the time and the presence, or absence, of protective features may also be influential. Conger, Rueter, and Elder (1999) showed that high marital support reduced the effect of economic pressure in adults, predisposing them to emotional distress, and that effective couple problem-solving reduced the adverse effect of marital conflict on marital distress. Jenkins and Smith (1990) showed that children whose parents had a discordant, conflict-ridden marriage were more likely to develop psychological disturbance than children whose parents had a harmonious marriage. However, this risk effect from a poor parental marriage was negligible in the case of children who had a very good close relationship with an adult (who might be one of the parents or might be someone outside the nuclear family). Either the good relationship buffered the children from the risk effects of a home characterized by discordant conflict or the main risk derived not from the overall atmosphere in the home, but rather from a negative relationship with a parent. In that connection, it is important to appreciate that family-wide risk influences (such as parental mental disorder or marital conflict) frequently do not impinge to the same extent (or even in the same way) on all children in the family (Carbonneau, Rutter, Simonoff, Silberg et al., 2001; Carbonneau, Eaves, Silberg, Simonoff et al., 2002; Carbonneau, Rutter, Silberg, Simonoff et al., 2002; Caspi et al., 2003; Jenkins, Rasbash, & O'Connor, 2003; Jenkins, Dunn, Rasbash, O'Connor, & Simpson, 2005). The evidence that, in these circumstances, one child is "scapegoated" but another child is treated more favorably, indicates that resilience may reflect this differential parental treatment. However, it should be noted that the differential treatment may come about from either child effects on the parent or from differences in parental attitude that arise in other ways.

Processing and Coping with Experiences

The factors involved with the development of resilience may also be apparent in individual differences in young people's immediate response to the stress situation. It is clear that all forms of stress or challenge need to be considered in terms of an interaction between people and their environments. It makes no sense to consider stress or adversity as if they impinged on a passive organism. They do not. From infancy onward, children process their experiences – thinking about them, developing concepts about what their experiences mean, and contemplating how they will affect their future. They consider how they will respond to the challenge with a response ranging from helpless resignation or acceptance that they can do nothing about their circumstances to a positive feeling that they are not going to allow the terrible experience to get them down. This, in turn, leads to forms of coping that may be adaptive or maladaptive in their effects. At one time, this used to be thought of in terms of "good" or "bad" defense mechanisms but it has become obvious that that is not an appropriate way of thinking about things (Rutter, 1981). To begin with, what suits one person may not suit another, and what is appropriate for one sort of adversity may not be appropriate for others.

It is probably more important that an individual has a range of coping strategies within his or her repertoire rather than routinely and reflexively always choosing one that is supposed to be "good." Rather, it is necessary to think of coping in terms of consequences. For example, it is likely to be better to adopt a problem-solving approach rather than having recourse to drugs or alcohol, which may suppress the negative symptoms in the short term but create a new set of problems through reliance on chemicals in the long run. In short, the individual differences in immediate response can be conceptualized in terms of the definition of the experience (as a challenge, opportunity, or threat); the response to the challenge (in terms of planning/coping versus resignation/acceptance); and adaptive versus maladaptive coping (as exemplified by problem solving versus recourse to drugs).

The evidence on these features is more limited than one would like but the evidence that exists supports the notion that features of this kind are influential. Thus, in a longitudinal study of young people who had been reared in group homes for most of their childhood and adolescence, Quinton and Rutter (1988) found that many developed a general feeling that they were at the mercy of fate. In the group homes, as part of a protective supportive environment, they had had very little opportunity to exercise autonomy or responsibility and all major decisions were made for them. The undesired and unexpected consequence of this, however, was that the young people had not developed a sense of self-efficacy or a determination that they would, somehow or other, find a way of overcoming difficulties. On the other hand, some of them had developed what was termed a "planning" tendency. This was measured in relation to planning for marriage and planning for work. In each case, the categorization was made not in terms of the quality of decision making but simply in terms of whether or not the young people exercised active choice. The findings showed that those who had this planning tendency were much less likely to become pregnant at age 18 or younger and much less likely to land up with a deviant partner (meaning someone who exhibited antisocial behavior or regularly misused drugs). The findings also showed that the development of a planning orientation was, to some extent, predictable. Very few of the young people had gained any kind of scholastic achievement but they did differ in terms of their success at school as measured in other ways – in terms of achieving positions of social responsibility within the school, with skills in music or sport, or some other activity. The implication was that, possibly, the experience of success and the ability to exert control, in one arena, had enabled them to develop a more positive self-concept and cognitive set to deal with life experiences. The findings from Clausen's longitudinal study paralleled these (Clausen, 1991; Clausen, 1993).

Harris, Brown, and Bifulco examined somewhat comparable features in terms of the long-term consequences of maternal loss in childhood in relation to the development of depression in adulthood (Harris, Brown, & Bifulco, 1990). They found that the risks accompanying maternal loss stemmed from the lack of parental care. The lack of care then served as an initiating point for two rather different indirect causal pathways that later predisposed individuals to depression. One pathway was concerned with the "practical real life" effects of a premarital pregnancy, which led to a later lack of marital support. Such a lack of support created a proximal risk factor for depression. The other pathway was the more psychological one, in which a lack of parental care predisposed an individual to a feeling of helplessness that went on to a more generalized feeling of hopelessness, which also created a proximal risk factor for depression.

IMPORTANCE OF LATER EXPERIENCES

The early literature on resilience, or "invulnerability" as it used to be termed, focused primarily on what happened at the time of the adverse experience. Recent research findings have made it clear that what happens after the experience is at least as important. Major recovery can take place after even the most severe adversity, stress, or deprivation provided that the later environment is of sufficiently high quality and represents a radical change. For example, Duyme, Dumaret, and Tomkiewicz (1999) showed this with respect to cognitive recovery in children removed from their parents because of abuse or neglect and adopted into well-functioning families at some point between the ages of 4 and 6 1/2. Although the provision of normal rearing did not begin until after age 4, major improvements in cognitive functioning were found.

Similarly, follow-up studies of children who spent their first few years in extremely depriving Romanian institutions, and who were subsequently adopted into British families, showed a major catch-up in physical growth, in cognitive functioning, and social and behavioral functioning (Rutter in press c; Rutter, Kreppner, O'Connor, & the English and Romanian Adoptees (ERA) Study Team, 2001a; Rutter & the English and Romanian Adoptees (ERA) Study Team, 1998).

IS DEVELOPMENTAL CATCH-UP USUALLY COMPLETE IF A GOOD REARING ENVIRONMENT IS PROVIDED?

The findings from these and other studies are very encouraging in terms of major positive changes that can and do occur, even after the most grossly depriving or abusive experiences, provided the later environment is of high quality. That is very encouraging and reassuring with respect to the potential for resilience, even in the most extreme circumstances. Nevertheless, it would be quite wrong to suppose that the psychological catch-up is always complete.

There may be lasting sequelae because of effects on the individual that can be quite persistent even if rearing circumstances are good (Rutter, 1989). For example, early adversities may set in motion altered patterns of interpersonal interactions, with such negative interactions predisposing individuals to the occurrence of further sets of psychosocial risk experiences. For example, in a classic follow-up study of children who attended a child guidance clinic in America, Robins (1966) showed that young people who exhibited disruptive behavior in childhood had a markedly increased risk of adverse experiences in adult life, of a kind that predisposed them to episodes of depression. These experiences included falling out with friends, lack of social support, multiple broken marriages, frequent changes of job, and frequent periods of unemployment. Similarly, in an 18-year follow-up study of a community sample in London, Champion, Goodall and Rutter (1995) showed that the children who exhibited disruptive behavior at age 10 had a markedly increased rate of severe and stressful experiences, both acute and chronic, in their late twenties. There was also some increase for children showing emotional disturbance at age 10, although the effects were less marked.

There may be similar self-perpetuating changes in people's styles of behavior. As already noted, young people reared in institutions often develop feelings of being at the mercy of circumstances and, because of that, they tend not to adopt effective coping strategies in relation to challenges and stresses.

The follow-up study of Romanian adoptees also suggested that biological programming effects on brain development might well be operative (Rutter in press c; Rutter, O'Connor, & the English and Romanian Adoptees Research Team, 2003). The strong effects of the duration of institutional deprivation on both cognitive and social outcomes were as marked at age 11 as they had been at age 6 and at age 4. The implication is that there was some change in the individual that was leading to persistence of adverse effects long after a good rearing environment was provided.

Another different sort of process is evident in the effects of both acute and chronic stress on the neuroendocrine system. As far as chronic stress is concerned, it is not primarily that adverse experiences lead to an up-regulation in the hormones that reflect emotional activation. Rather, it seems that experiences alter the normal diurnal variation in hormone levels (Carlson & Earls, 1997). It is not known what functional consequences result from this deregulation but the implication is that the sequelae may derive from a lack of normal modulation of endocrine activity rather than the hormone levels being absolutely too high or too low.

Animal studies have also shown that severe stress can damage neural structures, particularly those of the hippocampus (McEwen, 1999). There is growing evidence that the same occurs in humans. Once more, the functional consequences of these neural changes remain largely unknown. It certainly should not be assumed that the neural effects are irreversible but, equally, it would be unwise to assume that they don't have functional consequences.

As illustrated already in the causal model put forward by Harris (1990), a further route could lead to lasting consequences in the establishment of negative mental sets or negative self-concepts. There is no doubt that people develop mental sets about their experiences and about what these experiences mean in relation to themselves. It is quite possible that such mental sets, if negative, could provide one way of sequelae persisting.

PROMOTION OF RESILIENCE PRIOR TO ADVERSITY

In considering what may be done to promote resilience in terms of interventions before the occurrence of the adverse experiences, it is necessary to consider both the fostering of protective qualities in the individual and the provision of a range of adaptive experiences. Research findings have been reasonably consistent in highlighting the kinds of personal qualities that appear protective (Luthar, 2003; Masten, Best, & Garmezy, 1990; Rutter, 1999; 2000a). These include the following qualities: • good intelligence and high scholastic achievements; • secure attachments to caregivers, other family members, and individuals outside the family who have a loving continuous relationship with the child; • multiple harmonious relationships (reflecting the importance of a range of good relationships and therefore the protection that comes from multiplicity, rather than reliance on just one or two); • a sense of self-efficacy (meaning a feeling of confidence in one's own abilities to deal with situations and not just a general feeling good about oneself); • a range of social problem-solving skills (reflecting the fact that there is no one universally good coping strategy; rather protection comes from having a good repertoire of different skills that may be called upon in different circumstances); • a positive social interaction style (involving good humor, responsivity to other people's needs and feelings, and a sense of caring); • a flexible adaptive approach to new situations (reflecting the fact that adaptability is not a unitary quality but a key feature that derives from our evolutionary past is the capacity to learn from experience and to adapt to changing circumstances).

Some researchers who have adopted a strongly deterministic view of the ways in which genes and environment provide a complete account of all human behavior, have been skeptical about the possibility that there is such a thing as free will. Dennett (2003), adopting a strongly materialistic approach in relation to evolutionary theory, has convincingly shown that this is a wholly mistaken view. The basic point is that evolution has provided us with a nature that is designed for change and adaptability and which provides a set of thought processes that allow us to evaluate, plan, and shape what happens to us.

The provision of a range of adaptive experiences is equally important in promoting resilience. In essence, these seem to boil down to two main features: (1) opportunities to cope successfully with challenges and stresses within the individual's capacity at any particular point in development and in the prevailing social context, and (2) opportunities to succeed in a range of settings and circumstances. Many varied opportunities exist; they are to be found in families, schools, peer groups, and the community.

PROMOTION OF RESILIENCE AT TIME OF ADVERSITY

What happens at the time of the negative experience is equally important. Numerous studies suggest that five features are particularly important (Luthar, 2003; Masten et al., 1990; Rutter, 1999; 2000a): (1) Depending on the nature of the adversity, it may be possible to dilute its impact on the individual. For example, if the adversity lies in the occurrence of depression in a parent, this may be achieved by helping the depressed parent avoid focusing negative feelings on the children or by the other parent (or other family member) taking greater responsibility for child care; (2) It may be helpful to provide alternative sources of support in relationships. Taking again the example of mental illness in a parent, it may be helpful for the children to extend their range of activities outside the family when the family environment is pervasively stressful; (3) Children may be helped to develop better social problem-solving skills, greater self-efficacy, and more adaptive methods of coping; (4) Young people may be helped to develop a more positive and adaptive cognitive set to the challenging circumstances they are facing; (5) It is important to help young people avoid damaging coping strategies, such as reliance on drugs, destructive anger, or just "giving up."

PROMOTION OF RESILIENCE AFTER NEGATIVE EXPERIENCES

Attention has already been given to the substantial benefits that may follow the provision of a good rearing environment even after the most seriously damaging experiences in early childhood. Sometimes it is presumed that for these benefits to occur, the recuperative experiences must arise no later than in early or middle childhood. However, this is not the case. Many of the features that provide the development of later resilience are the same as those operating before adversity or during adversity, but there are additional features that are important. These may be illustrated by taking as examples turning-point experiences arising in late adolescence or early adult life. In our own studies of British children being reared in high-risk circumstances, we found that the existence of a warm supportive harmonious marital relationship greatly improved social functioning (Zoccolillo, Pickles, Quinton, & Rutter, 1992). Laub, Nagin, and Sampson (1998) found exactly the same results in a long-term follow-up of delinquent boys who had been in custodial institutions during their adolescence. Both of these studies dealt with individuals who showed antisocial behavior in childhood, and who were, therefore, at high risk of showing social problems in adult life. For obvious reasons, it was crucial to make sure that the apparent beneficial effects of a harmonious marriage were not simply a consequence of the individuals being at lesser risk or showing less behavioral disturbance in childhood, or of some other unmeasured variable. A variety of statistical techniques, applied to a wide range of risk and protective variables, satisfied us that the turning-point effect was indeed a real one. In another turning-point study, Osborn (1980) showed that a geographical move away from London was associated with a substantial drop in boys' delinquency, whether measured by self-report or by official crime records. Again, care was taken to ensure that this was not an artifact of the boys' prior experiences or prior behavior.

The available evidence suggests that positive turning-point experiences involve three key features: (1) the provision of new opportunities that involve a major break with the negative aspects of past experiences; (2) the opportunity for a change in mental set; and (3) circumstances that allow the development of improved coping strategies.

Summary of Promoters of Resilience

It cannot be claimed that the research evidence to date provides a comprehensive picture of the factors involved in promoting resilience, but it is possible to summarize the features that appear to play a major role. These features may conveniently be subdivided into key background factors and key resilience promoters.

The five key background factors that relate to resilience are: (1) the multiplicity of risk and protective experiences; (2) individual differences in sensitivity to risk (as influenced by both genes and environment); (3) mediating mechanisms that differ according to the type of risk; (4) mediating mechanisms that differ according to the psychological outcome; and (5) circumstances before, during, or after the risk experience.

The six key resilience promoters involve: (1) reduction of the impact of adversity on the individual; (2) reduction of negative chain reactions; (3) increasing, positive chain reactions; (4) opening up of advantageous opportunities; and (5) provision of experiences that in some way neutralize the key risk feature; and (6) promotion of positive cognitive processing of experiences so that individuals are better able to focus on the ways in which they have successfully met challenges rather than concentrating on all the things that went wrong.

Research Implications

The main implication for research that can be derived from extant studies of resilience is that much more attention needs to be given to examining the causal processes underlying individual differences in response to stress and adversity. The mechanisms are likely to vary according to the types of environmental hazard and the types of psychopathological outcome. No single answer should be expected. Note that the investigation of individual differences is not synonymous with a search for the causes of some hypothetical quality of general resilience. Individuals may be resilient with respect to some types of environmental hazard but not others, and such resilience may apply to some outcomes and not others. Moreover, the resistance to adversity may vary by developmental phase. Although some continuity over time is expected, it is most unlikely that resilience represents a fixed trait. Indeed, the evidence suggests that it would be a mistake to conceptualize resilience as necessarily residing in the individual. Rather, it may reflect the social context or social circumstances. In short, having argued for the importance of phenomena that characterize what has come to be called resilience, the accompanying recommendation is that research should abandon a focus on resilience, as such, and should concentrate on the processes underlying individual differences in response to environmental hazard.

The second implication for research concerns the importance of a life trajectory approach and the value of studying the causal mechanisms involved in turning-point effects. A rigorous quantitative research strategy will be needed to deal with a host of methodological hazards; the reality of the turning point must be established before determining its origins and consequences. Equally, qualitative research methods will be needed for an adequate evaluation of the personal meaning of the experiences that appear to have produced a turning point. But, having obtained data on such meaning, and the personal actions that result, it will be necessary to translate the findings into testable hypotheses that can be subjected to sound quantitative analysis that pits one explanation against others.

The third implication for research concerns the need to combine psychosocial with biological research approaches, using a diverse range of strategies. Attention was drawn to the molecular genetic research findings on gene-environment interaction (G × E). Psychosocial researchers have been inclined to dismiss such findings on the grounds that, however interesting they may be, they are of no practical importance because genes cannot be altered. However, that entirely misses the main point concerning G × E, namely the implication that the genes and the environment are operating on the same causal pathway. It is for that reason that G × E may be crucially informative with respect to the effects of E on the individual (Caspi et al., 2002; 2003).

Functional brain imaging may be similarly informative, as illustrated by the findings on both cognitive behavior therapy (Goldapple et al., 2004) and remedial interventions for dyslexia (Shaywitz et al., 2003). The goal is to bring together the cognitive processing and the brain-function changes to identify the factors mediating both therapeutic efficacy and individual differences in response.

Neuroendocrine studies represent a third potentially useful biological approach (Gunnar & Donzella, 2002). The goal of such approaches is to determine the individual differences in neuroendocrine response in order to relate them to successful coping as assessed behaviorally, and to use the findings together to test hypotheses on mediating mechanisms. It is relevant that successful adaptation is accompanied by alterations in neuroendocrine pattern, as the example of parachute jumping illustrates (Ursin, Badde & Levins, 1978).

The role of mental sets and models also warrants more detailed attention than it has received up to now. There is a widespread assumption that the ways in which people conceptualize negative experiences and incorporate them into their own self-concept greatly influence the psychopathological consequences (Bretherton & Munholland, 1999). The notion is plausible, but there are some findings that raise queries (Turton, Hughes & Fainman, in press) and there is a great need for research that puts the hypothesis of the crucial mediating role of cognitive internal-working models against alternative mediators.

Finally, animal models are potentially very informative about the possible mechanisms underlying individual differences in response to risk environments. For example, rhesus monkey studies by Suomi and his colleagues (e.g., Suomi, 2003) have shown the importance of gene-environment interactions. For obvious reasons, they cannot test hypotheses about mediating mechanisms that involve language or higher thought processes, but if they produce findings on low-level mediators this inevitably raises doubts about the need to involve mechanisms in humans that could not apply to organisms without the superior cognitive skills possessed by humans.

POLICY AND PRACTICE IMPLICATIONS

The evidence that even the most severe stresses and adversities do not have the same effects on everyone provides a message of hope. Some individuals succumb, but others survive and may even come through the negative experiences, strengthened as a result of having coped successfully. Prevention needs to be targeted not just on the reduction of risk and the enhancement of health promoting experiences but also on the processes that lead to positive functioning despite the experience of serious adversity – the phenomenon of resilience. The second message of hope is that the time frame for resilience is a long one; experiences, even in adult life, that provide a break from preceding disadvantage and which open up new opportunities can provide a beneficial turning point that can counter earlier adversities.

However, the positive message of hope must be accompanied by some message of caution. First, it is evident that some effects of experiences in early life can be quite difficult to reverse because they have resulted in some form of biological programming, or because they have brought about neural impairment. Second, it also has to be recognized that important areas of ignorance remain. This applies, for example to the causal processes underlying sex differences in susceptibility and some forms of psychopathology and the nature and extent of age-specific variations in vulnerability.

Probably, the most important policy practice implication is the need for a broadening of horizons on how resilience might be fostered. Thus, attention must be paid to experiences that do not involve major risks but which are protective for individuals who have suffered adversity. The adoption of children who have suffered chronic abuse or neglect is a case in point. Obviously, it would not be appropriate to view this as an acceptable general solution but the findings do underscore what can be achieved by a total change of environment, which brings about a combination of positive experiences and new opportunities.

Although the change is of an entirely different kind, the turning-point effects of a supportive marriage in later life serve a similar purpose. Of course, it is not possible to prescribe a supportive marriage, but there are lessons for prevention in the evidence on the origins of marital support and on the elements of its benefits. Thus, a harmonious marriage to a nondeviant spouse from a nondeprived background has been found to be more likely if the individual has acquired a style of planning key life changes (which, in turn, is more likely if the person had successful experiences at school); if marriage is postponed until after further education or work has broadened the social group of potential partners; and if the individuals are part of a peer group that is not antisocial in orientation (Quinton, Pickles, Maughan & Rutter, 1993, Sampson & Laub, 1993; Laub & Sampson 2003). The key seems to lie in real-life experiences that bring success (and thereby probably foster a concept of self-efficacy) and open up opportunities. The implication would seem to be that it is these sorts of experiences and opportunities that should be fostered, rather than relying on any form of intervention targeted on individual psychological qualities.

With respect to the elements that seemed to be implicated in beneficial turning-point effects, the most striking feature is that they involved far more than a dyadic relationship (the extended family of the nondeviant spouse, an altered peer group, and a work environment all appeared relevant), and that the supportive marriage also brought new role models, supervision, and control, and a changed life structure and set of activities. In short, there was a radical change in the person's whole social circumstances. Once more, the challenge is to provide real-life experiences that include these elements and these possibilities.

A second broadening of horizons, closely related to the first, derives from the evidence that the successful countering of adversity usually involves beneficial changes that combine effects in the individual, in the family, in the school, and in the community. That does not translate into a recommendation that interventions should separately target each of these; rather the implication is that success is likely to lie in interventions that may be expected to bring about a broadening of impact across social settings, with the kind of "knock-on" or indirect chain effects noted in relation to turning points.

A third broadening involves an appreciation that maladaptive responses to stress or adversity (such as reliance on drugs or alcohol or reacting with anger and aggression) can be appropriately targeted but that, if such targeting is to bring about the desired benefits, it is likely that the individuals will need to be helped to acquire alternative methods of coping (both emotionally and behaviorally). Experiences with problem-solving interventions suggest that these approaches are likely to work best if they are implemented in real-life circumstances rather than taught as a skill to be learned in the classroom (Compas, Benson, Boyer, Hicks et al., 2002; Pellegrini, 1994).

A fourth broadening stems from the recognition that societal influences may be critical in ensuring that everyone has the opportunity to exercise responsibility and judgment and to achieve success in some area that brings rewards and recognition. Thus, this has implications for the ways in which schools function (Rutter, Maughan, Mortimore, Ouston et al., 1979), but also it has similar implications for youth organizations and the work environment.

An entirely different broadening of horizons concerns the need to consider pharmacological interventions. That runs entirely counter to the whole ethos of the resilience movement but it would be a mistake to rule it out entirely. First, the evidence on gene-environment interactions points to the likelihood that, when they are present, environmental hazards are having effects on the same neurotransmitters, influenced by the genes (Caspi et al., 2003; Moffitt, Caspi & Rutter, submitted). Might resilience be fostered by drugs that affect the relevant neurotransmitters? We do not know, but the possibility should not be ruled out entirely. Second, studies with rats have shown that, in some circumstances, experiences may bring about their effects through epigenetic changes involving methylation and that these can be modified by drugs (Weaver, Cervoni, Champagne, D'Alessio et al., 2004). Once more, we are certainly not at a point at which drug treatment could be recommended, but however unlikely this approach may seem today, it should remain as an option on the long-term agenda.

The last point is that the findings on resilience clearly indicate that it would be a mistake to regard prevention as necessarily being restricted to either the reduction of adverse experiences or an increase in positive ones. The multifaceted nature of resilience shows many opportunities for preventative interventions to make a difference. These include steps taken before, during, and after adverse experiences. Clearly, we need to think creatively about how these steps may be used to construct improved preventive policies.

Of course, as always, it will be necessary to test whether or not our well-thought-through interventions do actually bring about the benefits that we expect. In evaluating effects, it will be crucial to go beyond the question of whether the intervention "works" to determine the mediating mechanisms for efficacy (Weersing & Weisz, 2002). Only in this way can we learn from the experience what is needed to devise improved methods of intervention in the future. In this connection, at an appropriate point, randomized controlled trials have an invaluable role to play. Sometimes it is argued that these only apply to medical interventions and not to social ones, but that is wrong. The history of social sciences indicates that it has actually provided leadership in this field (MacIntyre & Petticrew, 2000; Oakley & Roberts, 1996), even if that lesson tends to get overlooked.

References

Borge, A. I. H., Rutter, M., Côté, S., & Tremblay, R. E. (2003). Early childcare and physical aggression: Differentiating social selection and social causation. *Journal of Child Psychology and Psychiatry, 45*, 367–376.
Bretherton, I., & Munholland, K. A. (1999). Internal working models in attachment relationships: A construct revisited. In J. Cassidy & P. R. Shaver (Eds.), *Handbook of attachment: Theory, research and critical applications* (pp. 89–111). New York: Guilford.
Carbonneau, R., Eaves, L. J., Silberg, J. L., Simonoff, E., & Rutter, M. (2002). Assessment of the within-family environment in twins: Absolute versus differential ratings and relationship with conduct problems. *Journal of Child Psychology and Psychiatry, 43*, 1064–1074.
Carbonneau, R., Rutter, M., Silberg, J. L., Simonoff, E., & Eaves, L. J. (2002). Assessment of genetic and environmental influences on differential ratings of within-family experiences and relationships in twins. *Psychological Medicine, 32*, 729–741.

Carbonneau, R., Rutter, M., Simonoff, E., Silberg, J. L., Maes, H. H., & Eaves, L. J. (2001). The Twin Inventory of Relationships and Experiences (TIRE): Psychometric properties of a measure of the non-shared and shared environmental experiences of twins and singletons. *International Journal of Methods in Psychiatric Research, 10*, 72–85.

Carlson, M., & Earls, F. (1997). Psychological and neuroendocrinological sequelae of early social deprivation in institutionalized children in Romania. *Annals of the New York Academy of Sciences, 807*, 419–428.

Caspi, A. (2004). Life-course development: The interplay of social selection and social causation within and across generations. In P. L. Chase-Lansdale, K. Kiernan, & R. J. Friedman (Eds.), *Human development across lives and generations* (pp. 8–27). Cambridge: Cambridge University Press.

Caspi, A., McClay, J., Moffitt, T. E., Mill, J., Martin, J., Craig, I. W. et. al. (2002). Role of genotype in the cycle of violence in maltreated children. *Science, 297*, 851–854.

Caspi, A., Moffitt, T. E., Morgan, J., Rutter, M., Taylor, A., Arseneault, L., (2004). Maternal expressed emotion predicts children's externalizing behavior problems: Using MZ-twin differences to identify environmental effects on behavioral development. *Developmental Psychology, 40*, 149–161.

Caspi, A., Sugden, K., Moffitt, T. E., Taylor, A., Craig, I. W., Harrington, H. et al. (2003). Influence of life stress on depression: Moderation by a polymorphism in the 5-HTT gene. *Science, 301*, 386–389.

Champion, L. A., Goodall, G. M., & Rutter, M. (1995). Behaviour problems in childhood and stressors in early adult life. I. A 20-year follow-up of London school children. *Psychological Medicine, 25*, 231–246.

Cicchetti, D., Rogosch, F. A., Lynch, M., & Holt, K. D. (1993). Resilience in maltreated children: Processes leading to adaptive outcome. *Development and Psychopathology, 5*, 629–648.

Clausen, J. S. (1991). Adolescent competence and the shaping of the life course. *American Journal of Sociology, 96*, 805–842.

Clausen, J. S.(1993). *American lives: Looking back at the children of the Great Depression.* New York: Free Press.

Cohen, N. J. (2002). Adoption. In M. Rutter and E. Taylor (Eds.), *Child and adolescent psychiatry* (pp. 373–381). Oxford: Blackwell.

Cohen, S., Tyrrell, D. A. J., & Smith, A. P. (1991). Psychological stress and susceptibility to the common cold. *New England Journal of Medicine, 325*, 606–612.

Compas, B. E., Benson, M., Boyer, M., Hicks, T. V., & Konik, B. (2002). Problem-solving therapies. In M. Rutter & E. Taylor (Eds.), *Child and Adolescent Psychiatry* (pp. 938–948). Oxford: Blackwell.

Conger, R. D., Rueter, M. A., & Elder, G. H. Jr. (1999). Couple resilience to economic pressure. *Journal of Personality and Social Psychology, 76*, 54–71.

Dennett, D. C. (2003). *Freedom evolves.* London: Allen Lane.

Duyme, M., Dumaret, A.-C., & Tomkiewicz, S. (1999). How can we boost IQs of "dull children"?: A late adoption study. *Proceedings of the National Academy of Sciences of the United States of America, 96*, 8790–8794.

Duyme, M., Arseneault, L., & Dumaret, A-C (2004). Environmental influences on intellectual abilities in childhood: Findings from a longitudinal adoption study. In P. L. Chase-Lansdale, K. Kiernan, & R. J. Friedman (Eds.), *Human development across lives and generations: The potential for change* (pp. 278–292). Cambridge: Cambridge University Press.

Elder, G. H. (1974). *Children of the Great Depression*. Chicago: University of Chicago Press.

Fergusson, D. M., Horwood, L. J., & Lynskey, M. (1994). The childhoods of multiple problem adolescents: A 15-year longitudinal study. *Journal of Child Psychology and Psychiatry, 35*, 1123–1140.

Fergusson, D. M., Horwood, L. J., & Lynskey, M. T. (1992). Family change, parental discord and early offending. *Journal of Child Psychology and Psychiatry, 33*, 1059–1075.

Goldapple, K., Segal, Z., Garson, C., Lau, M., Bieling, P., Kennedy, S. et al., (2004). Modulation of Cortical-Limbic Pathways in Major Depression: Treatment-specific effects of cognitive behavior therapy. *Archives of General Psychiatry, 61*, 34–41.

Gunnar, M. R. & Donzella, B. (2002). Social regulation of the cortisol levels in early human development. *Psychoneuroendocrinology, 27*, 199–220.

Harris, T., Brown, G. W., & Bifulco, A. (1986). Loss of parent in childhood and adult psychiatric disorder: The role of lack of adequate parental care. *Psychological Medicine, 16*, 641–659.

Harris, T., Brown, G. W., & Bifulco, A. (1990). Loss of parent in childhood and adult psychiatric disorder: A tentative overall model. *Development and Psychopathology, 2*, 311–327.

Hennessey, J. W. & Levine, S. (1979). Stress, arousal, and the pituitary-adrenal system: A psychoendocrine hypothesis. In J. M. Sprague & A. N. Epstein (Eds.), *Progress in psychobiology and physiological psychology* (pp. 133–178). New York: Academic Press.

Hinde, R. A. & McGinnis, L. (1977). Some factors influencing the effect of temporary mother-infant separation: Some experiments with rhesus monkeys. *Psychological Medicine, 7*, 197–212.

Jaffee, S. R., Caspi, A., Moffitt, T. E., Dodge, K. A., Rutter, M., Taylor, A. et al., (in press). Nature × Nurture: Genetic vulnerabilities interact with child maltreatment to promote behavior problems. *Development and Psychopathology*.

Jenkins, J., Dunn, J., Rasbash, J., O'Connor, T. J., & Simpson, A. (2005). Mutual influence of marital conflict and children's behavior problems: Shared and nonshared family risks. *Child Development, 76*, 24–39.

Jenkins, J. M., Rasbash, J., & O'Connor, T. G. (2003). The role of the shared family in context in differential parenting. *Developmental Psychology, 39*, 99–113.

Jenkins, J. M. & Smith, M. A. (1990). Factors protecting children living in disharmonious homes: Maternal reports. *Journal of the American Academy of Child and Adolescent Psychiatry, 29*, 60–69.

Kendler, K. S., Kessler, R. C., Walters, E. E., MacLean, C., Neale, M. C., Heath, A. C. et al. (1995). Stressful life events, genetic liability, and onset of an episode of major depression in women. *American Journal of Psychiatry, 152*, 833–842.

Kosofsky, B. E. (1999). Effects of alcohol and cocaine on brain development. In D. S. Charney, E. J. Nestler, & B. S. Bunney (Eds.), *Neurobiology of mental illness* (pp. 601–615). New York: Oxford University Press.

Laub, J. H., Nagin, D. S., & Sampson, R. J. (1998). Trajectories of change in criminal offending: Good marriages and the desistance process. *American Sociological Review, 63,* 225–238.

Laub, J. H. & Sampson, R. J. (2003). *Shared beginnings, divergent lives: Delinquent boys to age 70.* Cambridge, MA: Harvard University Press.

Luthar, S. (2003). *Resilience and vulnerability: Adaptation in the context of childhood adversities.* New York: Cambridge University Press.

MacIntyre, S. & Petticrew, M. (2000). Good intentions and received wisdom are not enough. *Journal of Epidemiology and Community Health, 54,* 802–803.

Masten, A. S. (2001) Ordinary Magic: Resilience processes in development. *American Psychologist, 56,* 227–238.

Masten, A. S., Best, K. M., & Garmezy, N. (1990). Resilience and development: Contributions from the study of children who overcome adversity. *Development and Psychopathology, 2,* 425–444.

McEwen, B. S. (1999). The effects of stress on structural and functional plasticity in the hippocampus. In D. S. Charney, E. J. Nestler, & B. S. Bunney (Eds.), *Neurobiology of mental illness* (pp. 475–493). New York: Oxford University Press.

Moffitt, T. E., Caspi, A., & Rutter, M. (submitted). *Strategy for researching interactions between measured genes and measured environments.*

Oakley, A. & Roberts, H. (1996). *Evaluating social interventions: Report of two workshops funded by the Economic and Social Research Council.* London: Barnardos.

Osborn, S. G. (1980). Moving home, leaving London and delinquent trends. *British Journal of Criminology, 20,* 54–61.

Pellegrini, D. S. (1994). Training in interpersonal cognitive problem-solving. In M. Rutter, E. Taylor & L. Hersov (Eds.), *Child and Adolescent Psychiatry* (pp. 829–843). Oxford: Blackwell.

Petitto, J. M. & Evans, D. L., (1999) Clinical neuroimmunology: Understanding the development and pathogenesis of neuropsychiatric and psychosomatic illnesses. In D. S. Charney, E. J. Nestler, & B. S. Bunney (Eds.), *Neurobiology of mental illness* (pp. 162–169). New York: Oxford University Press.

Quinton, D. & Rutter, M. (1976). Early hospital admissions and later disturbances of behaviour: An attempted replication of Douglas' findings. *Developmental Medicine and Child Neurology, 18,* 447–459.

Quinton, D. & Rutter, M. (1988). *Parenting breakdown: The making and breaking of inter-generational links.* Aldershot: Avebury.

Quinton, D., Pickles, A., Maughan, B., & Rutter, M. (1993). Partners, peers, and pathways: Assortative pairing and continuities in conduct disorder. *Development and Psychopathology, 5,* 763–783.

Robins, L. (1966). *Deviant children grown up: A sociological and psychiatric study of sociopathic personality.* Baltimore: Williams & Wilkins.

Rotter, J. I. & Diamond, J. M. (1987). What maintains the frequencies of human genetic diseases? *Nature, 329,* 289–290.

Rutter, M. (1971). Parent-child separation: Psychological effects on the children. *Journal of Child Psychology and Psychiatry, 12,* 233–260.

Rutter, M. (1972). *Maternal deprivation reassessed.* Middlesex, England: Penguin Books.

Rutter, M. (1978). Family, area and school influences in the genesis of conduct disorders. In L. A. Hersov, M. Berger, D. Shaffer (Eds.), *Aggression and anti-social behaviour in childhood and adolescence* (pp. 95–113). Oxford: Pergamon Press.

Rutter, M. (1981). Stress, coping and development: Some issues and some questions. *Journal of Child Psychology and Psychiatry, 22,* 323–356.

Rutter, M. (1985). Resilience in the face of adversity: Protective factors and resistance to psychiatric disorder. *British Journal of Psychiatry, 147,* 598–611.

Rutter, M. (1987). Psychosocial resilience and protective mechanisms. *American Journal of Orthopsychiatry, 57,* 316–331.

Rutter, M. (1989). Pathways from childhood to adult life. *Journal of Child Psychology and Psychiatry, 30,* 23–51.

Rutter, M. (1990). Psychosocial resilience and protective mechanisms. In J. Rolf, A. Masten, D. Cicchetti, K. N., & S. Weintraub (Eds.), *Risk and protective factors in the development of psychopathology* (pp. 181–214). New York: Cambridge University Press.

Rutter, M. (1999). Resilience concepts and findings: Implications for family therapy. *Journal of Family Therapy, 21,* 119–144.

Rutter, M. (2000a). Resilience reconsidered: Conceptual considerations, empirical findings, and policy implications. In J. P. Shonkoff & S. J. Meisels (Eds.), *Handbook of early childhood intervention* (pp. 651–682). New York: Cambridge University Press,.

Rutter, M. (2000b). Psychosocial influences: Critiques, findings, and research needs. *Development and Psychopathology, 12,* 375–405.

Rutter, M. (2003). Genetic influences on risk and protection: Implications for understanding resilience. In S. Luthar (Ed.), *Resilience and vulnerability: Adaptation in the context of childhood adversities* (pp. 489–509). New York: Cambridge University Press.

Rutter, M. (in press a). Environmentally mediated risks for psychopathology: Research strategies and findings. *Journal of the American Academy of Child and Adolescent Psychiatry.*

Rutter, M. (in press b). Natural experiments, causal influences, and policy development. In M. Rutter & M. Tienda (Eds.), *Ethnicity and causal mechanisms.* New York: Cambridge University Press.

Rutter, M (in press c). The psychological effects of institutional rearing. In P. Marshall & N. Fox (Eds.), *The development of social engagement.* New York: Oxford University Press.

Rutter, M. & the English and Romanian Adoptees (E.R.A.) Study Team (1998). Developmental catch-up, and deficit, following adoption after severe global early privation. *Journal of Child Psychology & Psychiatry, 39,* 465–476.

Rutter, M., Kreppner, J., O'Connor, T. G., & the English and Romanian Adoptees (ERA) Study Team (2001 a). Specificity and heterogeneity in children's responses to profound institutional privation. *British Journal of Psychiatry, 179,* 97–103.

Rutter, M., O'Connor, T. G., & the English and Romanian Adoptees Research Team (2003). Are there biological programming effects for psychological development?: Findings from a study of Romanian adoptees. *Developmental Psychology, 40,* 81–94

Rutter, M., Maughan, B., Mortimore, P., Ouston, J., & Smith, A. (1979). *Fifteen Thousand Hours: Secondary schools and their effects on children*. Cambridge, MA: Harvard University Press.

Rutter, M., Pickles, A., Murray, R., & Eaves, L. (2001 b). Testing hypotheses on specific environmental causal effects on behavior. *Psychological Bulletin, 127,* 291–324.

Rutter, M. & Silberg, J. (2002). Gene-environment interplay in relation to emotional and behavioral disturbance. *Annual Review of Psychology, 53,* 463–490.

Sampson, R. J. & Laub, J. H. (1993). *Crime in the making: Pathways and turning points through life*. Cambridge, MA: Harvard University Press.

Shaywitz, S. E., Shaywitz, B. A., Fulbright, R. K. Skudlarski, P., Mencl, W. E., Constable, R. T., et al. (2003). Neural systems for compensation and persistence: Young adult outcome of childhood reading disability. *Biological Psychiatry, 54,* 25–33.

Stacey, M., Dearden, R., Pill, R., & Robinson, D. (1970). *Hospitals, children and their families: The report of a pilot study*. London: Routledge & Kegan Paul.

Stone, A. A., Bovbjerg, D. H., Neale, J. M., Napoli, A., Valdimarsdottir, H., Cox, D. et al. (1992). Development of common cold symptoms following experimental rhinovirus infection is related to prior stressful life events. *Behavioral Medicine, 18,* 115–120.

Streissguth, A. P., Barr, H. M., Kogan, J. & Bookstein, F. L. (1997). Primary and secondary disabilities in fetal alcohol syndrome. In A. Streissguth & J. Kanter (Eds.). *The challenge of fetal alcohol syndrome: Overcoming secondary disabilities* (pp. 25–39). Seattle: University of Washington Press.

Suomi, S. J. (2003). How gene-environment interactions influence emotional development in Rhesus monkeys. In C. Garcia-Coll, E. L. Bearer, & R. M. Lerner (Eds.), *Nature and nurture: The complex interplay of genetic and environmental influences on human development* (pp. 35–51). Mahwah, NJ: Erlbaum.

Thorpe, K., Rutter, M., & Greenwood, R. (2003). Twins as a natural experiment to study the causes of mild language delay: Vol. II Family interaction risk factors. *Journal of Child Psychology and Psychiatry, 44,* 342–355.

Turton, P., Hughes, P., & Fainman, D. (in press). PTSD and the unresolved-disorganized response to loss in the pregnancy after stillbirth: The link with disorganized attachment in the next-born infant. *Attachment and Human Development*.

Ursin, H., Badde, E., & Levins, S. (1978). *Psychobiology of stress: A study of coping men*. New York: Academic Press.

Weaver, I. C. G., Cervoni, N., Champagne, F. A., D'Alessio, A. C., Charma, S., Seckl, J. et al. (2004). Epigenetic programming by maternal behavior. *Nature Neuroscience, 7,* 847–854.

Weersing, V. R. & Weisz, J. R. (2002). Mechanisms of action in youth psychotherapy. *Journal of Child Psychology and Psychiatry, 43,* 3–29.

Werner, E. E. & Smith, R. S. (1982). *Vulnerable but Invincible: A Study of Resilient Children*. New York: McGraw-Hill Book Company.

Werner, E. E. & Smith, R. S. (1992). *Overcoming the odds: High risk children from birth to adulthood*. Ithaca & London: Cornell University Press.

Wüst, S., Van Rossum, F. C. E., Federenko, I. S., Koper, J. W., Kumsta, R., & Hellhammer, D. H. (2004). Common ploymorphisms in the glucocorticoid receptor gene are associated with adrenocortical responses to psychosocial stress. *The Journal of Clinical Endocrinology and Metabolism, 89,* 565–573

Williams, S., Anderson, J., McGee, R., & Silva, P. A. (1990). Risk factors for behavioral and emotional disorder in preadolescent children. *Journal of the American Academy of Child and Adolescent Psychiatry, 29,* 413–419.

Zoccolillo, M., Pickles, A., Quinton, D., & Rutter, M. (1992). The outcome of childhood conduct disorder: Implications for defining adult personality disorder and conduct disorder. *Psychological Medicine, 22,* 971–986.

3

Identifying Risk and Protective Factors For Healthy Child Development

Arnold Sameroff

Developmental problems of youth are a major social problem in the United States, with approximately 21 percent of 9- to 17-year-old children having diagnosable disorders (Shaffer et al., 1996). Although many of these have minimal impairment, four million children representing 11 percent of the population have significant impairment and another 4 percent have extreme impairment (Surgeon General, 1999). In an examination of how many children are at risk for mental disorders, the Centers for Disease Control and Prevention (2004) reported that during the previous 12 months, 29 percent of high school children felt blue or hopeless, 17 percent had considered suicide, and 9 percent had made an attempt. In terms of aggression, 33 percent had been in a physical fight and, in the year 2000 alone, 1.7 million youth were arrested. Academic problems in the United States were equally serious. Seventy percent of fourth graders were below proficiency levels in both reading and math, and 15 percent of adolescents dropped out of school before graduation. Although the majority of youth do not have such problems, the number who do is substantial. Reducing these numbers requires a clear understanding of the causes of these childhood problems. One of the clear correlates of increasing childhood problems is the declining quality of the child-family environment.

Concurrent with the high level of problems among children, family resources for coping with these problems have diminished in the United States. In 2000, 16 percent of children lived in families with incomes below the poverty line and 33 percent of children were born to unwed mothers (Children's Defense Fund, 2002). Moreover, 75 percent of mothers of school-aged children are in the workforce now, compared with about 50 percent in 1970 (U.S. Department of Health and Human Services, 1993). Family behavior also is a major problem. The Children's Defense Fund (2002) estimates that between 3 and 10 million children experience domestic violence yearly, with almost a million confirmed cases of child abuse or neglect.

The family figures prominently among the determinants of children's social competence. In addition, it has a major buffering effect on negative influences from other aspects of the social environment as well as an enhancing role by making positive social opportunities available for children. Families clearly matter in promoting youth development, but understanding how requires a comprehensive analysis of the etiology of problems in child development. A central requirement is the recognition that there are many contributors, in addition to the family, at multiple levels of children's social ecology. Moreover, there is a different balance of contributors for each child such that there are no universal treatments applicable to all children.

In a critical appraisal of efforts to reduce children's psychosocial disorders published 20 years ago, Rutter (1982) was led to conclude that our knowledge of the topic was limited because of unfounded beliefs. The two greatest intervention myths he identified were: (1) that there are single causes for disorders, and (2) that these causes can be eliminated by treating the individual child and ignoring the social context. Whatever substance can be found in this area of research points to multiple, not single causation, as the rule and to the need for intervening in the childrearing environment as of equal importance to treating the child. These issues are amplified by Rutter in Chapter 2 of this book, as he emphasizes the need to identify specific vulnerabilities in the biology and social context of the individual but also in the individual's personality. He elaborates on the importance of the individual's definition of challenging situations, coping responses, and adaptive and maladaptive resolutions.

In this chapter, I begin with an overview of the assessment of typical risk factors for poor developmental outcomes and explore the predictive efficacy of single- and multiple-risk indices. Then I try to identify social protective and individual resiliency factors that would allow the child to overcome adversity and achieve developmental competence. The role of the family in these considerations will be seen as one of the most important determinants.

ASSESSING RISKS

Where science is seen as the search for causes, a discussion of risk factors may appear to be a substitute for a more basic understanding of why individuals succeed or fail. Causes seem to represent truths, whereas risks represent only probabilities. However, the history of research into the etiology of all complex biological disorders has demonstrated that there are no single sufficient causes. The phrase "risk factors" itself arose from epidemiological research seeking the cause of heart disease (Kannel et al., 1961). In the most comprehensive of these efforts, the Framingham study of heart disease, high blood pressure, high blood cholesterol, smoking, obesity, diabetes, physical inactivity, and psychosocial issues all made small but significant contributions to heart disease at the population level. The Framingham researchers found that if they accumulated their risk variables they dramatically increased predictive efficiency (Dawber, 1963). The more risk factors an individual had, the more likely he or she was to get heart disease, but for any single affected individual there was a different combination of predictive factors.

We discover a similar result in our search for the causes of developmental problems in children and adolescents. It is not any single factor in the child, the family, or the social surround that causes difficulties, but a set of factors that probablistically contribute to the outcome.

Representative Risk Factors

Research aimed at identifying representative risk factors in the development of cognitive and social-emotional competence has focused on family mental health and socioeconomic status. For example, in a study of families with a high level of maternal psychopathology, children were followed from birth through high school in the Rochester Longitudinal Study (RLS). Socioeconomic status (SES) was found to have a great influence on youth mental health and intellectual achievement (Sameroff, Seifer, & Zax, 1982). However, to better understand the role of social status, a more differentiated view of environmental influences was necessary. The measures of a parent's educational and occupational achievement that are major constituents of SES scores needed to be transformed into variables that would illuminate the differences in experiences of children raised in different socioeconomic environments.

The circumstances of families within the same social class differed quite markedly. SES affects parenting, parental attitudes and beliefs, family interactions, and the availability of institutions in the surrounding community. From the data available in the RLS, we chose a set of variables that were related to economic circumstance but were not the same as SES (Sameroff, Seifer, Barocas, Zax et al., 1987a). We then tested whether poor preschool cognitive and social-emotional development was related to the risk factors associated with low socioeconomic circumstances. The 10 environmental risk variables were: (1) a history of maternal mental illness; (2) high maternal anxiety; (3) parental perspectives that reflected rigidity in the attitudes, beliefs, and values that mothers had in regard to their child's development; (4) few positive maternal interactions with the child observed during infancy; (5) head of household in unskilled occupation; (6) minimal maternal education; (7) disadvantaged minority status; (8) single parenthood; (9) stressful life events; and (10) large family size. Each of these risk factors has a large body of literature documenting its potential for deleterious developmental effects (Cichetti & Cohen, 1995; Damon & Eisenberg,

1998; Sameroff, Lewis, & Miller, 2000), but there are many other factors not included in our list. The effects of marital discord and divorce described in other chapters of this book by Amato (see Chapter 8 in this book) and Hetherington (see Chapter 9 in this book) are examples of additional family risk factors. Each of our ten variables turned out to be a risk factor for preschool competence. For both cognitive and mental health outcomes, the high-risk group for each factor had worse scores than the low-risk group.

Cumulative vs. Single Risk Studies

To take a broader perspective when examining the factors that may be targeted for intervention efforts, multiple settings and multiple systems must be examined because risk factors tend to cluster in the same individuals (Bronfenbrenner, 1994). Many investigators who started out examining a single risk factor soon realized that risk rarely occurs alone (Kalil & Kunz, 1999; Masten & Coatsworth, 1998). As children often experience many risks and recurring stressors, focusing on a single risk factor does not address the reality of most children's lives.

As a way of improving predictive power, Rutter (1979) argued that it was not any particular risk factor but the number of risk factors in a child's background that led to psychiatric disorder. Psychiatric risk for a sample of 10-year-olds rose from 2 percent in families with zero or one risk factor to 20 percent in families with four or more risk factors. The six risk factors considered included: severe marital distress, low socioeconomic status, large family size or overcrowding, paternal criminality, maternal psychiatric disorder, and admission of the child to foster care. Similarly, Williams, Anderson, McGee, and Silva (1990) related behavioral disorders in 11-year-olds to a cumulative disadvantage score based on number of residence and school changes, single parenthood, low SES, marital separation, young motherhood, low maternal cognitive ability, poor family relations, seeking marriage guidance, and maternal mental health symptoms. For the children with fewer than two disadvantages, only 7 percent had behavior problems whereas for the children with eight or more disadvantages the rate was 40 percent. Even more risk factors were used by Fergusson, Horwood, and Lynsky (1994) in a study of the effects of 39 measures of family problems on the adolescent mental health of a sample of New Zealand children. Again, the result was, the more risk factors, the more behavioral problems.

In the RLS, there were statistically significant differences between high- and low-risk groups for each variable, although most children with only a single risk factor did not have a major developmental problem. But when we used the new strategy and created a multiple risk score that was the total number of risks for each individual family, major differences were found on mental health and intelligence measures between those children with few risks and those with many. On the intelligence test, children with no environmental risks scored more than 30 points higher than children with eight or nine risk factors (Sameroff et al., 1987a). No preschoolers in the zero-risk group had IQs below 85; 26 percent of those in the high-risk group did. On average, each risk factor reduced the child's IQ score by four points. Four-year-olds in the high-risk group (five or more risk factors) were twelve times as likely to have clinical mental health symptoms (Sameroff, Seifer, Zax, & Barocas, 1987b).

Quantity vs. Quality

One of the important conclusions of the Framingham Study was that no one factor was either necessary or sufficient to cause heart disease (Dawber, 1980). For any single individual with heart disease there was a different combination of predictive factors. We decided to see if the same result would be found for the effects of environmental risk on psychological outcomes. Were the negative effects the result of the accumulation of risk factors or the action of a specific risk factor? We cluster-analyzed our risk data to determine which factors occurred together and whether specific combinations had worse effects than others (Sameroff et al., 1987a). The families fell into five groups with different combinations of high-risk conditions (see Table 3.1). Despite these differences, developmental competencies were the same for children in the five groups. No single factor was regularly related to either poor or good outcomes. Moreover, as in the Framingham study of heart disease, no single variable was either a necessary or sufficient

TABLE 3.1. *Average 4-Year IQ Scores of Children in Five Clusters of 4-Year Risk Factors*

Cluster	IQ Score	Defining Risks
1	97.7	Mental health
		Education
		Anxiety
		Social support
2	94.6	Mental health
		Infant interaction
		Anxiety
3	94.7	Single parent
		Minority
4	93.7	Minority
		Education
		Occupation
5	92.8	Developmental knowledge
		Education
		Minority

Source: Sameroff, Seifer, Barocas, Zax, & Greenspan (1987a).

determinant of good or bad outcomes. Only in families with multiple risk factors was the child's competence placed in serious jeopardy (Sameroff, Seifer, Baldwin, & Baldwin, 1993).

To establish a normative base for the prevalence of risk factors and their association with mental health outcomes, we require a study with a large representative sample and a clearly conceptualized model of risk. Unfortunately, as yet there has not been such an epidemiological study of children's mental health. Moreover, most studies of the effects of risk on development have not applied an ecological perspective in their conceptualization. As a consequence, ecological analyses are post hoc rather than a priori.

An example of such a study is an analysis of the progress of several thousand young children from kindergarten to third grade using community samples from 30 sites (Peck, Sameroff, Ramey, & Ramey, 1999). From the data collected, 14 risk factors were chosen that tapped ecological levels from parent behavior to neighborhood characteristics. The number of risk factors were summed and a linear relation was found between the multiple environmental risk score and school outcomes of academic achievement and social competence supporting the findings from the RLS. Although this study used a large sample in multiple sites, the children were not a representative sample of the community and the risk factors were selected from available data rather than planned in advance.

Predicting Youth Competence

A set of data on the effects of multiple environmental risks on adolescent development was provided by a study of a group of Philadelphia families (Furstenberg, Cook, Eccles, Elder et al., 1999). Mothers, fathers, and offspring were interviewed in close to 500 families, where there was a young person between the ages of 11 and 14.

In the Philadelphia project, a conceptual approach was taken to the design so that environmental measures were available for a number of ecological settings. To approximate an ecological model, 20 environmental risk variables reflecting six different contextual subsystems were built into the design (see Table 3.2). The subsystems were *Family Processes*, which included support for autonomy, behavior control, parental involvement, and family climate; *Parent Characteristics*, which included mental health, sense of efficacy, resourcefulness, and level of education; *Family Structure*, which included the parents' marital status, and socioeconomic indicators of household crowding and welfare status; *Family Management*, which comprised variables of institutional involvement, informal networks, social resources, and adjustments to economic pressure; *Peers*, including indicators of association with prosocial and antisocial peers, and *Community*, which included census tract information on average income and educational level of the neighborhood, parent report

TABLE 3.2. *Risk Variables in Domains of the Social Ecology in the Philadelphia Study*

Domain	Variable
Family process	Support for autonomy
	Discipline effectiveness
	Parental investment
	Family climate
Parent characteristics	Education
	Efficacy
	Resourcefulness
	Mental health
Family structure	Marital status
	Household crowding
	Welfare receipt
Management of community	Institutional involvement
	Informal networks
	Social resources
	Economic adjustment
Peers	Prosocial
	Antisocial
Community	Neighborhood SES
	Neighborhood problems
	School climate

of the number of neighborhood problems, and measures of the adolescent's school climate.

In addition to the larger number of ecological variables, we used a wider array of youth developmental outcomes than in the Rochester study. We assessed successful adolescence in five areas: *Psychological Adjustment, Self-Competence, Conduct Problems, Extracurricular Involvement,* and *Academic Performance.*

For a risk factor analysis, each of the 20 variables was dichotomized to produce a high- and low-risk condition. Generally, as in previous research, when there are continuous variables, the worst 25 percent are considered to be at risk. Although this is somewhat arbitrary and highly sample-specific, it generally works (Sameroff, 2000). Multiple risk scores were calculated for each family and ranged from zero to a maximum of 13 out of 20 possible risk factors. We normalized the five adolescent outcome scores and plotted them against the number of risk factors (see Figure 3.1). The results were very similar to the Rochester study in the negative relation between risk and competence. We found very large declines in outcome with increasing risk and a substantial overlap for each of the five outcomes (Sameroff, Bartko, Baldwin, Baldwin et al., 1998).

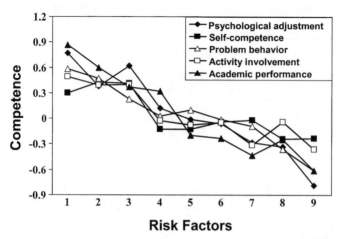

Risk Factors

FIGURE 3.1. Relation of five standardized youth outcome variables to multiple environmental risk score in the Philadelphia study (adapted from Sameroff et al., 1998).

Whether cumulative risk scores meaningfully increase predictive efficiency can be demonstrated by odds-ratio analyses – comparisons of the odds of having a bad outcome in a high-risk versus a low-risk environment. For the typical analysis of relative and attributable risk, the outcome variable is usually discrete, either succumbing to a disease or disorder, or not. For children, there are few discrete negative outcomes. They are generally too young to have many pregnancies or arrests and the rate of academic failure is not particularly high. In the Philadelphia study, bad outcomes were artificially created by identifying the 25 percent of adolescents who were doing the most poorly in terms of mental health, self-competence, problem behavior, activity involvement, or academic performance.

The relative risk in the high-risk group (eight or more risks) for each of the bad outcomes was substantially higher than in the low-risk group (three or fewer risks). The strongest effects were for Academic Performance, where the relative risk for a bad outcome increased from 7 percent in the low-risk group to 45 percent in the high-risk group, an odds ration of 6.7 to 1. The odds ratios for Psychological Adjustment, Problem Behavior, Self-Competence, and Activity Involvement were 5.7, 4.5, 3.4, and 2.7, respectively. For the important cognitive and social-emotional outcomes of youth, there seem to be powerful negative effects of the accumulation of environmental risk factors.

From these studies, one would hope that a standardized measure of ecological risk would have been developed. This is not yet the case. Each study used a slightly different set of variables sampling from various social domains. But what is compelling in the results of these studies is that whatever the set of variables used, the universal finding was that the more ecological risk factors, the worse the outcome for the child.

RESILIENCE, PROTECTIVE, AND PROMOTIVE FACTORS

A major counterpoint to changing the social circumstances of children's lives is the idea of changing the characteristics of the children themselves (see Rutter, Chapter 2, in this book). Resilience connotes positive adaptation by individuals despite severe adversity. Over the past three decades, studies of resilience have focused on individual variation in response to risky conditions such as stressful life events (Garmezy, Masten, & Tellegen, 1984; Weist, Freedman, Paskewitz, Proescher et al., 1995), exposure to community violence (White, Bruce, Farrell, & Kliewer, 1998), maltreatment (Moran & Eckenrode, 1992), urban poverty (Luthar, 1999), divorce (Hetherington, Chapter 9 in this book) and maternal mental illness (Sameroff et al., 1982).

These studies have brought sharper attention to the protective factors that influence stress resistance in children and adolescents. Although earlier studies focused primarily on personal attributes, such as high IQ (Garmezy et al., 1984), later research incorporated protective factors in the social context. For example, Garmezy (1993) identified three broad sets of variables that have been found to operate as protective factors in stress-resistant children including: (1) characteristics of the child such as temperament, cognitive skills, and positive responsiveness to others; (2) families that are marked by warmth, cohesion, and structure; and (3) the availability of external support systems.

Recently, however, there has been sharp criticism concerning the construct of resilience and the methods used by resilience researchers (see Luthar, Cicchetti, & Becker, 2000). One of the main criticisms concerns the absence of a unifying conceptual framework that encompasses its integration across disciplines and specialized areas. A scientific basis for intervention research necessitates precise terminology to build upon earlier classifications and to ensure its continued vitality (Luthar, in press). A consistent and systematic framework is essential to facilitate the work of researchers and practitioners who pursue work in this area, to integrate findings across diverse fields, as well as provide guidance for the identification and implementation of age-appropriate, optimal targets for preventive interventions (Sameroff & Gutman, 2004).

Many current research reports use the phrase "protective factor" as synonymous with competence-enhancing factor, but early pioneers of resilience research restricted the use of the term to situations where there was an interaction with a risk variable. In this sense, the effect of a protective factor would be minimal in low-risk populations but be magnified in the presence of one or more risk variables (Garmezy et al., 1984; Rutter, 1987). Studies have examined interactive effects models on a variety of outcomes including mental health (Moran & Eckenrode, 1992; White et al., 1998; Zimmerman, Ramirez-Valles, & Maton; 1998), cognitive competence

(Gutman, Sameroff, & Eccles, 2002), and behavior problems (Easterbrooks, Davidson, & Chazan, 1993; Weist, Freedman, Paskewitz, & Proescher, 1995).

There are many examples of reports using the term protective factors to describe factors associated with desirable outcomes independent of the occurrence of social disadvantage or adverse circumstances. In the findings from the National Longitudinal Study on Adolescent Health, for example, factors were labeled as protective if they were associated with lower levels of emotional distress, suicidality, involvement in violence, substance use, and sexual behaviors (Resnick, Bearman, Blum, Bauman et al., 1997). In another large study of school-aged children, social self-efficacy and social support were negatively associated with depression and, therefore, defined as protective factors (McFarlane, Bellissimo, & Norman, 1995). Although Rutter (1987) has argued that protective factors can only have meaning in the face of adversity, in these studies, protective factors were defined as simply the positive pole of risk factors (Stouthamer-Loeber et al., 1993). In this sense, I proposed that a better term for the positive end of the risk dimension would be *promotive* rather than protective factors (Sameroff, 2000). A promotive factor would have a positive effect in both high- and low-risk populations, reserving the term protective factor for variables that only facilitated the development of high-risk children.

Promotive Factors

To examine the different effects of risk and promotive influences in the Philadelphia study, we created a set of promotive factors by cutting each of our risk dimensions at the top quartile rather than at the bottom. So, whereas a negative family climate was a risk factor, a positive family climate now became a promotive factor; whereas the poor mental health of parents was a risk factor, their good mental health became promotive. We then summed these promotive factors and examined their relation to the five Philadelphia outcomes. The number of promotive factors for each family ranged from none to 15 out of a possible 20. The effects of the multiple promotive factor score mirrored the effects of the multiple risk score. Children from families with many promotive factors did substantially better than children from families with few promotive factors (see Figure 3.2). For the youth in the Philadelphia sample there did not seem to be much difference between the influence of risk and promotive variables. The more risk factors, the worse the child outcomes; the more promotive factors, the better the child outcomes. In short, when taken as part of a constellation of environmental influences on child development, most contextual variables in the parents, the family, the neighborhood, and the culture at large seem to be dimensional, aiding in general child development at one end and inhibiting it at the other. For intervention purposes, increasing promotive

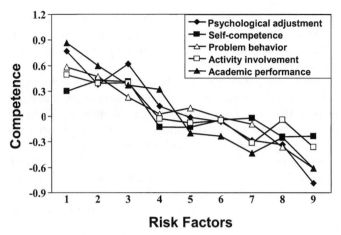

Risk Factors

FIGURE 3.2. Relation of five standardized youth outcome variables to multiple promotive factor score in the Philadelphia study.

factors has the same effect as reducing risks, but these factors are the same for most children, most of the time.

Protective Factors

Although most family and social factors seem to have linear effects on child competence, for intervention purposes it is worthwhile to determine whether there are some factors that show an interactive effect. One approach is to determine whether some environmental factor buffers the effects of other risks. Another approach is to search for factors in the child that would serve such functions.

On the environmental side, we examined the effect of two single risk factors that economists and sociologists have been very concerned about – income level and marital status (Sameroff et al., 1998). Although one would think that these factors should have powerful effects on the fate of children, we did not find such differences when these single variables were put into a broader ecological framework in the Philadelphia study. Differences in effects on child competence disappeared when we controlled for the number of other environmental risk factors in each family. To test the effects of different amounts of financial resources, we split our sample of families into those with high-, middle-, and low-income levels. For the family structure comparison, we split the sample into groups of children living in two-parent versus single-parent families. In each case there were no differences in the relation to child competence when we compared groups of children with the same number of risk factors raised in rich or poor families or families with one or two parents (Sameroff et al., 1998). There are many successful adults who were raised in poverty and unsuccessful ones who were raised in affluence; there are many healthy and happy adults who come from single-parent homes and unhappy ones who were raised by two parents.

What our analyses of these data reveal is that it is not single environmental factors that make a difference but the constellation of risks in each family's life. The reason that income and marital status seem to make major differences in child development is not that they are overarching variables in themselves but that they are strongly associated with a combination of other risk factors. For example, whereas 39 percent of poor children lived in high-risk families with more than seven risk factors, only 7 percent of affluent children did. Similarly, whereas 29 percent of single parent families lived in high-risk social conditions, only 15 percent of two-parent families did.

In a more recent study, we did find interactions with some family and peer variables (Gutman, Sameroff, & Eccles, 2002). We examined the effects of multiple risk and protective factors on the academic outcomes of African-American adolescents in a large county in Maryland that included both urban and suburban neighborhoods (Eccles, Early, Frasier, Belansky et al., 1997). Negative demographic and structural variables were defined as risk factors and parent interaction and social support variables were defined as positive factors to emphasize the interplay between these two sets of influences on adolescent development. A multiple risk score for each family was calculated based on factors shown to have deleterious effects on children and adolescents. These factors included maternal depression, family income, highest occupation in the household, maternal education, marital status, number of children living in the household, family stressful events, percent neighborhood poverty, percent neighborhood female-headed households, and percent neighborhood welfare recipients.

Parenting behavior and social support were defined as positive variables to examine whether they had promotive (i.e., direct) or protective (i.e., interactive) effects. Consistent with our past research (Sameroff et al., 1987; Sameroff, Seifer, Baldwin, & Baldwin, 1993), we found that the more risk factors adolescents experienced, the worse were their academic outcomes. As the number of risk factors increased, adolescents had lower grade point averages, more school absences, and lower math achievement test scores. The distinction between promotive and protective factors was helpful because different variables were found to have different effects depending on the achievement-related outcome assessed. Some factors were promotive only, such as parental school involvement, some had both promotive and protective effects, such as consistent discipline, and some were protective only, such as peer support. Peer support was associated with higher math achievement test scores for higher-risk adolescents, but did not affect the math achievement test scores of lower-risk adolescents.

A surprise in our data was that some family variables that were thought to be positive showed negative effects instead, such as democratic decision-making (Gutman et al., 2002). Fewer opportunities for adolescent democratic decision-making were associated with higher grade point averages and math achievement test scores for higher-risk African-American adolescents, whereas democratic decision-making had little or no effect on the grade point averages and math achievement test scores of adolescents with fewer risks. Parenting practices that emphasize democratic decision-making and foster a sense of autonomy may be more suitable for children from low-risk environments, whereas they may be inappropriate for, or even detrimental to, youth living in more risky environments. Children and adolescents who live in more dangerous environments may benefit from high levels of parental control, whereas children living in less risky neighborhoods may experience negative effects of such restrictive control (Baldwin, Baldwin, & Cole, 1990; Baumrind, 1972; Furstenberg et al., 1999; Gonzales, Cauce, Friedman, & Mason, 1996).

Detailing such studies is necessary to demonstrate the complexity of deciding how best to promote positive development for children and adolescents. To maximize the efficacy of intervention efforts to foster development, one must compare the positive and negative effects of social and individual factors. For example, based on the results of our study, intervention efforts aimed at increasing parental school involvement are important for all African-American students (a promotive effect), whereas enhancing peer networks is important for African-American youth exposed to multiple risks (a protective effect).

Resilience

Whether one should intervene with the child or the child's social context is a continuing question. Efforts to change the child should be based on information that child competencies are significant predictors of later success. To give some perspective on the individual contribution to the effects of risk, some child characteristics were included in the Philadelphia study (Furstenberg et al., 1999). Personal variables can be divided into demographic variables, such as gender and race, and behavioral domains, such as efficacy, mental health, and intelligence. For demographic variables the relation between risk scores and outcomes for separate groups of boys and girls and African Americans and Whites were examined and no differences were found. When the graphed relation between a summary competence measure and risk factors was compared for gender and racial groups the curves were essentially overlapping – the more risk factors the worse the developmental outcomes.

Like the SES variable on the environmental side, race and gender are not behavioral variables. Therefore it would be of greater interest to investigate the influence of variables with psychological content. A personality variable that is given great importance in discussions of successful development is resourcefulness. Is it possible that despite social adversity those children with high levels of "human capital," such as intelligence and social competence, (Coleman, 1988) are able to overcome minimal resources at home and in the community to reach levels of achievement comparable with children from more highly advantaged social strata.

In the Philadelphia study, we were able to measure this construct of resourcefulness with a set of questions asked of the parent and child about the young person's capacity to solve problems, overcome difficulties, and bounce back from setbacks. We divided the sample into high- and low-efficacy groups and looked at their adolescent outcomes. Indeed, high efficacious youth were more competent than those with low efficacy on our measures of adolescent competence.

But what happens to this effect when environmental adversity is taken into account? When we matched high- and low-efficacy children for the number of environmental risk factors, the difference in general competence between youth in the high- and low-environmental-risk conditions was far greater than between high and low resourceful groups. High-efficacious adolescents in high-risk conditions did worse than low-efficacious youth in low-risk conditions (Sameroff et al., 1998). It is probably not a surprise that even the less efficacious offspring of advantaged families have an easier developmental path than multi-risk children.

We did the same analysis using academic achievement as an indicator of competence and examined whether good work at school was related to adolescents' better mental health, more engagement in positive community activities, and less involvement in delinquent problem behavior. Again, for every outcome, high-academic-achieving adolescents in high-risk conditions did worse than youth with low school grades in low-risk conditions

One of the weaknesses in the Philadelphia study is that the data are cross-sectional. Finding causal factors is impossible unless one has longitudinal developmental data, and difficult even then. The Rochester study did have a series of assessments at different ages, which permitted a longitudinal view of the contribution of individual factors to developmental success. We could see how infant competence affected preschool competence, and then how preschool competence affected high school competence. For each infant we created a "multiple competence" score that included 12 factors from the data collected during the first year of life. These were scores from newborn medical and behavioral tests, temperament assessments, and developmental scales. We then divided the sample into groups of high- and low-competent infants and examined as outcomes their 4-year IQ and social-emotional functioning scores to determine if these personal

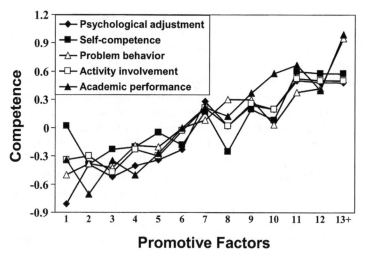

Promotive Factors

FIGURE 3.3. Relation of early social risk score to 4-year intelligence for groups of high- and low-competent infants (adapted from Sameroff et al., 1998).

characteristics could overcome the negative effects of social adversity. We found no relation between infant competence and 4-year IQ (Sameroff et al., 1998) or mental health problems (Sameroff & Fiese, 2000). The single predictor of 4-year mental health and IQ was the multiple environmental risk score (See Figures 3.3 and 3.4). Competent infants did no better than incompetent ones (Sameroff, 2000).

Infant developmental scales may be weak predictors because they assess different developmental functions than those captured by later cognitive and personality assessments. As many have argued, infant developmental scales do not incorporate aspects of mental functioning that are central to

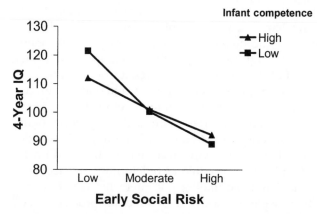

FIGURE 3.4. Relation of early social risk score to 4-year mental health for groups of high- and low-competent infants (adapted from Sameroff & Fiese, 2000).

later IQ tests. Perhaps, if we move up the age scale we would find that the mental health and intelligence of these children at 4 years of age, when more cognitive functions are incorporated into IQ tests, may be protective for later competence during adolescence.

To determine if 4-year competence might be protective for later achievements at 18 years, we divided the 4-year-olds into high- and low-mental-health groups and high- and low-IQ groups in two analyses. We then compared these groups on how they did at 18 years on their mental health and measures of school achievement. Competent preschoolers did better on average than less competent ones but, as in the Philadelphia data, when we controlled for environmental risk, the differences between children with high and low levels of early competence paled compared with the differences between children in high- and low-risk social environments. In each case we again found that high-competent children in high-risk environments did worse than low-competent children in low-risk environments.

If 4-year competence is still too ephemeral to resist the negative consequences of adverse social circumstance, would competent 13-year-olds fare better at 18-years-old? We divided the 13-year-olds into high- and low-mental-health groups and high- and low-intelligence groups and examined their 18-year behavior. Again, in each case, 13-year-old youth with better mental health and intelligence did better within the same social risk conditions, but groups of children with high levels of competence living in conditions of high environmental risk did worse than low-competent children in low-risk environments (Sameroff et al., 1998).

Developmental Trajectories

We have reported the effects of risk across two ages at a time, however interactive processes between risk and protective factors often rely on chains of connections over time rather than on a multiplicative effect at any single time point (see Rutter, Chapter 2 in this book). Understanding the factors that influence children's academic trajectories over many time points may help explain why some high-risk youth either catch up or fall further behind their more advantaged peers as they progress through school.

In the Rochester study, we examined school records and obtained grades and attendance records for the participants from first to twelfth grade. We used hierarchical linear modeling (HLM) to examine the trajectories of the children throughout their school careers (Gutman, Sameroff, & Cole, 2003). We could then determine how the growth curves were influenced by the children's 4-year multirisk scores. We could also determine the degree to which their early mental health and intelligence interacted with environmental risk to see if there were promotive (i.e., direct) or protective (i.e., interactive) effects of intelligence and mental health on school grades from the first to twelfth grades.

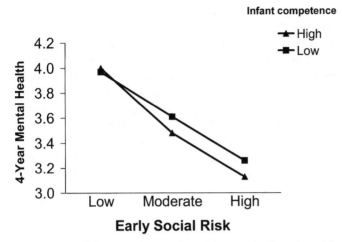

Infant competence

FIGURE 3.5. Effects of 4-year high and low multiple risk and high and low 4-year verbal intelligence on school grades (GPA) from first to twelfth grades (adapted from Gutman, Sameroff, & Cole, 2003).

These analyses confirmed our less sophisticated prior analyses – early risk had an adverse effect on academic trajectories during the entire period children were in school from the first to twelfth grades. For children in higher risk families, having a higher IQ score was not a protective factor. There were no differences between the growth curves (see Figure 3.5). But for children in low-risk families, higher IQ was a promotive factor and resulted in a higher grade point trajectory. But consistent with earlier analyses, low-competent 4-year-olds in low-risk conditions consistently had higher GPAs than the high-competent children in high-risk conditions.

Summary

Income level and marital status on the family side, and gender, race, efficacy, mental health, and achievement on the personal side, taken alone, may have statistically significant effects on adolescent behavior, but these differences are smaller than those resulting from the accumulation of multiple negative influences that characterize our high-risk groups. The overlap in outcomes for low-income versus high-income families, families with one versus two parents, boys versus girls, African Americans versus Whites, and high-resourceful versus low-resourceful youth is substantial for most psychological outcomes, but it is far less in comparisons of groups of children reared in conditions of high versus low levels of multiple risk. The important implication is that a focus on individual characteristics of individuals or families, such as gender, race, resourcefulness, or income, can never explain more than a small proportion of variance in behavioral development. To truly appreciate the determinants of competency requires attention to a broad constellation of ecological factors in which these individuals and families are embedded. Moreover, the search for resilience in select groups may be less efficient than seeking promotive influences that produce everyday competence in all children (Masten, 2001). The concern with preventing developmental failures has often clouded the fact that the majority of children in every social class and ethnic group are not failures. They get jobs, have successful social relationships, and raise a new generation of children. Masten concludes that the most surprising result of risk studies is the ordinariness of resilience; it is both common and arises from the normative functions of human adaptational systems, our promotive factors.

POLICY AND PRACTICE IMPLICATIONS

To fulfill a social agenda aimed at improving child competence requires consideration of the broad constellation of ecological factors in which individuals and families live. Moreover, the search for resilience in select groups may be less efficient than seeking promotive influences that produce everyday competence in all children (Masten, 2001). Research on risk and resilience can help practitioners design effective prevention and intervention programs. For example, as studies of resilience have shown that children typically experience multiple risks and resources in their lives, it is unlikely that a "magic bullet" for prevention or intervention will be found (Masten & Coatsworth, 1998). Prevention and intervention efforts emerging from this realization describe cumulative protection efforts to target multiple risks rather than single risk factors (Coie et al., 1993).

The assessment of multiple risks provides a list that is beyond the scope of most intervention programs, which are targeted at single family factors, school factors, or community factors. The utility of a multi-risk assessment can be seen as two-fold. First, is the identification of youth who are truly at high risk for developmental problems. This may be important for programs with limited resources that want to serve the most troubled families. Second, it provides an explanation for why targeting single risks frequently fails. A classroom intervention in an inner-city school might achieve good results in the classroom, but whether it will have an effect on the later development of the child will be a function of the number of other problems in the child's life. Recognizing the complexity of influences on child development is important in the design of successful interventions.

Successful Interventions

We have identified a variety of influences in many social contexts that can have positive influences on development. Increasingly, intervention programs with infants and young children have been utilizing a systems-oriented, ecological framework and a number of relatively successful efforts have been identified for improving their mental health and cognitive competence. A number of these have been described in the massive National Research Council study report, "From Neurons to Neighborhoods" edited by Shonkoff and Phillips (2000). The characteristics they share is that they are multi-system, long-term, and theory-driven. The multi-system aspect recognizes that many contexts of a child's ecology are involved in successful development. Long-term interventions are required because of the strong continuity of environmental risk factors that continue to impinge on successful development. Theory-driven implies that there needs to be a sufficient scientific understanding of developmental processes to know how best to intervene.

Early Head Start has incorporated many of these elements, and preliminary indications are that improvements are occurring in the children served (Chazan-Cohen et al., 2002). For older children, the Fast Track project is exemplary. It is a comprehensive intervention project designed to prevent serious antisocial behavior in children selected at being at high risk when entering first grade (Conduct Problems Prevention Research Group, 2002). The intervention is guided by a developmental theory positing the interaction of multiple influences on the development of antisocial behavior (Dodge et al., see Chapter 5 in this book). Because many of these studies are not randomized control trials, concerns have been raised about the validity claims of success. Despite these limitations there are many things to be optimistic about (Brooks-Gunn, 2003).

In a recent review of a number of approaches for improving infant mental health, we were able to delineate a coherent model of family process during development and identify interventions directed at specific problem domains (Sameroff, McDonough, & Rosenblum, 2004). Combining Stern's (1995) motherhood constellations as a structural model and Sameroff and Fiese's (2000) transactional intervention strategies as the process model, we illustrated many ports-of-entry into the family system that could alter targeted areas of dysfunction. These included the behavior of the mother, the child, the therapist, their interactions, their representations, and their resources. An emphasis from a systems perspective was that changes in any of these components could influence all the other components permitting interventions to seek the most expeditious entry point.

In our research on the probabilistic nature of risk factors, we found that most children with a single social risk factor have a low probability of disorder. But as the number of risk factors accumulates, the probability of disorder increases. The conclusion for intervention strategies is that the more risk factors that can be eliminated, the better the outlook. Although it might appear that changing single factors would prevent bad things from happening – for example, taking away guns from children to prevent their involvement in serious crimes or encouraging the use of contraceptives to prevent infection with a sexually transmitted disease – the reality is that for most children, most of the time, these risks are embedded in the context of many other risks. Therefore to prevent bad outcomes, other risk factors in the family and the community need to be addressed as well.

FUTURE RESEARCH DIRECTIONS

Because of the large range of risk and promotive factors considered in this chapter, there is no simple empirical next step. Family factors have a major impact on child development, but it may be their accumulation rather than their specificity that determines their effect. Researchers who focus on one of these influences must pay attention to others as well or at least offer a good explanation for not doing so. Otherwise we will be left with conclusions that may not be supported by more appropriately designed studies.

Studying an array of variables requires much larger samples than are found in the typical study of development. Large studies require larger groups of investigators and are more logistically complex, but occasionally they occur. The Fast Track (Conduct Problems Prevention Research Group, 2002) and NICHD Child Care Research Network (1999) studies are such examples. Larger samples permit more sophisticated statistical analyses, although HLM and Structural Equation Modeling have been found to be fruitful even in smaller samples where variables have powerful effects.

The evidence that multiple risk factors should be reduced if child outcomes are to improve means that clinical and intervention programs should be multifaceted. The discovery of promotive factors that affect many risk factors simultaneously could lead to simpler and less expensive interventions. Reducing poverty has been posited by many as such a factor, and more experimental studies where income levels were raised would aid in clarifying the pathways by which money helps and where more money makes no difference.

Clearly, more longitudinal data are necessary if we are to understand the processes of risk, protection, and promotion. From infancy to adulthood is a long time and whether the same factors affect development in the same way at each stage needs further research. Risk factor research is for the most part epidemiological and based on population probabilities for wellness and disorder. But for any single family the effects of a different combination of positive and negative factors need to be understood. Research methods focused on the search for universal influences are different from those that are more person-centered, and there is a great need to articulate where one approach may provide more fruitful answers than another. Improving the average developmental achievements of a whole society may require quite different approaches from improving the lot of a specific child.

References

Baldwin, A. L., Baldwin, C., & Cole, R. E. (1990). Stress-resistant families and stress-resistant children. In J. E. Rolf (Ed.), *Risk and protective factors in the development of psychopathology* (pp. 257–280). New York: Cambridge University Press.

Baumrind, D. (1972). An exploratory study of socialization effects on black children: Some black-white comparisons. *Child Development, 43,* 261–267.

Bronfenbrenner, U. (1994). Ecological models of human development. In T. Husten & T. N. Postlethwaite (Eds.), *International encyclopedia of education* (2nd ed., Vol. 3, pp. 1643–1647). New York: Elsevier Science.

Brooks-Gunn, J. (2003). Do you believe in magic?: What we can expect from early childhood intervention programs. *Social Policy Report, Society for Research in Child Development, 17*(1).

Centers for Disease Control and Prevention (2004). Youth Risk Behavior Surveillance – United States, 2003. *Morbidity & Mortality Weekly Report, 53,* 1–96.

Chazan-Cohen, R., Raikes, H., Kresh, E., Love, J. M., Kisker, E. E., & Jerald, J. (2002). Early Head Start findings: Significant benefits for children and families. *Head Start Bulletin, 74,* 43–44.

Children's Defense Fund (2002). *The state of children in America's union: A 2002 action guide to leave no child behind.* Washington, DC: Children's Defense Fund.

Cicchetti, D., & Cohen, D. (Eds.) (1995). *Developmental Psychopathology: Volume 2. Risk, disorder, and adaptation.* New York: Wiley.

Coie, J. D., Watt, N. F., West, S., Hawkins, J. D., Asarnow, J. R., Markman, H. J., Ramey, S. L., Shure, M. B., & Long, B. (1993). The science of prevention. *American Psychologist, 48,* 1013–1022.

Coleman, J. (1988). Social capital in the creation of human capital. *American Journal of Sociology, 94,* S95–S120.

Conduct Problems Prevention Research Group (2002). The implementation of the Fast Track program: An example of large-scale prevention science efficacy trial. *Journal of Abnormal Child Psychology, 30,* 1–18.

Damon, W., & Eisenberg, N. (Eds.) (1998). *Handbook of child psychology* (5th Ed.). *Vol. 3. Social, emotional, and personality development.* New York: Wiley.

Dawber T. R. (1963). Coronary heart disease; morbidity in the Framingham Study and analysis of factors of risk. *Bibliotheca Cardiologica, 13,* 9–24.

Dawber, T. R. (1980). The Framingham Study: The epidemiology of coronary heart disease. Cambridge, MA: Harvard University Press.

Eccles, J. S., Early, D., Frasier, K., Belansky, E., & McCarthy, K. (1997). The relation of connection, regulation, and support for autonomy to adolescents' functioning. *Journal of Adolescent Research, 12,* 263–286.

Easterbrooks, M. A., Davidson, C. E., & Chazan, R. (1993). Psychosocial risk, attachment, and behavior problems among school-age children. *Development and Psychopathology, 5,* 389–402.

Fergusson, D. M., Horwood, L. J., & Lynsky, M. T. (1994). The childhoods of multiple problem adolescents: A 15-year longitudinal study. *Journal of Child Psychology and Psychiatry, 35,* 1123–1140.

Furstenberg, F. F., Jr., Cook, T., Eccles, J., Elder, G. H., & Sameroff, A. J. (1999). *Managing to make it: Urban families and adolescent success.* Chicago: University of Chicago Press.

Garmezy, N. (1993). Children in poverty: Resilience despite risk. *Psychiatry, 56,* 127–136.

Garmezy, N., Masten, A. S., & Tellegan, A. (1984). The study of stress and competence in children: A building block of developmental psychopathology. *Child Development, 55,* 97–111.

Gutman, L. M., Sameroff, A. J., & Eccles, J. S. (2002). The academic achievement of African-American students during early adolescence: An examination of multiple risk, promotive, and protective Factors. *American Journal of Community Psychology, 30,* 367–399.

Gutman, L. M., Sameroff, A. J., & Cole, R. (2003). Academic growth curve trajectories from first to twelfth grades: Effects of multiple social risk and preschool child factors. *Developmental Psychology, 39,* 777–790.

Gonzales, N. A., Cauce, A. M., Friedman, R. J., & Mason, C. A. (1996). Family, peer, and neighborhood influences on academic achievement among African American adolescents: One-year prospective effects. *American Journal of Community Psychology, 24,* 365–388.

Kalil, A., & Kunz, J. (1999). First births among unmarried adolescent girls: Risk and protective factors. *Social Work Research,* 23(3), 197–208.

Kannel, W. B., Dawber, T. R., Kagan, A., Revotskie, N., Stokes, J. I. (1961). Factors of risk in the development of coronary heart disease – six year follow-up experience: The Framingham Study. *Annals of Internal Medicine, 55,* 33–50.

Luthar, S. S. (1999). *Poverty and children's adjustment.* Newbury Park, CA: Sage.

Luthar, S. S. (in press). Resilience in development): A synthesis of research across five decades. In D. Cicchetti & D. J. Cohen (Eds.), *Developmental psychopathology: Risk, disorder, and adaptation* (2nd edition). New York: Wiley.

Luthar, S. S., Cicchetti, D., and Becker, B. (2000). The construct of resilience: A critical evaluation and guidelines for future work. *Child Development, 71,* 543–562.

Masten, A. S. (1999). Resilience comes of age: Reflections on the past and outlook

Masten, A. S. (2001). Ordinary magic: Resilience processes in development. *American Psychologist, 56,* 227–238.

Masten, A. S., & Coatsworth, J. D. (1998). The development of competence in favorable and unfavorable environments: Lessons from research on successful children. *American Psychologist, 53,* 205–220.

McFarlane, A. H., Bellissimo, A., Norman, G. R. (1995). The role of family and peers in social self-efficacy: Links to depression in adolescence. *American Journal of Orthopsychiatry, 65,* 402–410.

Moran, P. B., & Eckenrode, J. (1992). Protective personality characteristics among adolescent victims of maltreatment. *Child Abuse and Neglect, 16,* 743–754.

NICHD Early Child Care Research Network (1999). Child care and mother-child interaction in the first three years of life. *Developmental Psychology, 35,* 1399–1413.

Peck, S., Sameroff, A., Ramey, S., & Ramey, C. (April 1999). Transition into school: Ecological risks for adaptation and achievement in a national sample. Paper presented at the Biennial Meeting of the Society for Research and Development, Albuquerque, NM.

Resnick, M., Bearman, P., Blum, R., Bauman, K., Harris, K., Jones, J. J., et al. (1997). Protecting adolescents from harm: Findings from the longitudinal study on adolescent health. *Journal of the American Medical Association, 278,* 823–832.

Rutter, M. (1979). Protective factors in children's responses to stress and disadvantage. In M. W. Kent & J. E. Rolf (Eds.), *Primary prevention of psychopathology: (Vol. 3): Social competence in children* (pp. 49–74). Hanover, NH: University Press of New England.

Rutter, M. (1982). Prevention of children's psychosocial disorders: Myths and substance. *Pediatrics, 70*, 883–894.

Rutter, M. (1987). Continuities and discontinuities from infancy. In J. Osofsky (Ed.), *Handbook of infant development* (2nd Ed.) (pp. 1256–1296). New York: Wiley.

Sameroff, A. J. (2000). Ecological perspectives on developmental risk. In J. D. Osofsky & H. E. Fitzgerald (Eds.), *WAIMH Handbook of Infant Mental Health: Vol. 4. Infant Mental Health in Groups at Risk* (pp. 4–33). New York: Wiley.

Sameroff, A. J., Bartko, W. T., Baldwin, A., Baldwin, C., & Seifer, R. (1998). Family and social influences on the development of child competence. In M. Lewis & C. Feiring (Eds.), *Families, risk, and competence*. Mahwah, NJ: Erbaum.

Sameroff, A. J., & Fiese, B. H. (2000). Transactional regulation: The developmental ecology of early intervention. In J. P. Shonkoff & S. J. Meisels (Eds.), *Handbook of early childhood intervention* (pp. 135–159). New York: Cambridge University Press.

Sameroff, A., & Gutman, L. M. (2004). Contributions of risk research to the design of successful interventions. In P. Allen-Meares & M. W. Fraser (Eds.), *Intervention with children and adolescents: An interdisciplinary perspective* (pp. 9–26). New York: Pearson, Allyn, & Bacon.

Sameroff, A., Lewis, M., & Miller, S. (Eds.) (2000). *Handbook of developmental psychopathology*. New York: Plenum.

Sameroff, A. J., McDonough, S. C., & Rosenblum, K. L. (Eds.) (2004). *Treating early relationship problems: Infant, parent, and interaction therapies*. New York: Guilford.

Sameroff, A. J., Seifer, R., & Zax, M. (1982). Early development of children at risk for emotional disorder. *Monographs of the Society for Research in Child Development, 47* (7, Serial No. 199).

Sameroff, A. J., Seifer, R., Baldwin, A., & Baldwin, C. (1993). Stability of intelligence from preschool to adolescence: The influence of social and family risk factors. *Child Development, 64*, 80–97.

Sameroff, A. J., Seifer, R., Barocas, B., Zax, M., & Greenspan, S. (1987a). IQ scores of 4-year-old children: Social-environmental risk factors. *Pediatrics, 79*, 343–350.

Sameroff, A. J., Seifer, R., Zax, M., & Barocas, R. B. (1987b). Early indices of developmental risk: The Rochester Longitudinal Study. *Schizophrenia Bulletin, 13*, 383–394.

Shaffer, D., Fisher, P., Dulcan, M. K., Davies, M., Piacentini, J., Schwab-Stone, M. E., Lahey, B. B., Bourdon, K., Jensen, P. S., Bird, H. R., Canino, G., & Regier, D. A. (1996). The NIMH Diagnostic Interview Schedule for Children Version 2.3 (DISC-2.3): Description, acceptability, prevalence rates, and performance in the MECA Study. Methods for the Epidemiology of Child and Adolescent Mental Disorders Study. *Journal of the American Academy of Child and Adolescent Psychiatry, 35*, 865–877.

Shonkoff, J., & Phillips, D. A. (Eds.). (2000). *Neurons to neighborhoods: The science of early childhood development*. Washington, DC: National Academies Press.

Stern, D. N. (1995). *The motherhood constellation: A unified view of parent-infant psychotherapy*. New York: Basic Books.

Stouthamer-Loeber M., Loeber, R., Farrington, D. P., Zhang, Q., van Kammen, W., & Maguin, E. (1993). The double edge of protective and risk factors for delinquency: interrelations and developmental patterns. *Developmental Psychopathology, 5,* 683–701.

Surgeon General (1999). *Mental health: A report of the surgeon general.* Washington, DC: Government Printing Office.

U.S. Department of Health and Human Services (1993). *Child health USA 1992.* Washington, DC: U.S. Government Printing Office.

Weist, M., Freedman, A., Paskewitz, D., Proescher, E., & Flaherty, L. (1995). Urban youth under stress: Empirical identification of protective factors. *Journal of Youth and Adolescence, 24,* 705–721.

White, K., Bruce, S., Farrell, A., & Kliewer, W. (1998). Impact of exposure to community violence on anxiety: A longitudinal study of family social support as a protective factor for urban children. *Journal of Child and Family Studies, 7,* 187–203.

Williams, S., Anderson, J., McGee, R., & Silva, P. A. (1990). Risk factors for behavioral and emotional disorder in preadolescent children. *Journal of the American Academy of Child and Adolescent Psychiatry, 29,* 413–419.

Zimmerman, M., Ramirez-Valles, J., & Maton, K. (1998). Resilience among urban African American male adolescents: A study of the prospective effects of sociopolitical control on their mental health. *American Journal of Community Psychology, 27,* 733–751.

PART TWO

PEERS AND PARENTS

4

The Influence of Family and Peer Relationships in the Development of Competence during Adolescence

W. Andrew Collins and Glenn I. Roisman

Adolescence has long been considered to "begin in biology and end in culture." This phrase traditionally refers to well-known psychological and behavioral markers of adolescent development, such as increasing parent-child conflict and intensified orientation to peers, which reflect both biological maturation and social and cultural expectations. Until recently, specialists in adolescence had given little attention to questions about the contributions of genetic or environmental effects to individual variation. Research with adolescents did have in common with other periods, however, an emphasis on questions of whether interpersonal forces influence adolescent development and, if so, which ones are especially important. Consequently, research before the late 1980s typically begged the question posed for this chapter: "How do parents and peers contribute to adolescent behavior?" Like other recent writers (e.g., Collins, Maccoby, Steinberg, Hetherington et al., 2000; Goodnow, 1992; Maccoby, 2000; Rutter et al., 1997), we propose that questions of *whether* and *which* now should be supplemented by the study of *how* (by what processes) and *when* (under what conditions) influences come about in the interpersonal experiences of adolescents.

We argue that the content and quality of relationships with both family members and other significant companions determine the nature and extent of their impact on development. The chapter is divided into three sections. In the first section, we briefly describe recent research findings on normative relationship networks in adolescence. In the second section, we focus on three types of research with adolescents that acknowledge the importance of the interplay of heredity and environment and provide a clearer basis for inferring potentially significant environmental influences such as interactions with parents and peers (Collins et al., 2000). Our third and final section draws on findings from these approaches to identify several emerging principles of influence in adolescents' relationships with parents and with peers (especially friends and romantic partners).

79

Relationships during Adolescence: Implications for Influence

Two hallmarks of development during adolescence are: (1) that social networks become more extensive and diverse, and (2) that relationships with peers intensify (Collins & Laursen, 2000). These phenomena are robust and highly significant, but commonly misunderstood. As an example, contrary to popular impressions, recent research findings document that parents remain prominent in adolescents' social networks and continue to serve as major influences on children, even after puberty. Moreover, parents and peers frequently influence adolescents' decisions in the same direction, rather than in contradictory directions. A long unrecognized, though now substantiated, factor in this implicitly two-sided contest is that adolescents' choices sometimes reflect independent decision making, influenced by neither parents nor peers (Collins, Gleason, & Sesma, 1997a). Nor does adolescence seem to undermine the affectional bonds between most parents and adolescents. Changes in parent-adolescent relationships primarily reflect declining dependence on parents, rather than erosion in the importance of these relationships (Allen & Land, 1999; Collins, 1995; Steinberg, 2001).

At the same time, relationships with both parents and peers change in ways that may alter the degree of influence of each relative to earlier periods. The proportion of time devoted to interactions with persons outside the family gradually increases during adolescence. Casual friendships are more numerous and diverse in adolescence than in childhood, perhaps because school and work provide relatively more opportunities to form new relationships. Romantic relationships also become increasingly common during adolescence (Brown, 2004; Collins, 2003; Collins & Laursen, 2004).

As relationships become more diverse, they also provide a wider range of potential experiences for adolescents. Eleven- and 13- year-olds differentiate reliably among family, peer, and teacher relationships as sources of instrumental help, intimacy, companionship, nurturance, and conflict. These different dyads overlap in their impact on adolescents, although some are relatively more important than others in specific areas (e.g., parents and best friends are especially prized by adolescents as sources of intimacy, relative to acquaintances and teachers). With respect to sources of social support, adolescents typically shift from reliance on relationships with parents in middle childhood, to same-sex friends in early and middle adolescence, and then to romantic partners at college age (Furman & Buhrmester, 1992). Similarly, perceptions of intimacy with close friends and romantic partners gradually overtake and then exceed perceived intimacy with parents (Hunter & Youniss, 1982). Both females and males report greater intimacy with same-sex friends than with members of the opposite sex, although the gap typically is smaller for 14- to 16-year-olds than for 10- to 12-year-olds (Sharabany, Gershoni, & Hoffman, 1981). By their middle twenties, many young adults report fewer, but more stable choices of individuals with whom they experience intimate relationships (Reis, Lin, Bennett, & Nezlek, 1993).

In comparison to childhood relationships, the lesser distance and greater intimacy in adolescents' peer relationships may both satisfy their needs for connections with others and also contribute to their preparation to engage effectively in relations among equals. In late adolescence and young adulthood, intimacy with parents often provides nurturance and support, but may be less important than friendships for socialization to roles and expectations in an increasingly adult world (Collins & Laursen, 2004; Laursen & Bukowski, 1997).

The overlapping functions of familial and extra-familial relationships may be one reason these dyads become increasingly interrelated over time. Despite the stereotype of incompatible or contradictory influences of parents and friends, parent-child relationships set the stage for both the selection of friends and the management of these relationships (Parke & Buriel, 1998). Links between qualities of friendships and romantic relationships, as well as between familial and romantic relationships, are equally impressive (Collins, 2003; Roisman, Madsen, Hennighausen, Sroufe et al., 2001).

The reorganization of social networks between childhood and early adulthood raises two related possibilities for developmental influences during this period. First, the importance and unique functions of parents and of peers imply that significant influences may occur in adolescents' relationships with both. Second, the degree of similarity and, sometimes, complementarity between parent-adolescent and peer relationships make it likely that influences from each combine, rather than contradict each other.

Beyond Correlations: Contemporary Research on Influences during Adolescence

Despite the potential for influences from diverse social relationships, skepticism is frequently expressed that these influences have a significant impact on the development of individual children. This skepticism largely stems from two historical facts. First, behavior-genetic research repeatedly has yielded findings that similarities and dissimilarities between individuals vary with their degree of genetic relatedness. Second, early socialization scholars unquestionably relied excessively on correlations between social influences and child or adolescent outcomes. Critiques of both research traditions are well known. Critics of behavior-genetic findings from traditional twin and adoption studies point to methods that bias results in favor of main effects for genetics while neglecting to allow for direct appraisals of the role of environment (e.g., Collins et al., 2000; Gottlieb, 1995; Maccoby, 2000; Rutter et al., 1997). Critics of socialization studies have charged that researchers fail to attend to issues of causal direction and to a number of plausible alternatives that could only be examined with genetically informed research designs (e.g., Harris, 1998; Rowe, 1994).

Contemporary researchers no longer rely exclusively on correlational designs, overly simple laboratory analogs, or simple additive models for assigning variance in outcomes to one source or another. Approaches today better capture real-world complexity without sacrificing the rigor necessary to infer causal relations, and conceptual models increasingly encompass multiple sources of influence. The result is a more complete and more differentiated picture of influences (Collins et al., 2000). Responsible reviewers agree on four conclusions from these newer studies. First, both twin studies following the additive model and simple correlations between parental characteristics and adolescent outcomes have been discredited as stand-alone methods (e.g., Gottlieb, 1995; Turkheimer, 1998). Second, more sophisticated, comprehensive designs have shown that both genetic and environmental influences are pervasive (Maccoby, 2000; Rutter et al., 1997). Third, interactions and correlations between the two explain social behavior and attitudes, personality, and motivation more satisfactorily than either heredity or environment alone (Collins et al., 2000; Maccoby, 2000). Finally, in contrast to the almost exclusive emphasis on parental effects in the past, other environmental influences, including extra-familial ones, play a significant role in development (Collins et al., 2000).

In this section we outline three types of evidence that close relationships between adolescents and their parents, their friends, and their romantic partners influence the development of competence during adolescence. These approaches begin with the assumption that both genetic and experiential forces contribute to the influences associated with these close relationships. The evidence of interest comes mostly from longitudinal research in which adolescents' behavior changes following certain types of experiences, while possible alternative reasons for the observed change are statistically controlled.

Interventions

Interventions of two types meet the standard of ethically sound experimental research. One type involves "natural experiments" in which children or adolescents with known temperamental or behavioral dispositions are exposed to different social influences. The other type consists of deliberate interventions in which the target is the behavior of parents or peers but not of the children or adolescents themselves.

Experiments of Nature. Natural experiments most often have occurred with infants and young children, although many researchers have followed the participants into middle childhood and some have tracked outcomes into adolescence (Rutter, 1996). Adoption is the most common example of a natural experiment (for a review, see Haugaard, 1998), and many studies of adoption have examined the possibility that adoptees are especially vulnerable to the physiological and the social changes of adolescence. Research on the development of children adopted in early life from Romanian orphanages shows that these children typically experienced minimal social contact in early life. If they were adopted within the first 6 months of life, children showed few lasting effects by age 6 years; later-adopted children showed signs that the neuroendocrine system involved in stress regulation had not developed normally by 6 years (e.g., Chisholm, 1998; Gunnar, 2000; Rutter & the ERA Study Team, 1998). Initial findings from an assessment at age 11, however, show the early-adopted group beginning to manifest clinical levels of emotional and behavioral problems. This apparent "sleeper effect" of early adversity actually may be a puberty-induced sign of inadequate development of the prefrontal cortex resulting from early adversity (Gunnar, personal communication, June 30, 2003). In either case, the emergence of difficulties during adolescence when none were apparent earlier makes a compelling case that parents can affect adolescents and their development.

Parenting Interventions. Further evidence of the efficacy of parents comes from findings that changes in parents' behavior can be linked with changes in the behavior of children or adolescents who themselves received no intervention. Few interventions have focused only on improving parental behavior and even fewer have assessed links between changes in parents' behavior and changes in child behavior (for reviews, see Cowan, Powell, & Cowan, 1998; McMahon & Wells, 1998). Exceptions come from recent parent training programs that are shown to affect children's behavior. In one example, Dishion, Patterson, and Kavanagh (1992) showed that a parent-training intervention to which parents were randomly assigned reduced coercive behavior toward their children. The authors next showed that, despite a history of aggressive behavior, the children of these parents subsequently showed a decline in antisocial behavior. In another intervention, Forgatch and DeGarmo (1999) were able to foster more effective parenting for recently divorced single mothers, which in turn resulted in improvements in the child's behavior at home and at school. Moreover, the degree of change in the mothers' behavior over the course of 12 months significantly forecast the degree of change in the children's behaviors. Changes in parenting practices were followed by decreased teacher-reported school adjustment problems, as well as less child-reported and parent-reported maladjustment.

Other interventions with parents have yielded similar evidence that increased parental effectiveness is linked to more positive child or adolescent behavior. Most efforts have been focused on the parents of infants and young children. Some of these studies document persistence of beneficial effects on children's behavior from early to late middle childhood (e.g., Cowan & Cowan, 1997; Forehand & King, 1977; Forehand, Wells, & Griest, 1980). When interventions with parents are effective, behavior changes for both parents and children tend to be long lasting (Kumpfer & Alvarado, 2003; Patterson, 1975).

Regrettably, no examples of rigorously conducted interventions focusing exclusively on adolescent peers, especially close peers, exist. Recent reviews of school-based intervention programs, however, show that programs with clear provisions for peer involvement tend to be more effective than school-based programs in which peer relationships are not involved (Greenberg et al., 2003).

Longitudinal Studies with Controls for Initial Child Characteristics

We also have found evidence of parental and peer influence in the results of longitudinal studies that began by estimating the initial relation between measures of the relationship and measures of child or adolescent adjustment in order to control for possible genetic factors. The degree to which behavior changed over time in connection with new relationship experiences could then be inferred. Although this approach assumes, perhaps erroneously, that genetic influences on social interactions are sufficiently static so that initial measures capture them adequately, the goal of these research designs is to approximate the controls that are imposed in experimental designs.

Several examples from recent longitudinal projects illustrate this reasoning. One example comes from a one-year longitudinal study of high school students (Steinberg, Lamborn, Darling, Mounts et al., 1994). Controlling for the initial association between parenting styles and adolescent competence, the researchers found that the relation persisted, and – for some outcomes such as antisocial behavior – strengthened, over time. A second example comes from evidence that protective effects of exposure to positive parenting increased over time when initial levels of exposure to harsh punishment were controlled (e.g., Pettit, Bates, & Dodge, 1997). In one of the longest-running longitudinal studies, Dubow, Huesmann, Eron, Boxer, and Slegers (in press) found an inverse relation between negative family interaction at age 8 and intellectual achievement at age 48, controlling for child's level of intelligence at age 8. By contrast, these investigators found direct relations between negative family relationships at age 8 and less desirable outcomes at age 48, especially for children from middle and higher socioeconomic backgrounds. Negative family interactions at age 8 significantly predicted aggressiveness 40 years later, and parental rejection at age 8 predicted lower occupational prestige scores. Findings were significant for boys, but not for girls, and for children from lower socioeconomic backgrounds.

We have found few longitudinal studies that both include estimates of peer-group influence and control for initial child characteristics. In one exception, Bagwell, Newcomb, and Bukowski (1998) assessed an array of child variables at age 11 (self-worth, school performance, future aspirations, relationship competence, and psychopathology). In addition, they determined whether children had reciprocated friendships and whether they were accepted by peers in general. By age 23, those individuals who earlier had experienced reciprocated friendships reported higher levels of relationship intimacy and feelings of self-worth and were less likely to report depressive symptoms relative to those without reciprocated friendships in early adolescence. These changes were attributable only to history of friendships. By contrast, general peer acceptance, but not friendship history, significantly predicted perceived job competence at age 23, as well as future aspirations. In another example of peer influence, peer group characteristics contributed significantly to changes in individual students' liking and enjoyment of school and their achievement over the school year. Risk of disengagement was greater when peers saw little intrinsic value in school and achievement, but less when perceptions of intrinsic value were high (Ryan, 2001). Peer *groups* were less important in shaping adolescents' belief in the utility of school and level of aspiration. Best friends, however, repeatedly have been found to influence these beliefs (Kandel, 1978). Similar findings from short-term longitudinal studies demonstrate the impact of peers on drinking and drug use (e.g., Kandel, 1973; Kandel & Logan, 1984) and on bullying and fighting (e.g., Espelage, Holt, & Henkel, 2003).

Studies of interpersonal influences are most informative when more than one source of potential influence is included. Recent analyses by Pettit and Bates (in press) documented unique contributions of low levels of childhood peer competence and acceptance to indicators of insecurity in relationships during late adolescence, after earlier and later family and peer factors were controlled. The same analyses showed that later insecurity about relationships was more likely for individuals who had experienced low levels of proactive parenting in childhood and high levels of parental intrusiveness during adolescence. Demonstrating that peer relationships predict insecurity over and above these clearly powerful parental influences strengthens the case that peer relationships are significant sources of influence.

Increasingly, researchers' use of multimethod, multi-informant assessments and more sophisticated statistical methods is overcoming shortcomings of traditional correlational studies of socialization and behavior-genetic studies using single informants (e.g., Conger & Elder, 1994; Forgatch, 1991; Kim, Hetherington, & Reiss, 1999). These more methodologically rigorous studies generally show that the effect size for relations between parenting behaviors and child or adolescent behavior range from small to medium. Even small effects of social influence, however, are likely to become large effects over time (Abelson, 1985). We believe this point is especially important in the case of parental behavior, which is highly stable across time (Holden & Miller, 1999). Thus, specific parental influences, consistently experienced, likely accumulate to produce larger meaningful outcomes over the childhood and adolescent years. Specific peer relationships are less stable over time (Brown, 2004), and that fact makes forecasting their long-term impact somewhat more difficult. It may be, however, that what matters is the experience of being in a voluntary close relationship, whether the other person remains the same over time or not, as long as the successive relationships are similar in quality and the characteristics of the adolescents' associates are similar (e.g., in how prosocial or antisocial they are) (Hartup, 1996).

Several further comments are important for evaluating the findings of longitudinal studies of parental and peer influence. One is that studies of the efficacy of particular sources of influence have focused on antisocial outcomes more often than on positive competence. Moreover, effect sizes for relations between interpersonal influences and antisocial outcomes generally have been larger for studies of antisocial behavior than for studies of positive competence. Scholars and funding agencies today are seeking possible ways to build a stronger body of findings regarding influences on positive outcomes. A second comment is that the few available studies vary in the timing of the measurement of influences from parent and peer relationships. Most rely on measures of influence taken before adolescence, rather than during adolescence. The emphasis on outcomes in and beyond adolescence is a key step toward answering questions of how parents and peers contribute to competent behavior and adjustment.

Analyses of Gene X Environment Effects

Traditional behavior-genetic approaches mask virtually ubiquitous correlations and statistical interactions between hereditary and environmental influences (Gottlieb, 1995; Maccoby, 2000; Turkheimer, 1998). Documenting the relevance of this point for studies of influence during adolescence is difficult, because most of the pertinent studies focus on temperamental differences during infancy and early childhood. Nevertheless, we have found several suggestive findings involving adolescents.

One point is that the processes linking parenting and children's predispositions and later behavior and adjustment almost certainly are not consistent with the linear causality that is implied in much discourse about developmental influences. As an example, O'Connor, Deater-Deckard, Fulker, Rutter, and Plomin (1998) found that adolescents at genetic risk for antisocial behavior elicited more negative parenting from adoptive parents than did adolescents who were not at risk (an *evocative* effect of heredity). They also found an environmentally mediated parental effect on children's behavior. This finding is consistent with the view that the behavior evoked from parents may also influence subsequent behavior patterns that are consistent with, or contrary to, hereditary influences alone (Rutter et al., 1997).

Parallels to these bidirectional relations between parenting and child behavior are also evident in studies of psychopathology. For example, parenting appears to be one avenue by which parental psychopathology contributes to child and adolescent symptoms of disorder (Conger, Ge, Elder, Lorenz et al., 1994; Ge, Conger, Lorenz, Shanahan et al., 1995; Ge, Lorenz, Conger, Elder et al., 1994). An especially striking finding was that adoptees with a schizophrenic biological parent were more likely to develop psychiatric disorders (including schizophrenia) than were adoptees who were not at genetic risk for mental disorder, only if the adolescents with a family history of disorder were adopted into dysfunctional families (Tienari et al., 1994; see also Cadoret, 1985). Similar findings have been reported from studies of adopted children whose biological parents had a history of criminality (Bohman, 1996). If adopted into well functioning families, 12 percent of these children displayed petty criminality in adulthood. If adopted into families carrying environmental risk, however, the rate of petty criminality in adulthood was 40 percent. These findings imply that well-functioning parents can buffer children who are at genetic risk and circumvent the processes that might ordinarily lead to negative outcomes. That genetic vulnerabilities (or strengths) may be expressed only in the presence of a pertinent environmental trigger, such as parenting or extrafamily contexts (e.g., peers), gives us further reason to conclude that interpersonal influences are highly significant in children's development.

Another compelling example comes from researchers studying the moderating role of a genetic variation on the link between maltreatment and outcome (Caspi et al., 2002). These authors sought to explain the sizable individual variations that have been reported in the likelihood that maltreatment is associated with later antisocial problems. They examined differences in one possible locus of genetic susceptibility, a functional polymorphism in the gene encoding the neurotransmitter-metabolizing enzyme monoamine oxidase A (MAOA). The polymorphism is X-linked, so that only males can manifest this susceptibility. Boys who were maltreated, but whose genotypes conferred high levels of MAOA expression, were less likely to develop antisocial problems. By contrast, boys with low levels of MAOA expression were more likely to do so. Thus, maltreatment may not be an exclusive cause of increased risk of antisocial behavior, but could work in concert with genetic susceptibility to influence an adolescent's behavior.

Studies of gene X environment effects, like longitudinal studies controlling for initial status, have emphasized antisocial (rather than positive) outcomes and adult (rather peer) influences. There are signs, however, that peer relationships might eventually be found to moderate risk-outcome links during adolescence. In a recent study of 5- and 7-year-old children, relationships with peers exacerbated or compensated for risks for aggression and poor psychological and school adjustment (Ladd & Burgess, 2001). Such findings with children raise the possibility that similar findings might emerge in parallel studies of adolescents.

These three broad approaches show that parents and peers are plausible and, in some instances, compelling sources of influence on adolescent development. The research described thus far, however, has yielded "phase one" findings (Collins, 1993): they provide evidence that influences are significant, but provide few insights regarding how such links come about. In the rest of this chapter we outline four themes that may move us toward a better understanding of the relevant processes.

Emerging Principles of Interpersonal Influence during Adolescence

The processes of interest reflect the contributions of the *relationships* between adolescents and their parents and peers.

Dyadic Processes. The impact of close relationships derives from the joint action patterns between the two people involved (Hartup & Laursen, 1991). In the case of adolescence, this realization has meant that researchers increasingly center on the dynamics of close relationships, rather than explaining outcomes exclusively in terms of personality constructs, situational constraints (including role-related demands), or the action of one person upon another (e.g., Ainsworth, 1989; Allen & Land, 1999; Collins, 1995). One sign of this shift is greater attention to bidirectional and reciprocal influences in adolescents' close relationships (e.g., Collins & Laursen, 2004; Smetana, 1996; Steinberg, 2001).

Characteristic patterns of joint actions between members of a relationship reveal how their distinctive influences might come about. For example, reciprocity, or the degree to which one party reacts in kind to the actions of the other party, occurs in both parent-adolescent interactions and friendships. A striking example can be seen in comparisons between pairs of delinquent adolescent males who are friends and pairs who are merely acquaintances. Compared with acquaintances, friends engage in more frequent reciprocity and mutual positive reinforcement (Dishion, Andrews, & Crosby, 1995). Within these established reciprocal patterns, members of the pair can both experience and exert influences on each other. Another example comes from studies of parent-adolescent pairs whose interactions include frequent reciprocal emotional negativity. Such pairs are more likely to increase rapidly in negative emotionality over time, even when researchers take into account the degree of negativity between them at the start (e.g., Kim, Conger, Lorenz, & Elder, 2001). Similarly, recent analyses of a well-known longitudinal sample in New Zealand revealed two-way effects between mothers' depression and their children's or adolescents' disruptive behavior and negative emotion. These two-way patterns could be seen beginning in middle childhood and continuing into early adolescence (Jaffee & Poulton, 2003). Reciprocities in adolescent relationships extend both over time and to other types of close relationships. For example, in the longitudinal study by Kim et al. (2001), the degree of negative emotionality in parent-adolescent dyads predicted degree of negative emotionality with romantic partners in late adolescence. This association appears to come about because of two characteristics of the parents' behavior toward the child: their frequent expressions of negative rather than positive emotion, and their ineffectiveness in monitoring and discipline.

In studies of influence in parent-adolescent relationships, variations in interactions from one parent-adolescent dyad to another traditionally have been described as differences in *parenting styles* (Baumrind, 1991; Darling & Steinberg, 1993; Maccoby & Martin, 1983). Although these contrasting patterns typically have been described in terms of the parents' actions, we believe that the link between parenting styles and adolescent behavior actually result from differing characteristics of interactions that occur in parent-adolescent relationships (Collins & Madsen, 2003). For example, the parenting style known as authoritativeness involves parent-adolescent interactions that typically are high in reciprocity and bidirectional communication. By contrast, authoritarian and indulgent parenting styles imply relationships in which the dominance of parent (in the authoritarian style) and of child (in the indulgent style) disrupts desirable levels of reciprocity and communication (Maccoby & Martin, 1983). Darling and Steinberg's (1993) distinction between parental *styles* (global attitudes and emotional stances that influence the quality of relationships with children) and parental *practices* (specific strategies for gaining children's compliance, maintaining control, and enforcing expectations) further clarifies the link to adolescent development.

The many findings that relationships differing in these ways are linked to child or adolescent skills and behaviors give us a clue to conditions under which positive and negative influences could occur. Longitudinal findings repeatedly have shown that high levels of bidirectional communication and acceptance in parent-child relationships during childhood and early adolescence are correlated positively with psychosocial maturity in later adolescence. Allen, Hauser, Bell, and O'Connor (1994) found that parents' (especially fathers') actions that made it more difficult for family members to discuss their own reasons for preferring one option over others were highly correlated with decreases in adolescents' ego development and self-esteem between the ages of 14 and 16. In a similar study, advances in adolescents' moral-reasoning levels over a two-year period were best predicted by earlier parent-child interactions characterized by supportive, but cognitively challenging, discussions of moral issues (Walker & Taylor, 1991). Conversely, resistance to delinquency and norm-breaking behavior in adolescence is less likely in families where monitoring of adolescents' out-of-home activities is accomplished by frequent two-way communication that encourages disclosure, than in families where parents rely on impersonal tracking and surveillance of activities (Stattin & Kerr, 2000). A related finding about the importance of relationship characteristics is that continuously high levels of conflict in relationships are associated with psychosocial problems and relationship dysfunction during adolescence and in later life (Laursen & Collins, 1994). Undoubtedly, these deleterious effects partly reflect the negative emotionality that parents and adolescents sometimes show during conflict. It is interesting, for example, that adolescents who report moderate levels of conflict with parents have better school grades and fewer adjustment problems than either adolescents who report frequent conflict or those who report no conflict (Adams & Laursen, 2001). In short, relationship properties probably play a role in determining whether specific experiences in relationships, such as conflicts, are detrimental in development.

Such correlational findings leave open the question of *how* variations in family relationships play a role in adolescent adjustment. The process undoubtedly is more complex than popular beliefs about the simple transmission of parents' values to the next generation imply (Grusec & Goodnow, 1994; Grusec, Goodnow, & Kuczynski, 2000). Certain parental behaviors clearly make a sizable impact, but that impact undoubtedly comes about through the dynamic properties of relationships between parent and child that foster the adolescents' desire or willingness to be influenced (Darling & Steinberg, 1993; Grusec et al., 2000). Maccoby (1984, 1992) has argued, for example, that a key step is gradually increasingly shared decision-making between parent and child in childhood and adolescence – in effect, training for effective interdependence, rather than independence. In her words, parenting that emphasizes collaborative interactions "... induct(s) the child into a system of reciprocity" (Maccoby, 1992, p. 1013), which is a key aspect of social competence (Hartup, 1986).

Interrelated Influences. Most research on adolescent adjustment has emphasized the role of family relationships, but relationships outside of the family such as those with peers have been found repeatedly to combine with parent-adolescent relationships in predicting behavior and adjustment. Brown, Mounts, Lamborn, and Steinberg (1993) found that parenting practices (e.g., emphasis on academic achievement, parental monitoring, and facilitation of joint parent-child decision-making) and parenting styles (e.g., variations along dimensions of demandingness and responsiveness) are associated with certain adolescent behaviors and predispositions. These behaviors in turn can guide adolescents into particular peer groups (e.g., "brains," "jocks," or "druggies"), and the norms of these groups further encourage the behaviors that brought the adolescent together with these peers in the first place. Other research further shows that adolescents who become increasingly susceptible to peers over time, compared with those who do not, often believe that parents not only are unreasonably strict, but that they don't allow the adolescent an appropriate role in making decisions that affect him or her (Fuligni & Eccles, 1993). On the other hand, chronic maltreatment by parents increases the risk that adolescents will be rejected by peers, largely because maltreated adolescents are especially likely to be quite aggressive (Bolger & Patterson, 2001).

These findings imply that, in well-functioning families, the stereotype that adolescents are more strongly influenced by peers than by parents is relatively unlikely. In fact, evidence from a sample followed from birth to age 26 in the Minnesota Longitudinal Study of Parents and Children shows that social competence with peers in adolescence and quality of relationships with romantic partners in early adulthood are predicted more strongly by a combination of earlier parent-child relationships and peer competence than by the quality of either earlier relationship alone. Sroufe, Egeland, and Carlson (1999) demonstrated that a history of supportive early relationships with caregivers significantly contributed to the development of competence in friendships in early adolescence. These authors further demonstrated that peer competence in early and middle childhood contributed significantly, over and above the contribution of early parental care.

Similar interrelations are apparent in adolescents' romantic relationships. In a Canadian sample of 12- to 13-year-olds, family stress, family separation, and poor psychological adjustment emerged as risk factors for very early involvement in romantic relationships (Connolly, Taradash, & Williams, 2001). In the Minnesota Longitudinal Study, a combination of early and later familial factors and peer-group behavior forecast being involved in romances in adolescence (Collins, Hennighausen, Schmit, & Sroufe, 1997b; Collins & Sroufe, 1999). Other studies have shown that both having an extensive peer network and experiencing intimacy and social support in relationships with peers correlate with having a romantic relationship that provides support and offers opportunities for sharing thoughts and feelings (Connolly & Johnson, 1996; Taradash, Connolly, Pepler, Craig et al., 2001). Prior relationship experiences also reflect expectancies regarding future relationships. The cognitive and behavioral syndrome known as rejection sensitivity arises from experiences of rejection in parent-child relationships and also in relations with peers and, possibly, romantic partners. Rejection sensitivity in turn predicts expectancies of rejection that correlate strongly with both actual rejection and lesser satisfaction in adolescent relationships (Downey, Bonica, & Rincon, 1999).

Finally, poor relationships with parents and peers contribute to the incidence of both physical and relational aggression between romantic partners in late adolescence (Linder & Collins, 2003; Linder, Crick, & Collins, 2002).

The significance of interrelated relationships likely will become even more apparent as peers, as well as parents, are included systematically in studies of influence. Research is needed especially to examine influences on the development of competence other than the regulation of antisocial behavior, which has dominated research on interrelated influences.

Moderator Effects and Mediator Processes. In addition to their direct impact on adolescent development, relationships with parents and peers also help to determine the impact of other social influences (Grotevant, 1998). Close relationships help to specify the conditions under which relations occur between close relationships and adolescent outcomes (*moderator effect*). Relationships also play a role in forming a connection between experiences and the adolescents' behavior (*mediator effects*) (Baron & Kenny, 1986). Below, we briefly describe examples of moderator and mediator effects.

An example of moderator effects of relationship qualities on the impact of specific parental actions comes from research showing that perceived quality of relationship with parents affected the likelihood that adolescents would imitate parents' substance use. Adolescents who had a relatively good quality relationship with parents tended to follow their parents' example more than if the relationship was relatively poor, implying that positive relationships with antisocial parents sometimes may be a source of risk (Andrews, Hops, & Duncan, 1997). Fuhrman and Holmbeck (1995) found that, when parent-adolescent affect was mostly positive, adolescents with high levels of emotional autonomy were more likely to show positive adjustment than adolescents whose emotional autonomy was low. The converse was true when parent-adolescent affect was relatively negative.

In the case of peer relationships, friends' influence frequently is moderated by the quality of the friendship, that is, the degree to which the friendship is marked by intimacy, prosocial behavior, and support for the other's self-esteem (Berndt & Keefe, 1995). Pre-delinquent and delinquent adolescents often have friendships of lower quality than other adolescents do, but variations in their friendships correlate positively with the degree of influence delinquent friends have on the involvement of the adolescent in deviant behavior (Dishion, Spracklen, Andrews, & Patterson, 1996; Hartup, 1996).

Parent-adolescent and peer relationships each frequently moderate the potential impact of the other on adolescent behavior and adjustment. For example, the degree to which mutual friendship contributes positively to psychological well-being depends on the degree to which the adolescent also experiences familial cohesion and adaptability (Gauze, Bukowski, Aquan-Assee, & Sippola, 1996). The potential complexity of moderating relationships is evident in a recent study following adolescents from grade 6 to grade 10. Parents' firm behavioral control appeared to halt the upward trajectory in externalizing problems among adolescents with deviant peers (Galambos, Barker, & Almeida, 2003). Lower levels of parental firm control and association with deviant peers predicted higher levels of internalizing behaviors. Conversely, friendship quality, peer group affiliations and peer antisocial behavior significantly moderated the link between negative parenting and adolescent externalizing behavior one year later (Lansford, Criss, Pettit, Dodge et al., 2003). Related findings on the links between parental behavior and deviance appear in the chapter by Dodge and colleagues (Chapter 5 in this book). High-quality friendships and peer affiliations attenuated the inverse correlation between negative parenting (defined as unilateral parental decision making, low supervision and awareness, and harsh discipline) and externalizing problems, whereas poor-quality peer relations and antisocial friends amplified the association.

The quality of parent-adolescent relationships also moderates the impact of stressors outside of the family. Junior-high-school students experiencing high levels of school "hassles" demonstrated more competent functioning and less evidence of psychopathology if they rated their familial relationships as high quality, rather than lower quality (Garber & Little, 1999). Moreover, the link between after-school self-care and involvement in problem behaviors was found to be buffered by parental acceptance and firm control, which are the dual hallmarks of relationships in authoritative families (Galambos & Maggs, 1991). Thus, a significant, but often neglected, aspect of influence from both parents and peers comes from their roles in amplifying or dampening other potential sources of influence.

As mediators, interactions in close relationships also often serve as conduits by which outside forces impinge on adolescent competence. A well-known example is the finding that the impact of a family's sudden economic losses on adolescents was mediated by deterioration of nurturant/involved parenting (e.g., Conger et al., 1992; Grant et al., 2003). In fact, the most significant impact of economic hardship in these studies was that of undermining parents' abilities to maintain effective relationships with their adolescent offspring. Familial conflicts serve a similar mediating role in the link between family economic hardship and adolescent aggression and anxiety/depression (Wadsworth & Compas, 2002).

Such mediator effects point to further possible avenues by which parent-adolescent relationships influence individual development. In a cross-sectional study of 10- to 16-year-old African-American adolescents (Connell, Spencer, & Aber, 1994), parents' engagement with their adolescents was related inversely to the degree to which their adolescents were disaffected from school. As parents' involvement lessened, adolescents were likely to become even more disaffected, partly because less parental engagement and support were associated with more negative self-appraisals by adolescents. This transactional process eventually could undermine adolescents' school performance.

These instances broaden simplistic cause-and-effect models of the impact of parent-adolescent relationships. Rather than focusing only on the assumption that parenting styles or specific practices cause the outcomes to which correlational findings have linked them, it now appears that parent-adolescent relationships influence adolescent development by modifying the impact of other sources of influence and transmitting them to adolescents through moment-to-moment exchanges between parents and children.

Expanded Outcomes. Developmental research has been dominated since the 1940s by outcome variables that reflect a highly individualistic view of mature competence, but the recent emphasis on relationships has brought about a shift toward a broader range of competences for participating in social life (Collins, 2002). Hartup (1986, p. 2) noted that relationships were significant contexts for socialization not only because they provide an opportunity for the inculcation of social norms, but because they constitute important templates or models for the construction of future relationships, and Maccoby (1992) further proposed that a relationship perspective means viewing outcomes as dynamic capacities for relating effectively to others. Although parental effectiveness has long been construed as a set of parental competencies for nurturing and regulating children's behavior, from a dyadic perspective, effective parenting also means creating a relationship with the child that serves as a prototype for other social reciprocities (Maccoby, 1992).

Increasingly, research findings imply that hallmark achievements of adolescence, such as autonomy and identity, "are most easily established not at the expense of attachment relationships with parents, but against a backdrop of secure relationships that are likely to endure well beyond adolescence" (Allen & Land, 1999, p. 319). Current views contend that the quality of parent-child exchanges and shared decision-making, over and above the specific content of parental teaching, contribute to the development of competencies for autonomous, responsible behavior, such as awareness of the perspectives of others, mature abilities for self-regulation, and active exploration of adult identity (Collins et al., 1997). More mature levels of these competencies are associated with parent-adolescent relationships that encourage both individuation (holding and expressing autonomous views, being one's "own person") and connectedness (feeling a bond with other family members) (e.g., Allen, Hauser, Bell, & O'Connor, 1994; Lamborn, Mounts, Steinberg, & Dornbusch, 1991). In short, relevant outcomes go beyond individual characteristics such as antisocial behavior and school achievement to include skills for cooperation, collaboration, and effectiveness in close relationships.

One implication of a more diverse set of competencies is that some features of close relationship experiences may predict more strongly to some outcomes than to others, as well as the converse. In the longitudinal study by Bagwell et al. (1998) described earlier, having a reciprocated friendship in early adolescence predicted changes in relationship intimacy, self-worth, and relatively low depression at age 23, relative to those with nonreciprocated friendships. Although peer acceptance was not a significant predictor of changes in these variables, acceptance (but not friendship) did predict perceived job competence and future aspirations at age 23.

A further example from the Minnesota Longitudinal Study of Parents and Children adds a developmental timing dimension to these confirmations of divergent predictions. To examine predictors of romantic relationship competence in adolescence and early adulthood, Collins and Madsen (2003) included quality of caregiving in infancy and early childhood, peer competence at grade 1 and grade 6, and characteristics of parent-child joint problem-solving at age 13. The two measures of parent-child functioning were based on videotaped behavior in laboratory tasks; the peer measures were teacher ratings. We then examined the role of these early relationship experiences in the development of two aspects of romantic relationships during adolescence and early adulthood.

The first variable was *involvement* in romantic relationships, including age at which participants began to date, the number of different dating partners, and so forth. The second variable was *quality of interactions* between participants and their romantic partners of four months or longer. The findings revealed that both peer competence in elementary school and parent-child effective conflict resolution and positive interaction at age 13 played a significant role in both later involvement in, and quality of, romantic relationships. For predictions of quality (though not involvement), quality of caregiving in infancy and early childhood also contributed significantly to adult relationship outcomes, over and above the contributions of later variables. This difference in the importance of very early relationships with parents could have been revealed only by considering several aspects of romantic relationships, and these would have been studied only within a framework in which relationships, rather than only individual attributes, were considered important in development.

Implications for Policy and Practice

In their futuristic view of adolescence in the twenty-first century, Larson, Wilson, Brown, Furstenberg, and Verma (2002) propose that the significance of competence in relationships may increase as youth face greater and more complex demands associated with living in an interdependent world. Research-based evidence that in childhood and adolescence, relationships with family members and peers are significant not only to the development of individual attributes, but to effective and satisfying relationships with others, implies that efforts to support families and schools in providing optimal relationship experiences should be a key concern of policymakers and practitioners.

Several possible models are implied by findings from intervention research. The success of intervention programs to change parental behavior for the better appears to be one avenue to improving both child behavior and parent-child relationships. Similarly, interventions to improve the behavior of individual children may be used as a basis for both school- and clinic-based programs to facilitate more positive interactions among children and adolescents. The research findings outlined in this chapter imply that improving some of a young person's relationships could have far-reaching effects through the interrelated networks of relationships that influence adolescent development.

CONCLUSION

This attempt to specify *how* parents and peers influence adolescent outcomes has underscored three key points about the nature of influence during adolescence, as well as in other age periods. The first is that contemporary research designs are more informative than the designs that were used to answer questions of *whether* parents and peers are significant forces in adolescent development. The second is that attempts to move beyond questions of whether influences occur to *how* they occur require attention to interpersonal processes between adolescents and the most important individuals in their social networks. The third is the importance of attending to interrelated influences from relationships with different partners and to the diverse contexts and domains of functioning in which influences may be operative.

Although these summary statements come from reliable information, important questions remain for future research. The emphasis in previous studies on the role of childhood experiences on adolescent behavior and adjustment should be supplemented by studies of the impact of familial and peer relationships during adolescence. The preoccupation with influences on antisocial behavior should be balanced by greater attention to the broad range of positive competencies outlined in this chapter, including motivations and skills that underlie effective participation in relationships with one's future spouses, children, neighbors, and co-workers. A more clearly interpersonal and transactional model of influence is the most promising avenue to understanding the broader range of relevant influences and outcomes involved in successful adolescent development.

ACKNOWLEDGMENTS

Preparation of the manuscript was supported in part by a grant from the National Institute of Mental Health to B. Egeland, L. A. Sroufe, and W. A. Collins.

References

Abelson, R. (1985). A variance explanation paradox: When a little is a lot. *Psychological Bulletin, 97*, 129–133.

Adams, R., & Laursen, B. (2001). The organization and dynamics of adolescent conflict with parents and friends. *Journal of Marriage and Family, 63*, 97–110.

Ainsworth, M. D. S. (1989). Attachments beyond infancy. *American Psychologist, 44*, 709–716.

Allen, J. P., Hauser, S. T., Bell, K. L., & O'Connor, T. G. (1994). Longitudinal assessment of autonomy and relatedness in adolescent-family interactions as predictors of adolescent ego development and self-esteem. *Child Development, 65*, 179– 194.

Allen, J. P., & Land, D. (1999). Attachment in adolescence. In J. Cassidy & P. R. Shaver (Eds.), *Handbook of attachment: Theory, research, and clinical applications* (pp. 319–335). New York: Guilford Press.

Andrews, J. A., Hops, H., & Duncan, S. C. (1997). Adolescent modeling of parent substance use: The moderating effect of the relationship with the parent. *Journal of Family Psychology, 11*, 259–270.

Bagwell, C. L., Newcomb, A. F., & Bukowski, W. M. (1998). Preadolescent friendship and peer rejection as predictors of adult adjustment. *Child Development, 69*, 140– 153.

Baron, R., & Kenny, D. (1986). The moderator-mediator variable distinction in social psychological research: Conceptual, strategic, and statistical considerations. *Journal of Personality and Social Psychology, 51*, 1173–1182.

Baumrind, D. (1991). Effective parenting during the early adolescent transition. In P. A. Cowan & M. Hetherington (Eds.), *Family transitions* (pp. 111–163). Hillsdale, NJ: Erlbaum.

Berndt, T. J., & Keefe, K. (1995). Friends' influence on adolescents' adjustment to school. *Child Development, 66*, 1312–1329.

Bohman, M. (1996). Predispositions to criminality: Swedish adoption studies in retrospect. In G. R. Bock & J. A. Goode (Eds.), *Genetics of criminal and antisocial behavior, Ciba Foundation Symposium 194* (pp. 99–114). Chichester, England: Wiley.

Bolger, K., & Patterson, C. (2001). Developmental pathways from child maltreatment to peer rejection. *Child Development, 72*, 549–568.

Brown, B. B. (2004). Adolescents' relationships with peers. In R. Lerner & L. Steinberg (Eds.), *Handbook of adolescent psychology*. New York: Wiley.

Brown, B., Mounts, N., Lamborn, S., & Steinberg, L. (1993). Parenting practices and peer group affiliation in adolescence. *Child Development, 64*, 467–482.

Cadoret, R. (1985). Genes, environment and their interaction in the development of psychopathology. In T. Sakai & T. Tsuboi (Eds.), *Genetic aspects of human development* (pp. 165–175). Tokyo: Igaku-Shoin.

Caspi, A., McClay, J., Moffitt, T. E., Mill, J., Martin, J., Craig, I. W., Taylor, A., & Poulton, R. (2002). Role of genotype in the cycle of violence in maltreated children. *Science, 297*, 851–854.

Chisholm, K. (1998). A three-year follow-up of attachment and indiscriminate friendliness in children adopted from Romanian orphanages. *Child Development, 69*, 1092–1106.

Collins, W. A. (1993). From phase 1 findings to phase 2 questions: New directions in research on fathers' roles in adolescent development. In S. Shulman & W. A. Collins (Eds.), *Father-adolescent relationships and their developmental significance. New Directions for Child Development*, No.62 (pp. 91–96). San Francisco: Jossey-Bass.

Collins, W. A. (1995). Relationships and development: Family adaptation to individual change. In S. Shulman (Ed.), *Close relationships and socioemotional development* (pp. 128–154). New York: Ablex.

Collins, W. A. (2002). Historical perspectives on contemporary research in social development. In P. Smith & C. Hart (Eds.), *Blackwell handbook of childhood social development* (pp. 3–23). London: Blackwell Publishers.

Collins, W. A. (2003). More than myth: The developmental significance of romantic relationships during adolescence. *Journal of Research on Adolescence, 13*, 1–24.

Collins, W. A., Gleason, T., & Sesma, A. (1997a). Internalization, autonomy, and relationships: Development during adolescence. In J. E. Grusec & L. Kuczynski (Eds.), *Parenting and children's internalization of values: A handbook of contemporary theory* (pp. 78–99). New York: Wiley.

Collins, W. A., Hennighausen, K. H., Schmit, D. T., & Sroufe, L. A. (1997b). Developmental precursors of romantic relationships: A longitudinal analysis. In S. Shulman & W. A. Collins (Eds.), *Romantic relationships in adolescence: Developmental perspectives. New Directions for Child Development*, No. 78 (pp. 69–84). San Francisco: Jossey-Bass.

Collins, W. A., & Laursen, B. (2000). Adolescent relationships: The Art of Fugue. In C. Hendrick & S. Hendrick (Eds.), *Close relationships: A sourcebook* (pp. 59–70). Thousand Oaks, CA: Sage.

Collins, W. A., & Laursen, B. (2004). Parent-adolescent relationships and influence. In R. Lerner & L. Steinberg (Eds.), *Handbook of adolescent psychology*. New York: Wiley.

Collins, W. A., Maccoby, E., Steinberg, L., Hetherington, E. M., & Bornstein, M. (2000). Contemporary research on parenting: The case for nature *and* nurture. *American Psychologist, 53*, 218–232.

Collins, W. A., & Madsen, S. D. (2003). Developmental change in parenting interactions. In L. Kuczynski (Ed.), *Handbook of dynamics in parent-child relations* (pp. 49–66). Thousand Oaks, CA: Sage.

Collins, W. A., & Sroufe, L. A. (1999). Capacity for intimate relationships: A developmental construction. In W. Furman, C. Feiring, & B. B. Brown (Eds.), *Contemporary perspectives on adolescent romantic relationships* (pp. 69–84). San Francisco: Jossey-Bass.

Conger, R., & Elder, G. E. (1994). *Families in troubled times: Adapting to change in rural America*. New York: Aldine.

Conger, R., Ge, X., Elder, G. H., Lorenz, F., & Simons, R. (1994). Economic stress, coercive family process and developmental problems of adolescents. *Child Development, 65*, 541–561.

Connell, J. P., Spencer, M. B., & Aber, J. L. (1994). Educational risk and resilience in African-American youth: Context, self, action, and outcomes in school. *Child Development, 65*, 493–506.

Connolly, J. A., Johnson, A. M.(1996). Adolescents' romantic relationships and the structure and quality of their close interpersonal ties. *Personal Relationships, 3,* 185–195.

Connolly, J. A., Taradash, A., & Williams, T. (2001). *Dating and sexual activities of Canadian boys and girls in early adolescence: Normative patterns and biopsychosocial risks for early onset of heterosexuality.* Working paper series. Applied Research Branch of Strategic Policy, Human Resources Development Canada.

Cowan, P. A., & Cowan, C. P. (1997). What an intervention design reveals about how parents affect their children's academic achievement and social competence. In J. Borkowski, S. Landesman-Ramey, & M. Bristol (Eds.), *Parenting and the child's world: Multiple influences on intellectual and social-emotional development.* Mahwah, NJ: Erlbaum.

Cowan, P. A., Powell, D., & Cowan, C. P. (1998). Parenting interventions: A family systems perspective. In W. Damon, I. Sigel, & K. A. Renninger (Eds.), *Handbook of child psychology: Child psychology in practice* (Vol. 4, pp. 3–72). New York: Wiley.

Darling, N., & Steinberg, L. (1993). Parenting style as context: An integrative model. *Psychological Bulletin, 113,* 487–496.

Dishion, T. J., Andrews, D. W., & Crosby, L. (1995). Antisocial boys and their friends in early adolescence: Relationship characteristics, quality, and interactional process. *Child Development, 66,* 139–151.

Dishion, T. J., Patterson, G. R., & Kavanagh, K. (1992). An experimental test of the coercion model: Linking theory, measurement, and intervention. In J. McCord & R. Tremblay (Eds.), *Interaction of theory and practice: Experimental studies of interventions* (pp. 253–282). New York: Guilford.

Dishion, T. J., Spracklen, K. M., Andrews, D. W., & Patterson, G. R. (1996). Deviancy training in male adolescent friendships. *Behavior Therapy, 27,* 373–390.

Downey, G., Bonica, C., & Rincón, C. (1999). Rejection sensitivity and adolescent romantic relationships. In W. Furman, B. B. Brown, & C. Feiring (Eds.), *The development of romantic relationships in adolescence* (pp. 148–174). New York: Cambridge University Press.

Dubow, E. F., Huesmann, L. R., Eron, L. D., Boxer, P., & Slegers, D. (in press). Middle childhood family contextual factors as predictors of adult outcomes. In A. Huston & M. Ripke (Eds.), *Building pathways to success: Research, policy, and practice on development in middle childhood.* Washington, DC: American Psychological Association.

Espelage, D. L., Holt, M. K., & Henkel, R. R. (2003). Examination of peer-group contextual effects on aggression during early adolescence. *Child Development, 74,* 205–220.

Forehand, R., & King, H. E. (1977). Noncompliant children: Effects of parent training on behavior and attitude change. *Behavior Modification, 1,* 93–108.

Forehand, R., Wells, K. C., & Griest, D. L. (1980). An examination of the social validity of a parent training program. *Behavior Therapy, 11,* 488–502.

Forgatch, M. S. (1991). The clinical science vortex: A developing theory of antisocial behavior. In D. Pepler & K. Rubin (Eds.), *The development and treatment of childhood aggression* (pp. 291–315). Hillsdale, NJ: Erlbaum.

Forgatch, M. S., & DeGarmo, D. S. (1999). Parenting through change: An effective prevention program for single mothers. *Journal of Consulting and Clinical Psychology, 67,* 711–724.

Fuhrman, T., & Holmbeck, G. N. (1995). A contextual-moderator analysis of emotional autonomy and adjustment in adolescence. *Child Development, 66,* 793–811.

Furman, W., & Buhrmester, D. (1992). Age and sex differences in perceptions of networks of personal relationships. *Child Development, 63*, 103–115.

Fuligni, A., & Eccles, J. (1993). Perceived parent-child relationships and early adolescents' orientation toward peers. *Developmental Psychology, 29*, 622–632.

Galambos, N., Barker, E., & Almeida, D. (2003). Parents do matter: Trajectories of change in externalizing and internalizing problems in early adolescence. *Child Development, 74*, 578–594.

Galambos, N. L., & Maggs, J. L. (1991). Out-of-school care of young adolescents and self-reported behavior. *Developmental Psychology, 27*, 644–655.

Garber, J., & Little, S. (1999). Predictors of competence among offspring of depressed mothers. *Journal of Adolescent Research, 14*, 44–71.

Gauze, C., Bukowski, W. M., Aquan-Assee, J., & Sippola, L. K. (1996). Interactions between family environment and friendship and associations with self-perceived well-being during early adolescence. *Child Development, 67*, 2201–2216.

Ge, X., Conger, R., Lorenz, F., Shanahan, M., & Elder, G. (1995). Mutual influences in parent and adolescent psychological distress. *Developmental Psychology, 31*, 406–419.

Ge, X., Lorenz, F., Conger, R., Elder, G., & Simons, R. (1994). Trajectories of stressful life events and depressive symptoms during adolescence. *Developmental Psychology, 30*, 467–483.

Goodnow, J. J. (1992). Families and development. In M. Bennett (Ed.), *Developmental psychology: Achievements and prospects* (pp. 72–88). Philadelphia: Psychology Press.

Gottlieb, G. (1995). Some conceptual deficiencies in "developmental" behavior genetics. *Human Development, 38*, 131–141.

Grant, K. E., Compas, B. E., Stuhlmacher, A. F., Thurm, A. E., McMahon, S. D., & Halpert, J. A. (2003). Stressors and child and adolescent psychopathology: Moving from markers to mechanisms of risk. *Psychological Bulletin, 129*, 447–466.

Greenberg, M. T., Weissberg, R., O'Brien, M. U., Zins, J., Fredericks, L, Resnik, H., & Elias, M. J. (2003). Enhancing school-based prevention and youth development through coordinated social, emotional, and academic learning. *American Psychologist, 58*, 466–474.

Grotevant, H. D. (1998). Adolescent development in family contexts. In W. Damon & N. Eisenberg (Eds.), *Handbook of child psychology: Vol. 3. Social, emotional, and personality development* (5th ed., pp. 1097–1150). New York: Wiley.

Grusec, J., & Goodnow, J. J. (1994). The impact of parental discipline methods on the child's internalization of values: A reconceptualization of current points of view. *Developmental Psychology, 30*, 4–19.

Grusec, J., Goodnow, J. J., & Kuczynski, L. (2000). New directions in analyses of parenting contributions to children's acquisition of values. *Child Development, 71*, 205–211.

Gunnar, M. R. (2000). Early adversity and the development of stress reactivity and regulation. In C. A. Nelson (Ed.), *Minnesota Symposia on Child Psychology: Vol. 31. The effects of adversity on neurobehavioral development* (pp. 163–200). Mahwah, NJ: Erlbaum.

Harris, J. R. (1998). *The nurture assumption: Why children turn out the way they do.* New York: Free Press.

Hartup, W. W. (1986). On relationships and development. In W. W. Hartup & Z. Rubin (Eds.), *Relationships and development* (pp. 1–26). Mahwah, NJ: Erlbaum.

Hartup, W. W. (1996). The company they keep: Friendships and their developmental significance. *Child Development, 67*, 1–13.

Hartup, W. W., & Laursen, B. (1991). Relationships as developmental contexts. In R. Cohen & A. W. Siegel (Eds.), *Context and development* (pp. 253–279). Hillsdale, NJ: Erlbaum.

Haugaard, J. (1998). Is adoption a risk factor for the development of adjustment problems? *Clinical Psychology Review, 18*, 47–69.

Holden, G. W., & Miller, P. C. (1999). Enduring and different: A meta-analysis of the similarity in parents' child rearing. *Psychological Bulletin, 125*, 223–254.

Hunter, F., & Youniss, J. (1982). Changes in the functions of three relations during adolescence. *Developmental Psychology, 18*, 806–811.

Jaffee, S. R., & Poulton, R. (2003). Reciprocal effects of mothers' depression and children's problem behaviors from middle childhood to early adolescence. In A. Huston & M. Ripke (Eds.), *Building pathways to success: Research, policy, and practice on development in middle childhood.* Washington, DC: APA.

Kandel, D. (1973). Adolescent marijuana use: Role of parents and peers. *Science, 181*, 1068.

Kandel, D. (1978). Homophily, selection, and socialization in adolescent friendships. *American Journal of Sociology, 84*, 427–436.

Kandel, D., & Logan, I. (1984). Patterns of drug use from adolescence to young adulthood: I. Periods of risk for initiation, continued use, and discontinuation. *American Journal of Public Health, 74*, 660–666.

Kim, J. E., Hetherington, E. M., & Reiss, D. (1999). Associations between family relationships, antisocial peers and adolescent's externalizing behaviors: Gender and family type differences. *Child Development, 70*, 1209–1230.

Kim, K. J., Conger, R. D., Lorenz, F. O., & Elder, G. H., Jr. (2001). Parent-adolescent reciprocity in negative affect and its relation to early adult social development. *Developmental Psychology, 37*, 775–790.

Kumpfer, K. L., & Alvarado, R. (2003). Family-strengthening approaches for the prevention of youth problem behaviors. *American Psychologist, 58*, 457–465.

Ladd, G. W., & Burgess, K. B. (2001). Do Relational risks and protective factors moderate the linkages between childhood aggression and early psychological and school adjustment? *Child Development, 72*, 1579–1601.

Lamborn, S. D., Mounts, N. S., Steinberg, L., & Dornbusch, S. M. (1991). Patterns of competence and adjustment among adolescents from authoritative, authoritarian, indulgent, and neglectful families. *Child Development, 62*, 1049–1065.

Lansford, J. E., Criss, M. M., Pettit, G. S., Dodge, K. A., & Bates, J. E. (2003). Friendship quality, peer group affiliation, and peer antisocial behavior as moderators of the link between negative parenting and adolescent externalizing behavior. *Journal of Research on Adolescence, 13*, 161–184.

Larson, R., Wilson, S., Brown, B. B., Furstenberg, F. F., Jr., & Verma, S. (2002). Changes in adolescents' interpersonal experiences: Are they being prepared for adult relationships in the twenty-first century? *Journal of Research on Adolescence, 12*, 31–68.

Laursen, B., & Bukowski, W. M. (1997). A developmental guide to the organisation of close relationships. *International Journal of Behavioral Development, 21*, 747–770.

Laursen, B., & Collins, W. A. (1994). Interpersonal conflict during adolescence. *Psychological Bulletin, 115,* 197–209.

Linder, J. R., & Collins, W. A. (2003). *Parent and peer predictors of physical aggression and conflict management in romantic relationships in early adulthood: A prospective developmental study.* Unpublished manuscript, Institute of Child Development, University of Minnesota, Minneapolis, MN USA.

Linder, J. R., Crick, N. R., & Collins, W. A. (2002). Relational aggression and victimization in young adults' romantic relationships: Associations with perceptions of parent, peer, and romantic relationship quality. *Social Development, 11,* 69–86.

Maccoby, E. E. (1984). Middle childhood in the context of the family. In W. A. Collins (Ed.), *Development during middle childhood: The years from six to twelve* (pp. 184–239). Washington, DC: National Academy Press.

Maccoby, E. E. (1992). The role of parents in the socialization of children: An historical perspective. *Developmental Psychology, 28,* 1006–1017.

Maccoby, E. E., & Martin, J. A. (1983). Socialization in the context of the family: Parent-child interaction. In P. H. Mussen (Ed.), *Handbook of child psychology* (Vol. 4, pp. 1–101). New York: Wiley.

Maccoby, E. E. (2000). Parenting and its effects on children: On reading and misreading behavior genetics. *Annual Review of Psychology, 51,* 1–27.

McMahon, R. J., & Wells, K. C. (1998). Conduct problems. In E. J. Mash & R. A. Barkley (Eds.), *Treatment of childhood disorders* (2nd ed., pp. 111–151). New York: Guilford Press.

O'Connor, T. G., Deater-Deckard, K., Fulker, D., Rutter, M. L., & Plomin, R. (1998). Genotype-environment correlations in late childhood and early adolescence: Antisocial behavioral problems and coercive parenting. *Developmental Psychology, 34,* 970–981.

Parke, R. D., & Buriel, R. (1998). Socialization in the family: Ethnic and ecological perspectives. In W. Damon & N. Eisenberg (Eds.), *Handbook of child psychology* (5th ed., Vol. 3, pp. 463–552). New York: Wiley.

Patterson, G. R. (1975). Multiple evaluations of a parent-training program. In T. Thompson & W. S. Dockens (Eds.), *Applications of behavior modification* (pp. 299–322). New York: Academic Press.

Pettit, G., & Bates, J. (in press). Aggression and insecurity in late-adolescent romantic relationships: Antecedents and developmental pathways. In A. Huston & M. Ripke (Eds.), *Building pathways to success: Research, policy, and practice on development in middle childhood.* Washington, DC: American Psychological Association.

Pettit, G., Bates, J., & Dodge, K. (1997). Supportive parenting, ecological context, and children's adjustment: A seven-year longitudinal study. *Child Development, 68,* 908–923.

Reis, H. T., Lin, Y., Bennett, E. S., & Nezlek, J. B. (1993). Change and consistency in social participation during early adulthood. *Developmental Psychology, 29,* 633–645.

Roisman, G. I. Madsen, S. D., Hennighausen, K. H., Sroufe, L. A., & Collins, W. A. (2001). The coherence of dyadic behavior across parent-child and romantic relationships as mediated by the internalized representation of experience. *Attachment and Human Development, 3,* 156–172.

Rowe, D. (1994). *The limits of family influence: Genes, experience, and behavior.* New York: Guilford Press.

Rutter, M. (1996). Transitions and turning points in developmental psychopathology as applied to the age span between childhood and mid-adulthood. *International Journal of Behavioral Development, 19,* 603–626.

Rutter, M., & The English and Romanian Adoptees (ERA) Study Team. (1998). Developmental catch-up, and deficit, following adoption after severe global early privation. *Journal of Child Psychology and Psychiatry and Allied Disciplines, 39,* 465–476.

Rutter, M., Dunn, J., Plomin, R., Simonoff, E., Pickles, A., Maughan, B., Ormel, J., Meyer, J., & Eaves, L. (1997). Integrating nature and nurture: Implications of person-environment correlations and interactions for developmental psychology. *Development and Psychopathology, 9,* 335–364.

Ryan, A. M. (2001). The peer group as a context for the development of young adolescent motivation and achievement. *Child Development, 72,* 1135–1150.

Sharabany, R., Gershoni, R., & Hofman, J. (1981). Girlfriend, boyfriend: Age and sex differences in intimate friendship. *Developmental Psychology, 27,* 800–808.

Smetana, J. G. (1996). Adolescent-parent conflict: Implications for adaptive and maladaptive development. In D. Cicchetti & S. L. Toth (Eds.), *Rochester Symposium on Developmental Psychopathology: Vol. 7. Adolescence: Opportunities and challenges* (pp. 1–46). Rochester: University of Rochester.

Sroufe, L. A., Egeland, B., & Carlson, E. A. (1999). One social world: The integrated development of parent-child and peer relationships. In W. A. Collins & B. Laursen (Eds.), *Relationships as developmental contexts: The Minnesota Symposia on Child Psychology: Vol. 30.* (pp. 241–261). Mahwah, NJ: Erlbaum.

Stattin, H., & Kerr, M. (2000). Parental monitoring: A reinterpretation. *Child Development, 71,* 1072–1085.

Steinberg, L. (2001). We know some things: Adolescent-parent relationships in retrospect and prospect. *Journal of Research on Adolescence, 11,* 1–19.

Steinberg, L., Lamborn, S. D., Darling, N., Mounts, N. S., & Dornbusch, S. M. (1994). Over-time changes in adjustment and competence among adolescents from authoritative, authoritarian, indulgent, and neglectful families. *Child Development, 65,* 754–770.

Taradash, A., Connolly, J. A., Pepler, D., Craig, W., & Costa, M. (2001). The interpersonal context of romantic autonomy in adolescence. *Journal of Adolescence, 24,* 365–377.

Tienari, P., Wynne, L. C., Moring, J., Lahti, I., Naarala, M., Sorri, A., ahlberg, K-E., Saarento, O., Seitma, M., Kaleva, M., & Lasky, K. (1994). The Finnish adoptive family study of schizophrenia: Implications for family research. *British Journal of Psychiatry, 23,* 20–26.

Turkheimer, E. (1998). Heritability and biological explanation. *Psychological Review, 105,* 782–791.

Wadsworth, M. E., & Compas, B. E. (2002). Coping with family conflict and economic strain: The adolescent perspective. *Journal of Research on Adolescence, 12,* 243–274.

Walker, L., & Taylor, J. (1991). Family interactions and the development of moral reasoning. *Child Development, 62,* 264–283.

5

Toward a Dynamic Developmental Model of the Role of Parents and Peers in Early Onset Substance Use

Kenneth A. Dodge, Patrick S. Malone, Jennifer E. Lansford, Shari Miller-Johnson, Gregory S. Pettit, and John E. Bates

Although most theories of deviant behavioral development explicitly acknowledge the roles of both parenting and peer relations, few theories, and even fewer empirical analyses, have articulated the manner in which these factors relate to each other and operate dynamically across childhood. The chapter by Collins and Roisman (Chapter 4 in this book) provides an excellent general overview of how these factors operate in adolescence. This chapter identifies aspects of parenting and peer relations across the life span that may play a role in the onset of illicit drug use in adolescence and the manner in which these factors may influence each other and operate in concert across development.

The enormous social, psychological, and economic costs of substance use among adolescents in the United States over the past four decades (Kendall & Kessler, 2002; Kessler et al., 2001) have led to unprecedented attempts at interdiction, prosecution, and treatment, mostly without much success. Epidemiologic studies have directed attention toward prevention. This research has taken largely a risk-factor approach following from the methods of Rutter (Rutter & Garmezy, 1983), in which individual-difference variables in childhood are statistically linked to later substance use. Empirical research has identified several dozen factors in childhood that enhance risk for substance use during adolescence (reviewed by Hawkins, Catalano, & Miller, 1992; Weinberg, Rahdert, Colliver, & Glantz, 1998), but a laundry list of risk factors has not yet led to efficacious prevention programs. Although numerous theories have been offered that compile factors into a list of risks for substance-use onset (e.g., Brook, Brook, Gordon, Whiteman et al., 1990; Catalano, Kosterman, Hawkins, Newcomb, & Abbott, 1996; Simons, Conger, & Whitbeck, 1988), none has sufficiently explained the developmental-transactional relations among risk factors and the ecological transitions that a child goes through on a path toward substance use in order to guide strategic preventive intervention (see Petraitis, Flay, & Miller, 1995, for a review of theories). In this chapter, we : (1) build a developmental theory that integrates the dynamic impact that both parents and peers have in the onset of drug use among adolescents, (2) subject the proposed model to rigorous empirical testing through prospective inquiry, and (3) provide implications of the findings for prevention practice and public policy.

DEVELOPMENTAL PATTERNS IN ADOLESCENT SUBSTANCE USE

By age 18, between 83 and 90 percent of American adolescents experiment with alcohol consumption in social circumstances (Costa, Jessor, & Turbin, 1999; Johnston, O'Malley, & Bachman, 1998), about 61 percent of adolescents try smoking cigarettes or chewing tobacco (National Institute on Drug Abuse, 2002), and about 50 percent try an illicit substance such as marijuana (Johnston, O'Malley, & Bachman, 1998; Kosterman, Hawkins, Guo, Catalano et al., 2000). Very few children initiate use prior to age 8, but the risk of onset rises steadily for each year between ages 10 and 18 and then declines sharply thereafter (Kandel & Logan, 1984; Kandel & Yamaguchi, 1985).

Several perspectives suggest the importance of distinguishing early (prior to age 15) from later onset of substance use, including different prevalence rates, different long-term outcomes, and possibly different etiologies. The nearly ubiquitous nature of late-teenage drinking implies that merely experimenting with this behavior in a high school cultural context of social drinking is not a strong predictor of adult problem outcomes, even though almost all adult alcoholics begin drinking before adulthood. As Clark and Winters (2002, p. 1214) concluded, "experimentation with alcohol, tobacco, and other drugs is part of the normal developmental trajectory for adolescents . . . The developmental timing of early substance use is important in distinguishing normative from problematic use". Thus, early initiation of drinking or illicit substance use, prior to age 15 and during elementary or middle school, may be especially diagnostic of later problem outcomes. The U.S. nationwide Monitoring the Future study indicates that, by the eighth grade, 54 percent of youth report drinking alcohol and 23 percent report using marijuana (Johnston, O'Malley, & Bachman, 1998). In French-speaking Montreal, Canada, by age 15 years, 48 percent of boys report being drunk in the past year and 31 percent report using some other drug (Masse & Tremblay, 1997). These prevalence rates indicate that early-onset illicit substance use, although not rare, is less prevalent than rates during the high school years, whereas substance use during high school surpasses 50 percent.

Whereas later adolescence-onset substance use has received relatively little attention and has been dismissed as socially normative, explaining early-onset substance use (prior to ninth grade) is a matter of great controversy. Cloninger (1986, 1987) has argued that early-onset alcohol use is due to an inherited personality pattern that consists of high novelty-seeking, low harm-avoidance, and low reward-dependence. These characteristics reflect actions of neurally-mediated behavioral activation, inhibition, and maintenance systems, respectively. Evidence consistent with this theory is plentiful. In a sample of 431 Swedish males, these three personality dimensions were significantly related to early-onset alcoholism (Cloninger, Sigvardsson, & Bohman, 1988). Wills, Vaccaro and McNamara (1994) found that these characteristics predicted early-onset cigarette smoking, alcohol use, and marijuana use. Pomerleau, Pomerleau, Flessland and Basson (1992) found that novelty-seeking and harm-avoidance, but not reward-dependence, were correlated with cigarette smoking in adulthood. Masse and Tremblay (1997) found that novelty-seeking and harm-avoidance, but not reward dependence, measured by teacher ratings at age 6 predicted self-reports of early-onset alcohol and marijuana use between the ages of 10 and 15. The theoretical thrust of these findings is that inherited personality characteristics are responsible for early-onset substance use. Implied is the assertion that environmental events exert little impact on substance-use development.

In contrast , Dishion, Capaldi, and Yoerger (1999) have offered a more ecological perspective. They suggested that features of the home, school, and neighborhood settings (such as stigmatization, victimization, behavioral norms, and economic resources) provide a context that leads to early behaviors (such as antisocial behavior, negative affect, and problematic temperament) that might appear as inherent child characteristics. The same settings were hypothesized to foster the development of substance use. Further, Dishion et al. hypothesized and found that family management practices of harsh discipline and poor monitoring and peer experiences of social rejection and association with deviant friends have a direct impact on the development of early onset marijuana use and partially mediate the effect of early context. Unfortunately, their measures of child characteristics were confounded in time with their measures of parenting, so that strong correlations between a child's antisocial behavior at age 9 and early onset substance use between ages 10 and 15 could not be interpreted definitively. They concluded that both genetic and environmental theorists might endorse their findings as supportive. Furthermore, they could not distinguish (in time or statistically) the separate impacts of family versus peer experiences on substance-use development. They ultimately aggregated all of these factors into a parsimonious but theoretically unsatisfying single construct that they called "childhood risk structure," which accounted for 34 percent of the variance in substance use .

TOWARD A DYNAMIC DEVELOPMENTAL MODEL OF THE ONSET OF YOUTH SUBSTANCE USE

A review of the literature on risk factors for youth substance use reveals six types of factors that contribute to the onset of youth substance use.

They are reviewed here and integrated into a dynamic developmental model.

Child Factors

In spite of the strong gender and race correlations with externalizing behaviors (Coie & Dodge, 1998), late-adolescent substance use does not show similar biases. Unlike studies of conduct problems (which find that African Americans are at greater risk than European Americans, Coie & Dodge, 1998), surveys indicate slightly lower rates of substance use among African American adolescents than European Americans (Costa, Jessor, & Turbin, 1999; Johnston, O'Malley, & Bachman, 1995; Maddahian, Newcomb, & Bentler, 1988), or no differences (Chilcoat & Anthony, 1996; Wills, Sandy, Yaeger, & Shinar, 2001). In contrast, Kosterman et al. (2000) found higher rates among African-American youth than European-American youth. Kaplow, Curran, Dodge, and the Conduct Problems Prevention Research Group (2002) found that African-American children are at higher risk than European Americans for very early onset alcohol and substance use. It may be that minority ethnicity (and its disadvantages) is correlated with early onset substance use but not more normative use in adolescence. Whether predictors of substance use vary across ethnic groups is a matter of debate, with some studies indicating that peer factors play a relatively stronger role in cigarette smoking for European Americans (Landrine, Richardson, Klonoff, & Flay, 1994) and family factors play a stronger role in illicit substance use for African Americans (Krohn & Thornberry, 1993).

Males appear to be at slightly greater risk than females for early onset alcohol and illicit substance use (Costello, Erkanli, Federman, & Angold, 1999; Kaplow et al., 2002; Liu & Kaplan, 1996; Thomas, 1996) and for serious substance-use disorder that is comorbid with other psychiatric disorders (Lewinsohn, Rohde, & Seeley, 1995), but some studies find no differences (Chilcoat & Anthony, 1996). The differences tend to be so small and study-specific that Armstrong and Costello (2002) concluded that the similarities between the sexes are more remarkable than the differences. Recent data show that girls' use is almost equal to that of boys', particularly at younger ages (National Center on Addiction and Substance Abuse [NCASA], 2003). Data from the National Household Survey on Drug Abuse (NHSDA) show an increase in alcohol initiation among early adolescent girls (SAMHSA, 1997). In addition, while the age of first usage is getting younger for both boys and girls, it is dropping at a faster rate for girls. To illustrate, three decades ago, initiation of alcohol use in the group of young teen girls aged 10 to 14 was only 7 percent. However, in the last decade, this initiation rate has increased to 31 percent. This increase for girls contrasts with a relative increase from 20 percent to 35 percent for boys.

Heritability has been posited as a driving force in problematic and early-onset substance use. The evidence is consistently supportive for alcoholism in males but not in females or for illicit substance use. Twin studies (Hrubec & Omenn, 1981) reveal higher concordance among male monozygotic twins than dyzogotic twins, and adoption studies (Cadoret, Cain, & Grove, 1980) indicate rates of alcoholism up to 27 percent for adopted sons of alcoholics compared with only 6 percent for adopted sons without a biologic alcoholic parent. However, studies of girls have found no such effects (Murray & Stabenau, 1982), and studies evaluating genetic transmission of early-onset illicit substance use have yet to reveal consistent patterns (Hawkins, Catalano, & Miller, 1992). More likely than a direct genetic effect on illicit substance use is a genetic effect on factors that affect the development of substance use, such as cognitive capabilities and molecular markers of tolerance and susceptibility to addiction (Institute of Medicine, 1994; Nestler & Landsman, 2001; Tarter et al., 1999). Furthermore, genetic effects may vary across gender groups and may be moderated by life experiences. This conceptualization suggests that heritable risk requires specific life experiences to potentiate and mediate the risk.

Behavior-genetic findings notwithstanding, constitutionally endowed temperament constructs have been posited as risk factors for alcohol and substance use (Tarter & Vanyukov, 1994). Two factors derive from Gray's (1987) theory of neural control. A strong behavioral activation system is reflected in exhilaration that is activated by novel stimuli (high novelty-seeking). The behavioral inhibition system adaptively heightens responsiveness to aversive stimuli, and a weak system will fail to facilitate the inhibitive behaviors that avoid harm (low harm-avoidance). Zuckerman (1987) has found that novelty-seeking (which he calls sensation-seeking) is linked biochemically to platelet monoamine oxidase activity, which is correlated with early onset alcoholism (Tabakoff & Hoffman, 1988). Cloninger, Sigvardsson and Bohman (1988), Pomerleau et al. (1992), and Wills, Vaccaro and McNamara (1994) have found correlations between both high novelty-seeking and low harm-avoidance and substance use. Most impressively, Masse and Tremblay (1997) reported that these two factors assessed at age 6 predicted onset of alcohol and illicit substance use between 10 and 15 years of age.

Other related temperament factors have been examined as well, most notably the "difficult temperament" constellation of high activity level, negative withdrawal responses to new stimuli, arrhythmicity, rigidity, and distractibility (Weinberg & Glantz, 1999). Windle (1991) and Wills, DuHammel and Vaccaro (1995) found that these factors correlated significantly with adolescent substance use. Using the Revised Dimensions of Temperament Survey (Windle & Lerner, 1986) and the Emotionality, Activity, and Sociability Inventory (Buss & Plomin, 1984), Wills et al. (2001) found that difficult temperament (combination of high activity level and negative emotionality) correlated significantly with a combined measure of self-reported alcohol, tobacco, and other drug (ATOD) use among sixth through eighth graders surveyed in school. Because the substance use measure combined types of substances, it is not clear whether difficult temperament related significantly to illicit substance use. Likewise, prospective follow-up of 5-year-old children into young adulthood revealed that early difficult temperament, indexed by slow adaptability to change, negative mood, and withdrawal responses to new stimuli, predicted adolescent ATOD use (Lerner & Vicary, 1984). Dishion et al. (1999) found that mothers' nine-item ratings of a child's "early difficulties" in the first five years of life (e.g., sleep problems, physical development problems) predicted later alcohol and marijuana use.

Early Family Social-Ecological Factors

Equally important as risk factors for early-onset illicit substance use are social-ecological factors within the family context during the child's early life. Although there is outdated evidence that high parental education and upper levels of income are associated with slightly greater marijuana use among high-school seniors (Bachman, Lloyd, & O'Malley, 1981; Zucker & Harford, 1983), extreme economic poverty is also a risk factor for alcohol and illicit drug use (Robins & Ratcliff, 1979). Recently, Costa et al. (1999) and Dishion et al. (1999) found a negative correlation between family socioeconomic status (SES) and problem drinking in adolescence. Kaplow et al. (2002) found that children from the lowest SES group were at higher risk for very early onset (before age 13) alcohol or substance use than other children.

In addition to family socioeconomic disadvantage, other early family contexts that have been demonstrated to enhance risk for early onset substance use include being reared in a family missing a biological parent (Costa et al., 1999), parental disorganization and emotional instability (Block, Block, & Keyes, 1988; Brook et al., 1990), and parental stress as indexed by childcare problems, family medical conditions, unemployment, and the ratio of children to adults in the household (Dishion et al., 1999).

One of the most potent family-context risk factors is living with a parent who abuses alcohol or illicit substances (Merikangas et al., 1998; Weinberg & Glantz, 1999). Parental alcoholism (Cloninger, Bohman, Sigvardsson, & von Knorring, 1985; Goodwin, 1985) and substance use (Brook et al., 1990; Hops, Tildesley, Lichenstein, Ary, & Sherman, 1990; Johnson, Schoutz, & Locke, 1984) substantially increase a child's likelihood of early-onset alcohol use (Chassin, Curran, Hussong, & Colder, 1996) and illicit substance use (Costello et al., 1999). Dishion et al. (1999) followed 206 boys in the Oregon Youth Study and found that parental alcohol use as assessed by the Michigan Alcoholism Screening Test (MAST) and marijuana use (but not over-the-counter drug use) when the boy was in fourth grade significantly predicted boys' alcohol and marijuana use by age 15. Kaplow et al.

(2002) followed 387 kindergarten boys and girls from four geographic sites and found that parental substance use, as well as maternal depression, predicted substance use by age 12. Although parental substance use indexes an empirically important risk factor, the causal mechanism of this effect is unclear and could variously reflect genetic influences, a family context of psychopathology, or parental modeling of deviant behavior.

Early Parenting Factors

As found by Dishion et al. (1999), the development of early onset substance use is more directly predicted by family interactions that a child experiences during his or her early years than the context into which that child is born. The most-studied early parenting behavior is discipline style. Dishion et al. (1999) observed parent-child interaction at home at age 9 and indexed a poor-discipline factor that included nattering (nonexplosive negative parenting behavior), abusive parenting (verbal attacks, physical strikes, and threats), and erratic discipline skills. This poor-discipline construct predicted boys' alcohol and illicit substance use by age 15.

At the extreme of harsh discipline is physical abuse. Child maltreatment, which encompasses physical abuse, neglect, and sexual abuse, has been found to pose risk for substance use, especially substance-use disorder, in numerous studies (Kilpatrick, Acierno, Saunders, Resnick et al., 2000; Widom, Ireland, & Glynn, 1995). Early sexual abuse enhances risk for substance-use problems in girls (Kendler, Bulik, Silberg, Hettema et al., 2000) and boys (Clark, Lesnick, & Hegedus, 1997). Physical abuse in the absence of sexual abuse also poses enhanced risk for substance-use problems (Kaplan et al., 1998), although not as strongly. Distinct from a harsh discipline style is the use of nonviolent discipline practices that involve verbal reasoning and discussion. Kaplow et al. (2002) found that this parenting behavior protects children from early-onset substance use, and Kosterman et al. (2000) found that a proactive family management style protected children from later marijuana use .

Yet another relevant early-parent factor is warmth and involvement between parent and child. Kandel and Andrews (1987) and Penning and Barnes (1982) found that lack of maternal involvement with a child increases risk for substance use. Shedler and Block's (1990) direct observations of mothers' cold nonresponsiveness and lack of encouragement of their child at age 5 predicted frequent marijuana use in adolescence. Kaplow et al. (2002) found that parents' lack of involvement in their kindergarten child's education at school also predicted later substance use. Brook et al. (1990) reported a causal pathway in which early strong parent-child attachment led to the child's internalization of mainstream norms and values which, in turn, led the child to associate with nondeviant peers and to non-use of drugs.

Other early parenting behaviors that have been correlated with the child's onset of illicit substance use include parental inconsistent permissiveness (Baumrind, 1983), mothers' unclear rules for child behavior (Brook et al., 1990), and the lack of family rules about daily chores, homework, and so on (Costa et al., 1999). Parental failure to discourage deviant behavior early in life (the inverse is sometimes labeled as parental approval for drug use, although few parents directly encourage substance use before age 15) has also been associated with adolescent substance use in numerous studies (Barnes & Welte, 1986; Brook, Gordon, Whiteman, & Cohen, 1986; Hansen, Graham, Sobel, Shelton et al., 1987) that span multiple ethnic groups (Jessor, Donovan, & Windmer, 1980).

Less direct early parenting behaviors that enhance risk for a child's early onset substance use include modeling of deviant behaviors such as parental substance use (noted above), marital discord (Simcha-Fagan, Gersten, & Langner, 1986), and marital transitions (Dishion et al., 1999).

Early Peer Relations and Child Social-Adaptation Factors

Perhaps as important in substance-use development as the parent-child relationship is the young child's relationship with peers. Because the interactions with peers are reciprocal, both the peer group's actions toward the child and the child's behavior toward peers are included here. Kaplow et al. (2002) found that social rejection by the first-grade peer group, indexed by the social preference score (liking nominations minus disliking nominations) predicted very early onset use of illicit substances. Likewise, Dishion, Capaldi, Spracklen, and Li (1995) used the same score collected in fourth grade and found that it predicted tobacco, alcohol, and marijuana use by age 15.

Features of the child's behavior toward peers during this period may lead to the peer group's reactions or may be a response to peer group rejection, but in either case they have been found to be important markers of later substance use. Greene et al. (1997, 1999) found that early social impairment predicted later substance-use disorder even after controlling for conduct disorder, other psychiatric disorders, and social class. Early social competence, indexed in various ways, has been a consistent protective factor in substance-use development. Kaplow et al. (2002) found that first-grade peers' nominations of a child as prosocial ("cooperates, helps others, shares") protected a child from later substance use. Jackson, Henriksen, Dickenson, and Levine (1997) found that third- and fifth-grade children with low teacher-rated competence (separate ratings of social skills, self-confidence, and academic abilities) were at least twice as likely to report early use of alcohol as children with high competence. Other measures of social competence that have predicted later substance use include social problem-solving deficits and hostile attributional biases measured by responses to hypothetical vignettes (Kaplow et al., 2002), poor behavioral self-control skills (Griffin, Botvin, Epstein, Doyle et al., 2000), and expectations and aspirations for success in life (Costa, Jessor, & Turbin, 1999; Newcomb & Felix-Ortiz, 1992).

The importance of social competence is further highlighted by findings of two related constructs that do not consistently predict substance use, intelligence and self-esteem. High scores on intelligence tests predicted *earlier and more* frequent use of alcohol in an inner-city sample (Fleming, Kellam, & Brown, 1982); in contrast, low scores on the Wechsler Intelligence Scale for Children (Revised) in first grade predicted earlier substance use in Kaplow et al.'s (2002) four-site sample. In their review, Hawkins, Catalano, and Miller (1992, p. 84) concluded, "The available evidence suggests that social adjustment is more important than academic performance in the early elementary grades in predicting later drug abuse." However, social-behavioral factors such as a low degree of commitment to school (Johnston, O'Malley, & Bachman, 1985), disliking of school (Kelly & Balch, 1971), poor academic achievement (Dishion et al., 1999), and truancy (Gottfredson, 1988), which are related to school performance, have been identified as risk factors. Measures of self-esteem have also yielded contradictory findings: Although Costa et al. (1999) found that low self-esteem marked risk for alcohol use, Dishion et al. (1999) found no such relation.

Of all early child behaviors that have been examined in this context, aggression toward peers has been most consistently predictive of later substance use. Kellam, Ensminger, and Simon (1980) found that aggressive behavior in the first-grade classroom predicted later drug use, whereas shyness did not (unless coupled with aggressive behavior). Kaplow et al. (2002) reported a similar relation for first-grade aggressive behavior as indexed by parents' daily reports, and Dishion et al. (1999) found a similar relation for fourth-grade antisocial behavior. Supportive findings have been reported by Boyle, Offord, Racine, Szatmari, Fleming, and Links (1992), Lewis, Robins, and Rice (1985), and Reinherz, Giaconia, Hauf, Wasserman, and Paradis (2000), among others. Both community studies (Armstrong & Costello, 2002) and clinical studies (Clark, Parker, & Lynch, 1999; Disney, Elkins, McGue, & Iacono, 1999) support the temporal relation between early disruptive behavior disorders and early onset substance use. In fact, of all early child psychiatric disorders that have been linked to adolescent substance use, conduct disorder stands out as the most consistent and strongest marker of risk (Glantz & Lashner, 2000), so much so that Glantz (2002) has called for randomized trials of interventions to reduce conduct disorder as a test of substance-abuse prevention.

Attention-deficit hyperactivity disorder (ADHD; Mannuza, Klein, Bessler, Malloy et al., 1998) has also been linked to later substance-use problems, but this relation has been attributed to its comorbidity with conduct disorder. Farmer, Compton, Burns, and Robertson (2002, p. 1267) concluded, "ADHD may indirectly increase risk of substance use disorders by increasing risk for antisocial disorders." Likewise, early medication treatment for ADHD has been correlated with early onset substance use (Kaplow et al., 2002), but medication may be a risk factor simply because it marks the presence of ADHD. A recent meta-analysis (Wilens, Faraone, Biederman, & Gunawardene, 2003) suggests that stimulant treatment for ADHD actually reduces the risk of later substance use disorder, controlling for ADHD itself.

Internalizing disorders have been correlated with substance-use problems in adolescence (Kandel et al., 1999) and may immediately precede substance use in the short term (Deykin, Buka, & Zeena, 1992), but little evidence exists that internalizing problems early in childhood mark risk for early onset substance use. In fact, early anxiety and other internalizing symptoms in the absence of disruptive behavior may actually protect a child from early alcohol use (Kaplow, Curran, Angold, & Costello, 2001), substance use (Kaplow et al., 2002), and tobacco use (Costello et al., 1999). In contrast, one type of adult-onset alcoholism may be associated with anxiety.

Parenting Factors in Early Adolescence

As a child moves into early adolescence, parenting factors continue to mark risk for substance-use development, but the nature of important parenting factors shifts away from harsh discipline to overall supervision and monitoring. Chilcoat and Anthony (1996) followed 926, 8- to 10-year-old urban-dwelling children into adolescence and found that a ten-item child-report measure of parental supervision and monitoring predicted later marijuana, cocaine, and inhalant use. Furthermore, decreases in parental monitoring across time signaled a subsequent increase in risk of initiating illicit substance use. Numerous other studies support the importance of parental monitoring in protecting early adolescents from moving toward substance use (Baumrind, 1985; Dielman, Butchart, Shope, & Miller, 1991; McCarthy & Anglin, 1990), although Dishion et al. (1999) were surprised that their measure of monitoring, which predicted tobacco use, did not reach significance for marijuana use. It is possible that parental supervision is especially important in particular settings, such as neighborhoods that provide ready access to drugs, or for particular children who are prone to deviance (Pettit, Bates, Dodge, & Meece, 1999). Thus, interaction effects might prove stronger than main effects of parenting factors.

Parental knowledge of a child's whereabouts, activities, and friends, which is a direct outcome of monitoring behaviors, has also been found to predict ATOD initiation (Barnes, Reifman, Farrell, & Dintcheff, 2000; Dishion et al., 1995; Flannery, Vaszonyi, Torquati, & Fridrich, 1994; Fletcher, Darling, & Steinberg, 1995). Finally, quality of the parent-child relationship in early adolescence continues to mark risk (Hundleby & Mercer, 1987). Hawkins et al. (1992) refer to "low bonding to family" as the critical construct in characterizing early adolescents at risk for becoming involved with illicit substances.

Adolescent Peer Relations Factors

In early adolescence, ecological factors such as the presence of deviant forces in one's neighborhood take on importance in predicting deviant behavior (Pettit et al., 1999). Peer relations become even stronger predictors of later substance-use initiation, as peers grow in influence relative to parents (Bogenschneider, Wu, Raffaelli, & Tsay, 1998). Like parenting, though, the important aspect of peer relations shifts away from overall acceptance by the mainstream peer group to association with deviant peers. Early-adolescent involvement with friends and peers who display deviant behavior, especially substance use, is perhaps the strongest predictor of subsequent initiation of substance use (Hawkins et al., 1992), presumably through processes of peer modeling and pressure (Bray, Adams, Getz, & McQueen, 2003). Dishion et al. (1999, p. 199) suggest that, "Smoking may serve as a mechanism by which boys with troubled peer relations have commerce in a peer group . . . One may hypothesize that early onset smoking is a peer adaptation and has functional use in the life of the at-risk youth." Supportive findings come from studies across a wide range of ethnic groups and geographic contexts (Brook et al., 1990; Dishion et al., 1999; Elliott, Huizinga, & Ageton, 1985; Griffin et al., 2000; Jessor et al., 1980; Kosterman et al., 2000).

In spite of these strong correlations, the causal status of peer influence remains under debate. First, the relation between self-deviance and peer deviance has been found to be reciprocal. Changes in peers' use of substances increase a child's risk for substance-use initiation, but a child's initiation of deviant behavior also influences the peer group (Curran, Stice, & Chassin, 1997). Second, gravitation toward deviant peers is predictable from earlier peer rejection and externalizing problems (Laird, Jordan, Dodge, Pettit et al., 2001), suggesting that association with deviant peers might be epi-phenomenal to substance-use development. Third, strong relationships with one's parents have been found to buffer a child from the effects of associating with peers who are deviant (Brook et al., 1990). Finally, not all young adolescents are susceptible to peer influence, even in the context of association with deviant peers. The concept of resistance efficacy has been introduced to understand moderation effects involving association with deviant peers and has been targeted by prevention programs as a way to enhance resistance to substance use (Botvin, 1986).

THEORETICAL INTEGRATION

The diversity in risk factors that have been associated with later substance use calls for empirical integration. Rutter and Garmezy's (1983) risk-factor counting approach has been used successfully to tighten the number of predictor variables. For example, Kaplow et al. (2002) used an array of variables to find that, although any single risk factor increased risk of adolescent substance use from less than 10 percent (for zero risk factors) to 30 percent, a child with two risk factors had greater than a 50 percent risk and a child with three risk factors had more than 60 percent risk.

Theoretical integration is also needed. Simons et al. (1988) have suggested a multi-stage social learning model that posits initial risk from parental modeling of substance abusing behaviors, through the child's experimentation, followed by peer-group reward for using substances, and further increases in substance use. This model has not been tested empirically. Dishion, Capaldi, and Yoerger (1999) also suggest a multi-component model that includes risk factors of ecological context, family management, and peer environment. Although these models are encouraging, they do not account for the full diversity of risk factors reviewed here, they do not account for the different ways that parents and peers influence youth at different points in development, and they do not suggest reciprocal relations in an ongoing transaction between the youth and the social world.

We propose a multi-stage, incremental, transactional social learning model that is depicted in Figure 5.1. This model integrates diverse risk factors in a sequential fashion that posits the manner in which risk factors build upon each other to lead to early-onset substance-use initiation in adolescence. The model begins with child and family socio-ecological factors in very early life, including demographics, temperament, and SES. It posits that a difficult-temperament child who is born into a family of poverty and stress, headed by a single, socially isolated, teenage, alcohol-using mother who gave birth following an unplanned pregnancy with medical complications, is at heightened risk for substance use 15 years later. These factors place a child empirically at risk for later use of substances, but they tell us little about the mechanisms through which that development occurs.

The next step of the model involves early parenting and caregiving. The model posits that: (1) Negative parenting experiences in the first 5 years of life increase a child's risk for later substance use, above and beyond the risk imposed by previous child and family factors; and (2) These parenting factors partially mediate the effect of previous factors on substance-use development. Thus, as with models of other youth problem behaviors (e.g., McLoyd, 1990), it is posited that risk induced by structural and child factors operates partially through their effect on early care giving. Children who are born into poverty and stress are likely to receive care characterized by harsh discipline (even physical abuse) and lack of positive parenting, accompanied by inter-parental conflict, exposure to violence and values that support deviant behavior, and a high rate of nonparental child care. In turn, these experiences increase a child's risk for using drugs in adolescence

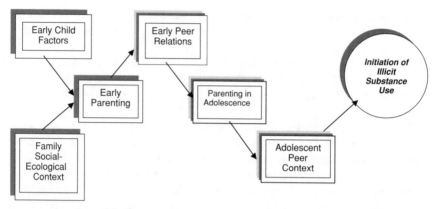

FIGURE 5.1. A multi-stage transactional social learning model of substance-use development.

and describe the processes through which early poverty and adversity are transformed into substance use.

At the next step, children who have received this kind of deficient early parenting are likely to enter elementary school displaying aggressive conduct problems that lead them to be socially rejected by the classroom peer group. The experience of peer rejection, in turn, exacerbates the child's risk for later substance use and is a mechanism that partially accounts for the effects of early deficient parenting on later substance-use outcomes.

As the child moves into early adolescence, parenting factors once again exert an influence, but in a different manner than previously believed. The conduct-problem child who is rejected by peers is likely to continue to be in conflict with parents, who begin to give up attempts at socialization and instead withdraw from monitoring and supervising their young teen. The youth is left to roam the neighborhood during after-school and week-end hours with no one charting her or his whereabouts. These adolescent parental and sociocultural risk factors increase the child's risk for initiating substance use and partially mediate the effects of early peer experiences on subsequent substance use.

The final step prior to initiating the use of substances is association with deviant peers, although some adolescents may initiate substance use even prior to this stage. Adolescents whose parents do not monitor their behavior, especially those who have not succeeded in mainstream peer relations and who live in dangerous neighborhoods, are likely to gravitate toward deviant peers. The deviant peer group, in turn, exposes the youth to new deviant activities and culture, including illicit substances. Whether the motive is sensation seeking, self-medication, or group acceptance, the youth's ready access to drugs through the deviant peer group affords the opportunity that makes using drugs a high probability. Deviant peer associations partially mediate the impact of adolescent parenting on substance use.

EMPIRICALLY TESTING THE PROPOSED MODEL IN THE CHILD
DEVELOPMENT PROJECT

The model in Figure 5.1 is useful because it suggests several empirically testable hypotheses:

1. The set of early child and sociocultural factors predicts adolescent substance use.
2a. The set of early parenting factors increments the prediction of adolescent substance use, even controlling for child and sociocultural factors.
2b. The set of early parenting factors partially mediates the effect of child and sociocultural factors on adolescent substance use.
3a. The set of early peer relations factors increments the prediction of adolescent substance use, even controlling for early parenting factors.
3b. The set of early peer relations factors partially mediates the effect of early parenting on adolescent substance use.
4a. The set of adolescent parenting factors increments the prediction of adolescent substance use, even controlling for early peer relations factors.
4b. The set of adolescent parenting factors partially mediates the effect of early peer relations on adolescent substance use.
5a. The set of adolescent peer relations factors increments the prediction of adolescent substance use, even controlling for adolescent parenting factors.
5b. The set of adolescent peer relations factors partially mediates the effect of adolescent parenting on adolescent substance use.

The Design of the Child Development Project

We undertook a prospective study called the Child Development Project (Dodge, Bates, & Pettit, 1990) in order to understand the development of substance use through longitudinal inquiry of a community sample followed from childhood through adolescence. The participants were recruited when the children registered for public kindergarten in 1987 or 1988 at each of three sites: Knoxville, TN, Nashville, TN, and Bloomington, IN. The sample consisted of 585 families at the first assessment (58 percent boys; 81 percent European American, 17 percent African American, 2 percent other). The Hollingshead (1979) index of families' SES indicated a wide range, from 11 to 66, with a mean in the low-middle class ($M = 39.59$,

$SD = 13.96$). Follow-up assessments were conducted annually through grade 12. For the basic outcome measure of drug use in adolescence, which is based on scores that are aggregated across indicators at grades 7, 9, 10, 11, and 12, 87 percent of participants contributed at least one of the component measures. Higher percentages contributed to every other variable.

During the summer before children started kindergarten or within the first weeks of school, in-depth clinical interviews were conducted with mothers in their homes. Early risk factors were measured within the context of these interviews either through mothers' direct reports or through interviewer ratings made following mothers' responses to open-ended questions (see Deater-Deckard, Dodge, Bates, & Pettit, 1998). During the initial home interview, mothers reported their child's *race* and *gender* and completed the Retrospective Infant Characteristics Questionnaire (Bates & Bayles, 1984; Bates et al., 1998) to derive a measure of *difficult temperament*. Mothers described the child's health during the prenatal through early postnatal period (*medical complications*). *Socioeconomic status* was based on the Hollingshead (1979) Four-Factor Index of Social Status. Families were coded as headed by a *single mother* and a *ratio of children to adults* in the household was computed on the basis of mothers' reports of who lived in the household at the time of the initial assessment. Mothers' *teenage pregnancy* and the *planfulness of the pregnancy* were noted. A *family stress* scale was created by summing responses to 30 questions. Maternal *social isolation* was coded by the interviewer following a series of questions regarding mothers' social contact and who was available to help them in times of need. Finally, the *mother's history of alcoholism* was assessed through the 13-item Short Michigan Alcoholism Screening Test (SMAST; Selzer, Vinokur, & Van Rooijen, 1975).

During the prekindergarten interviews, mothers reported the extensiveness of *nonparental child care in the child's early years of life* (see Bates, Marvinney, Kelly, Dodge et al., 1994). Mothers reported the biological *father's involvement and support*, the child's *exposure to interparental conflict*, and *exposure to violence*. Following a series of questions, interviewers rated the extent to which the child had experienced *harsh discipline, physical abuse,* and *positive parenting*. Finally, *mothers' support of aggression* was assessed through the Culture Questionnaire (Dodge et al., 1994).

Sociometric nominations were made by children's peers annually from kindergarten through third grade and used to derive scores for peer social preference, peer rejection, the number of years rejected, *and* peer group stability. Children's kindergarten teachers completed the 113-item Teacher Report Form of the *Child Behavior Checklist* (CBCL; Achenbach & Edelbrock, 1986). Items were summed to create separate scales reflecting *internalizing* and *externalizing behavior problems*.

At age 11, *mother-reported parental monitoring* was scored from mother reports which were adapted from other measures of parental monitoring

(Capaldi & Patterson, 1989; Dishion, Patterson, Stoolmiller, & Skinner, 1991). In the seventh grade, a measure of *adolescent-reported parental monitoring* was created from a similar instrument for youth. When adolescents were in the sixth grade, their mothers rated the level of neighborhood safety for the child based on their knowledge and observation.

When adolescents were in the sixth grade, *mother-reported peer drug use* and *child-reported peer drug use* were assessed. In seventh grade, *peer group deviance, peer group drug use,* and *best friend deviance* were scored from youth reports. Adolescents' susceptibility to peer pressure was measured using the Doing Things with Your Friends interview. Finally, seventh-grade teachers reported the *peer deviance level* of the child's peer group.

When adolescents were in the seventh and ninth through twelfth grades, they reported whether they had used various illicit substances, including marijuana, cocaine, crack, LSD, heroin, inhalants, or other drugs. Annual dichotomous scores for use or non-use were created and used as the outcome of interest.

What We Found

By grade 12, 51 percent of the participants reported to us that they had used an illicit substance at some time in their lives. This rate is comparable to nationwide estimates generated by the Monitoring the Future Study (Johnston et al., 1998). Analyses followed a general template that attempted to test the hypotheses implied in Figure 5.1. First, each of the variables in a class was tested independently for prediction of the onset of substance use. Next, the set of variables in the class was tested as a group in a multiple predictor model. Finally, each block of variables was tested as a potential mediator of the relations between the temporally precedent block and the substance-use outcome.

Finding 1. Early child and sociocultural risk factors predict adolescent substance use. The child-factor predictors, as a set, were marginally significantly related to onset of drug use, but no single variable was significant. In contrast, the set of sociocultural risk factors was significantly predictive of onset. A child was at increased likelihood of using drugs later in adolescence if he or she was born into a context of low SES, a family with a single mother or a teen mother, a household with a high ratio of children to adults, and high family stress.

Finding 2. Early parenting factors predict adolescent substance use and account for the way that socioeconomic factors operate on youth outcomes. Onset of drug use was significantly predicted from the set of early parenting factors, notably early nonparental care of the child, the father's level of involvement in early life, inter-parental conflict, physical abuse, and mother's values supporting the use of aggression. Furthermore, the early parenting composite was significantly predicted by the sociocultural risk composite: Problematic parenting grows out of adverse sociocultural contexts. Next, the early parenting risk composite score was tested as a mediator of the effect of sociocultural context on later drug-use onset. The indirect effect of early sociocultural risk on the onset of substance use as mediated by early parenting risk was significant. In addition, the direct effect of sociocultural risk became only marginally significant. Thus, the effect of early sociocultural risk appears to operate on the onset of substance use indirectly, by affecting the early parenting that a child receives.

Finding 3. Early peer relations and aggression predict adolescent substance use and account for the way that problematic parenting leads to substance use. The next step in the proposed model concerns the child's peer relations and adjustment during the elementary school years. Three of the six peer relations factors were found to predict later onset of drug use: peer rejection, low social preference, and externalizing behavior problems. The set of six risk factors also showed significant prediction.

As hypothesized, the peer relations composite was significantly predicted by the early parenting composite, indicating that aggressive behavior and problems in peer relations grow out of previous problems in parenting. The mediational model at this step indicated that the effect of early parenting on later onset of substance use is significantly mediated by the peer relations factor. That is, the effect of early parenting on later substance-use onset appears to operate indirectly by affecting the child's adjustment with peers during the elementary school years.

Finding 4. Parenting factors in early adolescence predict substance use and partially account for the way that early child problems lead to adolescent substance use. Both parent report and child report of the parent's monitoring of the child's behavior in early adolescence were significantly related to later onset of drug use, as was the set of parenting risk factors. In fact, parental monitoring of a young adolescent's whereabouts, supervision of the child's after-school and weekend hours, and knowledge of the child's social and academic functioning were among the strongest predictors of the onset of substance use.

The proposed dynamic model does not posit that parenting and peer relations are unidirectionally related. Rather, the hypothesis is that a child's emergent peer relations, which grow out of early parenting experiences as evidenced above, also affect subsequent parenting. This hypothesis was tested next. Low parental monitoring, in turn, was predicted from previous child peer-relations problems. Although perhaps counterintuitive, this finding indicates that children who display externalizing and peer problems are likely to act in ways that lead parents to decrease their monitoring and supervision. Two mechanisms for this effect are plausible. It is possible that children who display externalizing problems begin to hide their misbehavior from parents, making it more difficult for parents to monitor their behavior effectively. It is also possible that parents who have been in conflict with a misbehaving child for a long period of time grow weary of the overt conflict and seek to reduce that conflict by monitoring their child less arduously. These hypotheses should be tested in future studies. Finally, the mediation model indicated a significant indirect effect of early peer problems on later drug-use onset as mediated by the parent's lack of monitoring. In this model, the direct effect of early peer problems remained significant, indicating that the mediation effect was only partial. Thus, the best-fitting empirical model includes both an indirect path from early peer problems to later onset of drug use as mediated by lowered parental monitoring and a direct path from early peer problems to drug-use onset.

Finding 5. Deviant peer associations predict adolescent substance use and account for the way that parenting factors lead to substance use. The final step proposed was that association with drug-using deviant peers in early adolescence would lead to initiation of substance use. Six of the seven predictors in this set were significantly related to onset of drug use, as was the composite. Further, the effect of adolescent-reported peer group drug use on an individual's later onset of drug use showed some evidence of moderation by respondent gender. Although the effect was significant and positive for both males and females, it was stronger for males.

In turn, association with deviant peers was significantly predicted from a lack of parental monitoring. The transactional relations between parenting and peer relations are evidenced again here, in that low parental monitoring in early adolescence, which grew out of the child's earlier peer relations problems, now exerts an impact on the child's tendency to associate with deviant peers. The mediation model indicated a significant indirect effect of adolescent parenting risk as mediated by deviant peer associations, with no significant direct effect remaining.

CONCLUSIONS AND CAVEATS

The empirical findings are remarkably consistent with a dynamic developmental model of sequential effects that lead to the onset of drug use in adolescence. Numerous significant bivariate correlations can be reduced to the significant paths depicted in Figure 5.1. This streamlined figure tells a parsimonious story. Early child and sociocultural risk factors set the stage for adolescent onset of drug use, by making it difficult for parents to provide consistent discipline and loving care. In turn, these early parenting failures lead the child to come to school ready to behave aggressively and to experience social rejection by peers. Escalating problems in peer conflicts make family life aversive, so that parents respond by lowering their monitoring and supervision of the child, allowing the child to interact freely with deviant peers. Deviant peer associations are the most proximal factor, leading the child to initial drug use.

Although this developmental model is plausible and consistent with clinical evidence, future empirical analyses should test key features even more rigorously. These tests are necessitated by the fact that the sequential tests described and supported here are also consistent with a model in which *most recent* factors account for previous factors, no matter what they are. Statistical control of similar risk factors at different points in development could test whether the occurrence of a risk event is crucial at a particular point in development. For example, when testing the effect of early harsh parenting, one might control statistically the effect of later harsh parenting. Likewise, when testing the effect of early family poverty, one could control family poverty during adolescence. One limit on these tests will be the fact that not all risk factors have the same meaning at different points in development. Harsh parenting in toddlerhood may be indicated by spanking and inconsistent discipline, whereas in adolescence it may be indicated by yelling and screaming. Deviant peer associations in adolescence have no counterpart in toddlerhood.

Several other caveats must be noted. The proposed model and empirical tests address initial onset of drug use in adolescence and say little about the progression from initial use to abuse and to disorder. It is likely that different predictors and course may apply to those outcomes. Another caveat is that, although the sample includes both boys and girls from multiple ethnic groups at three different geographic sites, tests have only relatively weak power to detect interactions among these factors. Thus, it is not necessarily the case that the model will prove robust about disparate groups or generalize to other contexts.

Nonetheless, the findings reported here provide an example of how complicated, multi-step developmental models involving transactional relations between parenting and peer relations can be tested in a single study. These findings provide robust support for transactional relations, not merely of a reciprocal-influence model but of a sequencing of events that escalate problematic interactions in the onset of drug use. The findings suggest a dynamic interplay among parents, children, and peer groups, in which each of these parties both influences and is influenced by the other parties over time.

PUBLIC POLICY AND PRACTICE IMPLICATIONS

These findings suggest that the problem of illicit substance use in adolescence begins many years earlier. Rather than wait until after-the-fact of problem use, policies could be initiated that interrupt this development and prevent initiation in the first place. The first point of intervention, and perhaps the most challenging, could come with economic and social supports to the family during early life. It is ironic that economic benefits carry their greatest impact on children if provided during the first several years of life, but the average family is poorest during those years. That is, most families become wealthier as children grow older, because parents have more hours available for work and are more senior and skilled to earn higher wages. Families need economic supports early in children's lives, rather than later. Policies should be set in place that enhance family economic status early in children's lives, or at least allow families to borrow against their own future in the way that college loans allow students to borrow against their future earnings.

The rationale for this recommendation is the cascade of life events that ensues following early economic hardship. As depicted in Figure 5.1 and supported by the empirical findings of the Child Development Project, economic hardship impairs the family's ability to provide consistent, effective discipline and develop warm parent-child relationships during the preschool years. These problems in parenting, in turn, ignite a series of problems in the child's peer relations and conduct at school, which eventually evolve into association with deviant peers and illicit drug use. It is hypothesized that this cascade can be aborted early through economic support for families during a child's first 5 years of life.

Other points for intervention are also implied by the model and findings. Schools can play a greater role in substance-use prevention by delivering curricula for social-cognitive skills training to enhance children's social competence and success. The findings of this study suggest that these curricula might have long-term impact if administered as early as the elementary school years. Finally, parents can play a greater role in preventing their adolescents from initiating substance use by increasing their monitoring and supervision of those adolescents, especially by keeping them from associating with deviant peers.

FUTURE RESEARCH DIRECTIONS

The policy and practice suggestions noted above must first be tested through implementation and rigorous testing in intervention experiments before they are adopted on a wide scale. The findings of the current study require replication and extension in stronger research designs than the correlational design utilized here. Intervention experiments afford both the scientific control to tease apart factors in child development and prototypes for broader implementation. We recommend the proliferation of these intervention experiments.

References

Achenbach, T. M., & Edelbrock, C. S. (1986). *Manual for the Teacher's Report Form and Teacher Version of the Child Behavior Profile.* Burlington, VT: University of Vermont.

Armstrong, T. D., & Costello, E. J. (2002). Community studies on adolescent substance use, abuse, or dependence and psychiatric comorbidity. *Journal of Consulting and Clinical Psychology, 70,* 1224–1239.

Bachman, J. G., Lloyd, D. J., & O'Malley, P. M. (1981). Smoking, drinking, and drug use among American high school students: Correlates and trends, 1975–1979. *American Journal of Public Health, 71,* 59–69.

Barnes, G. M., Reifman, A. S., Farrell, M. P., & Dintcheff, B. A. (2000). The effects of parenting on the development of adolescent alcohol misuse: A six wave latent growth model. *Journal of Marriage and the Family, 62,* 175–186.

Barnes, G. M., & Welte, J. W. (1986). Patterns and predictors of alcohol use among 7–12th grade students in New York State. *Journal of Studies on Alcohol, 47,* 53–62.

Bates, J. E., & Bayles, K. (1984). Objective and subjective components in mothers' perceptions of their children from age 6 months to 3 years. *Merrill-Palmer Quarterly, 30,* 111–130.

Bates, J. E., Marvinney, D., Kelly, T., Dodge, K. A., Bennett, D. S., & Pettit, G. S. (1994). Child care history and kindergarten adjustment. *Developmental Psychology, 30,* 690–700.

Bates, J. E., Pettit, G. S., Dodge, K. A., & Ridge, B. (1998). Interaction of temperamental resistance to control and restrictive parenting in the development of externalizing behavior. *Developmental Psychology, 34,* 982–995.

Baumrind, D. (1983, October). *Why adolescents take chances – And why they don't.* Paper presented at the National Institute for Child Health and Human Development, Bethesda, MD.

Baumrind, D. (1985). Familial antecedents of adolescent drug use: A developmental perspective. In C. L. Jones & R. J. Battjes (Eds.), *Etiology of drug abuse: Implications for prevention.* Rockville, MD: National Institute on Drug Abuse.

Block, J., Block, J. H., & Keyes, S. (1988). Longitudinally foretelling mental precursors. *Child Development, 59,* 336–355.

Bogenschneider, K., Wu, M., Raffaelli, M., & Tsay, J. (1998). Parental influences on adolescent peer orientation and substance use: The interface of parenting practices and values. *Child Development, 69,* 1672–1688.

Botvin, G. (1986). Substance abuse prevention research: Recent developments and future directions. *Journal of School Health, 56,* 369–374.

Boyle, M. H., Offord, D. R., Racine, Y. A., Szatmari, P., Fleming, J. E., & Links, P. (1992). Predicting substance use in late adolescence: Results of the Ontario Child Health Study follow-up. *The American Journal of Psychiatry, 149,* 761–767.

Bray J. H., Adams, G. J., Getz, J., & McQueen, A. (2003). Individuation, peers, and adolescent alcohol use: A latent growth analysis. *Journal of Consulting and Clinical Psychology, 71,* 553–564.

Brook, J. S., Brook, D. W., Gordon, A. S., Whiteman, M., & Cohen, P. (1990). The psychosocial etiology of adolescent drug use: A family interactional approach. *Genetic, Social, and General Psychology Monographs, 116,* 111–267.

Brook, J. S., Gordon, A. S., Whiteman, M., & Cohen, P. (1986). Some models and mechanisms for explaining the impact of maternal and adolescent characteristics on adolescent stage of drug use. *Developmental Psychology, 22*, 460–467.

Buss, A., & Plomin, R. (1984). *Temperament: Early developing personality traits.* Hillsdale, NJ: Erlbaum.

Cadoret, R. J., Cain, C. A., & Grove, W. M. (1980). Development of alcoholism in adoptees raised apart from alcoholic biologic relatives. *Archives of General Psychiatry, 37*,561–563.

Capaldi, D. M., & Patterson, G. R. (1989). *Psychometric properties of fourteen latent constructs from the Oregon Youth Study.* New York: Springer-Verlag.

Catalano, R. F., Kosterman, R., Hawkins, J. D., Newcomb, M. D., & Abbott, R. D. (1996). Modeling the etiology of adolescent substance use: A test of the social development model. *Journal of Drug Issues, 26*, 429–455.

Chassin, L., Curran, P. J., Hussong, A. M., & Colder, C. R. (1996). The relation of parent alcoholism to adolescent substance use: A longitudinal follow-up study. *Journal of Abnormal Psychology, 105*, 70–80.

Chilcoat, H. D., & Anthony, J. C. (1996). Impact of parent monitoring on initiation of drug use through late childhood. *Journal of the American Academy of Child and Adolescent Psychiatry, 35*, 91–100.

Clark, D. B., Lesnick, L., & Hegedus, A. M. (1997). Traumas and other adverse life events in adolescents with alcohol abuse and dependence. *Journal of the American Academy of Child and Adolescent Psychiatry, 36*, 1744–1751.

Clark, D. B., Parker, A. M., & Lynch, K. G. (1999). Psychopathology and substance-related problems during early adolescence: A survival analysis. *Journal of Clinical Child Psychology, 28*, 333–341.

Clark, D. B., & Winters, K. C. (2002). Measuring risks and outcomes in substance use disorders prevention research. *Journal of Consulting and Clinical Psychology, 70*, 1207–1223.

Cloninger, C. R. (1986). A unified biosocial theory of personality and its role in the development of anxiety states. *Psychiatric Developments, 3*,167–226.

Cloninger, C. R. (1987). Neurogenetic adaptive mechanisms in alcoholism. *Science, 236*, 410–416.

Cloninger, C. R., Bohman, M., Sigvardsson, S., & von Knorring, A. L. (1985). Psychopathology in adopted-out children of alcoholics: The Stockholm Adoption Study. *Recent Developments in Alcoholism, 3*, 37–51.

Cloninger, C. R., Sigvardsson, S., & Bohman, M. (1988). Childhood personality predicts alcohol abuse in young adults. *Alcoholism, 12*, 494–503.

Coie, J. D., & Dodge, K. A. (1998). Aggression and antisocial behaviour. In N. Eisenberg (Ed.), *Handbook of child psychology: Vol. 3. Social, emotional and personality development* (pp. 779–862). New York: John Wiley and Sons.

Costa, F. M., Jessor, R., & Turbin, M. S. (1999). Transition into adolescent problem drinking: The role of psychosocial risk and protective factors. *Journal of Studies on Alcohol, 60*, 480–490.

Costello, E. J., Erkanli, A., Federman, E., & Angold, A. (1999). Development of psychiatric comorbidity with substance abuse in adolescents: Effects of timing and sex. *Journal of Clinical Child Psychology, 28*, 298–311.

Curran, P. J., Stice, E., & Chassin, L. (1997). The relation between adolescent alcohol use and peer alcohol use: A longitudinal random coefficients model. *Journal of Consulting and Clinical Psychology, 65*, 130–140.

Deater-Deckard, K., Dodge, K. A., Bates, J. E., & Pettit, G. S. (1998). Multiple-risk factors in the development of externalizing behavior problems: Group and individual differences. *Development and Psychopathology, 10,* 469–493.

Deykin, E. Y., Buka, S. L., & Zeena, T. H. (1992). Depressive illness among chemically dependent adolescents. *American Journal of Psychiatry, 149,* 1341–1347.

Dielman, T. E., Butchart, A. T., Shope, J. T., & Miller, M. (1991). Environmental correlates of adolescent substance use and misuse: Implications for prevention programs. *International Journal of Addictions, 25,* 855–880.

Dishion, T. J., Capaldi, D., Spracklen, K. M., & Li, F. (1995). Peer ecology of male adolescent drug use. *Development and Psychopathology, 7,* 803–824.

Dishion, T. J., Capaldi, D. M., & Yoerger, K. (1999). Middle childhood antecedents to progressions in male adolescent substance use: An ecological analysis of risk and protection. *Journal of Adolescent Research, 14,* 175–205.

Dishion, T. J., Patterson, G. R., Stoolmiller, M., & Skinner, M. L. (1991). Family, school, and behavioral antecedents to early adolescent involvement with antisocial peers. *Developmental Psychology, 27,* 172–180.

Disney, E. Y., Elkins, I. J., McGue, M., & Iacono, W. G. (1999). Effects of ADHD, conduct disorder, and gender on substance use and abuse in adolescence. *American Journal of Psychiatry, 156,* 1515–1521.

Dodge, K. A., Bates, J. E., & Pettit, G. S. (1990). Mechanisms in the cycle of violence. *Science, 250,* 1678–1683.

Dodge, K. A., Pettit, G. S., & Bates, J. E. (1994). Socialization mediators of the relation between socioeconomic status and child conduct problems. *Child Development, 65,* 649–665.

Elliot, D. S., Huizinga, D., & Ageton, S. S., (1985). *Explaining delinquency and drug use.* Beverly Hills, CA: Sage.

Farmer, E. M. Z., Compton, S. N., Burns, B. J., & Robertson, E. (2002). Review of the evidence base for treatment of childhood psychopathology: Externalizing disorders. *Journal of Consulting and Clinical Psychology, 70,* 1267–1302.

Flannery, D. J., Vaszony, A. T., Torquati, J., & Fridrich, A. (1994). Ethnic and gender differences in risk for early adolescent substance use. *Journal of Youth and Adolescence, 23,* 195–213.

Fleming, J. P., Kellam, S. G., & Brown, C. H. (1982). Early predictors of age at first use of alcohol, marijuana and cigarettes. *Drug and Alcohol Dependence, 9,* 285–303.

Fletcher, A. C., Darling, N., & Steinberg, L. (1995). Parental monitoring and peer influences on adolescent substance use. In J. McCord (Ed.), *Coercion and punishment in long term perspectives* (pp. 259–271). New York: Cambridge University Press.

Glantz, M. D. (2002). Introduction to the special edition on the impact of childhood psychopathology interventions on subsequent substance abuse: Pieces of the puzzle. *Journal of Consulting and Clinical Psychology, 70,* 1203–1206.

Glantz, M. D., & Lashner, A. I. (2000). Drug abuse and developmental psychopathology. *Development and Psychopathology, 12,* 795–814.

Goodwin, D. W. (1985). Alcoholism and genetics: The sins of the fathers. *Archives of General Psychiatry, 42,* 171–174.

Gottfredson, D. C. (1988). *Issues in adolescent drug use.* Unpublished final report to the U.S. Department of Justice, Johns Hopkins University, Center for Research on Elementary and Middle Schools, Baltimore, MD.

Gray, J. A. (1987). *The psychology of fear and stress* (2nd ed.). New York: McGraw Hill.

Greene, R. W., Biederman, J., Faraone, S. V., Sienna, M., & Garcia-Jetton, J. (1997). Adolescent outcome of boys with attention deficit/hyperactivity disorder and social disability: Results from a 4-year longitudinal follow-up study. *Journal of Consulting and Clinical Psychology, 65,* 758–767.

Greene, R. W., Biederman, J., Faraone, S. V., Wilens, T. E., Mick, E., & Blier, H. K. (1999). Further validation of social impairment as a predictor of substance use disorders: Findings from a sample of siblings of boys with and without ADHD. *Journal of Consulting and Clinical Psychology, 62,* 410–414.

Griffin, K. W., Botvin, G. J., Epstein, J. A., Doyle, M. M., & Diaz, T. (2000). Psychosocial and behavioral factors in early adolescence as predictors of heavy drinking among high school seniors. *Journal of Studies on Alcohol, 61,* 603–606.

Hansen, W. B., Graham, J. W., Sobel, J. L., Shelton, D. R., Flay, B. R., & Johnson, C. A. (1987). The consistency of peer and parent influences on tobacco, alcohol, and marijuana use among young adolescents. *Journal of Behavioral Medicine, 10,* 559–579.

Hawkins, J. D., Catalano, R. F., & Miller, J. Y. (1992). Risk and protective factors for alcohol and other drug problems in adolescence and early adulthood. *Psychological Bulletin, 112,* 64–105.

Hollingshead, A. A. (1979). *Four-Factor Index of Social Status.* Unpublished manuscript, Yale University, New Haven, CT.

Hops, H., Tildesley, E., Lichenstein, E., Ary, D., & Sherman, L. (1990). Parent-adolescent problem solving interactions and drug use. *American Journal of Drug and Alcohol Abuse, 16,* 239–258.

Hrubec, Z., & Omenn, G. S. (1981). Evidence of genetic predisposition to alcoholic cirrhosis and psychosis: Twin concordances for alcoholism and its biological end points by zygosity among male veterans. *Alcoholism, 5,* 207–215.

Hundleby, J. D., & Mercer, G. W. (1987). Family and friends as social environments and their relationship to young adolescents' use of alcohol, tobacco, and marijuana. *Journal of Clinical Psychology, 44,* 125–134.

Institute of Medicine (1994). *Reducing risks for mental disorders: Frontiers for preventive intervention research.* Washington, DC: National Academy Press.

Jackson, C., Hendrikson, L., Dickinson, D., & Levine, D. W. (1997). The early use of alcohol and tobacco: Its relation to children's competence and parents' behavior. *American Journal of Public Health, 87,* 359–364.

Jessor, R., Donovan, J. E., & Windmer, K. (1980). *Psychosocial factors in adolescent alcohol and drug use: The 1980 National Sample Study and the 1974–78 Panel Study.* Unpublished final report, University of Colorado, Institute of Behavioral Science, Boulder.

Johnson, C. A., Schoutz, F. C., & Locke, T. P. (1984). Relationships between adolescent drug use and parental drug behaviors. *Adolescence, 19,* 295–299.

Johnston, L. D., O'Malley, P. M., & Bachman, J. G. (1985). *Use of licit and illicit drugs by America's high school students. 1975–1984.* Rockville, MD: National Institute of Drug Abuse.

Johnston, L. D., O'Malley, P. M., & Bachman, J. G. (1995). *National survey results on drug use from the Monitoring the Future Study, 1975–1994: Vol. 1. Secondary school students.* Rockville, MD: National Institute on Drug Abuse.

Johnston, L. D., O'Malley, P. M., & Bachman, J. G. (1998). *National survey results on drug use from the Monitoring the Future Study, 1975–1997: Vol. 1. Secondary school students.* Rockville, MD: National Institute on Drug Abuse.

Kandel, D. B., & Andrews, K. (1987). Processes of adolescent socialization by parents and peers. *International Journal of Addictions, 22,* 319–342.

Kandel, D. B., Johnson, J. G., Bird, H. R., Weissman, M. M., Goodman, S. H., Lahey, B. B., Regier, D. A., & Schwab-Stone, M. E. (1999). Psychiatric comorbidity among adolescents with substance use disorders: Findings from the MECA study. *Journal of the American Academy of Child and Adolescent Psychiatry, 38,* 693–699.

Kandel, D. B., & Logan, J. A. (1984). Patterns of drug use from adolescence to young adulthood: I. Periods of risk for initiation, continued use, ad discontinuation. *American Journal of Public Health, 74,* 660–666.

Kandel, D. B., & Yamaguchi, K. (1985). Developmental patterns of the use of legal, illegal, and medically prescribed psychotropic drugs from adolescence to young adulthood. In C. L. Jones & R. J Battjes (Eds.), *Etiology of drug abuse: Implications for prevention* (pp. 193–235). Rockville, MD: National Institute on Drug Abuse, NIDA research monograph 56.

Kaplan, S. J., Pelcovitz, D., Salzinger, S., Weiner, M., Mandel, F. S., Lesser, M. L., & Labruna, V. E. (1998). Adolescent physical abuse – Risk for adolescent psychiatric disorders. *American Journal of Psychiatry, 155,* 954–959.

Kaplow, J. B., Curran, P. J., Angold, A., & Costello, E. J. (2001). The prospective relation between dimensions of anxiety and the initiation of adolescent alcohol use. *Journal of Clinical Child Psychology, 30,* 316–326.

Kaplow, J. B., Curran, P. J., Dodge, K. A., & the Conduct Problems Prevention Research Group. (2002). Child, parent, and peer predictors of early-onset substance use: A multisite longitudinal study. *Journal of Abnormal Child Psychology, 30,* 199–216.

Kellam, S. G., Ensminger, M. E., & Simon, M. B. (1980). Mental health in first grade and teenage drug, alcohol, and cigarette use. *Drug and Alcohol Dependence, 5,* 273–304.

Kelly, D. H., & Balch, R. W. (1971). Social origins and school failure: A reexamination of Cohen's theory of working-class delinquency. *Pacific Social Review, 14,* 413–430.

Kendall, P. C., & Kessler, R. C. (2002). The impact of childhood psychopathology interventions on subsequent substance abuse: Policy implications, comments, and recommendations. *Journal of Consulting and Clinical Psychology, 70,* 1303–1306.

Kendler, K. S., Bulik, C. M., Silberg, J., Hettema, J. M., Myers, J., & Prescott, C. A. (2000). Childhood sexual abuse and adult psychiatric and substance use disorders in women: An epidemiological and cotwin control analysis. *Archives of General Psychiatry, 57,* 953–959.

Kessler, R. C., Aguilar-Gaxiola, S., Andrade, L., Bijl, R., Borges, G., Carveo-Anduaga, J. J., et al. (2001). Mental-substance comorbidities in the ICPE surveys. *Psychiatria Fennica, 32,* 62–80.

Kilpatrick, D. G., Acierno, R., Saunders, B., Resnick, H. S., Best, C. L., & Schnurr, P. P. (2000). Risk factors for adolescent substance abuse and dependence: Data from a national sample. *Journal of Consulting and Clinical Psychology, 68,* 19–30.

Kosterman, R., Hawkins, J. D., Guo, J., Catalano, R. F., & Abbott, R. D. (2000). The dynamics of alcohol and marijuana initiation: Patterns and predictors of first use in adolescence. *American Journal of Public Health, 90,* 360–366.

Krohn, M. D., & Thornberrry, T. P. (1993). Network theory: A model for understanding drug abuse among African-American and Hispanic youth. In M. R. De La Rosa & J. R. Adrados (Eds.), *Drug abuse among minority youth: Advances in research and methodology* (pp. 102–127). Rockville, MD: National Institute on Drug Abuse.

Laird, R. D., Jordan, K., Dodge, K. A., Pettit, G. S., & Bates, J. E. (2001). Peer rejection in childhood, involvement with antisocial peers in early adolescence, and the development of externalizing problems. *Development and Psychopathology, 13,* 337–354.

Landrine, H., Richardson, J., Klonoff, E., & Flay, B. (1994). Cultural diversity in the predictors of adolescent cigarette smoking: The relative influence of peers. *Journal of Behavioral Medicine, 17,* 331–346.

Lerner, J., & Vicary, J. (1984). Difficult temperament and drug use: Analysis from the New York longitudinal study. *Journal of Drug Education, 14,* 1–8.

Lewinsohn, P. M., Rohde, P., & Seeley, J. R., (1995). Adolescent psychopathology: III. The clinical consequences of comorbidity. *Journal of the American Academy of Child and Adolescent Psychiatry, 34,* 510–519.

Lewis, C. E., Robins, L. N., & Rice, J. (1985). Association of alcoholism with antisocial personality in urban men. *Journal of Nervous and Mental Disease, 173,* 166–174.

Liu, X., & Kaplan, H. B., (1996). Gender-related differences in circumstances surrounding initiation and escalation of alcohol and other substance use/abuse. *Deviant Behavior, 17,* 71–106.

Maddahian, E., Newcomb, M. D., & Bentler, P. M. (1988). Adolescent drug use and intention to use drugs: Concurrent and longitudinal analyses of four ethnic groups. *Addictive Behaviors, 13,* 191–195.

Mannuza, S., Klein, R. G., Bessler, A., Malloy, P., & LaPadula, M. (1998). Adult psychiatric status of hyperactive boys grown up. *American Journal of Psychiatry, 155,* 493–498.

Masse, L. C., & Tremblay, R. E. (1997). Behavior of boys in kindergarten and the onset of substance use during adolescence. *Archives of General Psychiatry, 54,* 62–68.

McCarthy, W. J., & Anglin, M. D. (1990). Narcotics addicts: Effect of family and parental risk factors on timing of emancipation, drug use onset, pre-addiction incarcerations and educational achievement. *Journal of Drug Issues, 20,* 99–123.

McLoyd, V. C. (1990). The impact of economic hardship on black families and children: Psychological distress, parenting, and socioemotional development. *Child Development, 61,* 311–346.

Merikangas, J., Stolar, M., Stevens, D., Goulet, J., Preisig, M., Fenton, B., Zhang, H., O'Malley, S., & Rounsaville, B. (1998). Familial transmission of substance use disorders. *Archives of General Psychiatry, 55,* 973–979.

Murray, D. M., & Stabenau, J. R. (1982). Genetic factors in alcoholism predisposition. In *Encyclopedic handbook of alcoholism* (pp. 135–144). New York: Gardner Press.

National Center on Addiction and Substance Abuse [NCASA]. (2003). *The formative years: Pathways to substance abuse among girls and young women ages 8–22.* Available http://www.casacolumbia.org/Absolutenm/articlefiles/151006.pdf

National Institute on Drug Abuse. (2002). *2002 Monitoring The Future Survey shows decrease in use of marijuana, club drugs, cigarettes and tobacco.* Retrieved September 8, 2003, from http://www.nida.nih.gov/Newsroom/02/NR12-16.html

Nestler, E. J., & Landsman, D. (2001). Learning about addiction from the genome. *Nature, 409,* 834–835.

Newcomb, M. D., & Felix-Ortiz, M. (1992). Multiple protective and risk factors for drug use and abuse: Cross-sectional and prospective findings. *Journal of Personality and Social Psychology, 63,* 280–296.

Penning, M., & Barnes, G. E. (1982). Adolescent marijuana use: A review. *International Journal of Addictions, 17*, 749–791.

Petraitis, J., Flay, B. R., & Miller, T. Q. (1995). Reviewing theories of adolescent substance use: Organizing pieces in the puzzle. *Psychological Bulletin, 117*, 67–86.

Pettit, G. S., Bates, J. E., Dodge, K. A., & Meece, D. W. (1999). The impact of after-school peer contact on early adolescent externalizing problems is moderated by parental monitoring, neighborhood safety, and prior adjustment. *Child Development, 70*, 768–778.

Pomerleau, C. S., Pomerleau, O. F., Flessland, K. A., & Basson, S. M. (1992). Relationship of TPQ scores to smoking variables in female and male smokers. *Journal of Substance Abuse, 4*, 143–153.

Reinherz, H. Z., Giaconia, R. M., Hauf, A. M., Wasserman, M. S., & Paradis, A. D. (2000). General and specific childhood risk factors for depression and drug disorders by early adulthood. *Journal of the American Academy of Child and Adolescent Psychiatry, 39*, 223–231.

Robins, L. N., & Ratcliff, K. S. (1979). Continuation of antisocial behavior into adulthood. *International Journal of Mental Health, 7*, 96–116.

Rutter, M., & Garmezy, N. (1983). Developmental psychopathology. In P. H. Mussen & E. M. Hetherington (Eds.), *Handbook of child psychology: Vol. 4. Socialization, personality and social development* (pp. 775–911). New York: Wiley.

Selzer, M. L., Vinokur, A., & Van Rooijen, C. (1975). A self-administered Short Michigan Alcoholism Screening Test (SMAST). *Journal of Studies on Alcohol, 36*, 117–126.

Shedler, J., & Block, J. (1990). Adolescent drug use and psychological health: A longitudinal inquiry. *American Psychologist, 45*, 612–630.

Simcha-Fagan, O., Gersten, J. C., & Langner, T. (1986). Early precursors and concurrent correlates of illicit drug use in adolescents. *Journal of Drug Issues, 16*, 7–28.

Simons, R. L., Conger, R. D., & Whitbeck, L. B. (1988). A multistage social learning model of the influences of family and peers upon adolescent substance abuse. *Journal of Drug Issues, 24*, 9–24.

Substance Abuse and Mental Health Services Administration [SAMHSA]. (1997). *Preliminary results from the 1996 National Household Survey on Drug Abuse.* Available http://www.oas.samhsa.gov/nhsda/PE1996/HTTOC.HTM

Tabakoff, B., & Hoffman, P. L. (1988). Genetics and biological markers of risk for alcoholism. *Public Health Reports, 103*, 690–698.

Tarter, R. E., & Vanyukov, M. (1994). Alcoholism: A developmental disorder. *Journal of Consulting and Clinical Psychology, 62*, 1096–1107.

Tarter, R. E., Vanyukov, M., Giancola, P. R., Dawes, M. A., Blackson, T., Mezzich, A. C., & Clark, D. (1999). Etiology of early age onset substance use disorder: A maturational perspective. *Development and Psychopathology, 11*, 657–683.

Thomas, B. S. (1996). A path analysis of gender differences in adolescent onset of alcohol, tobacco and other drug use (ATOD), reported ATOD use and adverse consequences of ATOD use. *Journal of Addictive Disorders, 15*, 33–52.

Weinberg, N. Z., & Glantz, M. D. (1999). Child psychopathology risk factors for drug abuse: Overview. *Journal of Clinical Child Psychology, 28*, 290–297.

Weinberg, N. Z., Rahdert, E., Colliver, J. D., & Glantz, M. D. (1998). Adolescent substance abuse: A review of the past 10 years. *Journal of the American Academy of Child and Adolescent Psychiatry, 37*, 252–261.

Widom, C. S., Ireland, T., & Glynn, P. J. (1995). Alcohol abuse in abused and neglected children followed-up: Are they at increased risk? *Journal of Studies on Alcohol, 56,* 207–217.

Wilens, T. E., Faraone, S. V., Biederman, J., & Gunawardene, S. (2003). Does stimulant therapy of attention-deficit/hyperactivity disorder beget later substance abuse? A meta-analytic review of the literature. *Pediatrics, 111,* 179–185.

Wills, T. A., DuHammel, K., & Vaccaro, D. (1995). Activity and mood temperament as predictors of adolescent substance use. *Journal of Personality and Social Psychology, 68,* 901–916.

Wills, T. A., Sandy, J. M., Yaeger, A., & Shinar, O. (2001). Family risk factors and adolescent substance use: Moderation effects for temperament dimensions. *Developmental Psychology, 37,* 283–297.

Wills, T. A., Vaccaro, D., & McNamara, G. (1994). Novelty seeking, risk taking, and related constructs as predictors of adolescent substance use: An application of Cloninger's theory. *Journal of Substance Abuse, 6,* 1–20.

Windle, M. (1991). The difficult temperament in adolescence: Associations with substance use, family support, and problem behaviors. *Journal of Clinical Psychology, 47,* 310–315.

Windle, M., & Lerner, R. M. (1986). The Revised Dimension of Temperament Survey. *Journal of Adolescent Research, 1,* 213–229.

Zucker, R. A., & Harford, T. C. (1983). National study of the demography of adolescent drinking practices in 1980. *Journal of Studies on Alcohol, 44,* 974–985.

Zuckerman, M. (1987). Biological connection between sensation seeking and drug abuse. In J. Engel & L. Oreland (Eds.), *Brain reward systems and abuse* (pp. 165–176). New York: Raven Press.

PART THREE

WORK AND FAMILY

6

Mothers and Fathers at Work

Implications for Families and Children

Ann C. Crouter

Mothers' and fathers' employment is of fundamental importance to families and children in two distinct ways. First, parents' work connects families to the larger social system. Because of their choices of jobs and workplaces, mothers and fathers are exposed to trends in the local, national, and global economy; to economic and social policy in such areas as international trade, parental leave, health insurance coverage, and social welfare; and to technology and technological change, including computerization, high speed communication, and robotics. In a more immediate way, mothers' and fathers' work situations connect them to a work culture that encourages certain values and behaviors and discourages others, to work-based friendships and social networks and, sometimes, to certain child care arrangements.

A second way in which parents' employment is important for families and children is that, through the nature of the work that parents do and the workplace in which those work activities take place, parents are exposed to a set of occupational conditions that have implications for how they interact with and socialize their children. Some occupational conditions, such as how much time a parent spends on the job or when those work hours are scheduled, are important because they shape the parent's availability to the child. Others, such as the extent to which the job offers the worker autonomy and self-direction (or encourages conformity) or the extent to which the parent experiences work-related pressures and strains, affect the child in indirect ways; that is, they influence the parent's own development or psychological well-being in ways that have implications for parenting. In this chapter, I focus on the second area because it has received more research attention. Before exploring this set of issues, however, I raise several caveats included to provide a cautionary filter for the reader by emphasizing the complexity inherent in this research area.

RESEARCH CAVEATS: AN INTRODUCTION TO COMPLEXITY

The field of work and family research has grown dramatically in the past three decades, but much of the research, including my own, has ignored some of the complexities inherent in this area of study. I highlight three caveats that need to be kept in mind when thinking about the connections between work and family life. The first has to do with bi-directional linkages and selection effects. These two related concepts remind us that individuals and families are not passive recipients of work-related influences but play an active role choosing jobs and work situations and, sometimes, influencing the workplace. The second caveat underscores the curious bifurcation between research on "work and family" and research on "child care and its effects." The third caveat pertains to the complexity inherent in studying dual-earner families because these families are linked to the world of work in two ways: through the father's work and through the mother's work.

Bi-Directional Linkages and Selection Effects

As in other areas of human development, research on work and family has tended to favor linear, unidirectional models in which work is seen as shaping the employed parent and, in turn, his or her family. There is increasing recognition, however, that the linkages between these two central arenas of adult life are bi-directional. The nature of the work that people do has an impact on them and, through them, their children, but in addition, individuals and families exert influences on the workplace (Crouter, 1984). A good example comes from research on home-to-work stress contagion by Bolger, DeLongis, Kessler, and Wethington (1989). Using data that included six weeks of daily assessments of husbands' and wives' overloads and arguments both at work and at home, they found that when men engaged in arguments with their spouses at home, they were more likely to have arguments with co-workers or supervisors at work the next day. Presumably, arguments at home activate an arousal system that is hard for men to turn off when they head off to work.

Some of the clearest evidence for reciprocal linkages comes from sociological research on occupational self-direction by Kohn and Schooler (1983). Using longitudinal survey data on a national sample of employed men in the United States, they found that, over a 10-year period, men in self-directed jobs (i.e., jobs that involved low levels of supervision and routinization and high levels of complexity) developed greater intellectual flexibility. They also found, however, that men selected in and out of jobs as a function of their initial levels of intellectual flexibility.

Indeed, selection effects would seem to be a ubiquitous feature of work-family research, but they are often ignored. Work-related selection effects occur at two levels: the individual and the workplace. Individuals make choices about education, job training, occupation, and specific employers or places of work. Within constraints imposed by the employer, employees may also make choices about work hours (e.g., working full- or part-time), work shift (e.g., day, afternoon, night, or rotating), and whether or not to work overtime. Other selection effects occur at the level of the work context. Employers try to hire and promote the most competent and reliable employees and to weed out those who are not productive. Discrimination on the basis of sex, age, race, and ethnicity represents the "dark side" of workplace selection effects.

The net effect of individual and workplace selection processes is that people are distributed nonrandomly in fields and specific occupations. The clearest example of this is widespread gender segregation within the U.S. labor market, both between and even within jobs (Baron & Bielby, 1985). Presumably, in addition to gender, other personal qualities such as risk-taking, intelligence, achievement motivation, social skills, and physical prowess are also correlated with job choices. Thus, associations between job qualities and personal qualities or parenting behaviors cannot be easily attributed to "occupational socialization." Selection effects undoubtedly play a role in those associations.

The same logic can be extended to child outcomes. Some of the qualities on the basis of which mothers and fathers are "sorted" into careers and jobs are probably heritable. Thus, correlations between parents' job characteristics and children's outcomes may not simply reflect the effect of parents' work on children but, instead (or in addition), the fact that parents selected, and were selected for, those jobs because they had certain characteristics, characteristics that are shared by their offspring. Researchers who are interested in work and family rarely acknowledge this implication of the selection effect issue. To address it satisfactorily would require data that combine detailed information on parental work and parents' and children's psychosocial functioning with a behavior genetics design.

BIFURCATION OF LITERATURES ON PARENTAL EMPLOYMENT AND CHILD CARE ARRANGEMENTS

Children growing up in dual-earner families are influenced by at least three important social contexts: family, child care (or, for older children, school), and parents' work (see chapter on child care by McCartney, Chapter 7 in this book). It is very rare, however, to find a research study that has paid close attention to all three. Researchers interested in parental work typically pay little attention to where children are when their parents are working, and experts in child care seldom include information on the quality of parents' jobs or work experiences when considering the implications of child care arrangements for children.

This oversight is particularly important in light of the selection effect issues described above. Some occupational conditions may have implications not only for parents' individual psychosocial functioning and the ways in which they socialize their children but also for the kinds of child care arrangements they select for their children. Henly and Lambert (in press), for example, note that low-income, employed parents often encounter workplace practices such as "just-in-time scheduling" that wreak havoc with their need for stable, consistent child care arrangements. They argue that, in part in response to the ubiquitous, last-minute scheduling changes at work, low-income parents, at least in certain occupations (Henly and Lambert studied the retail sector), often favor informal child-care provided by relatives and friends rather than formal child care. Thus, for some parents, work conditions and child care arrangements may be confounded in important ways that we know little about.

Work-Family Complexity Inherent in Dual-Earner Families

Although empirical research on the interface between work and family can be traced back to the 1930s (Bronfenbrenner & Crouter, 1982), the literature became more defined and took off as an area of research in the 1960s and 70s. During this period, women entered the labor force in unprecedented numbers, and many continued to participate in the paid labor force even after becoming mothers of infants and young children. Initially, and even today (e.g., Brooks-Gunn, Han, & Waldfogel, 2002; National Institute of Child Health and Human Development of Early Child Care Research Network, 2003), this demographic trend was seen as a potential threat to children's well-being. The fear was that paid employment would usurp mothers' time, energy, and attention, and that children would be the losers. For the most part, however, this fear proved to be unjustified (see review by Bianchi, 2000).

Note that developmental researchers initially focused not on parents' occupational conditions, but on mothers' employment status. Framing the issue in this way oversimplified matters in two ways. First, the attention to maternal employment *status* equated maternal work with maternal absence and directed attention away from the nature of mothers' jobs and the diversity in employed mothers' work experiences. Second, by framing the issue as *maternal* employment, developmental researchers set themselves up to ignore fathers and, in doing so, to ignore the complexity inherent in the *combination* of mothers' and fathers' work circumstances. As a result, there has been a paucity of research that has examined employed mothers and fathers as dyads.

A dyadic approach recognizes that dual-earner families are connected to the workplace and to the larger economic system via two jobs – his and hers (Crouter & Helms-Erikson, 1997). Recognizing this means acknowledging the possibility of another layer of selection effects because some work and family circumstances reflect dyadic decisions. In some dual-earner families, for example, one partner, often but not always the father, takes on the role of primary provider, the one whose job is most important to the economic well-being of the family (Bernard, 1981). Opportunities to maximize the primary provider's success (e.g., promotions that entail geographic moves) may come at the expense of the other partner's career, leading over time to widening inequality between the two spouses' economic resources, a difference that sets the stage for power dynamics in the home. Another dyadic decision involves the timing of work. In some families, the two spouses elect to work "split shifts" (Presser & Cain, 1983), meaning that one partner works day shift, and the other works afternoons or evening shift. This strategy enables the couple to provide care for their children and to avoid the expense, inconvenience, and unreliability of nonparental care. This particular dyadic work arrangement, however, appears to have unintended negative consequences in the form of increased marital distress and risk for divorce (Perry-Jenkins, Goldberg, Pierce, & Haley, under review; Presser, 2000, 2003; White & Keith, 1990).

Researchers have taken two approaches to studying employed fathers and mothers as dyads. One approach has been to include characteristics of both parents' work circumstances, as well as interaction terms that cross mothers' and fathers' circumstances, in models predicting child outcomes. For example, Parcel and Menaghan (1994) reported that the *combination* of both parents working overtime was associated with higher levels of problem behavior in children and lower levels of verbal competence (i.e., vocabulary) than was the case when only one parent worked overtime. Another approach has been to develop typologies of families based on the patterning of mothers' and fathers' work characteristics using an approach such as cluster analysis (Crouter & Manke, 1997; Bumpus, Crouter, & McHale, 1999).

In sum, although there is considerable research on the implications of parents' work for children's psychosocial functioning, that research must be scrutinized carefully because it virtually never covers the full spectrum of relevant issues. The next generation of researchers in this area will need to pay attention to bi-directional and selection effects, to the experiences children have at child care or school when their parents are working, and to the dyadic combination of maternal and paternal employment circumstances. That said, there is a body of research that convincingly indicates that parents' work situations are important for families and children. In the remainder of this chapter, I focus on three occupational conditions and review what is known about their links to family and child well-being. These occupational conditions are: (1) parents' work time and the timing of employment, (2) parents' autonomy and self-direction on the job, and, (3) parents' occupational stress and strain.

IMPLICATIONS OF PARENTS' OCCUPATIONAL CONDITIONS
FOR FAMILIES AND CHILDREN

I limit my review to literature based on U.S. samples and, with a few exceptions, to dual-earner families. Cross-cultural differences in labor markets, social policies in areas such as parental leave, norms about men's and women's roles, and the availability and quality of child care give work and family issues a different "flavor" in different countries (Davidson & Cooper, 1984). The United States is an interesting country to focus on because, compared with many European countries, it has traditionally provided little in the way of government supports for working parents. Some of the findings reviewed here might not generalize to parents living in societies in which there is greater support for parents to combine work and family life. The focus on dual-earner families is useful because it highlights the importance of fathers and their jobs for families, but it is important to note that work and family issues are also important for single-parent families, perhaps especially for low-income families headed by single mothers. The United States has recently instituted "welfare reform," a set of policies that limit the number of years a mother can receive welfare over her lifetime and that encourage low-income parents (typically unmarried mothers) to enter the labor force. Often poorly educated, unskilled, and lacking in seniority, mothers making the transition from welfare to work typically lack the credentials to get good jobs. The work dimensions that are reviewed below from the perspective of dual-earner families may be even more important in the lives of low-income mothers who are rearing children alone (Lambert, 1999).

Temporal Dimensions of Parents' Jobs: How Much and When Parents Work

About 25 years ago, Kanter (1979) identified the "time and timing of work" as an important influence on families and children, and there has been a steady stream of research in this area ever since. As a backdrop to our discussion, it is important to note that, in dual-earner families, fathers work longer hours on average than mothers do (Jacobs & Gerson, 2001), even when both parents work full-time. This reflects the tendency in many families for the father to take the role of the primary economic provider for the family and for the mother to take on the responsibility for housework and childcare. The traditional division of paid and unpaid work along gender lines is both a cause and a consequence of the tendency for men to be paid more than women in the market economy (Coltrane, 1996; England & Farkas, 1986).

Until recently, the literature has suggested that, in general, the sheer number of hours that mothers work per week is *not* linked to family or child outcomes (Harvey, 1999; Parcel & Menaghan, 1994). In recent years, however, a handful of studies have appeared that indicate that there may be some negative effects of longer hours. Generally, the effects are small and are focused on the very early years. For example, Brooks-Gunn, Han, and Waldfogel (2002), using data from the National Institute of Child Health and Human Development Study of Early Child Care, found that children scored lower on a test of school readiness if their mothers had returned to work by 9 months (see chapter by McCartney, Chapter 7 in this book, for additional findings from this multisite, longitudinal study). The negative effects were particularly pronounced when mothers had worked 30 hours per week or more. These effects were partially (but not entirely) accounted for by child care quality, the quality of the home environment, and maternal sensitivity, each of which can be thought of as a possible buffer. Interestingly, in light of the paucity of research that examines both parental work and childcare, Brooks-Gunn et al., (2002) reported that children whose mothers worked full-time during the first year of life were more likely than other children to experience poor quality child care during their first three years.

Mothers' work hours are also important because they appear to pull fathers into a more active parenting role. For example, in a study of dual-earner families with school-aged children, my colleagues and I found that mothers who worked longer hours were as knowledgeable about their children's daily activities, whereabouts, and companions as mothers who worked fewer hours were, but the husbands of the women who devoted more time to work were significantly more knowledgeable about their children's daily experiences compared with fathers married to women who worked fewer hours (Crouter, Helms-Erikson, Updegraff, & McHale, 1999). We observed a similar pattern in a short-term, longitudinal study of dual-earner families with school-aged children that compared families in which both parents worked across a year with families in which fathers worked consistently across the year but mothers cut back their involvement in paid work significantly during the summer months (Crouter & McHale, 1993). In the former group, mothers and fathers maintained a somewhat egalitarian division of parenting across the year, and fathers retained a consistent and reasonably high level of knowledge about their children's daily activities. In the group in which mothers greatly reduced their work time during the summer months, however, the division of parenting became markedly more traditional over the summer, and, perhaps reflecting their reduced level of involvement with their children, fathers became less knowledgeable during the summer months. Consistent with the idea that longer maternal work hours pull fathers into a greater involvement in family life, we found that fathers returned to their prior levels of involvement in parenting and became more knowledgeable about their children's ongoing activities again during the subsequent school year, once their wives had resumed their prior levels of involvement in paid work.

Fathers' work hours are also potentially important for children. In a summary of a program of research based on data from the National

Longitudinal Survey of Youth (NLSY), Parcel and Menaghan (1994), for example, found that a pattern of part-time paternal work hours in children's early years was linked not only to lower levels of reading and math skills but to higher rates of marital disruption, which in turn had direct effects on children's subsequent problem behavior. Interestingly, Parcel and Menaghan (1994) also found a link between fathers' overtime schedules and lower achievement in the areas of vocabulary and arithmetic. They attributed the former finding to economic hardship and related stresses and strains that families experience when men are underemployed and the latter finding to reductions in stimulation and supervision that may ensue when a parent is working very long hours. Parcel and Menaghan (1974) also examined the *dyadic patterning* of spouses' work hours, finding that when *both* parents held part-time work schedules, they provided their children with lower quality home environments than was the case when only one parent worked part-time. Likewise, the combination of two parents on overtime work schedules was associated with higher levels of problem behavior in children and lower levels of verbal competence than was the case when only one parent worked overtime.

Our research team has examined the implications of long paternal hours for the quality of fathers' relationships with their adolescent offspring (Crouter, Bumpus, Head, & McHale, 2001). Specifically, we examined the associations between overwork (i.e., working more than 60 hours per week), overload (i.e., fathers' subjective perceptions that they had too much to do in the limited time available), and fathers' and adolescent children's perceptions of relationship quality. The combination of overwork and overload was consistently linked to reports of diminished relationship quality from both fathers and youth. When men worked long hours *and* felt highly overloaded, fathers and offspring reported lower intimacy, higher levels of conflict, and lower levels of perspective taking in their relationship. When fathers worked long hours but did not perceive themselves to be overloaded, negative relationship outcomes were not evident.

The timing of parents' work also matters. A handful of studies on the implications of shift work for children suggests that, controlling for a host of possible selection effects, children exhibit higher levels of conduct problems and lower levels of academic achievement when a parent works a nonstandard shift, meaning any shift other than a day shift (Bogen & Joshi, 2002; Heyman, 2000). For example, using a 6-year span of NLSY data, Heyman (2000) reported that children with poor educational outcomes were significantly more likely to have had a parent who had worked evenings or nights at least some of the time over the 6-year period. These findings held up after controlling for family income, parental education, marital status, child gender, and the total number of hours the parent worked. Similarly, in what appears to be the only large-scale study of the effects of mothers' nonstandard schedules on children growing up in low-income, primarily mother-headed households, Bogen and Joshi (2002) analyzed data from the Welfare, Children, and Families Study, an ambitious multimethod study of welfare reform in three U.S. cities. Controlling for a variety of possible confounding variables, they found that the higher the propensity for nonstandard work, the more likely mothers were to report high levels of problem behavior and low levels of positive behavior in their 2- to 4-year-old children.

Why is having a parent working a nonstandard shift problematic for children? Possible explanations focus on the stressful nature of shift work and on parenting as a potential mediator. Working nonstandard shifts is inherently stressful for several reasons. It disrupts people's biological rhythms, which may increase irritability and make people more susceptible to illness (Smith, Folkard, & Fuller, 2003). People on nonstandard schedules are also out of synch with the social clocks of their communities. Depending on the nature of the shift, for example, it may be difficult to maintain involvement in children's schools, attend children's extracurricular events, schedule health appointments, and run errands that are important for the smooth running of family life (Presser, 2003). In two-parent families, research suggests that there is increased marital tension when one partner works a nonstandard shift (Perry-Jenkins et al., under review; Presser, 2000; White & Keith, 1990), especially when a parent works the night shift, which is typically from 11 p.m. to 7 a.m. (Presser, 2000). The stress and strains occasioned by working a nonstandard shift may distract parents from providing quality care and supervision for their children. It also may make them more irritable, less patient, and less able to provide sensitive, contingent parenting.

Evidence for this idea is found in a three-year longitudinal study by White and Keith (1990). They compared families in which one parent had originally worked a nonstandard shift but over time had changed to a standard shift with families in which both parents consistently worked standard, day shifts. The first group exhibited a significant decrease in child-related stresses and strains, suggesting that working a nonstandard shift may have made it more difficult to provide quality parenting. Additional evidence of the possible importance of parenting comes from Bogen and Joshi (2002), who found that the associations between work shift and child psycho-social functioning were partially mediated by mothers' perceived parenting challenges (e.g., low feelings of parenting competence and satisfaction, reports of irritability, anger, and impatience toward children).

Occupational Self-Direction: The Nature of Work Matters

Although the time and timing of parents' work is important, it is not the whole story. It is also essential to consider the nature of parents' work. One important dimension of work that has been found to matter for parents and children is the extent to which the job offers the employed parent a chance to exercise autonomy and self-direction (Kohn & Schooler, 1983; Luster, Rhoades, & Haas, 1989; Parcel & Menaghan, 1994).

Interest in occupational self-direction grew out of Melvin Kohn's pioneering sociological research on social class in which he took the position that, "Members of different social classes, by virtue of enjoying (or suffering) different conditions of life, come to see the world differently – to develop different conceptions of social reality, different aspirations and hopes and fears, different 'conceptions of the desirable'" (Kohn, 1977, p. 7). Although quick to acknowledge the importance of education as a key antecedent of people's place in the social hierarchy, Kohn highlighted *work* as a pivotal feature of social class, arguing that work socializes employees to hold certain values, values that in turn have implications for the qualities they seek to instill in their children. Kohn and Schooler (1983) argued that the key feature that distinguishes between middle and working class jobs is "occupational self-direction," defined in terms of complexity, closeness of supervision, and routinization. Jobs high in self-direction offer workers complexity autonomy, and challenge, whereas jobs low in self-direction typically feature highly routinized, closely supervised work that is not particularly complex or challenging.

Several researchers have extended Kohn and Schooler's ideas and illustrated the ways in which parents' access to complex, self-directed work is linked to how they approach child rearing. In a small-scale study of 65 mother-infant dyads, Luster, Rhoades, and Haas (1989) focused on some of the mechanisms that may link social class and parenting behavior during the first year of life. These researchers replicated Kohn's (1969, 1977) finding that social class is related to parents' values of conformity and self-direction in their children. They also identified a set of specific parental beliefs that mediated the relation between parental values and parenting behavior. Global parenting values were related to specific attitudes about spoiling babies, giving babies freedom to explore the home environment, discipline, and the importance of verbal stimulation. These specific beliefs, in turn, were related to mothers' supportive and constraining behaviors toward their babies as reported by the mothers themselves and as rated by interviewers.

Parcel and Menaghan (1994) operationalized occupational complexity by matching NLSY mothers' occupations with objective data on work demands provided by the *Dictionary of Occupational Titles*. Arguing that, "having a parent in a complex job can be a resource for children in that it sets a high level of expectation regarding self-direction and intellectual flexibility" (Parcel & Menaghan, 1994, p. 14), they found that, even controlling for mothers' education, age, measured mental ability, income and other possible confounds, mothers employed in jobs with greater substantive complexity created more stimulating home environments for their children.

Longitudinal analyses by Menaghan and Parcel (1995) also illuminate the importance of job complexity. Children's home environments deteriorated over time if mothers, for whatever reason, moved into jobs low in substantive complexity but improved if mothers moved into more substantively complex jobs. Declines in the home environment were particularly pronounced for unmarried women who took on jobs low in complexity *and* low in wages. The quality of home environments in turn was related to children's receptive vocabulary at ages 3 to 6 and reading and math skills at ages 5 to 8 (Parcel & Menaghan, 1994). Interestingly, Parcel and Menaghan (1994) did *not* find statistical evidence that the quality of the home environment *mediated* the effects of occupational self-direction on child outcomes; the processes through which occupational complexity affects children's development remain unclear.

Parents' occupational self-direction may also be linked to how they socialize their children around gender. Using a sample of dual-earner couples with adolescent offspring, Klute, Crouter, Sayer, and McHale (2001) examined the links between husbands' and wives' occupational self-direction, their values for self-direction, and two features of family life that have implications for children's gender socialization: parents' gender role attitudes and their division of female-typed household tasks (i.e., cooking, washing dishes, cleaning, and laundry). Controlling for parents' education and work hours, Klute et al., (2001) found that husbands and wives enjoying higher levels of occupational self-direction held less traditional attitudes and adopted a less traditional division of labor. Consistent with Kohn's (1969, 1977) thinking, the links between occupational self-direction and parents' attitudes and division of housework were mediated by parents' values for self-direction. The more self-direction parents reported experiencing at work, the more they valued self-direction; higher values for self-direction were in turn associated with less traditional gender role attitudes and a more egalitarian division of housework. Other research has demonstrated a link between parents' and children's gender role attitudes (Tenenbaum & Leaper, 2002). Thus, an interesting question for future research is whether children endorse less sex-typed (i.e., less conformist) gender role attitudes when their parents have more opportunity to exercise self-direction on the job.

Occupational Pressure and Strain

A third dimension of work that matters for working parents and their children is the emotional climate of the workplace (Kanter, 1979). Two jobs may be very similar in terms of the hours and shifts required and opportunities for self-direction but may differ considerably in terms of the extent to which they are stressful places in which to work. The literature that addresses the issue of how stressful work impinges families takes two different approaches (see review by Crouter & Bumpus, 2001). In one approach, researchers rely on parents' global reports about their work environments. Often parents are asked to think about their work situation over the last year. Studies using this global approach have focused on a variety of phenomena including perceptions of pressure, pace, and deadlines (e.g., Crouter, Bumpus, Maguire, & McHale, 1999) and co-worker and supervisor support (e.g., Greenberger, Goldberg, Hamill, O'Neil et al., 1989). The second approach focuses on intra-individual variation in daily overloads (e.g., Bolger et al., 1989; Repetti & Wood, 1997) or daily arguments with co-workers and supervisors (e.g., Bolger et al., 1989). Studies using this daily approach make repeated assessments of work and family experiences and treat the occasion as the unit of analysis, rather than the individual. Analyses compare how parents behave at home following workdays that vary in terms of stress and strain.

Research following the global approach suggests that the process through which stress experienced by parents on the job is linked to their children's psychosocial functioning is indirect, much like a series of dominos. Crouter et al. (1999), for example, found that high levels of perceived pressure at work increased parents' feelings of role overload (a general measure of stress and strain), which, in turn, predicted higher levels of parent-adolescent conflict and, as a consequence, lower levels of adolescent well-being (see Galambos et al., 1995, for findings suggesting a similar scenario). Interestingly, fathers' work pressure predicted not only their own feelings of role overload, but their wives' as well. In contrast, mothers' work pressure predicted only mothers' own role overload, not their husbands'. At least in this way, fathers' work stress may be thought of as exerting more influence on the emotional tenor of the family than mothers' work stress.

Studies that take a global approach generally support a generalization model in which stressful experiences on the job predict stressful experiences at home. In contrast, studies that examine daily fluctuations in stress suggest that parents may cope with daily work-related stress by *withdrawing* from spousal and parent-child interaction. Repetti and Wood (1997), for example, collected data on 30 mother-preschool dyads over five consecutive weekdays. They also videotaped mother-child reunions at the child's work-site child care center. (Note that studying reunions at a work-site child care center is an ingenious way of getting around the methodological problem that long commutes between work and home may dissipate work-related moods that might influence family interaction.) Repetti and Wood reported that, on days when mothers had experienced heavy workloads or negative social interactions on the job, they were less likely to interact, positively or negatively, with their child. The pattern of withdrawal in the face of negative social interactions at work was more pronounced for mothers reporting higher levels of Type A behavior, suggesting that individual differences in parents' personalities and coping styles play a role in shaping how they respond to stressful work conditions.

Together, the two approaches to research on the connections between work stress and family interaction suggest a scenario in which, over the short-run, stressful days on the job lead to withdrawal from social interaction with children. Withdrawal means that the parent is engaging in less positive behavior with the child but also less negative behavior. Over the long run, however, when parents perceive their work to be generally stressful they engage in more aversive behavior with their children. It is important to point out that the global studies have generally been based on studies of parents raising adolescents (e.g., Crouter et al., 1999; Galambos, et al., 1995) whereas the research of Repetti and Wood focused on mothers raising preschoolers. Thus, there may be a developmental explanation for the disparity in findings for the two approaches. Parents who experience high levels of work pressure may not be able to regulate their emotions in the face of the adolescent provocation but may be able to do so when dealing with younger children. Some support for this idea comes from a study by Almeida, Wethington, and Chandler (1999), who were interested in transmission of emotions within families. They found that both mothers and fathers were more likely to engage in tense interactions with their children if they had experienced marital tension the previous day, and, for mothers, negative emotional transmission was heightened when they had adolescent offspring. (For fathers, interestingly, negative emotional transmission was heightened when their wives held full-time jobs.)

Work, Families, and Children: The Big Picture

Looking across the three dimensions of work explored here – time and timing, occupational self-direction, and work-related stress – several themes can be distilled. First, the effects of parents' work on family processes or child psychosocial functioning are rarely direct. They are usually mediated (or moderated) by what the parent is like or how the parent behaves. Parents' reactions to work in the form of feelings of stress and strain and experiences of parenting stress are the important linchpins connecting the world of work to children's lives. In other words, to understand the effect of parents' work on children, we have to understand the effect of parents' work on parents themselves. Experts on work and family must think developmentally not only about children but about parents.

There is some suggestion in the literature reviewed that fathers' work is at least as important to families as mothers' work is, if not more important. As discussed, for example, mothers' hours of employment are generally not linked to child outcomes (except, perhaps, in the first year of life) whereas children do less well on certain cognitive outcomes when their fathers work either part- or over-time (Parcel & Menaghan, 1994). Similarly, Crouter et al. (1999) found that fathers' work pressure mattered for fathers and mothers, whereas mothers' perceptions of pressure were related only to their own feelings of overload.

Why are fathers' jobs especially important? Fathers frequently take on the role of the primary provider and are seen that way by other family members, giving fathers' work special "clout" that mothers' work may simply not have. Reflecting provider role norms, fathers and mothers also are often involved in the workforce at different levels (Jacobs & Gerson, 2001). Even in families in which both parents work full-time, fathers are more likely than mothers to put in long work hours. This means that the variability in how much parents' work is at different ends of the distribution for mothers and fathers. For mothers in dual-earner families, there tends to be variability at the part-time end. For fathers, part-time work is rare; indeed, for fathers, variability is more likely to be found at the high end of the work hours distribution, and it may be at the high end that we see the most potential for "spillover" into family life.

NEXT STEPS IN THE RESEARCH AGENDA

In the United States today, the typical two-parent family is a dual-earner family (Hernandez, 1997), making mothers *and* fathers' jobs important features of family life for many children. Although not the focus of this chapter, the occupational conditions of single parents may be particularly important influences on family and child well-being because so much depends upon that job and the resources it brings the parent and the family. Thus, in future research, it will be important to extend and enrich our knowledge about how parents' work makes its mark on these families and children.

Another important area to address head-on in future research is the issue of selection effects. As I suggested in my initial caveats, associations between work and family life may be due in part to the tendency for individuals with certain personal and family characteristics to choose certain jobs or to be selected by certain employers. Traditionally, there have been disciplinary differences in how researchers have dealt with this issue of "niche-picking" (Scarr & McCartney, 1983). Psychologists have tended to use small, homogeneous samples (often focused on professional or middle-class families) and to ignore selection effects. Sociologists and economists have tended to try to statistically control for the myriad characteristics that might underlie a phenomenon such as maternal work hours. It is rare, however, that a data set contains the full spectrum of variables one would need to address.

As a first step, we need to build questions about selection effects into our research protocols and report that information in our publications. For example, in addition to finding out how many hours parents work and what shifts they work, we need to find out why they work those hours and schedules. For parents who are not working the hours and schedules they prefer, we need to get a read on the impediments. Do they lack seniority? Do their child-care arrangements limit their work hours or schedule? What roles do spouses or partners play in these decisions, some of which may reflect dyadic trade-offs? Henly and Lambert's (in press) insights into the work-related conditions that underlie some parents' choices of child care arrangements are also important. More research of this kind is needed to examine parents in different lines of work and living in communities that offer different choices in terms of child-care arrangements.

Although research on selection effects will provide important information, we also need to implement or take advantage of experiments or quasi-experiments in the workplace and trace whether and how those changes make a difference for families and children. Such changes could involve potentially positive changes such as the introduction of so-called "family-friendly" benefits like flexible work hours, or they could involve changes triggered by economic forces, such as instituting policies requiring that workers work overtime (common in U.S. factories during boom economic times) or stepping up productivity demands (a change that presumably would heighten deadlines, pace, and pressure). The advantage of such "natural experiments" (Bronfenbrenner, 1979) is that, over time, the employed parent serves as his or her own control, and the researcher can see whether and how the changes instituted in the workplace are related to changes in employed parents' psychological well-being or parenting and in turn to changes in children's psychosocial functioning.

Another important area that has not received sufficient attention is how work and family are experienced by parents and children living in working-class and low-income families (Lambert, 1999). Much of the literature to date has focused on middle-class, professional families. This is in part due to researchers' interest in the phenomenon of dual-earner families. In two-parent families, if both parents hold paying jobs, it is less likely that the family will be struggling economically. Understanding the consequences of low-income occupational conditions is important for several reasons. Large numbers of children are growing up in working poor and low-income families, many of which are headed by single mothers. Low-income and working-class parents' jobs are undoubtedly an important influence on the quality of their family environments. In addition, such research can inform social policy. For example, welfare reform in the United States has pushed large numbers of single-parent mothers into the paid labor force, under the assumption that, in the long run, this policy will not only save taxpayers money but benefit low-income women and their families. Menaghan and Parcel's (1995) study of the impact of changes in mothers' occupational conditions on the quality of their home environments underscored the potential implications of mothers making the transition from welfare to work. Noting that the quality of the home environment declined when mothers entered jobs that were low in wages and occupational complexity, Menaghan and Parcel (1995, p. 82) remarked:

> Despite the negative short term costs we detect, mothers' movement into such employment may be better for families in the long run if the low-complexity, low-wage jobs are part of "internal labor markets" or job ladders that allow progressively more responsibility and higher pay as workers ascend over time. Unfortunately, such a scenario may be unduly optimistic, given what we know about continuities in parental advantage or disadvantage over time . . .

The jury is still out on the impacts of welfare reform on children. Early evaluations of welfare-to-work programs by Duncan and his colleagues (see Duncan, 2003) suggest that school-aged children are generally not adversely affected by their mothers' transition from welfare to work, but there are consistent, negative effects for adolescents in areas such as school achievement. Perhaps this is because many newly employed, low-income, single mothers rely heavily on their teenagers for help with child care and housework, responsibilities that may conflict with school attendance, school-related extracurricular activities, and homework completion (Dodson & Dickert, 2004). Given the clear connection between educational attainment and subsequent occupational status, it is a concern that policies encouraging mothers to move from welfare to work are inadvertently hindering their adolescent offspring's ability to succeed in school and, in the long run, gain a competitive advantage in the labor market.

IMPLICATIONS FOR POLICY AND PRACTICE

Although the field has accumulated considerable knowledge about the connections between work and family, it is difficult to make specific, empirically supported suggestions for policy. To address gaps in current knowledge, the National Institute of Child Health and Human Development is currently developing a funding initiative to encourage research that uses rigorous experimental or quasi-experimental designs to examine whether (and how) so-called "family friendly policies" in the workplace enhance the well-being of employed parents and their families and children, as well as productivity in the workplace. The kinds of policies that have traditionally been referred to as family-friendly include parental leave, flexible work schedules, opportunities for part-time employment and job sharing, and employer-supported child care (including after-school care, summer programs, and care for sick children). There is also growing interest in whether stress management programs or health promotion programs in the workplace enhance employee psychosocial functioning and, in so doing, strengthen parenting and family dynamics.

Not all employees are parents who are actively raising children, however. This means that it may be difficult to target special policies or programs to employed parents that are not relevant to or accessible to people in other life circumstances, including people who have no children or those whose children are grown. There could be a backlash of employee resentment, for example, if employers were to favor parents of young children when assigning work shifts, approving part-time schedules, or assigning over-time. The strategy of offering "flexible benefits" in which employees choose from an array of benefits those most important to them allows employed parents and nonparents alike to benefit from a workplace ethos that acknowledges and supports employees' lives off the job (Ferber, O'Farrell, & Allen, 1991).

CONCLUSION

The central tenet of this chapter is that parents' work matters for families and children. In the domains of inquiry reviewed here, mothers' and fathers' jobs are linked in important ways to parents' temporal availability to their children, parents' values, and parents' moods when they return home from work, phenomena that in turn are linked to how parents socialize and interact with their offspring. To move the field of work and family forward, researchers need to broaden their samples to include families struggling to make ends meet and to adopt experimental and quasi-experimental designs that attempt to minimize the ubiquitous influences of selection effects.

References

Almeida, D. M., Wethington, E., & Chandler, A. L. (1999). Daily transmission of tensions between marital and parent-child dyads. *Journal of Marriage and the Family, 61*, 49–61.

Baron, J. N., & Bielby, W. T. (1985). Organizational barriers to gender equality: Sex segregation of jobs and occupations. In A. S. Rossi (Ed.), *Gender and the life course* (pp. 233–251). New York, Aldine.

Bernard, J. (1981). The good provider role: Its rise and fall. *American Psychologist, 36*, 1–12.

Bianchi, S. M. (2000). Maternal employment and time with children: Dramatic change or surprising continuity? *Demography, 37*, 401–414.

Bogen, K., & Joshi, P. (2002). *Bad work or good move: The relationship of part-time and nonstandard work schedules to parenting and child behavior in working poor families.* Paper presented at a conference entitled, "Working Poor Families: Coping as Parents and Workers" sponsored by the National Institute of Child Health and Human Development.

Bolger, N., DeLongis, A., Kessler, R. C., & Wethington, E. (1989). The contagion of stress across multiple roles. *Journal of Marriage and the Family, 51*, 175–183.

Bronfenbrenner, U. (1979). *The ecology of human development*. Cambridge, MA: Harvard University Press.

Bronfenbrenner, U., & Crouter, A. C. (1982). Work and family through time and space. In S. Kamerman & C. Hayes (Eds.), *Families that work: Children in a changing world* (pp. 39–83). Washington, DC: National Academy Press.

Brooks-Gunn, J. Han, W., & Waldfogel, J. (2002). Maternal employment and child cognitive outcomes in the first three years of life: The NICHD Study of Early Child Care. *Child Development, 73*, 1052–1072.

Bumpus, M. F., Crouter, A. C., & McHale, S. M. (1999). Work demands of dual-earner couples: Implications for parents' knowledge about children's daily lives in middle childhood. *Journal of Marriage and the Family, 61*, 465–475.

Coltrane, S. (1996). *Family man: Fatherhood, housework, and gender inequality*. New York: Oxford University Press.

Crouter, A. C. (1984). Spillover from family to work: The neglected side of the work-family interface. *Human Relations, 37*, 425–442.

Crouter, A. C., & Bumpus, M. F. (2001). Linking parents' work stress to children's and adolescents' psychological adjustment. *Current Directions in Psychological Science, 10*, 156–159.

Crouter, A. C., Bumpus, M. F., Head, M. R., & McHale, S. M. (2001). Implications of overwork and overload for the quality of men's family relationships. *Journal of Marriage and Family, 63*, 404–416.

Crouter, A. C., Bumpus, M. F., Maguire, M. C., & McHale, S. M. (1999). Linking parents' work pressure to adolescents' well-being: Insights into dynamics in dual-earner families. *Developmental Psychology, 35*, 1453–1461.

Crouter, A. C., & Helms-Erikson, H. (1997). Work and family from a dyadic perspective: Variations in inequality. In S. Duck (Ed.), *Handbook of personal relationships*. New York: Wiley.

Crouter, A. C., Helms-Erikson, H., Updegraff, K., & McHale, S. M. (1999). Conditions underlying parents' knowledge about children's daily lives in middle childhood: Between- and within-family comparisons. *Child Development, 70*, 246–259.

Crouter, A. C., & Manke, B. (1997). Development of a typology of dual-earner families: A window into differences between and within families. *Journal of Family Psychology, 11*, 62–75.

Crouter, A. C., & McHale, S. M. (1993). Temporal rhythms in family life: Seasonal variation in the relation between parental work and family processes. *Developmental Psychology, 29*, 198–205.

Davidson, M. J., & Cooper, C. L. (1984). *Working women: An international survey*. New York: Wiley.

Dodson, L., & Dickert, J. (2004). Girls' family labor in low-income households: A decade of qualitative research. *Journal of Marriage and Family, 66*, 318– 332.

Duncan, G. (2003, June). *What can welfare experiments tell us about family and child well-being?* Paper presented at the Family Research Consortium III Summer Institute, Santa Ana Pueblo, New Mexico.

England, P., & Farkas, G. (1986). *Households, employment, and gender: A social, economic, and demographic view*. New York: Aldine de Gruyter.

Ferber, M. A., & O'Farrell, B. with L. Allen (1991). *Work and family: Policies for a changing workforce.* Washington, DC: National Academy Press.

Galambos, N. L., Sears, H. A., Almeida, D. M., Kolaric, G. (1995). Parents' work overload and problem behavior in young adolescents. *Journal of Early Adolescence, 5*, 201–223.

Greenberger, E., Goldberg, W. A., Hamill, S., O'Neil, R., & Payne, C. K. (1989). Contributions of a supportive work environment to parents' well-being and orientation to work. *American Journal of Community Psychology, 17*, 755–783.

Harvey, E. (1999). Short-term and long-term effects of early parental employment on children of the National Longitudinal Survey of Youth. *Developmental Psychology, 35*, 445–459.

Henly, J., & Lambert, S. (in press). Linking workplace practices to child care requirements: Lower-level workers in lower-skilled jobs. Chapter to appear in Bianchi, S. M., Casper, L. M., Christensen, K. E., & King, R. B. (Eds.), *Workforce/workplace mismatch? Work, family health, and well-being.*

Hernandez, D. J. (1997). Child development and the social demography of childhood. *Child Development, 68*, 149–169.

Heyman, J. (2000). *The widening gap: Why American's working families are in jeopardy – and what can be done about it.* New York: Basic Books.

Jacobs, J. A., & Gerson, K. (2001). Overworked individuals or overworked families? Explaining trends in work, leisure, and family time. *Work and Occupations, 28*, 40–63.

Kanter, R. M. (1979). *Work and family in the United States: A critical review and agenda for research and policy.* New York: Russell Sage Foundation.

Klute, M. M., Crouter, A. C., Sayer, A. G., & McHale, S. M. (2001). Occupational self-direction, values, and egalitarian relationships: A study of dual-earner couples. *Journal of Marriage and Family, 64*, 139–151.

Kohn, M. L. (1969). *Class and conformity: A study in values.* New York: Dorsey Press.

Kohn, M. L. (1977). *Class and conformity: A study in values.* (2nd. ed.). Chicago: University of Chicago Press.

Kohn, M. L., & Schooler, C. (1983). *Work and personality: An inquiry into the impact of social stratification.* Norwood, NJ: Ablex.

Lambert, S. J. (1999). Lower-wage workers and the new realities of work and family. *The Annals of the American Academy of Political and Social Science, 562*, 174–190.

Luster, T., Rhoades, K., & Haas, B. (1989). Relations between parenting values and parenting behavior. *Journal of Marriage and the Family, 51*, 139–147.

Menaghan, E. G., & Parcel, T. L. (1995). Social sources of change in children's home environments: The effects of parental occupational experiences and family conditions. *Journal of Marriage and the Family, 57*, 69–84.

National Institute for Child Health and Human Development Early Child Care Research Network (2003). Does amount of time spent in child care predict socioemotional adjustment during the transition to kindergarten? *Child Development, 74*, 976–1005.

Parcel, T. B., & Menaghan, E. G. (1994). *Parents' jobs and children's lives.* New York: Aldine de Gruyter.

Perry-Jenkins, M., Goldberg, A., Pierce, C., & Haley, H. (under review). Employment schedules and the transition to parenthood: Implications for mental health and marriage.

Presser, H. B. (1999). Toward a 24-hour economy. *Science, 284,* 1778–1779.

Presser, H. B. (2000). Nonstandard work schedules and marital instability. *Journal of Marriage and Family, 62,* 93–110.

Presser, H. B. (2003). *Employment in a 24/7 economy: Challenges for American families.* New York: Russell Sage Foundation.

Presser, H. B., & Cain, V. S. (1983). Shift work among dual-earner couples with children. *Science, 219,* 876–879.

Repetti, R. L., & Wood, J. (1997). Effects of daily stress at work on mothers' interactions with preschoolers. *Journal of Family Psychology, 11,* 90–108.

Scarr, S., & McCartney, K. (1983). How people make their own environments: A theory of genotype → environment effects. *Child Development, 54,* 424–435.

Smith, C. S., Folkard, S., & Fuller, J. (2003). Shiftwork and working hours. Chapter in J. C. Quick & L. E. Tetrick (Eds.). *Handbook of occupational health psychology* (pp. 163–183). Washington, DC: American Psychological Association.

Tenenbaum, H. R., & Leaper, C. (2002). Are parents' gender schemas related to their children's gender-related cognitions? A meta-analysis. *Developmental Psychology, 38,* 615–630.

White, L., & Keith, B. (1990). Effect of shift work on quality and stability of marital relations. *Journal of Marriage and the Family, 52,* 453–462.

7

The Family-Child-Care Mesosystem

Kathleen McCartney

The family's influence on individual differences in context is part of a larger question, an old question – older than developmental science: What is the role of experience in development? Consideration of the importance of any influence on development inevitably leads to considerations of nature and nurture, because these are the only two mechanisms that can explain individual differences in development. From the beginning, theorists have questioned whether the effects of experience can be isolated. In 1934, Gesell and Thompson concluded that nature and nurture could be separated "only in analytical thinking." More recently, Gottlieb, Wahlsten, and Lickliter (1998) argued that attempts to separate the two were "nonsensical." Yet, polarizing claims continue. One example is Harris's (1995) thesis that families do not matter. This conclusion was based primarily on the failure to find strong shared environmental effects for children's psychological development. Critiques of Harris's thesis have focused on the likelihood that family influences are largely not shared, because parents respond to individual differences among their children (Rutter, 2002; Vandell, 2000). The most promising research today on the family's influence concerns genotype-environment interplay, rather than research that promotes one over the other.

I have recently argued that theory and conceptualization in developmental science far exceed methodology (McCartney, 2003). This is hardly controversial. Behavior genetics and socialization methods are each limited, for reasons that are well known to developmentalists (Collins, Maccoby, Steinberg, Hetherington et al., 2000). As a result, these methods can only produce evidence that is *suggestive* of genetic or socialization effects. Although augmented behavior genetics designs that include rich assessments of the environment are undoubtedly the strongest methods available to study the role of experience in development, these methods are still limited. Developmental science has produced convincing evidence that genetic and environmental factors each play a substantial role in the origins of individual differences. Nevertheless, our estimates of effects are "very approximate" (Rutter, 2002). A significant association tells us little more than there might be something there – a kind of signal amidst the noise (McCartney, 2003).

Socialization researchers are also preoccupied with questions about the size of effects. These estimates, too, can only be approximate. There are at least two problems associated with the assessment of environmental effects in any context experienced by the developing child. The first is that the environment is extraordinarily complex. Sensibly, social scientists focus on constructs hypothesized to be important predictors of child competence, from indicators of the physical environment to the social environment to the environment produced by the child through choice and evocation. When researchers isolate a variable from the environment, including an indicator of parenting, we need to be mindful of the fact that this indicator is associated with myriad other environmental variables (Scarr, 1985). In other words, we can isolate a variable for study, however we cannot necessarily isolate its effects.

Thus, a focus on effect size is premature. "All aspects of behavioral development are multiply and redundantly determined, and, as a result, the absolute magnitude of each individual influence is likely to be quite small when all important factors are taken into account simultaneously" (Lamb, 1998, p. 116). It is no wonder that focusing on an identified indicator of the environment typically produces small effects. Variables are mere indicators of environmental experience, indicators with considerable measurement error. Consider the child-care environment as an example. Researchers have developed observational coding instruments that focus on caregiving behaviors such as sensitivity and stimulation of cognitive development. Even in the best studies, observers try to capture the complexity of a child's experience by coding variables based on one or two days of observation. This kind of time-sampling produces an indicator of experience to be sure, but only a coarse one. Developmentalists have not conducted comprehensive assessments of children's experience in context, perhaps because this is painstaking work of a technical nature with few incentives from the scientific community.

Questions about "how much" sometimes cloud questions about "how." How questions are at the level of description, and this is the level that reflects state-of-the-art, nonexperimental work on the importance of experience. I begin this chapter with the assumption that parents matter for the developing child to some extent, an assumption derived from one hundred years of developmental research in behavior genetics as well as on socialization. By including the phrase "to some extent," questions about how much are no longer the focus of inquiry. Instead, our task is to describe identified relations between experience and development, mindful that development is indeed multiply and redundantly determined.

HOW FAMILIES MATTER IN THE CHILD-CARE CONTEXT

Papers on child care typically begin with a description of the rising trend in maternal employment that began in the 1970s, followed by the concomitant increase in the use of nonmaternal child care for infants, toddlers, and preschoolers. Researchers then argue that this represents a dramatic change in how families raise their children. In fact, shared child rearing has been the norm throughout the long evolution of human history, while exclusive maternal care has been practiced for a relatively short period of time, specifically since the industrial revolution (McCartney & Phillips, 1988). The myth of motherhood is powerful in our culture, such that deviations from exclusive mother care are perceived as potentially harmful (Lamb, 1998; Scarr, 1984). Many cultural explanations have been advanced to explain the focus on child care as a risk for young children, especially the influence of psychoanalysis and its emphasis on early experience.

It is fair to say that the type of child care used by families has shifted in recent history, from less formal to more formal arrangements. Less formal child care includes care by siblings, relatives, and neighbors. These kinds of child-care arrangements have enabled women to work for ages. Weisner and Gallimore (1977) have described how child care in social-agricultural groups is provided by girls and older women, so that younger women can work in the fields and still tend to their babies as needed. More formal arrangements are found in school-like settings, including center-based child care, nursery school, Head Start, and public pre-kindergarten programs. The primary purpose of some programs is to support maternal employment, whereas the primary purpose of other programs is to provide early education to prepare children for school entry; however, the boundaries among all child-care programs are blurring because most programs now support both goals (Phillips & McCartney, in press).

Although definitions of child care may be elusive, it is clear that researchers view child care as a pervasive context in which early development unfolds, second only to the immediate family (Shonkoff & Phillips, 2000). Research on child care has generally focused on isolating its effects from family effects by controlling statistically for contributions from the family. As a result, important questions about the interconnections between these two contexts have been sidestepped or addressed indirectly. Connections among contexts for the developing child comprise the mesosystem, a term coined by Bronfenbrenner to refer to "interrelations among major settings containing the developing person at a particular point in his or her life" (Bronfenbrenner, 1977, p. 515). In an effort to bring into focus how families matter for their children's development in relation to their children's child-care experience, I review four bodies of literature that demonstrate interconnections between the family and child care contexts: family selection of child care, quality effects and family moderation, the predictive power of the family across child-care contexts, and child care as a family support.

Family Selection of Child Care

Not surprisingly, maternal employment status often drives decisions about child care. Clearly, other factors influence these decisions as well. For example, nonemployed mothers, both rich and poor, do enroll their children in child-care programs such as nursery schools and intervention programs to foster school readiness skills. However, child care is used most often to support maternal employment. Recent work shows that hours in child care over the first 4 $\frac{1}{2}$ years of a child's life predicts higher maternal wages when children are in first grade, especially for more educated mothers (Bub & McCartney, 2004). Thus, the relation between maternal employment and child care is best described as interdependent or synergistic. Note, however, that it may be better to consider mothers' and fathers' employment status as well as their employment conditions when assessing child-care decisions (see Crouter, Chapter 6 in this book).

If parents decide to use child care, numerous decisions remain – decisions about the age at which their children will begin child care, decisions about the type of care, decisions about the amount of time spent in care, and decisions about the quality of care. Ultimately, parental choices about child care reflect parental values, needs, and circumstances (Lamb, 1998). Surely these decisions constitute a primary means through which families influence their children's development. Nevertheless, parent choices are sometimes constrained by economic considerations (Fuller, Holloway, & Liang, 1995).

The family's ability to pay for care is strongly associated with child-care choices. Mothers who earn more are more likely to enroll their children in child-care settings earlier and for more hours than mothers who earn less (Leibowitz, Klerman, & Waite, 1992; Symons & McLeod, 1993). Families with more economic resources are more likely to select center-based care (Blau, 2001; Fuller, Holloway & Liang, 1995; Hofferth & Wissoker, 1992). There is some evidence, however, that the relation between income and child-care quality is curvilinear (Bolger & Scarr, 1995; McCartney, 1984). Children from high- and low-income families receive higher quality care than those from families with moderate incomes (Phillips, Voran, Kisker, Howes et al., 1994; Waite, Leibowitz, & Witsberger, 1991), because access to high-quality care is available to high-income families by virtue of their wages and to low-income families via subsidies and other social programs. Not surprisingly, parent satisfaction with child-care arrangements varies by income level. For example, 43 percent of low-income single mothers report that they would use a different child-care arrangement if they could afford to do so (Phillips, 1995).

Interestingly, the price-quality relation is "quite idiosyncratic," varying greatly by location (Blau, 2001, p. 123). There are bargains to be had for educated consumers. Unfortunately, experts agree that parents are not skilled consumers of the child-care market. Parents often lack information about what constitutes quality care. In fact, both Gormley (1995) and Blau (2001) consider parents' lack of information to be a major reason for U.S. child-care problems, from market failure to the lack of quality programs. Parents typically rely on informal networks to identify child-care options for their children, rather than on knowledge about child care (Gable & Cole, 2000). Moreover, parents are constrained in their ability to select quality programs for their children by their own needs with respect to location and hours of operation.

Even educated consumers may have difficulty identifying quality programs because of lack of availability. Quality programs are in the minority, ranging from 30 percent in the Cost, Quality, and Outcomes study (Cost, Quality, & Outcomes Team, 1995) to 56 percent in a survey of family and relative care (Kontos, Howes, Shinn, & Galinsky, 1995) to 44 percent of settings across all types of care in the National Institute for Child Health and Human Development Study of Early Child Care and Youth Development (NICHD ECCRN, 2000b). Taken together, these studies paint a grim picture of typical child care in the United States, where child-care providers are the second lowest paid workers, controlling for education and experience (Gormley, 1995). Low wages compromise the quality of the work force, because they make it difficult to recruit and retain qualified providers (Phillips, Howes, & Whitebook, 1992).

Parental values also influence decisions about child-care quality. Parents who have authoritarian child-rearing beliefs and who provide less sensitive care are less likely to select high-quality child care (Bolger & Scarr, 1995; Howes & Stewart, 1987; Vandell & Corasaniti, 1990). This association between parenting values and child-care quality is one of the most consistent findings in the literature on child-care selection. Child characteristics also influence parents' decision making. Parents prefer informal arrangements for children under 3 years and formal arrangements, like center-based care, for children 3 years and older (Gable & Cole, 2000). Latino families prefer informal arrangements as well, however, selection effects associated with ethnicity are generally quite small (Singer, Fuller, Keiley, & Wolf, 1998).

Parental choice of child care escaped the consideration of the earliest child-care researchers. As such, early research suffers from omitted variables bias, meaning that identified child-care effects reflected, to some extent, confounded family effects. Since the early 1980s, researchers have considered the role of parental selection in child-care experience by controlling for family variables in statistical models. In the first effort to control for selection, McCartney (1984) regressed child-care quality on a wide range of family variables and included significant predictors of quality, for example mother's education, as controls in subsequent models that estimated child outcomes from child-care quality. This conservative strategy has not been adopted in most research. Instead, researchers tend to include family variables hypothesized to predict parental choice. Economists have been critical of this developmental research on child care and recommend increasing the number and type of family controls (Duncan & Gibson, 2000).

In contrast, Newcombe (2003) has argued that controlling for family variables when the goal is "to understand the lives of families" may lead to "misleading" conclusions about the effects of child care. She used a recent paper by the NICHD Early Child Care Research Network (NICHD ECCRN, 2003) to make her point. In that paper, maternal income and maternal depression, along with other family variables, were used as controls when modeling children's behavior problems from total number of child-care hours. Hours in care were positively associated with child behavior problems, controlling for maternal income and depression. The question is whether hours in care truly function as a risk factor, when maternal income is negatively associated with behavior problems and maternal depression is positively associated with behavior problems. Newcombe argued that suppressing variables in models that cannot be suppressed in real life can lead to erroneous conclusions concerning identified effects and suggested that some controls control too much. This argument can be applied broadly to all nonexperimental research.

Quality Effects and Family Moderation

Reviewers frame the child-care research literature in three waves (Belsky & Steinberg, 1978; McCartney & Galanopoulos, 1988; Lamb, 1998). The first wave consisted of comparisons of children in child care with children in exclusive maternal care to assess risks associated with child care per se. Because these studies did not consider family confounds of child-care experience, they are not interpretable and therefore of little use. Furthermore, this first wave of studies treated child care as a uniform experience. Clearly, children's experiences across child-care settings differ, just as their experiences across family settings differ. Moreover, children's experiences within child-care settings differ, again as experiences within families differ. Thus, it is critical to assess individual children's experiences in child care.

The second wave of studies focused on variations in child-care experience by assessing the role of quality of care. Quality is typically assessed via structural or process measures. Structural characteristics, such as child-staff ratio, group size, and caregiver education and training, are distal indicators of children's experience, albeit relevant to policy. Process characteristics, such as caregiver sensitivity and cognitive stimulation, more directly reflect developmentalists' conceptions about environmental mechanisms that promote children's development, but are less easily regulated than structural characteristics. Not surprisingly, the two sets of variables are related, such that children experience more sensitive interactions that support their learning in settings with lower child-staff ratios, smaller group sizes, and more-educated as well as better-trained teachers.

Two studies ushered in this second wave, the National Day Care Study (Ruopp, Travers, Glantz & Coelen, 1979), which assessed quality via structural characteristics of child care and the Bermuda Day Care Study (McCartney, Scarr, Phillips, Grajek et al., 1982), which assessed quality via process characteristics of child care. There is now a large body of literature that documents positive associations between quality indicators and children's cognitive, language, and social outcomes (for a review, see Lamb, 1998). For the most part, these studies assessed quality at the level of the group, so that comparisons could be made across settings, but not within settings. Although researchers hoped to examine components of quality, quality indicators tended to be highly intercorrelated, and therefore, researchers created global measures. For the most part, child-care quality measures reflected the views of early childhood educators, specifically that quality programs are more likely to be developmentally appropriate, to offer varied and interesting activities, to offer activities that promote sustained attention, to provide children with opportunities to exercise choice in learning, and to foster achievement motivation (Bryant, Burchinal, Lau, & Sparling, 1994).

The third wave of research is characterized by large, multi-site, longitudinal studies. Large studies are needed so that researchers have sufficient power to identify interactions between family and child-care effects; multi-site studies are needed to reflect the diversity of child-care options across states with varying regulations; and longitudinal studies are needed so as to relate children's experiences to their developmental trajectories. The Cost, Quality and Outcomes Study (Peisner-Feinberg, Burchinal, Clifford, Culkin et al., 2001) and the NICHD Study of Early Child Care and Youth Development (SECCYD; NICHD ECCRN, 2001) both exemplify this third wave. In the former, 418 children, recruited from 176 child-care centers, randomly selected from four regions in the United States, were followed through second grade. Child-care quality was assessed via two variables, teacher-child closeness and the classroom practices index, a composite measure consisting of global quality and teacher responsiveness. There were modest effects of quality through second grade on a wide range of outcomes, including receptive language ability, math ability, cognitive and attention skills, problem behaviors, and sociability. There was also some evidence of differential effects, with teacher-child closeness predicting social outcomes better than cognitive outcomes.

The SECCYD is a prospective study of 1,364 children from birth through sixth grade (for a summary, see NICHD ECCRN, 2001). It is the most comprehensive U.S. study to date about connections among child-care experiences, family factors, and children's early development. The NICHD ECCRN developed a process quality measure that could be used across child-care contexts, both formal and informal. The Observational Record of the Caregiving Environment (ORCE; NICHD ECCRN, 1996) focuses on interactions between caregivers and focal children to assess positive caregiving. Thus, the ORCE assesses individual children's experiences within a setting, rather than characteristics of the setting itself. This instrument provides data on both children and caregivers. In particular, frequency counts of specific child and caregiver behaviors are recorded as are qualitative ratings of caregiver-child interactions and caregivers' behaviors. Positive caregiving is associated with a wide range of cognitive, language, and social outcomes. Again, there is some evidence of differential effects, such that the amount of language stimulation provided is more strongly associated with language outcomes than is positive caregiving per se (NICHD ECCRN, 2000a).

According to Burchinal and colleagues, three implicit conceptual models have been used to describe the effect of child-care quality on children's development (Burchinal, Peisner-Feinberg, Bryant, & Clifford, 2000). The first is a main effects model in which quality care enhances development similarly for all children. Much of the existing research on child-care effects is, in fact, consistent with this model. The second is an interaction model, first advanced by Caughy, DiPietro, and Strobino (1994), which predicts that higher-quality child care will enhance the development of children from less-responsive home environments, while poorer-quality child care will impair the development of children from more-responsive home environments. The third model comes from Garcia-Coll (1990), who believes that optimal child care is not universal but rather varies as a function of parental values and beliefs. Burchinal et al. (2000) assessed these three models by combining data from three large child-care data sets: the Cost, Quality, and Outcomes Study, the North Carolina Head Start Partnership Study, and the Public Preschool Evaluation Project. Not surprisingly, children attending high-quality child-care programs were rated as having fewer behavior problems and scored higher on tests of language and academic skills than children in average- or low-quality programs. Tests for interactions between quality and poverty, gender, and ethnicity revealed only one significant interaction, namely that between quality and ethnicity for language skills, such that children of color profited more from high-quality care than did white children. There was no evidence that discrepancies between parents' and child-care providers' values were associated with child outcomes in any way. Thus, the preponderance of evidence supports a main effects model.

As Burchinal et al. (2000) note, their study is among the few child-care investigations with sufficient power to test interactions. It is more difficult to detect interactions in field studies than in experimental studies because the predictor variables in a field study, unlike the independent variables in an experiment, are typically correlated. For example, in the data set used by Burchinal et al. (2000), child-care quality and family income are negatively related. McClelland and Judd (1993, p. 388), have outlined the statistical difficulties associated with detecting interactions in field studies and warn non-experimental researchers that "the odds are against them."

Nevertheless, there is some evidence that child-care quality can serve as a protective factor for children from families in poverty. Using data from the National Longitudinal Survey of Youth, Caughy et al. (1994) reported greater effects of child-care participation for children from low-income families with respect to reading ability. Specifically, there were significant interactions between the number of years in child care and family income as well as between type of care and family income, such that children from low-income families had higher reading scores than other low-income children when they attended child care for more years and when they attended center-based programs, in particular.

Caughy et al.'s (1994) interaction findings have not been replicated by the NICHD ECCRN, perhaps because they did not test quality-by-income interactions in a targeted way. Instead, quality-by-income interactions were assessed in blocks along with home-by-income, gender-by-income, and ethnicity-by-income interactions. The NICHD ECCRN (2000a, p. 975), reported that only three of the 27 blocks tested were significant, "yielding no apparent patterns." McCartney, Dearing, and Taylor (2003) respecified models to test income-by-quality interactions directly. Because significant interactions could not reveal whether high-quality child care protected children from poverty or whether poverty and low-quality child care operated as dual risks, we included a group of children with no child-care experience in the analysis sample. We found that high-quality child care protected children from the negative effects of low income with respect to school readiness, receptive language, and expressive language. Specifically, children at or near the poverty level who attended high-quality child care, unlike middle-class children, had higher scores on cognitive and language tests than did children in low-quality child care or children not in care. The effects are of practical importance. Consider that the negative effects of poverty were between 31 percent and 60 percent smaller for children in high-quality child care compared with their peers who were not in care.

Two other studies that demonstrate compensatory effects of child care for children from less advantaged homes are particularly impressive because the range of child-care quality was restricted in each. The first study was conducted in 32 rural Head Start classrooms, where the vast majority of programs were rated in the middle range on the Early Childhood Environment Rating Scale (Bryant et al., 1994). Children in high-quality programs performed better on cognitive tests of problem solving and reasoning. Moreover, children from better home environments benefited more from high-quality child-care programs, presumably because some learning supports must be available in the home for children to profit from quality child care. The second study was conducted in Sweden, a culture with a fairly uniform and high standard of care (Hagekull & Bohlin, 1995). Even with a restricted range of quality at the high end, children from families with fewer economic resources benefited more from high-quality care. In particular, children from low-income families who attended high-quality child-care programs were less aggressive at 4 years of age than children from low-income families who attended low-quality child care. Two interactions between child-care quality and gender were identified as well, such that boys in high-quality programs had lower internalizing scores and higher ego strength scores than boys in low-quality programs. The authors speculate that the gender effect may reflect caregivers' efforts to foster adaptive behaviors in boys who may be at risk for school failure due to behavior problems.

There is some recent evidence to demonstrate that center-based care may promote cognitive skills better than less formal arrangements. For example, in the Goteborg Child Care Study, second grade cognitive performance was predicted by the number of months children had spent in center-based child care before $3^{1}/_{2}$ years of age (Broberg, Wessels, Lamb, & Hwang, 1997). In the NICHD SECCYD, cognitive and achievement outcomes were predicted by participation in center-based child care in the third and fourth years of life (NICHD ECCRN & Duncan, 2003). It is likely that the advantages of center-based programs result from the curricula offered in more formal settings, which are designed to foster school readiness skills.

The Predictive Power of the Family

There are several studies that test whether extensive child-care experience attenuates the effect of family processes on child functioning. Specifically, researchers have examined whether the predictive power of family factors varies across child-care niches or contexts, that is across groups that vary in their exposure to child care. For example, Howes (1990) demonstrated that parenting practices were associated with a range of developmental outcomes in kindergarten, including ratings of behavior problems and verbal intelligence, for children who had no early child-care experience; in contrast, the association was essentially zero for children with child-care experience. Similarly, Dunham and Dunham (1992) reported that the association between maternal utterances and children's vocabulary was three times as large for children with nonemployed mothers compared with employed mothers. Other researchers have failed to identify differential associations as a function of child-care experience. In her Chicago study, Clarke-Stewart and colleagues examined a range of family factors, including demographic, behavioral and attitudinal characteristics of parents, as well as physical characteristics of the home, and found no evidence for differential influence of the family across child-care niches on a wide range of outcomes (Clarke-Stewart, Gruber, & Fitzerald, 1994).

The NICHD ECCRN (1998) also examined whether associations between family predictors and child outcomes are larger for children with less exposure to early child care. Specifically, it compared associations between parenting variables and a range of child outcomes for two groups, children in exclusive parental care and children in full-time child care. The matrix of correlations between family predictors and child outcomes was not different for the two groups, a finding that is consistent with the view that developmental processes operate similarly for children with and without extensive early child-care experience.

Related to the question of whether parenting effects are attenuated by child-care experience, is the debate about whether early and extensive child care disrupts mother-child attachment. Daily separations have been hypothesized to reduce opportunities for "ongoing tuning of the emerging infant-caregiver interactive system" (Sroufe, 1988, p. 286). Although early studies (e.g., Belsky & Rovine, 1988) and meta-analytic work (e.g., Clarke-Stewart, 1989; Lamb & Sternberg, 1990) demonstrated that 20 or more hours of child care are associated with insecurity, especially avoidance, more recent, better-controlled studies have failed to replicate this finding (e.g., NICHD ECCRN, 1998; Roggman, Langlois, Hubbs-Tait et al., 1994). Data from the SECCYD are particularly convincing for two reasons: (1) the diverse sample, consisting of 1,201 15-month-olds from ten sites around the country, and (2) the coding method for the Strange Situation, involving double-coded assessments from researchers who were blind to children's child-care history. There were no significant differences in attachment security related to child-care participation as indexed by four parameters: age of entry into child care, continuity of care, amount of care, and quality of care. Even for children in extensive, early, unstable, or poor-quality care, the risk of insecure attachment was not higher than that for other children.

Instead, attachment security was related to mother's sensitivity and responsiveness, especially observed in the natural setting of the home, and to her overall positive psychological adjustment. Interactions between low maternal sensitivity and low-quality care, more hours in care, and many care arrangements were associated with increased insecurity, findings that support a dual-risk model of development (Werner & Smith, 1992). There was also some indication that high-quality child care served a compensatory function for children with less sensitive mothers. Overall, the results demonstrate that child care in and of itself constitutes neither a risk nor a benefit for attachment security. Although mothers whose infants were in child care for 30 or more hours per week spent about 32 percent less time with their infants than mothers whose infants were not in care, there were no differences in the quality of parenting provided by these two groups of mothers; nor was there a difference between the two groups of infants on cognitive development, attachment security, language use, or engagement with their mothers (Booth, Clarke-Stewart, Vandell, McCartney et al., 2002).

In general, the influence of parent variables exceeds the influence of child-care variables in regression models predicting children's cognitive, language, and social abilities. It is difficult to compare effect sizes across contexts, however, because the measurement of family and child-care quality indicators is typically not equivalent. Nevertheless, effect sizes for home variables are often substantially larger than those for child-care variables. In fact, in the NICHD study, child-care quality indicators were only 27 percent as strong as parenting variables when predicting children's 54-month achievement test scores (NICHD ECCRN, 2002). It is not surprising that parenting variables account for more variance than child-care variables for at least three reasons: the family provides the primary environment based on exposure; the family provides the most consistent environment over time; and measures of the family reflect genetic as well as contextual influence.

Child Care as a Family Support

Implicit in conceptions of family support is the notion that professionals, including early childhood educators, should partner with parents to support the needs of the developing child. Weissbourd (1990) has offered a set of principles that define family support, including the belief that parents are the primary influence in their children's lives and that parents' need for support transcends social class and cultural differences. Child care supports parents in at least three ways: by child-care resource and referral agencies that help them identify services; by child-care services that support their employment; and by informal parent education from child-care providers. Most parent education consists of the promotion of knowledge concerning child development. Informal education occurs through conversations between parents and child-care providers that typically occur during drop off and pick up times as well as through modeling by providers of caregiving, teaching, and behavior management. Formal education occurs via numerous mechanisms, including home visits, workshops, study groups, books and periodicals, organizational activities, and lectures (Bowman, 1997). In addition, parent education can extend beyond child development to job training and self-esteem programs (Benasich, Brooks-Gunn, & Clewell, 1992).

There is good evidence that parent education programs have helped to reduce health risks through dissemination of public health information, however, it is less clear that parent education can or should change parenting practices, which may reflect cultural differences in values. Historically, parents have been subjected to "a barrage of inconsistent and changing advice that was sometimes destructive and almost always expensive" (Bowman, 1997, p. 167). For example, at present, parents are wondering whose advice to believe regarding whether hours of care, even moderate amounts, pose a risk for the development of behavior problems.

Parent education remains an important component of many intervention models for at-risk families. Benasich, Brooks-Gunn, and Clewell, (1992) identified 27 evaluation studies of educational intervention programs for disadvantaged children that provided treatment to children or their parents. Based on these studies they concluded that mothers who participated in programs were less likely to be on welfare, more likely to be employed, and more likely to seek educational opportunities. There was also some evidence that intervention participation was associated with a decrease in family size and an increase in birth spacing between children, both of which are indicative of a shift from family dependency towards family autonomy. Consistent with this view is the finding that program mothers were more likely to rate themselves higher on measures of internal locus of control, compared with other mothers. Intervention participation was also associated with improvements in mother-child interaction, such that program mothers were less critical of their children and more likely to use reasoning as a behavior management strategy.

Recent evidence suggests that high-quality community child care can serve as an intervention for low-income parents by leading to improvements in the home environment. Using the NICHD SECCYD data set, McCartney Dearing, and Taylor (2003) predicted home quality from the interaction between income and child-care quality. The interaction was significant, revealing no association between income and home quality for children in high-quality care and a positive association between income and home quality for children in low-quality care. Thus, high-quality care protected children from the effects of low income on home quality, which was assessed with the Home Observation for Measurement of the Environment (HOME; Caldwell, & Bradley, 1984), a gold standard measure that assesses a variety of household characteristics, from quality of parent-child interactions (e.g., maternal responsiveness) to level of cognitive stimulation available and educational resources provided in the home (e.g., number of books the child owns). Although the mechanism for such a link is not easily determined, the authors speculate that children's participation in high-quality programs led to increases in mothers' knowledge about childrearing as well as decreases in parenting stress.

SUMMARY OF RESEARCH ON THE FAMILY-CHILD
CARE MESOSYSTEM

In this chapter, I have reviewed four bodies of literature. The first concerned family selection of child care. An extensive body of literature in this area documents how maternal employment and family economic resources influence family decisions about child-care choices. Not surprisingly, employed mothers are more likely to use child care not only to support their careers but also to provide early education for their children. To some extent, family economics drives child-care choices, although the relation between family economics and child-care quality is more idiosyncratic than one might think. Instead, family values drive decision-making, such that authoritarian parents are less likely to choose quality child care. The second body of literature concerns family moderators of child-care quality effects. Researchers have been able to demonstrate that quality matters more for children from at-risk families, especially families in poverty. As such, community child care can function as a form of intervention for children. The third, body of literature concerns the predictive power of the family. There is no evidence that child care attenuates the effects of the family or disrupts the development of infant-attachment relationships with parents. The fourth, body of literature concerns the ability of child care to function as a family support, influencing parenting, job training, and self esteem. An interest in isolating child-care effects on children's development has blinded researchers to questions concerning the family-child care mesosystem. Isolating the effects of child care from the effects of family may be as nonsensical as isolating the effects of nature from nurture. Describing *how* the family matters in the child-care context offers a means of addressing neglected questions about the interconnections between the two primary contexts for the developing child.

IMPLICATIONS FOR CHILD-CARE POLICY

It is tempting to discuss the policy implications that might follow from these findings. For example, a sensible person might conclude that families with fewer economic resources need subsidies to ensure that their children have access to high-quality programs. Instead, I argue that the findings summarized here are policy-relevant, but that the policy implications are far from clear. The main reason for this is that policy is influenced by more than scientific evidence. Social scientists may give priority to data as a basis for policy but others do not (Shonkoff, 2000). Instead, policymakers view data alongside compelling testimonies from ordinary citizens, newspaper exposés, and partisan politics (McCartney & Weiss, in press). Even when policymakers embrace research findings, they need to balance multiple competing demands for funds. Research can and does inform decisions not only of policymakers, but also of ordinary citizens, including parents. Thus, research showing that children spend large amounts of time in low-quality care can be expected to factor into decisions about child care.

In the final analysis, child-care policy is dictated by cultural values. Thus, the family-child care mesosystem operates within a larger ecological context. Specifically, child-care policy influences the quality of care generally as well as a parent's ability to access quality programs for their children. In Bronfenbrenner's terminology, child-care policy functions as an exosystem, that is, a major societal institution that affects the developing child. Exosystems can be formal or informal, although policies typically constitute formal systems, documented in laws and regulations. A comparative analysis reveals the extent to which varying policies influence children's experiences within a culture.

Policies surrounding child care vary greatly across industrialized countries as a function of the degree to which child care is viewed as a public or a private responsibility. Gormley (1995, p. 1) has described child care in the United States as a "private headache, only fitfully addressed by public policies" despite the fact that reliable child care is critical to the health of the U.S. economy. This stands in stark contrast to most northern and western European countries, where policymakers and citizens have been willing to invest in their child-care systems through subsidies, regulations, and government programs and services. In fact, universal child care is available for children in many European countries, beginning at age 3 and continuing through compulsory school age (Kamerman & Kahn, 1995).

The historian, Sonya Michel (1999), offers two explanations for the U.S. child-care crisis. The first concerns the history of child care in the United States, where there has always been a divided constituency between low-income families in need of "custodial" care and middle-class families in search of "developmental" care. Policy debates about child care are typically embroiled in broader issues of public policy pertaining to the poor, including immigration, unemployment, tax equity, and welfare reform (Phillips & McCartney, in press). These links between child care and issues pertaining to the poor have hurt efforts aimed at promoting publicly supported child care.

The second explanation requires a comparative analysis of political environments. Countries like the United States and Australia emphasize free competition and tend not to commit public resources to social programs. In contrast, Scandinavian states adhere to a more social democratic philosophy, as evidenced by principles of universalism, full employment, and equality. Countries such as France, Germany, Austria, and Italy lie somewhere in the middle; they are willing to allow states to displace markets as providers of welfare, but they are not "strongly redistributive" (Kamerman & Kahn, 1995). The bottom line is that economic beliefs guide child-care policies in all cultures. Considerations of the benefits of child care for child development play, at best, a secondary role. An understanding of the cultural context must guide the study of the family-child care mesosystem.

FUTURE DIRECTIONS

Studies on the family-child care mesosystem offer the opportunity to describe more completely the child-rearing context for the developing child. With respect to selection effects, the resolution of important methodological concerns is critical. Economists have challenged whether developmental models adequately address issues of causality, while developmentalists have expressed concern about suppressing variables that cannot be suppressed in real life. Perhaps hope lies in better methods, for example longitudinal models (Duncan & Gibson, 2000) and propensity score analysis (D'Agostino, 1998). More likely, hope lies in experimental studies of child care. With respect to family moderation, here again experimental studies offer a means of identifying effects, because independent variables will not be confounded, as they tend to be in observational studies. In addition, there is a need to extend research on child care to the study of mediator variables. There is evidence that parenting styles mediate associations between maternal employment and children's academic achievement; in fact, the failure to consider parenting as a mediator accounts for some of the inconsistencies of the maternal employment literature (Beyer, 1995). Child-care researchers should take heed of this lesson. Parents' ability to cope with the demands of multiple roles may be a particularly important mediator of child care's influence (Ozer, 1995). These studies may well direct interventionists to the families most in need of support. With respect to the predictive power of the family, fewer questions remain because studies consistently show stronger family effects compared with child-care effects. Lastly, studies on child care as a form of family support should be conducted in light of cultural values. We know that parents lack information on what constitutes quality care. Evaluations of parent education programs would reveal whether knowledge contributes to family empowerment, especially among the poor, and whether informed parents would pressure child-care producers to improve their services (Gormley, 1995). Cross-cultural work is needed to inform policymakers' decisions about the benefits as well as the costs of investing in child care, not only for children and families but also for local economies.

ACKNOWLEDGMENTS

This work was supported by a grant from the National Institute of Child Health and Human Development (HD 25441). The author is grateful for feedback provided by the editors of this volume, Alison Clarke-Stewart and

Judy Dunn; by the other participants in the Jacobs Foundation conference that resulted in this volume; and by Kristen Bub, Eric Dearing, Lisa Hohmann, and Erin O'Connor.

References

Belsky, J., & Rovine, M. (1988). Nonmaternal care in the first year of life and the security of infant-parent attachment. *Child Development, 59,* 157–167.

Belsky, J., & Steinberg, L. D. (1978). The effects of daycare: A critical review. *Child Development, 49,* 929–949.

Benasich, A. A., Brooks-Gunn, J., & Clewell, B. C. (1992). How do mothers benefit from early intervention programs? *Journal of Applied Developmental Psychology, 13,* 311–362.

Beyer, S. (1995). Maternal employment and children's academic achievement: Parenting styles as mediating variable. *Developmental Review, 15,* 212–253.

Blau, D. M. (2001). *The child care problem: An economic analysis.* New York: Russell Sage Foundation.

Bolger, K. E., & Scarr, S. (1995). *Not so far from home: How family characteristics predict child care quality.* Unpublished manuscript, University of Virginia, Charlottesville.

Booth, C. L., Clarke-Stewart, K. A., Vandell, D. L., McCartney, K., & Owen, M. T. (2002). Child-Care usage and mother-infant "quality time." *Journal of Marriage and Family, 64,* 16–26.

Bowman, B. T. (1997). Preschool as family support. In C. Dunst & M. Wolery (Eds.), *Advances in Early Education and Day Care* (pp. 157–172). Greenwich, CT: JAI Press.

Broberg, A. G., Wessels, H., Lamb, M. E., & Hwang, C. P. (1997). The effects of day care on the development of cognitive abilities in eight-year olds: A longitudinal study. *Developmental Psychology, 33,* 62–69.

Bronfenbrenner, U. (1977). Towards an experimental ecology of human development. *American Psychologist, 32,* 513–531.

Bryant, D. M., Burchinal, M., Lau, L. B., & Sparling, J. J. (1994). Family and classroom correlates of Head Start children's developmental outcomes. *Early Childhood Research Quarterly, 9,* 289–309.

Bub, K. L., & McCartney, K. (2004). On child care as a support for maternal employment. *Journal of Social Issues, 60,* 819–835.

Burchinal, M. R., Peisner-Feinberg, E., Bryant, D. M., & Clifford, R. (2000). Children's social and cognitive development and child-care quality: Testing for differential associations related to poverty, gender, or ethnicity. *Applied Developmental Science, 4,* 149–165.

Caldwell, B. M., & Bradley, P. H. (1984). *Home Observation for Measurement of the Environment.* Little Rock: University of Arkansas.

Caughy, M. O., DiPietro, J. A., & Strobino, D. M. (1994). Day-care participation as a protective factor in the cognitive development of low-income children. *Child Development, 65,* 457–471.

Clarke-Stewart, K. A. (1989). Infant day care: Maligned or malignant? *American Psychologist, 44,* 266–273.

Clarke-Stewart, K. A., Gruber, C., & Fitzgerald, L. (1994). *Children at home and in day care.* Hillsdale, NJ: Erlbaum.

Collins, W. A., Maccoby, E. E., Steinberg, L., Hetherington, E. M., & Bornstein, M. H. (2000). Contemporary research on parenting: The case of nature and nurture. *American Psychologist, 55,* 218–232.

Cost, Quality, & Outcomes Team. (1995). *Cost, Quality, and Child Outcomes in Child Care Centers.* Denver CO: University of Colorado.

D'Agostino, R. B., Jr. (1998). Propensity score methods for bias reduction in the comparison of a treatment to a non-randomized control group. *Statistics in Medicine, 17,* 2265–2281.

Duncan, G., & Gibson, C. (2000). Selection and attribution in the NICHD Childcare Study's analyses of the impacts of childcare quality on child outcomes. Unpublished manuscript, Northwestern University, Evanston, IL.

Dunham, P., & Dunham, F. (1992). Lexical development during middle infancy: A mutually driven infant-caregiver process. *Developmental Psychology, 28,* 414–420.

Fuller, B., Holloway, S. D., & Liang, X. (1995). *Which families use nonparental child care and centers? The influence of family structure, ethnicity, and parental practices.* Cambridge, MA: Department of Human Development and Psychology, Harvard University.

Gable, S., & Cole, K. (2000). Parents' child care arrangements and their ecological correlates. *Early Education & Develoment, 11,* 549–572.

Garcia-Coll, C. T. (1990). Developmental outcome of minority infants: A process-oriented look into our beginnings. *Child Development, 61,* 270–289.

Gesell, A., & Thompson, H. (1934). *Infant behavior: Its genesis and growth.* New York: McGraw-Hill.

Gormley, W. T., Jr. (1995). *Everybody's children: Child care as public problem.* Washington, DC: Brookings.

Gottlieb, G., Wahlsten, D., & Lickliter, R. (1998). The significance of biology for human development: A developmental psychobiological systems view. In R. M. Lerner (Ed.), *Handbook of child psychology,* Vol. 1 (pp. 233–274). New York: Wiley.

Hagekull, B., & Bohlin, G. (1995). Day care quality, family and child characteristics and socioemotional development. *Early Childhood Research Quarterly, 10,* 505–526.

Harris, J. R. (1995). Where is the child's environment? A group socialization theory of development. *Psychological Review, 102,* 458–489.

Hofferth, S. L., & Wissoker, D. A. (1992). Price, quality, and income in child care choice. *Journal of Human Resources, 27,* 70–111.

Howes, C. (1990). Can the age of entry into child care and the quality of child care predict adjustment in kindergarten? *Developmental Psychology, 26,* 292–303.

Howes, C., & Stewart, P. (1987). Child's play with adults, toys, and peers: An examination of family and child-care influences. *Developmental Psychology, 23,* 423–430.

Kammerman, S. B., & Kahn, A. J. (1995). Innovations in toddler day care and family support services: An international overview. *Child Welfare, 74,* 1281–1300.

Kontos, S., Howes, C., Shinn, M., & Galinsky, E. (1995). *Quality in family child care and relative care.* New York: Teachers College Press.

Lamb, M. E. (1998). Nonparental child care: Context, quality, correlates, and consequences. In W. Damon (Ed.), *Handbook of child psychology: Vol 4* (pp. 73–133). New York: Wiley.

Lamb, M. E., & Sternberg, K. J. (1990). Do we really know how day care affects children? *Journal of Applied Developmental Psychology, 11*, 351–379.

Leibowitz, A., Klerman, J. A., & Waite, L. J, (1992). Employment of new mothers and child-care choice: Differences by children's age. *Journal of Human Resources, 27*, 112–133.

McCartney, K. (1984). Effect of quality of day care environment on children's language development. *Developmental Psychology, 20*, 244–260.

McCartney, K. (2003). On the meaning of models: A signal amidst the noise. In A. Booth & A. C. Crouter (Eds.), *Children's influence on family dynamics: The neglected side of family relations*. Mahwah, NJ: Erlbaum.

McCartney, K., Dearing, E., & Taylor, B. A. (2003). *Is higher-quality child care an intervention for children from low-income families?* Paper presented at the Biennial Meetings of the Society for Research in Child Development, Tampa, Florida.

McCartney, K., & Galanopoulos, A. (1988). Child care and attachment: A new frontier the second time around. *American Journal of Orthopsychiatry, 58*, 16–24.

McCartney, K., & Phillips, D. (1988). Motherhood and child care. In B. Birns & D. F. Hay (Eds.), *The different faces of motherhood: Perspectives in developmental psychology* (pp. 157–183). New York: Plenum.

McCartney, K., & Weiss, H. (in press). Data in a democracy: The evolving role of evaluation in policy and program development. In J. L. Aber, S. J. Bishop-Josef, S. M. Jones, K. T. McLearn & D. A. Phillips (Eds.). *Child development and social policy: Knowledge for action*. Washington, DC: American Psychological Association.

McCartney, K., Scarr, S., Phillips, D., Grajek, S., & Schwarz, J. C. (1982). Environmental differences among day care centers and their effects on children's development. In E. F. Zigler & E. W. Gordon (Eds.), *Day care: Scientific and social policy issues* (pp. 135–156). Boston: Auburn House.

McClelland, G. H., & Judd, C. M. (1993). Statistical difficulties of detecting interactions and moderator effects. *Psychological Review, 114*, 376–390.

Michel, S. (1999). *Children's interests/mother's rights: The shaping of America's child care policy*. New Haven, CT: Yale University Press.

Newcombe, N. S. (2003). Some controls control too much. *Child Development 74*, 1050–1052.

NICHD Early Child Care Research Network. (1996). Characteristics of infant child care: Factors contributing to positive caregiving. *Early Childhood Research Quarterly, 11*, 269–306.

NICHD Early Child Care Research Network. (1998). Relations between family predictors and child outcomes: Are they weaker for children in child care? *Developmental Psychology, 43*, 1119–1128.

NICHD Early Child Care Research Network. (2000a). The relation of child care to cognitive and language development. *Child Development, 71*, 960–980.

NICHD Early Child Care Research Network. (2000b). Characteristics and quality of child care for toddlers and preschoolers. *Applied Developmental Science, 4*, 116–135.

NICHD Early Child Care Research Network. (2001). Nonmaternal care and family factors in early development: An overview of the NICHD Study of Early Child Care. *Journal of Applied Developmental Psychology, 22*, 559–579.

NICHD Early Child Care Research Network. (2002). Early child care and children's development prior to school entry: Results from the NICHD Study of Early Child Care. *American Education Research Journal, 39*, 133–164.

NICHD Early Child Care Research Network. (2003). Does amount of time spent in child care predict socioemotional adjustment during the transition to kindergarten. *Child Development, 74*, 976–1005.

NICHD Early Child Care Research Network, & Duncan, G. (2003). Modeling the impacts of child care quality on children's preschool cognitive development. *Child Development, 74*, 1485–1506.

Ozer, E. M. (1995). The impact of childcare responsibility and self-efficacy on the psychological health of professional working mothers. *Psychology of Women Quarterly, 19*, 315–335.

Peisner-Feinberg, E. S., Burchinal, M. R., Clifford, R. M., Culkin, M. L., Howes, C., Kagan, S. L., & Yazejian, N. (2001). The relation of preschool child-care quality to children's cognitive and social developmental trajectories through second grade. *Child Development, 72*, 1534–1553.

Phillips, D. A. (Ed.). (1995). *Child care for low-income families*. Washington, DC: National Academy Press.

Phillips, D. A., Howes, C., & Whitebook, M. (1992). The social policy context of child care: Effects on quality. *American Journal of Community Psychology, 20*, 25–51.

Phillips, D., & McCartney, K. (in press). Lessons learned from the disconnect between research and policy on child care. In D. B. Pillemer & S. H. White (Eds.), *Developmental psychology and the social changes of our time*. New York: Cambridge University Press.

Phillips, D. A., Voran, M., Kisker, E., Howes, C., & Whitebook, M. (1994). Child care of children in poverty: Opportunity or inequality? *Child Development, 65*, 472–492.

Roggman, L., Langlois, J., Hubbs-Tait, L., & Rieser-Danner, L. (1994). Infant day care, attachment, and the "file drawer problem." *Child Development, 65*, 1429–1443.

Ruopp, R., Travers, J., Glantz, F., & Coelen, G. (1979). *Children at the cente.* Cambridge, MA: Abt Associates.

Rutter, M. (2002). Nature, nurture, and development: From evangelism through science toward policy and practice. *Child Development, 73*, 1–21.

Scarr, S. (1984). *Mother care, other care*. New York: Basic Books.

Scarr, S. (1985). Constructing psychology: Making facts and fables for our times. *American Psychologist, 40*, 499–512.

Shonkoff, J. P. (2000). Science, policy, and practice: Three cultures in search of a shared mission. *Child Development, 71*, 181–187.

Shonkoff, J. P., & Phillips, D. A. (Eds.). (2000). *From neurons to neighborhoods: The science of early childhood development*. Washington, DC: National Academy Press.

Singer, J. D., Fuller, B., Keiley, M. K., & Wolf, A. (1998). Early child-care selection: Variation by geographic location, maternal characteristics, and family structure. *Developmental Psychology, 34*, 1129–1144.

Sroufe, L. A. (1988). A developmental perspective on day care. *Early Childhood Research Quarterly, 3*, 283–291.

Symons, D. K., & McLeod, P. J. (1993). Maternal employment plans and outcomes after the birth of an infant in a Canadian sample. *Family Relations, 42,* 442–446.

Vandell, D. L. (2000). Parents, peer groups, and other socializing influences. *Developmental Psychology, 36,* 699–710.

Vandell, D. L., & Corasaniti, M. A. (1990). Variations in early child care: Do they predict subsequent social, emotional, and cognitive differences? *Early Childhood Research Quarterly, 5,* 555–572.

Waite, L. J., Leibowitz, A., & Witsberger, C. (1991). What parents pay for: Child-care characteristics, quality, and costs. *Journal of Social Issues, 47,* 33–48.

Weisner, T. S., & Gallimore, R. (1977). My brother's keeper: Child and sibling caretaking. *Current Anthropology, 18,* 971–975.

Weissbourd, B. (1990). Family resource and supported programs: Challenges in human services. In D. Under & D. Powell (Eds.), *Families as nurturing systems* (pp. 157–174). New York: Haworth Press.

Werner, E. E., & Smith, R. S. (1992). *Overcoming the odds.* Ithaca, NY: Cornell University Press.

PART FOUR

DISCORD AND DIVORCE

8

Marital Discord, Divorce, and Children's Well-Being

Results from a 20-Year Longitudinal Study of Two Generations

Paul R. Amato

Studies consistently show that chronic discord between parents is a risk factor for a variety of child problems, including poor emotional adjustment, low self-esteem, aggression in peer relationships, and delinquency (Davies & Cummings, 1994; Emery, 1999). In most of these studies researchers have observed children during middle childhood or adolescence. Few studies have traced the implications of marital conflict after children have reached adulthood. Several studies have shown that adults who recall frequent conflict between their parents while growing up also report a disproportionately large number of psychological and marital problems in their own lives (Adams, Bouckoms, & Streiner, 1982; Kessler & Magee, 1993; Overall, Henry, & Woodward 1974). Reliance on retrospective data, however, limits our confidence in these findings. Emotionally troubled individuals are primed to recall aversive events from childhood, including instances of conflict between parents. Because the same individuals report on events in their families of origin and their current level of well-being, common method variance is likely to inflate the magnitude of associations in these studies.

Other studies show that parental divorce is associated with problematic outcomes in adulthood. Compared with adults who grew up with two continuously married parents, adults who experienced parental divorce complete fewer years of education (Amato & Keith, 1991; McLanahan & Sandefur, 1994), have weaker ties with parents (Zill, Morrison, & Coiro, 1993), experience more conflict in their own marriages (Tallman, Gray, Kullberg, & Henderson, 1999; Ross & Mirowsky, 1999), are more likely to see their own marriages end in divorce (Bumpass, Martin & Sweet 1991; Wolfinger 1999), and report less happiness with life and more symptoms of psychological distress (Cherlin, Chase-Lansdale, & McRae, 1998; Ross & Mirowsky, 1999). Presumably, recollections of parental divorce are more reliable than are recollections of discord between parents. For this reason, it is tempting to view these findings as evidence that marital discord has long-term negative consequences for children. This conclusion would be premature, however, because not all high-discord marriages end in divorce, and not all divorces are preceded by an extended period of overt discord between parents (Amato & Booth, 1997). Prospective studies that collect information on the parents' marriage when children are growing up, as well as information on children's well-being in adulthood, are necessary to draw conclusions about the long-term effects of marital discord.

Only a handful of prospective studies on this topic are available. Caspi and Elder (1988) used longitudinal data from the Berkeley Guidance Study ($N = 182$) and found that interparental conflict was associated with an elevated number of behavior problems among children. Later, as adults, these offspring exhibited a problematic interpersonal style that affected the quality of their marriages negatively. Conger, Cui, Bryant, and Elder (2000) drew on longitudinal data from 193 families in Iowa and found that interpersonal behavior between parents in 1989 to 1992 (when offspring were young adolescents) predicted their offspring's interpersonal behavior with romantic partners in 1997 (when offspring were young adults). When parents were warm and supportive toward one another, offspring were warm and supportive toward their romantic partners; these offspring behaviors, in turn, were linked with greater relationship satisfaction among offspring and their partners. Finally, in a series of reports drawing on a panel study of two generations ($N = 691$), we found that parents' reports of marital discord (when children were growing up) predicted adult offspring's reports of psychological distress, marital discord, risk of divorce, and feelings of closeness to mothers and fathers (Amato & Booth, 1997; Amato & Booth, 2001; Amato & DeBoer, 2001; Amato & Sobolewski, 2001; Booth & Amato, 2001). Overall, existing evidence indicates that both parental divorce *and* parental discord predict a variety of problems for offspring in later adulthood.

Why should exposure to high levels of conflict between parents have negative long-term consequences for children? Several mechanisms appear to be responsible. First, observing overt conflict between parents is a direct stressor for children. Observational studies show that children react to conflict between adults with fear, anger, aggression, or the inhibition of normal behavior (Cummings, 1987). Preschool children – who tend to be egocentric – may attribute blame for marital conflict to themselves, which results in feelings of guilt and lowered self-esteem (Grych & Fincham, 1990). Conflict between parents also tends to spill over and affect the quality of parents' interactions with their children (Hetherington, 2001; Hetherington, Chapter 9 in this book). Moreover, children often are drawn into conflict between parents, resulting in further deteriorations in parent-child relationships and general family cohesiveness (Davies & Cummings, 1994). Furthermore, through modeling verbal or physical aggression, parents indirectly teach their children that disagreements are resolved through conflict rather than discussion. As a result, children may not learn the social skills (such as the ability to negotiate and reach compromises) that are necessary to form successful relationships with peers (Amato & Booth, 2001).

These explanations assume that problems experienced by adults from discordant or divorced families of origin represent continuations of problems that first appeared during childhood. It is also likely, however, that circumstances and events in early adulthood exacerbate earlier problems or create new sources of stress. Early adulthood is a critical stage in the life course – a time when people make decisions that have lasting implications, such as decisions about education, employment, marriage, and parenthood. During the last few decades, the transition to adulthood has become more complex, and youth have become increasingly reliant on their parents, not only for economic support, but also for practical assistance and guidance (Arnett, 2000; Furstenberg, 2000). Because youth from troubled families tend to have weak ties with parents, they are disadvantaged during these critical years. For example, offspring from high-conflict families tend to leave home at relatively young ages (Aquilino, 1991). An early departure from the parental home, combined with a lack of financial assistance from parents, often requires youth to find full-time employment and curtail future educational plans. Moreover, these young adults often marry or become parents at early ages – decisions that increase the risk of poor economic, marital, and psychological outcomes.

An alternative explanation refers to genetics. Certain parental traits, such as a predisposition toward antisocial behavior or an inability to establish close bonds with others, may be direct causes of marital discord and divorce, as well as child problems. The discovery that concordance (similarity between siblings) for divorce among adults is higher among monozygotic than dizygotic twins suggests that genes predispose some people to engage in behaviors that increase the risk of divorce (McGue & Lykken, 1992; Jockin, McGue, & Lykken, 1996). Consequently, some children from discordant or divorced families may exhibit psychological and interpersonal problems because they have inherited genetic traits from their (presumably troubled) parents. To the extent that parents' genetically transmitted predispositions are causes of parent and child problems, the apparent "effects" of discord and divorce on children are spurious.

Consistent with this perspective, Capaldi and Patterson (1991) found that mothers' antisocial personality traits accounted for the association between mothers' marital transitions and boys' adjustment problems. Contrary to this perspective, however, other studies have found significant effects of divorce even after controlling for relevant aspects of parents' personality, such as depression (Demo & Acock, 1996) and antisocial behavior (Simons and Associates, 1996). Several studies have shown that the associations between parental divorce and many child problems are similar for adopted and biological children (Brodzinsky, Hitt, & Smith, 1993;

O'Connor, Caspi, DeFries, & Plomin, 2000) – a finding that cannot be explained by genetic transmission. Another study based on a sample of twins (Kendler, Neale, Kessler, Heath et al., 1992) found that parental divorce predicted offspring depression in adulthood, even with genetic resemblance controlled statistically. These studies suggest that although genetic factors may predispose parents and children to exhibit emotional and behavioral problems, interparental discord and divorce bring about new conditions that exacerbate children's distress.

In this chapter, I provide new information about the links between marital discord, divorce, and children's long-term well-being. To accomplish this task, I draw on the most recent waves of longitudinal data from the Marital Instability Over the Life Course study. This chapter has three goals: (1) to estimate the effects of growing up with discordant but continuously married parents on multiple dimensions of adult well-being, (2) to compare the effects of growing up in a high-discord family with the effects of parental divorce, and (3) to determine some of the conditions under which exposure to parental discord and divorce are more (or less) problematic for children. For example, I consider whether the effects of discord and divorce vary with children's gender and age at exposure, whether the effects of discord are linear or curvilinear, and whether the effects of divorce vary with the level of pre- and post-divorce conflict between parents. I draw on these analyses to cast new light on an old question: When parents have a discordant relationship, are children better off if their parents remain together or divorce?

These data are not well suited to distinguish family environment effects from genetic effects. Despite this limitation, however, the analyses control for a variety of variables that are likely to have a genetic component, such as parents' antisocial behavior (alcohol abuse and getting in trouble with the police) and a family history of divorce prior to the marriage that produced the focal child. Although adjusting for a broad array of background characteristics does not preclude the possibility of observing spurious associations, these adjustments strengthen our confidence that the associations are the result of experiences in the family of origin rather than genetic factors.

THE MARITAL INSTABILITY STUDY

The Marital Instability Over the Life Course study began as a national sample of married individuals in the United States in 1980. The total sample consisted of 2,033 married persons (not couples) who were representative of the married population with respect to age, race, household size, home ownership, and presence of children. These individuals were interviewed again in 1983, 1988, 1992, 1997, and 2000. In 1992, 1997, and 2000, interviews were conducted with a total of 691 adult offspring (19 years of age or older) of the main respondents. In 2000, the ages of these offspring ranged from 22 to 50, with a median age of 30. The typical child was 10 years old in 1980 when the study began.[1]

Measuring Parental Divorce and Discord

Of the 691 adult offspring in the analysis, 132 (19 percent) experienced a parental divorce by the age of 22. This cutting point represents a common age at college graduation – a consideration consistent with the growing trend for young people to depend on parents for economic and social support well into the third decade of life, as noted earlier (Arnett, 2000; Furstenberg, 2000).

In 1980, 1983, 1988, and 1992, parents provided information on three aspects of marital discord: conflict, relationship problems, and divorce proneness. Marital conflict was a five-item scale that referred to arguments over the household division of labor, arguments over the children, the frequency of disagreements in general, the total number of "serious quarrels" that had occurred in the past two months, and whether spouses had ever hit, shoved or thrown objects at one another. Marital problems was a seven-item scale that referred to recurring interaction problems, including being critical, getting angry easily, being moody, having feelings that are easily hurt, being domineering, being jealous, and refusing to talk with one's spouse. Divorce proneness was a 13-item scale that assessed cognition (thinking about getting a divorce) as well as behavior (discussing the possibility of a divorce with one's spouse, friends, or family members). To provide a broad estimate of marital discord, these three scores were equally weighted and averaged within each survey year and across all four waves of data.[2]

---

[1] The target population for this study consisted of all married individuals in households in the contiguous United States in 1980 with a telephone, both spouses present, and both spouses 55 years of age or younger. Telephone interviewers used random digit dialing to select a sample of households and a second random procedure to determine whether to interview the husband or wife. The overall response rate for the study was 65 percent, and the final sample consisted of 2,033 married persons (not couples). When compared with U.S. Census data, the sample was representative with respect to age, race, household size, home ownership, and presence of children. These individuals were interviewed again in 1983, 1988, 1992, 1997, and 2000. In 1992, 1997, and 2000, we interviewed the adult offspring (19 years of age or older) of the main respondents. We obtained completed interviews with 80 percent of eligible offspring, resulting in a sample of 691 cases. In 2000, the ages of these offspring ranged from 22 to 50, with a median age of 30. (The typical child was 10 years old in 1980, when the study began.) The sample was almost evenly divided between men and women, and most offspring (92%) were White.

[2] Reliability coefficients for measures described in this section were .92 for parents' marital discord, .71 for parents' postdivorce conflict, .83 for offspring's psychological well-being, .87 for offspring's relations with mothers, .90 for offspring's relations with fathers, and .80 for offspring's marital discord.

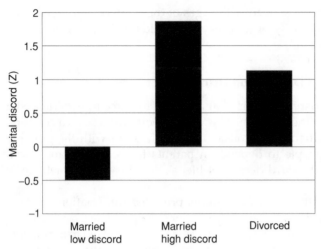

FIGURE 8.1. Mean levels of marital conflict in three types of families.

Marital discord scores for parents who divorced during the study were based on all interviews conducted prior to separation. For example, if parents separated in 1987, their discord scores were based on the 1980 and 1983 interviews. The median discord score for parents who later divorced was used to create a high-discord, non-divorced group. That is, parents who remained continuously married throughout the study but had discord scores *equal to or higher than* the median score of couples who later divorced formed the high-discord group. This group of 105 parents represented 15 percent of the total sample and 19 percent of all parents who remained continuously married.

Figure 8.1 shows the mean marital discord scores for three groups: parents who divorced during the study ($N = 132$), parents in high-discord marriages that did not end in divorce ($N = 105$), and parents in low-discord marriages that did not end in divorce ($N = 454$). Not surprisingly, the means for the high-discord and the divorced group were considerably higher than the mean for the rest of the sample. Moreover, the mean level of discord was greater in the high-discord (but continuously married) group than in the divorced group – a difference of about three-fourths of a standard deviation. This difference reflects the fact that many couples do not report a prolonged period of intense conflict prior to divorce (Amato & Booth, 1997; Hetherington, 2001).

To assess conflict between parents following divorce, adult offspring rated the frequency of parental disagreements over four topics: where children lived, the payment of child support, visitation arrangements, and how children were raised.

Measuring Offspring Well-Being

Educational attainment was coded as the total number of years of education offspring had obtained by 2000. Almost all offspring (98 percent) had completed their education by this year. Four scales measured aspects of children's *psychological well-being* in 1997: the Rosenberg (1965) self-esteem scale, the Langner (1962) scale of psychiatric distress symptoms, a 7-item scale of satisfaction with various domains of life (including job, home, friends, and neighborhood), and a single-item rating of overall happiness with life. These measures were equally weighted and averaged to form a composite measure of psychological well-being. *Perceived social support* was based on a series of questions that asked about the total number of close friends and relatives (excluding parents) with whom offspring could talk about a personal problem. The typical offspring reported about five individuals (two family members and three close friends) in their support networks. This variable was assessed in 1997. With respect to the quality of *parent-child relationships*, offspring rated their mothers and fathers on five items in 1997 dealing with understanding, respect, trust, fairness, and the overall closeness of the relationship. In 1997, 316 offspring were married, and these offspring completed the marital conflict, marital problems, and divorce proneness scales described earlier. The three scores were equally weighted and added to produce an overall measure of offspring's *marital discord*. A measure of *relationship disruptions* was based on the number of disrupted cohabiting relationships and marriages that offspring had experienced prior to the 2000 interview. The number of disrupted relationships ranged from zero to five, although only 35 percent of offspring had experienced one or more disruptions.

LINKS BETWEEN DISCORD, DIVORCE, AND OFFSPRING WELL-BEING

Table 8.1 shows the results of seven regression analyses.[3] Parental divorce was related significantly to six of the seven outcomes. Compared with children who grew up with continuously married, low-discord parents,

---

[3] To reduce the possibility of observing spurious associations, all analysis included the following control variables: parents' education, family income when growing up, parents' welfare use, parents' divorces prior to the marriage that produced the focal child, grandparents' divorces, parents' attitudes toward divorce, parents' age at marriage, parents' cohabitation prior to marriage, parents' religiosity, parents' problems with alcohol abuse, parents' problems with the law, the duration of the parents' marriage, offspring's gender, offspring's race, offspring's age, and the number of children in the household when children were growing up. Although it was not possible to control for genetic factors, some of the control variables (such as a family history of divorce, alcohol abuse, and getting into trouble with the law) are likely to have a genetic component.

TABLE 8.1. *Associations between Parental Discord, Parental Divorce, and Dimensions of Children's Well-Being in Early Adulthood*

				Children's Well-Being			
Models	Years of Education	Psychological Well-Being	Social Support	Close to Mother	Close to Father	Marital Discord	Relationship Disruptions
Parental divorce	-.28**	-.28**	-.18	-.22*	-.93***	.29*	.33**
High discord marriage	.06	-.31**	-.19*	-.14	-.27**	.24*	.07

Note: $N = 691$ children for all equations, except for marital discord ($N = 316$). Of all children, 129 experienced a parental divorce and 101 grew up with continuously married but discordant parents. Table values are unstandardized b coefficients (effect sizes). All models control for offspring gender, offspring race, offspring age, number of siblings, parents' education, parents' prior divorces, grandparents' divorces, parents' age at marriage, parents' cohabitation prior to marriage, parents' religiosity, parents' problems with alcohol use, parents' problems with the law, parents' attitudes toward lifelong marriage, and the duration of parents' marriages. Models also include a Heckman correction to adjust for panel attrition. Children's well-being variables were measured in 1997, except for years of education and relationship disruptions, which were measured in 2000.

* $p < .05$.
** $p < .01$.
*** $p < .001$.

children who experienced divorce obtained less education, reported lower psychological well-being, were less close to their mothers, were less close to their fathers, and experienced a larger number of disrupted intimate relationships. Moreover, among offspring who were married in 1997, divorce was associated with greater marital discord. Most of the effect sizes ranged from about one-fifth to one-third of a standard deviation – a range that reflects modest but nontrivial associations. The exception involved relations with fathers. The effect size for this variable was nearly one standard deviation – a large difference by any criterion.[4] Finally, the coefficient for perceived social support approached significance ($p = .06$). These results indicate that divorce predicts a broad range of negative outcomes for children in adulthood. Hetherington, (see Chapter 9 in this book) shows comparable results for parental divorce among adolescents. Walper & Beckh (see Chapter 10 in this book) show that recent family transitions, rather than being in a stable single-parent or step-parent family, appear to be especially problematic for adolescents.

Table 8.1 also indicates that children with continuously married but discordant parents experienced many of the same problems as did children with divorced parents. Compared with children with low-discord parents, children with discordant parents had a lower level of psychological well-being, reported less perceived social support, had weaker ties with fathers, and (among those who were married in 1997) reported more discord in their own marriages. Hetherington (see Chapter 9 in this book) and Walper & Beckh (see Chapter 10 in this book) also report negative effects of family conflict on adolescents. For some outcomes, such as psychological well-being, the effect sizes for divorce and discord were comparable.

Because offspring were not interviewed until 1992, sample attrition between 1980 and 1992 may have made the sample less representative of the population, thus compromising the generalizability of findings. To address this issue, I relied on Heckman's (1979) method to correct for attrition bias. This procedure involved constructing a probit regression equation to model the attrition of parents from the panel. Based on the significant predictors, I calculated *lambda* to reflect the probability of dropping out of the panel. This variable also served as a control in all analyses.

Information on some variables was missing – a common problem in survey research. The usual method of dealing with missing data (casewise deletion) tends to bias parameter estimates. To deal with missing data, I imputed values for all variables using the expectation maximization (EM) algorithm (Allison, 2001). This procedure has been shown to generate accurate maximum likelihood estimates with up to 50 percent missing data.

[4] To facilitate the interpretation of results, I standardized each of the dependent variables to have a mean of zero and a standard deviation of one. Because parental discord and divorce were represented as dichotomous variables in the analysis, the unstandardized *b* coefficients reflect the mean differences between these two groups and the omitted comparison group (offspring with continuously married, low-discord parents). For this reason, the *b* coefficients can be interpreted as effect sizes, that is, standardized mean differences between groups, adjusted for all control variables.

For relations with fathers, however, the effect size for divorce was substantially larger than the effect size for discord. Moreover, discord was not related to as many outcomes as was divorce. For example, offspring with unhappily married parents did not appear to differ from offspring with happily married parents in terms of educational attainment or relationship disruptions.

Further comparisons revealed that children with divorced parents had significantly poorer relationships with fathers than did children with discordant but nondivorced parents ($p < .01$). Similarly, children with divorced parents were marginally lower in educational attainment ($p < .10$) and marginally higher in relationship disruptions ($p < .1$). In general, these results suggest that parental divorce *and* growing up with discordant parents increase the risk of a variety of problems in adulthood. The estimated effects of parental discord, however, do not appear to be as strong or as pervasive as the effects of divorce.

Gender Differences

To assess gender differences in the estimated effects of parental discord and divorce, I added multiplicative terms to the models in Table 8.1. These analyses revealed two significant interactions. First, the estimated effect of parental divorce on the father-child relationship was stronger for daughters than for sons ($p < .001$). Second, the estimated effect of parental discord on the number of relationship disruptions was stronger for daughters than for sons ($p < .05$).

Figure 8.2 shows the means of these variables for sons and daughters, adjusted for all of the control variables. Parental divorce appeared to lower the quality of father-child relationships for children of both genders, but the decline was twice as large for daughters: 0.65 of a standard deviation for sons versus 1.36 of a standard deviation for daughters. As a result, although sons and daughters were equally close to their fathers in nondivorced families, daughters were less close to their fathers than were sons in divorced families. This finding is consistent with research showing that the father-daughter relationship is more vulnerable than the father-son relationship, in general, and with research showing that nonresident fathers are more likely to maintain contact with sons than with daughters (Hetherington, 1993; Manning & Smock, 1999).

Figure 8.2 also shows that the estimated effect of parental discord on children's relationship disruptions was stronger for daughters than for sons. In fact, parental discord appeared to increase relationship disruptions among daughters only, with the increase representing about one-third of a standard deviation. Prior research has shown that women are more likely than men to monitor the status of their intimate relationships (Thompson & Walker, 1989), attempt to repair relationship problems (Gottman, 1994),

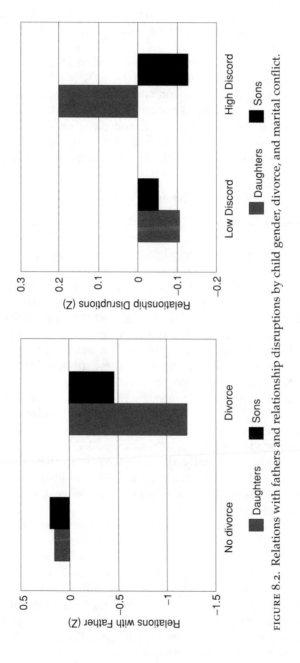

FIGURE 8.2. Relations with fathers and relationship disruptions by child gender, divorce, and marital conflict.

and leave relationships that are unsatisfying (Kitson, 1992). If children from discordant families reach adulthood with fewer relationship skills or with a weak commitment to marriage, then it is not surprising that the long-term consequences of parental discord for relationship stability are stronger for daughters than for sons.

Although these findings are plausible, readers should note that out of 14 interaction terms involving gender (parental divorce × seven outcomes plus parental discord × seven outcomes), only two attained significance. In general, most of the long-term consequences of parental discord and divorce appear to be similar for sons and daughters. Hetherington (see Chapter 9 in this book) and Walper & Beckh (see Chapter 10 in this book) also note the general absence of child gender × family type interactions.

Age at Time of Divorce and Exposure to Parental Discord

As noted earlier, the ages of children at the time of parental divorce ranged from the first year of life to age 22. To determine whether age at the time of divorce was related to well-being in adulthood, I limited the analysis to the 132 children who experienced a parental divorce. This analysis revealed that age at the time of divorce was related to three outcomes: educational attainment, perceived social support, and relations with fathers.

Figure 8.3 shows these results. To construct the figure, I divided age at divorce into four categories: the preschool years (0–4), childhood (5–11), adolescence (12–18), and early adulthood (19–22), with the bars in the figure representing the adjusted means for these groups. The figure reveals that children's educational attainment was relatively low (about half of a standard deviation below the mean) when divorce occurred during the preschool or elementary school years. In contrast, children's educational attainment was close to the mean for the overall sample when divorced occurred during adolescence or early adulthood. Presumably, divorces that occur when children are relatively young have the greatest potential to disrupt children's early educational progress. At an older age, when children already have established themselves as strong or weak students, divorce appears to be less disruptive.

The association between age at divorce and father-child relations was approximately linear. When divorce occurred during the preschool years, children's relationships with fathers were especially weak. But when divorce occurred during the early adult years, father-child relations were only modestly impacted. Presumably, it is difficult for fathers and children to form close emotional bonds when they are physically separated early in children's lives. (In this sample, 85 percent of children were in sole mother custody following divorce.) But if separation occurs when children are older, then children and fathers have spent more time living together – time when close emotional bonds can be formed and solidified.

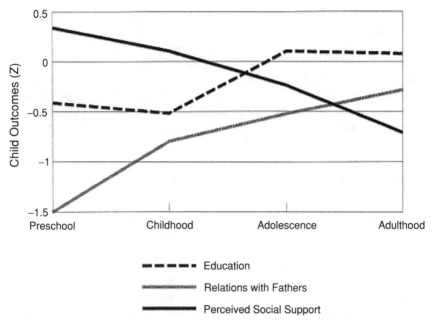

FIGURE 8.3. Children's education, relations with fathers, and perceived social support by age at time of divorce.

The opposite trend appeared for perceived social support, with the estimated effect of parental divorce appearing to be strongest in early adulthood. These results suggest that more recent divorces are especially corrosive for young adults' social ties. During late adolescence and the early adult years, youth develop their identities, clarify their values, become self-reliant, and form plans for the future. Dealing with a parental divorce at this point in the life course may interfere with young people's progress toward independence and lead them to focus on their parents' problems rather than their own social development. Preoccupation with parental divorce may lead youth to become less involved with friends and romantic partners. Similarly, offspring who feel estranged from one parent may become less close to that parents' kin, resulting in further restrictions in social networks. Irrespective of the explanation, the findings shown in Figure 8.3 do not lead to a simple conclusion that parental divorce is more or less difficult for children at particular ages. Young children from divorced families may do less well in school and develop weaker ties to their fathers but develop normal social support networks in later life. Older children, in contrast, may do well in school and retain ties with their fathers but experience disruptions in other social bonds.

I also attempted to see if age at the time of exposure to marital discord was related to children's long-term well-being. Exposure to parental discord at any age appeared to weaken children's ties with fathers and to lower children's psychological well-being. Exposure to parental discord during the preschool and elementary school years appeared to be most detrimental to children's perceived social support, whereas exposure to parental discord during childhood and adolescence (but not during the preschool years or adulthood) appeared to increase offspring's marital discord. In general, these results suggest no period during which children are immune to (or especially vulnerable to) the negative effects of interparental conflict.

Are the Estimate Effects of Marital Discord Linear?

The analysis in Table 8.1 was based on a dichotomous indicator of discord – a procedure that made it possible to compare children with divorced parents to children with discordant but continuously married parents. This procedure raises the question, however, of whether marital conflict has a continuous, linear association with children's well-being or whether this association takes a nonlinear form. It may be, for example, that marital conflict involves a threshold effect, with exposure having relatively few implications for children until a critical level is reached. Alternatively, a ceiling may exist, with conflict being related to child outcomes to a certain point, but with higher levels of conflict having no further implications. To assess these possibilities, I restricted the analysis to children raised with married parents and used the continuous version of the parental discord variable. To show how discord was related to children's outcomes, I calculated the best fitting lines through scatterplots of discord and the child outcome variables.[5]

Figure 8.4 shows the results for marital discord and the quality of children's relationships with mothers and fathers. (The continuous discord variable was significantly related to mother-child relations, although the dichotomous version of this variable in Table 8.1 was not.) In both cases, the associations were approximately linear, with increases in conflict being related to declines in parent-child relationships throughout the full range of the conflict scale.

Figure 8.4 also reveals that the association between parents' marital discord and children's psychological well-being also was approximately linear, with greater levels of discord being associated with lower levels of well-being. The one exception to this pattern involved offspring's marital discord. Among married offspring, parents' marital discord was positively associated with children's marital discord, but only up to the mean

---

[5] I relied on locally weighted polynomial regression – also knows as Lowess modeling (Mutulsky & Christopoulos, 2003). This technique uses regression methods to fit a line through the points in a scatterplot, based on a shifting 50 percent sample of cases. The resulting line (which can be any shape) provides the best fit to the data.

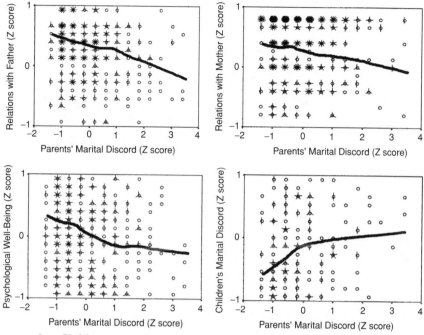

FIGURE 8.4. Child outcomes by level of marital conflict.

of the scale. After this point, increases in parents' marital discord appeared to have only minor implications for the quality of offspring's marriages. (A statistical test revealed that the deviation from linearity was significant at $p < .05$). These results suggest that children benefit from growing up with parents who have harmonious marriages, perhaps because these parents have especially positive relationship skills. The difference between growing up with parents with average levels of conflict and parents with high levels of conflict appeared to be minimal. This result suggests that marital quality may be transmitted across generations, not so much because children with discordant parents learn negative interpersonal behaviors, but because children with harmonious parents learn skills for resolving disagreements amicably.

Patterns of Parental Discord Over Time

Although some parents have chronically discordant marriages and other parents have generally harmonious marriages, other patterns also occur. For example, some parents report relatively low levels of discord early in their marriages but show increases in discord over time. Other parents report high levels of discord early in their marriages but show declines

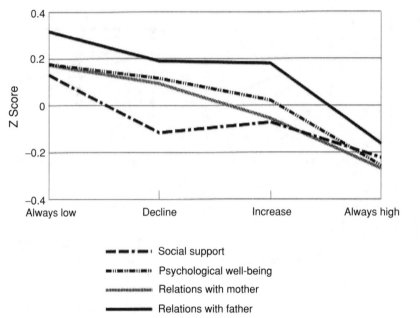

FIGURE 8.5. Child outcomes by pattern of marital conflict.

in discord over time. To capture these different patterns, I relied on the k-means clustering algorithm – one of the most commonly used clustering techniques (Bailey, 1994). A cluster analysis of the 1980, 1983, 1988, and 1992 discord scores revealed four underlying clusters: parents who reported decreasing level of discord between 1980 and 1992 ($n = 118$), parents who reported increasing levels of discord ($n = 117$), parents who reported a consistently high level of discord throughout this period ($n = 57$), and parents who reported a consistently low level of discord ($n = 267$).[6]

I then used membership in these four groups to predict children's well-being in 1997. This analysis revealed that the four discord categories were related significantly ($p < .05$) to four offspring outcomes: psychological well-being, perceived social support, relations with mothers, and relations with fathers. The means for families that fell into these four groups (adjusted for all control variables) appear in Figure 8.5.

Figure 8.5 reveals that all four outcomes were related to parental discord in a similar fashion. Children raised with consistently discordant parents had the lowest mean scores on all four outcomes, whereas children raised with consistently harmonious parents had the highest mean scores on all

---

[6] In a cluster analysis, some cases fit into the resulting categories better than others. To deal with this problem, I weighted the sample by the distance of each case from the cluster center, with cases that fit well into one category receiving a higher weight than cases that did not fit well into any category.

four outcomes. In general, there were few differences between children who experienced increases in parental discord and children who experienced declines in parental discord. Offspring in these two groups had moderate levels of well-being on each outcome. These results suggest that it is the cumulative exposure to parental discord that disadvantages children. Offspring exposed to high levels of discord for only part of their childhoods (irrespective of whether it was early or late) were better off than offspring exposed to chronic discord and worse off than offspring exposed to little discord. These results are consistent with the conclusion, noted earlier, that age at exposure to discord has few implications for children's long-term well-being.

Conflict Before and After Parental Divorce

Another factor relevant to children's long-term adjustment is the level of conflict between parents prior to and following marital dissolution. Given that discord and divorce both appear to affect children negatively, one might assume that the worse possible scenario involves a high level of conflict followed by divorce. Contrary to this assumption, however, earlier reports using these data suggested that parental divorce is especially detrimental to children when it is preceded by a *low* level of marital discord (Amato, Loomis, & Booth, 1995; Amato & Booth, 1997; Booth & Amato, 2001). Although counter-intuitive at first glance, two other studies have replicated this finding using different data sets (Hanson, 1999; Jekielek, 1998).

Although many people believe that most divorces are preceded by a prolonged period of conflict, this pattern does not occur for most couples. Instead, the Marital Instability data indicate that divorce is usually preceded by a period of mutual disengagement, with little positive affect – but little overt hostility – between parents. Hetherington (2001) reported comparable findings from her longitudinal data. Under these circumstances, parental separation comes as an unwelcome surprise to most children. Moreover, parental separation often leads to a series of stressful transitions (moving, declines in standard of living, losing touch with fathers, and parental remarriage) with few compensating benefits for children. In contrast, when divorce is preceded by a long-term pattern of fighting and yelling (and perhaps violence), parental separation comes as a relief to many children.

To illustrate this pattern, I included an interaction term between marital discord and divorce in the regression equations. As noted earlier, marital discord was based on interviews conducted before separation in cases of marital dissolution. These interactions were significant for three outcomes: psychological well-being ($p < .01$), relationship disruptions ($p < .01$), and marital discord ($p < .05$).

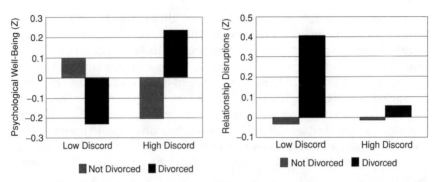

FIGURE 8.6. Children's psychological well-being and relationship disruptions by marital discord and divorce.

Figure 8.6 illustrates this pattern. This figure shows that children with continuously married and discordant parents were about one-third of a standard deviation lower than children with continuously married and harmonious parents ($p < .05$). In contrast, when marriages ended in dissolution, children's psychological well-being was lower (nearly half of a standard deviation) when separation was preceded by a low rather than a high level of discord ($p < .05$). Although children with discordant parents who later divorced appeared to have the highest level of well-being, the mean for children in this group did not differ significantly from the mean for children with continuously married, low-discord parents. Similarly, Figure 8.6 indicates that parental divorce appeared to increase the risk of relationship dissolutions among children only when it was preceded by a relatively low level of discord. In this analysis, the mean for children in the low-discord divorced group was significantly higher than the means for the other three groups (all $p < .05$). Although not shown in the figure, the results for offspring's marital conflict was similar to the pattern shown in Figure 8.6.

I also considered the role of post-divorce conflict between parents. This variable, however, was unrelated to any measure of offspring well-being. This result seems surprising, given that several studies have shown that post-divorce conflict is a good predictor of children's adjustment (e.g., Guidubaldi, Cleminshaw, Perry, Nastasi, & Lightel, 1986; Johnston, Kline, & Tschann, 1989). In the present study, however, the length of time since divorce was considerable. Although discord between parents following divorce may be stressful for children, communication between parents tends to decline after a few years (Kitson, 1992). Indeed, most parents in the present study had little or no contact once post-divorce routines were established. Given that post-divorce conflict between parents had ended for virtually all offspring in the present study, it is not surprising that this variable had few lingering consequences. Incidentally, the correlation between pre-divorce conflict and post-divorce conflict was not significant – a finding that suggests little continuity in the social environments of children with divorced parents. (Hetherington, 2001, also comments on this point.)

CONCLUSIONS

Documenting the long-term consequences of parental discord and divorce for adult offspring requires the use of prospective, longitudinal data. In the analyses described in this chapter, information on marital discord and divorce (and the control variables) came from interviews with parents in 1980, 1983, 1988, and 1992. Correspondingly, information on child outcomes came from interviews with offspring in 1997 and 2000. This procedure ensured that variables were measured in the correct temporal order, and that different sources of information were used for independent and dependent variables.

In a study of this nature, the greatest threat to internal validity is the inability to control for factors that may be causes of marital discord as well as children's later well-being. These factors include economic factors, with low parental income increasing the risk of divorce as well as problematic outcomes (such as low educational attainment) among children. Similarly, parents with particular personality traits (such as a tendency to exhibit antisocial behavior or an inability to bond with others) may divorce and also pass this trait to their children, either through inept parenting or genetic transmission. It is not possible to control for all possible confounding variables with survey data. Nevertheless, the current study controlled for a broad range of factors that captured not only parents' socioeconomic status (parents' education, income, and use of public assistance), but also traits that may reflect difficulties in forming stable relationships (parents' prior divorces, grandparents' divorces, antisocial behavior).

The analyses in this paper lead to several conclusions. First, growing up with chronically discordant parents appears to increase the risk of multiple problems for children in adulthood, including low psychological well-being, restricted social support networks, weak ties with fathers, and discord in children's own marriages. Most of these associations are modest rather than large, ranging from one-fifth to one-third of a standard deviation. Readers should keep in mind, however, that the typical child was only 10 years old in 1980 (the first year of data collection) and 30 years old in 2000 (the last year of data collection). Given the length of time involved between measurements, the existence of any significant associations is striking.

Second, divorce, like marital discord, is associated with multiple problematic outcomes among adult offspring. Of the two childhood risk factors, parental divorce is associated with a broader range of child problems. For example, although divorce appears to reduce children's educational attainment, discord has no comparable effect. Moreover, the estimated effect of divorce on the father-child relationship is considerably stronger than the estimated effect of marital discord (nearly one standard deviation versus one-quarter of a standard deviation).

Additional analyses revealed few gender differences in the estimated effects of discord and divorce, although two findings suggest that daughters are more vulnerable than sons. With respect to age, divorce appears to be especially detrimental to children's educational attainment and relationships with fathers when it occurs early in childhood, although no comparable effects appear for exposure to discord. Finally, divorce and marital discord appear to interact, with the estimated effect of divorce being more detrimental when it is preceded by a low – rather than a high – level of discord.

Implications for Interventions and Policy

Do these findings have implications for whether parents should be counseled to "stay together for the sake of their children"? On the one hand, if the choice for parents is between divorcing and remaining in a high-conflict marriage (assuming no possibility that the marriage can be improved through therapy or counseling), then it may be preferable to end the marriage. Growing up with chronically discordant parents predicts a number of long-term problems for children. Divorce, in these cases, may ameliorate some of these negative effects, presumably by removing children from dysfunctional, conflict-ridden households. In the present study, among offspring with chronically discordant parents, those who experienced a parental divorce had better psychological well-being, experienced fewer relationship disruptions, and reported more harmonious marriages than did those whose parents remained together. This result is consistent with the finding that children with continuously married parents were better off, in general, if the level of discord declined between 1980 and 1992. In general, these results suggest that attempts to restrict couples' access to no-fault divorce are likely to harm children trapped in homes with mutually hostile, and perhaps violent, parents.

On the other hand, divorce is a high-risk strategy. Irrespective of the level of discord prior to dissolution, divorce still appears to lower children's educational attainment, particularly if it occurs when children are young. (Recall that discord between parents was not related to children's educational attainment.) Similarly, the estimated effects of divorce on the father-child relationship are considerably stronger than the estimated effects of marital discord (especially for daughters). Consequently, even in high-discord homes, divorce is a mixed blessing. Although it lowers children's exposure to overt conflict, it also exposes children to new risk factors.

The best choice for parents contemplating divorce might be to postpone separation until children are older adolescents – a time when children's educational trajectories and relationships with fathers are less vulnerable to the stress of family disruption.

The case is clearer for parents in low-discord marriages who are contemplating divorce. Living in a marriage marked by mutual disengagement is a less-than-satisfying experience for parents. But for most children, this arrangement is satisfactory. In these families, children have ready access to both parents, a standard of living based on both parents' income, and a predictable and stable home environment. Divorce in these cases appears to increase the risk of a number of problems for offspring in adulthood, including an elevated level of psychological distress, a high level of marital discord, and a history of disrupted intimate relationships. In addition, these children (like all children of divorce) are at risk of educational problems and having weak ties with parents, although waiting until children are older may lessen these risks somewhat.

Overall, if parents in disengaged marriages wish to minimize the risks to their children, then their best option is to attempt to strengthen their relationships through counseling or therapy. Consequently, any policies that increase people's access to these services are likely to be in children's best interests. Alternatively, disengaged parents can be encouraged to choose a "wait and see" approach. Many marriages go through difficult times, and these periods can last for years. But among marriages that do not end in divorce, many eventually improve again. Although some people may view this option as a long-shot, it is a choice consistent with the promise that couples made to each other on the day they married.

Future Research Needs

Although we have learned a great deal about marital conflict, divorce, and children's well-being during the last three decades, there is still much that we do not understand. First, although there are strong reasons for believing the marital conflict and divorce have negative effects on children, additional research with genetically informed designs is necessary to determine whether these linkages are (at least partly) genetically mediated. Second, most of the research in this field has involved either relatively small samples of white middle-class offspring, or large probability samples that reflect the general population. Because few studies have focused specifically on families of color or low-income families, the extent to which the effects of marital conflict and divorce on children vary across subpopulations is unknown. Third, research has shown that some interventions to facilitate children's adjustment to divorce are promising, especially school-based programs that emphasize social support from peers and the use of active coping strategies (see Emery, 1999, for a review). Nevertheless, additional evaluation research that delineates the usefulness of specific interventions for children would be of great practical value. Finally, this research literature leads to a fundamental, but as yet unanswered, question: If marital conflict and divorce increase the risk of a variety of problems for children, then is it possible to implement policies that improve the quality and stability of marriage in the population? Currently in the United States, many state governments are experimenting with policies to strengthen marriage, such as Oklahoma, which provides free premarital education to individuals planning to marry (Ooms, Bouchet, & Parke, 2004). Although it is not yet known whether these programs can improve the quality of marriage or lower the rate of divorce in the general population, the U.S. federal government has recently funded large-scale evaluations of these programs. In time, we may know if it is possible for large-scale interventions to lower the general level of marital discord, decrease the risk of divorce, and, in the process, improve children's long-term well-being.

References

Adams, K. S., Bouckoms, A., & Streiner, D. (1982). Parental loss and family stability in attempted suicide. *Archives of General Psychiatry, 39*, 1081–1085.

Allison, P. D.(2001). Missing data. Thousand Oaks, CA: Sage.

Amato, P. R., & Booth, A.(1997). *A generation at risk: Growing up in an era of family upheaval*. Cambridge, MA: Harvard University Press.

Amato, P. R., & Booth, A. (2001). The legacy of marital discord: Consequences for children's marital quality. *Journal of Personality and Social Psychology, 81*, 627–638.

Amato, P. R., & DeBoer, D. (2001). The transmission of divorce across generations: Relationship skills or commitment to marriage? *Journal of Marriage and Family, 63*, 1038–1051.

Amato, P. R., & Keith, B. (1991). Separation from a parent during childhood and adult socioeconomic attainment. *Social Forces, 70*, 187–206.

Amato, P. R., Loomis, L. S., & Booth, A. (1995). Parental divorce, marital conflict, and offspring well-being in early adulthood." *Social Forces, 73*, 895–916.

Amato, P. R., & Sobolewski, J. M. (2001). The effects of divorce and marital discord on adult children's psychological well-being. *American Sociological Review, 66*, 900–921.

Aquilino, W. S.(1991). Family structure and home-leaving: A further specification of the relationship. *Journal of Marriage and the Family, 53*, 999–1010.

Arnett, J. 2000. Emerging adulthood: A theory of development from the late teens through the twenties. *American Psychologist, 55*, 469–480.

Bailey, K. D.(1994). *Typologies and taxonomies: An introduction to classification techniques*. Thousand Oaks, CA: Sage.

Booth, A., & Amato, P. R. (2001). Parental predivorce relations and offspring postdivorce well-being. *Journal of Marriage and the Family, 63*, 197–212.

Brodzinsky, D., Hitt, J. C., & Smith, D. (1993). Impact of parental separation and divorce on adopted and nonadopted children. *American Journal of Orthopsychiatry, 63*, 451–461.

Bumpass, L. L., Martin, T. C., & Sweet, J. A. (1991). The impact of family background and early marital factors on marital disruption. *Journal of Family Issues, 12,* 22–42.

Capaldi, D. M., & Patterson, G. R. (1991). The relation of parental transitions to boys' adjustment problems: I. A linear hypothesis, and II. Mothers at risk for transitions and unskilled parenting. *Developmental Psychology, 27,* 489–504.

Caspi, A., & Elder, G. H. Jr. (1988). Emergent family patterns: The intergenerational construction of problem behavior and relationships. In R. A. Hinde & J. Stevenson-Hinde (Eds.), *Relationships within families* (pp. 218–240). New York: Oxford University Press.

Cherlin, A., Chase-Lansdale, J. P. L., & McRae, C. (1998). Effects of divorce on mental health throughout the life course. *American Sociological Review, 63,* 239–49.

Conger, R. D., Cui, M., Bryant, C. M., & Elder, G. H. Jr. (2000). Competence in early adult romantic relationships: A developmental perspective on family influences. *Journal of Personality and Social Psychology, 79,* 224–237.

Cummings, E. M.(1987). Coping with background anger in early childhood. *Child Development, 58,* 976–984.

Davies, P. T., & Cummings, E. M. (1994). Marital conflict and child adjustment: An emotional security hypothesis. *Psychological Bulletin, 116,* 387–411.

Demo, D. H., & Acock, A. C. (1996) Family structure, family process, and adolescent well-being. *Journal of Research on Adolescence, 6,* 457–488.

Emery, R. E.(1999). *Marriage, divorce, and children's adjustment.* (2nd ed). Beverly Hills, CA: Sage.

Furstenberg, F. F.(2000). The sociology of adolescents and youth in the 1990s: A critical commentary. *Journal of Marriage and the Family, 62,* 896–910.

Gottman, J. M.(1994). What predicts divorce? Hillsdale, NJ: Lawrence Erlbaum.

Grych, J. H., & Fincham, F. D. (1990). Marital conflict and children's adjustment: A cognitive-contextual framework. *Psychological Bulletin, 108,* 267–290.

Guidubaldi, J., Cleminshaw, H. K., Perry, J. D., Nastasi, B. K., & Lightel, J. (1986). The role of selected family environment factors in children's post-divorce adjustment. *Family Relations, 35,* 141–151.

Hanson, T. L.(1999). Does parental conflict explain why divorce is negatively associated with child welfare? *Social Forces, 77,* 1283–1316.

Heckman, J. J.(1979). Sample selection bias as a specification error. *Econometrics, 47,* 153–161.

Hetherington, E. M.(1993). An overview of the Virginia Longitudinal Study of Divorce and Remarriage with a focus on early adolescence. *Journal of Family Psychology, 7,* 39–56.

Hetherington, E. M. (2001). *Intimate pathways: Changing patterns in close personal relationships across time.* Paper presented at the annual meeting of the National Council on Family Relations, Rochester, New York.

Jekielek, S. M.(1998). Parental conflict, marital disruption and children's emotional well-being. *Social Forces, 76,* 905–935.

Jockin, V., McGue, M., & Lykken, D. T. (1996). Personality and divorce: A genetic analysis. *Journal of Personality and Social Psychology, 71,* 288–299.

Johnston, J. R., Kline, M., & Tschann, J. M. (1989). Ongoing postdivorce conflict: Effects on children of joint custody and frequent access. *American Journal of Orthopsychiatry, 59,* 576–592.

Kendler, K. S., Neale, M. C., Kessler, R. C., Heath, A. C., & Eaves, L. J. (1992). Childhood parental loss and adult psychopathology in women. *Archives of General Psychiatry, 49*, 109–116.

Kessler, R. C., & Magee, W. J. (1993). "Childhood adversities and adult depression: Basic patterns of association in a U.S. national sample." *Psychological Medicine, 23*, 679–90.

Kitson, G. C.(1992). *Portrait of divorce: Adjustment to marital breakdown.* New York: Guilford Press.

Langner, T. S.(1962). A twenty-two item screening score of psychiatric symptoms indicating impairment. *Journal of Health and Human Behavior, 3*, 269–76.

Manning, W. D., & Smock, P. J. (1999). New families and nonresident father-child visitation. *Social Forces, 78*, 87–116.

McGue, M., & Lykken, D. T. (1992). Genetic influence on risk of divorce. *Psychological Science, 3*, 368–373.

McLanahan, S., & Sandefur, G.(1994). *Growing up in a single-parent family: What helps, what hurts.* Cambridge, MA: Harvard University Press.

Mutulsky, H., & Christopoulos, A.(2003). *Fitting models to biological data using linear and nonlinear regression.* San Diego, CA: Graphpad Software.

O'Connor, T. G., Caspi, A., DeFries, J. C., & Plomin, R. (2000). Are associations between parental divorce and children's adjustment genetically mediated? An adoption study. *Developmental Psychology, 36*, 429–437.

Ooms, T., Bouchet, S., & Parke, M.(2004). *Beyond marriage licenses: Efforts in states to strengthen marriage and two-parent families.* Washington, DC: Center for Law and Social Policy.

Overall, J. E., Henry, B. W., & Woodward, A. (1974). Dependence of marital problems on parental family history. *Journal of Abnormal Psychology, 83*, 446–50.

Rosenberg, M.(1965). *Society and adolescent self-image.* Princeton, NJ: Princeton University Press.

Ross, C. E., & Mirowsky, J (1999). Parental divorce, life-course disruption, and adult depression. *Journal of Marriage and the Family, 61*, 1034–45.

Simons, R. L. and Associates. (1996). *Understanding differences between divorced and intact families.* Thousand Oaks, CA: Sage.

Tallman, I., Gray, L. N., Kullberg, V., & Henderson, D. (1999). The intergenerational transmission of marital conflict: Testing a process model. *Social Psychology Quarterly, 62*, 219–239.

Thompson, L., & Walker, A. J. (1989). Gender in families: Women and men in marriage, work, and parenthood. *Journal of Marriage and the Family, 51*, 845–871.

Wolfinger, N. H.(1999). Trends in the intergenerational transmission of divorce. *Demography, 33*, 415–420.

Zill, N., Morrison, D. R., & Coiro, M. J. (1993). Long-term effects of parental divorce on parent-child relationships, adjustment, and achievement in young adulthood. *Journal of Family Psychology, 7*, 91–103.

9

The Influence of Conflict, Marital Problem Solving and Parenting on Children's Adjustment in Nondivorced, Divorced and Remarried Families

E. Mavis Hetherington

In this chapter, I examine how marital conflict, divorce, and remarriage affect parenting, parent-child and sibling relationships, and the adjustment of children as they move from early to mid-adolescence.

The association between marital and family discord, marital transitions and child adjustment is well established. Children and adolescents living in contentious homes or divorced or remarried families in comparison with those in harmonious nondivorced families are higher in externalizing behavior problems (antisocial behavior, aggression, noncompliance) and internalizing behavior problems (inhibited, withdrawn behavior, anxiety, depression) and lower in social responsibility, self-esteem, and social and cognitive competence (see Amato, 2001; Amato & Keith, 1991a; Cummings, Goeke-Morey, & Rapp, 2001; Hetherington, Bridges, & Insabella, 1998; Hetherington & Stanley-Hagan, 2000; 2002; McLanahan, 1999, for reviews).

Although conduct disorders decline in young adulthood, substance abuse, alcoholism and troubles with the law remain higher in youths from conflicted, divorced and remarried families. Youths who have experienced their parent's marital transitions also are more likely to be single parents, to experience lower socioeconomic and educational attainment and to be on welfare. In addition, they have more problems with family members, in intimate relations, in marriage and in the workplace. Their divorce rate is higher and their reports of general well-being and life satisfaction are lower (Amato, 1999; 2001; see Chapter 8, in this book); Amato & Booth, 1996; Amato & Keith, 1991b; Hetherington, 1999a; 2003; Hetherington & Kelly, 2002).

It is not surprising then that most researchers have pathogenic models of conflict, divorce and remarriage focusing on stresses and problems in the adjustment of children. However, although disagreements and conflict in families are inevitable they do not inevitably lead to adverse outcomes. Some conflicts have no negative effects or have positive effects on child development (Cummings et al., 2001). Conflicts that involve hostility, contempt, coercion, abuse and withdrawal, that are unresolved, or that are accompanied by strong negative emotions are more destructive. Those that are about the child, that make the child feel caught in the middle, or that are seen by the child as a threat to the stability of the family are more likely to undermine the child's emotional security. In contrast, disagreements and conflicts that are accompanied by mutual respect, positive or emotionally regulated affect, explanations, information seeking, compromise and problem resolution may be constructive.

Children may learn to be competent effective problem solvers by being exposed to socially skilled role models. In addition, an almost completely stress- or conflict-free environment may not prepare children to deal with conflicts they are likely to encounter outside of the family with peers, in romantic relationships, and in the workplace. There is some evidence that children, under moderate levels of stress, with a close supportive relationship with a parent, may be strengthened and exhibit a "steeling" effect (Rutter, 1987). They become stronger and are better able to adapt to future stresses than children who have experienced little stress or those who have been exposed to very high stress with little social support or few personal resources (Hetherington, 1991a).

Marital transitions may bring marked positive and negative life changes; both new challenges and new opportunities occur. Although divorce leads to an increase in stressful life events, such as poverty, psychological and health problems in parents, and inept parenting, it also may be associated with escape from conflict, the building of new more harmonious fulfilling relationships, and the opportunity for personal growth and individuation (Hetherington & Kelly, 2002).

Similarly, remarriage is associated with potential risks and benefits. Both an increase in negative and positive life events occur following a remarriage (Anderson, Greene, Hetherington, & Clingempeel, 1999; Bray, 1999; Hetherington, & Clingempeel, 1992; Hetherington, Henderson, & Reiss, 1999; O'Connor, Hetherington, & Reiss, 1998).

Remarriage is the fastest route out of poverty for divorced women and their children, and a remarriage offers the possibility not only of economic but also of emotional and childrearing support from a stepparent. However, the adjustment of children in divorced single parent families and in stepfamilies is remarkably similar (Anderson et al., 1999; Cherlin & Furstenberg, 1994; Hetherington & Clingempeel, 1992; Hetherington & Stanley-Hagan, 2000; 2003; O'Connor, Dunn, Jenkins, Pickering, & Rasbash, 2001). It has been argued that the effects of the stresses associated with marital break up and life in a single parent family may be persistent and difficult to reverse or that new stresses in a stepfamily may counter benefits for children that may accrue to a remarriage. Certainly unique challenges arise in stepfamilies as parents try to build a marital relationship in the presence of children and develop constructive relationships between biological parents, stepparents and children, between step siblings and between residential and nonresidential family members. Papernow (1984, p. 360) commented that the typical starting point for the remarried couple would be considered risky in any family – "a weak couple subsystem, a tightly bonded parent-child alliance, and potential interference in family functioning from an outsider."

THE SPILLOVER HYPOTHESIS

The marital relationship often is viewed as the cornerstone of family functioning. When it is weak it erodes the functioning of the entire family system. To explain the association between marital conflict, parenting, and adjustment problems in children, family researchers have proposed a "spillover" model (see Figure 9.1). Destructive conflict in the couple relationship spills over and undermines the quality of parenting, which in turn erodes parent child and sibling relationships and child adjustment (Buchanan & Waezenhofer, 2001; Cummings et al., 2001; Cowan & Cowan, 1992; Hetherington, 1999b; Hetherington et al., 1999; Kanoy, Ulku-Steiner, Cox, & Burchinal, 1993; McHale, 1997). In contrast, constructive conflict in which couples communicate and work through their disagreements may enhance both family relationships and the well-being of children. Although gender differences have been reported in spillover effects, with distressed marital relations being more likely to undermine the parenting of fathers, especially with daughters, these effects are not consistently obtained (Cowan & Cowan, 1992; Cummings et al., 2001; Hetherington & Kelly, 2002; Kanoy et al., 1993).

THREE STUDIES OF MARITAL TRANSITIONS

The data on which this chapter is based are drawn from three longitudinal studies of divorce and remarriage involving more than 1,400 families and 2,800 children (i.e., The Virginia Longitudinal Study of Divorce and Remarriage (Hetherington, 1987, 1991b, 1993, 2003; Hetherington, Cox, & Cox 1985; Hetherington & Kelly, 2002), the Hetherington and Clingempeel study of Divorce and Remarriage (Hetherington & Clingempeel, 1992) and the Nonshared Environmental Study of Adolescent Adjustment (Hetherington et al., 1999; Reiss, Neiderhiser, Hetherington, & Plomin, 2000). More details on methods can be obtained from the citations above.

All three studies used multi-measure, multi-method, multi-informant assessments including questionnaires, standardized tests, and observations to gather information on family demographics, history and functioning, and on the adjustment of family members including adolescents. Composite variables combining parent, adolescent and sibling reports and observations were used in assessing conflict, family relationships, and adjustment in the analyses in this chapter.

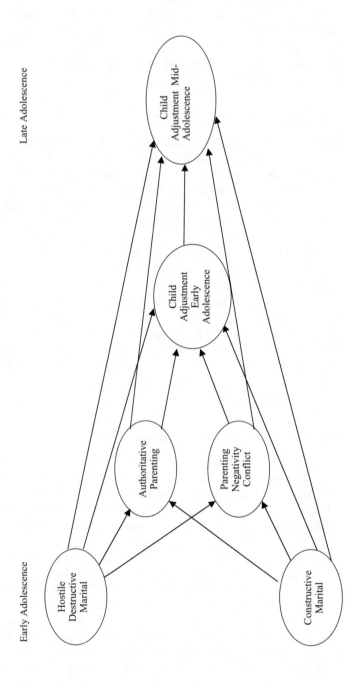

FIGURE 9.1. A theoretical model for predicting adolescent adjustment.

Assessments of common constructs and many shared measures were used in all studies, often permitting the combining of data from the three studies. Some of the analyses in this paper include families and offspring drawn from all three studies and some only from the Virginia Longitudinal Study of Divorce and Remarriage, therefore sample sizes vary widely.

In this chapter, I examine the changes in family relationships and the adjustment of adolescents as they move from early adolescence (average age 11.7 years) to late adolescence (average age 15.6 years) to show how different types of marital conflict and parenting are associated with these changes. Because the chapter is aimed at a broad audience and not necessarily a research audience, methodological and data analytic methods are not reported in detail but are available from the author and in previous publications (see Hetherington, 1987; 2003; Hetherington, Cox, & Cox, 1985; Hetherington & Clingempeel, 1992; Hetherington et al., 1999; Reiss et al., 2000).

The Adjustment of Children in Nondivorced, Divorced and Remarried Families

In this section, I address three major questions. First, are there differences in the adjustment of adolescents in different kinds of families? Second, are there differences between boys and girls in adjustment and are these differences related to what kind of family they live in? Third, how does the adjustment of boys and girls change as they move from early adolescence to dealing with the physical, social, emotional, and cognitive challenges of mid adolescence? Both positive aspects of development such as social responsibility, cognitive agency, sociability, autonomy and self worth, and negative aspects of development such as internalizing and externalizing are examined.

Family type was divided into nondivorced families with high or low marital conflict, divorced families, and simple and complex stepfamilies. Simple stepfamilies are stepfamilies where all the siblings in the family share the same biological relationship with their parents. In most cases they are stepfather families where the children are biologically related full siblings from a mother's previous marriage. Complex stepfamilies are families in which siblings do not share the same relationship with their parents. Thus, blended families in which one sibling comes from a mother's previous marriage and one from a father's previous marriage or families in which a new child is born to the remarried couple in a stepfamily are complex stepfamilies.

Table 9.1 presents the average levels of adjustment and significant differences for 790 adolescents in different types of families drawn from the three longitudinal studies. It is important to note that although there is great variability in the time since divorce or remarriage, on the average most are

TABLE 9.1. *Family Type and Gender Differences in Adjustment in Early and Mid-Adolescence*

	High Conflict Nondivorced		Low Conflict Nondivorce		Divorced		Simple Step		Complex Step		Significant Main Effects and Interactions	Significant Differences
	Boys	Girls	Boys	Girls	Boys	Girls	Boys	Girls	Boys	Girls		
Social responsiblity												
Early adolescence	-.19	-.02	.38	.53	-.32	-.12	-.07	.13	-.29	-.15	Family	LCND>SS >HCND>D,CS
Mid-adolescence	-.21	.00	.36	.48	-.39	-.23	.10	.13	-.27	-.13	Gender	G > B
Sociability												
Early adolescence	-.11	.08	-.14	.02	-.09	.03	-.02	.07	-.03	.14	Gender	G > B
Mid-adolescence	-.14	.10	-.16	.04	-.12	.07	-.03	.09	-.07	.03		
Cognitive agency												
Early adolescence	.01	.21	.24	.43	-.16	-.09	-.04	.15	-.26	-.10	Family	LCND>HACND, SS>D,CS
Mid-adolescence	-.03	.18	.27	.36	-.14	-.08	-.01	.08	-.20	-.08	Gender	G > B
Autonomy												
Early adolescence	-.09	.12	-.14	.15	-.03	.36	-.06	.34	.07	.30	Family	D,SS, CS > HCNS,LDND; G > B
Mid-adolescence	-.03	.28	-.09	.27	.06	.39	.11	.41	.18	.36	Gender Age	M > E
Self-worth												
Early adolescence	.14	-.01	.14	-.02	.10	.05	.14	-.01	-.03	.04	Age	E > M
Mid-adolescence	-.09	-.10	-.11	-.12	-.14	-.19	-.19	-.08	-.11	-.14		
Externalizing												
Early adolescence	.20	.02	-.17	-.38	.28	.14	-.01	-.07	.32	.18	Family	D,SD > HCND > SS > LCND
Mid-adolescence	.13	.01	-.25	-.35	.32	.39	-.06	-.05	.33	.21	Gender; Family × Gender × Age	B > G; M,DG > E,DG
Internalizing												
Early adolescence	.19	.14	-.25	-.21	.31	.17	-.01	-.07	.16	.22	Family	HCND, D, CS >SS> LCND
Mid-adolescence	.11	.21	-.38	-.06	.10	.22	-.09	.01	.12	.29	Gender × Age Age	B,E > M,G; M > E

Family type: HCND = High conflict nondivorced; LCND = Low conflict nondivorced; D = divorced; SS = Simple stepfamily; CS = Complex stepfamily; Gender: G = Girls, B = Boys; Age: E = Early adolescence, M = Mid-adolescence.

past the early crisis period of the 2 to 3 years to adapt to divorce and 4 to 6 years to adapt to remarriage reported to be normative by clinicians and researchers. They are in what we would consider stabilized divorced or remarried families, not in the tumultuous early years of a marital breakup or repartnering. When these children were in early adolescence, the average length of time since divorce in the divorced group was 5.4 years and the average length of time since remarriage in the stepfamilies was 6.1 years.

Gender differences were found in the adjustment of boys and girls, but only a few of these gender differences were associated with the type of family. Girls were consistently more competent than boys; they were more sociable, socially responsible, autonomous and higher in cognitive agency and lower in externalizing than boys. Despite their higher levels of competence, girls also exhibited more internalizing characterized by depressive symptoms and anxiety and this increased as they moved into mid-adolescence.

On the average, as boys and girls moved from early to mid-adolescence, they increased in sociability and autonomy and decreased in feelings of self worth. Moreover, girls increased and boys decreased in internalizing. Patterns of change were similar for adolescents in different family groups. However, one of the few exceptions to the similarity in changes in adjustment from early to late adolescence for children in different family types was a greater surge in antisocial rebellious externalizing behavior in girls from divorced families. In fact, at this time externalizing was as high in girls as in boys from divorced families.

Overall, the effect of marital conflict and transitions on the adjustment of adolescent boys and girls is similar. With younger children we have found that being in a divorced high-conflict family or a mother-headed family was more detrimental for boys than for girls, whereas being in a stepfamily was more harmful for girls (Hetherington, 1993; Hetherington & Jodl, 1994). This was not found for these adolescents.

It can be seen in Table 9.1 that adolescents from low-conflict, nondivorced families exhibited more competent behaviors and fewer problem behaviors than those in the other family groups, with children in divorced families and complex stepfamilies showing more difficulties. Children in divorced families and in complex stepfamilies were somewhat more poorly adjusted than even those in high-conflict, nondivorced families. However, adolescents in simple stepfamilies were better adjusted than those in high-conflict, nondivorced families. Adolescents in divorced families and complex stepfamilies were lower in social responsibility and cognitive agency and higher in externalizing and autonomy than those in nondivorced families. However, those in high-conflict, nondivorced families exhibited less responsible behavior and more externalizing and internalizing than those in low-conflict, nondivorced families or those in simple stepfamilies. In addition, adolescents in simple stepfamilies were more responsible, higher in cognitive agency, and lower in externalizing than those in complex step-families. It should be noted that most of the areas in which children from divorced, remarried, or conflicted families are disadvantaged over those in a low-conflict, nondivorced family are those that require self regula-tion – social responsibility, externalizing, and cognitive agency. Our mea-sures of cognitive agency included not only academic performance but also persistence and goal-directed behavior. No family-type differences were obtained for sociability or self-worth.

The finding of greater autonomy in children from divorced and remar-ried families is congruent with reports that children whose parents have divorced grow up faster (Weiss, 1979). Children in divorced families receive less adult supervision and less adequate monitoring and control than those in nondivorced families. Furthermore, these children, especially daughters, are more likely to be assigned the responsibility for household chores and the care of younger siblings as well as providing emotional support for depressed or emotionally needy divorced mothers (Hetherington, 1999b).

We also found that children in divorced and remarried families and high-conflict families disengage more from their families than do children in low-conflict, nondivorced families, spending little time in the home or in family activities (Hetherington, 1999b; Hetherington & Jodl, 1994). If this disengagement involves the association with an antisocial peer group, increases in delinquent activities and decreases in academic achievement occur. If a caring authoritative adult such as a grandparent, teacher, coach, or parent of a friend is actively involved in the adolescent's life for a sus-tained period, disengagement is sometimes a successful way of coping with an unhappy, contentious home life.

In summary, these findings suggest that the most salutary family set-ting for adolescents is a harmonious, nondivorced family environment. In the area of regulated socially responsible behavior both conflict and mar-ital transitions undermine child adjustment. However, perhaps the most intriguing finding was that adolescents in simple stepfamilies were func-tioning relatively well, especially in comparison with those in high-conflict, nondivorced families and in complex stepfamilies. In our previous research on some of these same children when they were in the early years of a remarriage, children in simple stepfamilies were found to be as troubled as those in divorced families and more than those in nondivorced families (Hetherington, 1993; Hetherington & Clingempeel, 1992). In these long-established simple stepfamilies, adolescents are eventually able to benefit from the presence of a stepparent and the resources the stepparent is able to provide. Previous research has demonstrated that loyalty conflicts and conflictual distressed family relations as well as problems in adjustment are more likely to occur in complex families (Bray & Berger, 1993; Hetherington et al., 1999). The findings presented in this paper suggest that the challenges in complex stepfamilies are persistent and place children at greater long-term risk.

It is important to note that although on average our adolescents in divorced and complex stepfamilies show more problems than those in harmonious nondivorced families, still the vast majority are resilient in coping with their new life situation and emerge as reasonably competent individuals falling within the normal nonclinical range of well being and adjustment. For example, on a standardized test of children's adjustment, the Child Behavior Checklist (Achenbach & Edelbrock, 1983), about 20 to 25 percent of adolescents in divorced and remarried families in contrast to 10 to 15 percent in nondivorced families score in the clinical range. That is a two-fold increase but still it means 75 to 80 percent are within the normal range (Hetherington & Clingempeel, 1992). A substantial number of women and girls are enhanced by dealing with the challenges of divorce and emerge as exceptionally able and well adjusted (Hetherington, 2003; Hetherington & Kelly, 2002). Enhancement and marked personal growth occurs less often for men and boys in response to divorce (Hetherington & Kelly, 2002). It is the diversity rather than the inevitability of adverse outcomes associated with family conflict, divorce, and remarriage that is striking.

Problems Anteceding Divorce

Although it would be tempting to conclude that the problems in adjustment found in children following marital dissolution are attributable to divorce, problems in the adjustment of parents and children and in disrupted inept parenting practices are present long before a divorce occurs (Amato, 2001; Block, Block, & Gjerde, 1988; Hetherington, 1999b). Higher rates of alcohol, substance abuse, antisocial behavior, depression, economic problems, and stressful life events are found in adults who will later divorce (Capaldi & Patterson, 1991; Davies, Avison & McAlpine, 1997; Hope, Power, & Rodgers, 1999; Kitson, 1992; Kurdek, 1990). In their interactions with marital partners, they have poor problem-solving skills and exhibit escalation and reciprocation of negative affect, contempt, denial, withdrawal, and negative attributions about their spouses' behavior, which in turn significantly increase their risk for marital dissolution and multiple divorces (Bradbury & Fincham, 1990; Fincham, Bradbury, & Scott, 1990; Gottman, 1993; 1994; Gottman & Levenson, 1992; Gottman & Notarius, 2001; Hetherington, 1999a, b; Matthews, Wickrama, & Conger, 1996). In addition, more conflict, negativity, irritability and less warmth and control are found in the parenting of mothers and fathers who will later divorce compared to those who remain married (Amato, 2001; Amato & Booth, 1996; Block et al., 1988; Hetherington, 1999b). Their children also exhibit more problems before the marital breakup such as conduct disorders

(Amato & Booth, 1996; Cherlin, Furstenberg, Chase-Lansdale, Kiernan, Robins, Morris, & Tietler, 1991; Sun, 2001), substance abuse (Doherty & Needle, 1991), internalizing, and diminished social competence, self-esteem and achievement (Aseltine, 1996; Cherlin et al., 1991; Hetherington, 1999b; Sun, 2001). When predivorce levels of parent and child adjustment and parenting are controlled it greatly diminishes the size of problem behaviors attributable to divorce.

It is not surprising that living in an unhappy marriage and in what often is a conflictual family situation may have taken its toll on the well-being of family members before a marital breakup occurs. Furthermore, the presence of a difficult child with behavior disorders may undermine a fragile marital relationship and contribute to the divorce. However, how mates are selected must also be considered as a contributing factor to marital dissension, poor parenting, and divorce. Mate selection is not random. Antisocial individuals are more likely to select an antisocial partner (Amato, 2001; Hetherington, 2003). People who have adjustment problems such as antisocial behavior, impulsivity, and depression are more likely to encounter stressful life events, to have problems in interpersonal relationships, to be inept parents, to have difficulty in building successful intimate relationships, and to divorce. Selection of a high-risk partner exacerbates the negative effects of personal factors that contribute to marital instability (Hetherington, 2003).

It has been argued that there may be an underlying genetic substrate to divorce that links personality problems in parents, inadequate parenting practices, and behavior problems in children (D'Onofrio, 2004; Neiderhiser, 2004). The concordance for divorce and similarity on personality characteristics such as antisocial or impulsive behavior or depression that erodes marriage and parent child relationships is greater in identical twins, who share 100 percent of their genes than in fraternal twins who share only 50 percent of their genes (Jocklin, McGue, & Lykken, 1996; McGue & Lykken, 1992). Therefore children from divorced families may have more problems both because they have inherited these characteristics from their parents and because of their exposure to genetically influenced inept parenting, not because of divorce. These partially genetically based personality traits in adults and problems in interpersonal interactions are likely to carry over and contribute to difficulties in a remarriage. However, a recent twin study indicates that the impact of divorce on children's externalizing and antisocial behavior, where the greatest effects are usually obtained, are largely attributable to environmental not genetic effects (D'Onofrio, 2004). These environmental effects are likely to include conflict, poverty, residential moves and incompetent parenting. The question of genetic effects on differences found in different domains of child adjustment between children in divorced and nondivorced families remains open.

Selection and genetic factors may contribute to divorce but longitudinal studies also show that an unhappy marriage, conflict, divorce, and remarriage, at least temporarily, increase problems in adjustment in adults and children and lead to less authoritative parenting (Amato, 2001; Bray, 1999; Hetherington, 1991b; 1993; 2003; Hetherington & Clingempeel, 1992; Hetherington & Jodl, 1994; Hetherington & Kelly, 2002; McLanahan, 1999).

Hostile-Confrontational, Hostile-Withdrawn, Engaged and Avoidant Marital Problem-Solving Styles

Most researchers have focused on the negative effects of marital conflict and divorce. However, disagreements are inevitable in close personal relationships and it is not so much the frequency of conflict but the emotions and problem-solving behavior exhibited by couples that influence the responses of spouses and children to marital conflict. I now turn to an examination of how different strategies and styles in dealing with disagreements and conflict affect family relations and the behavior and adjustment of family members (Cummings et al., 2001; Katz & Woodin, 2002; McHale, 1997).

When couples have conflicts they exhibit a wide array of behaviors – some conciliatory and constructive and some that escalate ill will and confrontation. In our research, composite variables were derived from observational ratings and spouses' reports of their own and their partner's different behaviors – positive and negative emotion, belligerence, criticism, contempt/sarcasm, withdrawal, denial, reciprocated negativity, validation, affection, attending, humor, self disclosure, explanation and reasoning, compromise, and frequency of agreement. When the behaviors husbands and wives exhibited in attempting to deal with disagreements and conflicts were examined, four different patterns of coping with marital conflict were identified. The first was a *hostile-confrontational* style found in 34 percent of wives and 20 percent of husbands. It was characterized by negative emotion, criticism, contempt and sarcasm, belligerence, reciprocated negativity and escalation of aversive behavior, failure to agree, and low affection and validation of the partner. These couples often shouted down their partners, didn't listen to their arguments and demeaned their partners with remarks like "Only an idiot could say that," or "Don't be such a bloody fool." Hostility and lack of respect and affection were rampant in these relationships. The second was a *hostile withdrawn* style (20 percent of wives, and 38 percent of husbands) again characterized by negative emotion, low support of the partner, low affection and failure to agree but not by the overt threats and belligerence and escalation of negativity found in spouses with hostile-confrontational styles. These spouses tended to deny culpability then withdraw in sullen silence. Contempt was also high in these spouses but it tended to be manifested nonverbally in eye rolling, lip curling, raised eyebrows and smug, self-satisfied smiles rather than by sarcasm or demeaning verbalizations. The third style an *engaged* style

(36 percent of women and 30 percent of men) was characterized by positive affect, humor, affection, validation of the partner, explanation and reasoning, compromise and more frequent conflict resolution than was found in the other groups. Anger was at about the average level in these spouses but hostility manifested in belligerence, contempt, and sarcasm was low. These spouses were willing to confront their differences. The verbalization of disagreements (e.g., "I don't see it that way" or "I'm not so sure about that") was higher in this group than in the hostile-withdrawn group but not as high as in the hostile-confrontational group. A fourth small cluster, a *conflict avoidant cluster* (10 percent of women and 12 percent of men), characterized by infrequent conflict, neutral affect in women, and moderately positive affect in men and high withdrawal was also identified.

Problem-Solving Style and the Marital Relationship

How might these problem-solving styles differ in men and women and in different types of families, and how might different problem-solving styles be associated with differences in the quality of the marital relationship? Men were more likely to be hostile-withdrawn and less likely to be hostile-confrontational than were women. This combination yielded the familiar pursuer-distancer couple in which wives want to confront and discuss problems and emotional issues in the relationship and men want to avoid confrontations and resort to denial, withdrawal, and stonewalling. This often evolves into a chronic pattern of wives carping, nagging, and becoming frustrated and husbands denying, withdrawing, and becoming sullen, resentful, and angry. Hostile confrontational behavior was more common in divorced women with their ex-spouse and in remarried women in complex stepfamilies than in their partners or in husbands and wives in first marriages.

Although there was greater hostile confrontational behavior in remarried women, on the whole there were more similarities than differences between remarried and first married couples. Their reports of marital satisfaction were similar and marital satisfaction decreased and hostile confrontational conflict increased in both types of couples as their children moved further into adolescence. Many of their conflicts were about the behavior and activities of their adolescent children.

In both husbands and wives, in first marriages and remarriages, in comparison with an engaged or avoidant problem-solving style, both a hostile-confrontational style and a hostile-withdrawn style in self or partner were associated with lower marital satisfaction, higher marital instability (thinking critically about the relationship or about separation and divorce, talking to friends and family about problems in the relationship or possible divorce, separations, consulting a lawyer, etc.), more frequent disagreements about child rearing, and also with depression in women. It is interesting that no differences in the couples' reports of marital instability or satisfaction or depression were found between those with an engaged or an avoidant style of dealing with conflict, although disagreements about childrearing were less frequent in the avoidant group.

A hostile-withdrawn style in the partner was associated with higher rates of marital infidelity in both husbands and wives but a hostile-confrontational style in the partner was associated with infidelity for men only. Women in first marriages and remarriages reported being less maritally satisfied when their husbands were hostile avoidant than when they were hostile confrontational. For women, a disengaged, stonewalling husband is harder to accept than a more tempestuous husband. An exception to this occurs when physical violence is involved. Women with physically violent husbands reported less satisfaction, more instability and greater depression than those in avoidant relationships.

Overall, it is apparent that marital conflict resolution style is related to marital satisfaction and instability and psychological well-being, which have been associated both with the quality of parenting and with the adjustment of children.

PROBLEM-SOLVING STYLES AND SPILLOVER EFFECTS IN PARENT-CHILD RELATIONSHIPS

I turn now to an examination of parent-child relations in nondivorced, divorced, and remarried families as children move from early to mid-adolescence. Then I explore whether there is a spillover effect from the specific type of problem solving exhibited in the marital relationship to parenting behavior and the parent-child relationship. When parenting in stepfamilies is discussed, consideration is given to whether the parent is dealing with his or her own biological child or a stepchild, since our previous work has demonstrated that biological "owness" plays an important role in parent-child relationships and spillover effects (Hetherington et al., 1999).

Parenting in Different Types of Families

Problems in the adjustment of children associated with divorce and remarriage are often attributed to inept parenting practices found in these families as parents attempt to deal with their new life situation. In the immediate aftermath of a divorce or remarriage, biological mothers become less attentive and affectionate and more irritable, harsh, and inconsistent in discipline. Their parenting becomes more authoritative as the new family stabilizes, still on average, divorced mothers remain less competent parents than those in harmonious nondivorced families. Relationships between divorced mothers and preadolescent sons are especially problematic with sons being noncompliant and coercive and mothers being harsh, erratic, and ineffectual in discipline. In contrast, divorced mothers and preadolescent daughters often have close, companionate relationships. However, such relationships change as children grow older.

In the families we studied, parent-child conflict increased and parental warmth, control, and monitoring decreased as children moved into mid-adolescence. This pattern held for relations in all family groups but the increase in conflict between early and mid-adolescence was greatest for mothers with early maturing daughters and for divorced mothers and daughters. Differences in divorced mothers' relationships with sons and daughters disappeared as the adolescents grew older. With early adolescents, divorced mothers were more aggressive and exhibited more negative affect toward sons than either nondivorced or remarried mothers did and were more negative toward sons than daughters. By mid-adolescence, these gender differences in frequency of conflict and in hostile, punitive, confrontational maternal behavior disappeared as divorced mothers' relationships with their daughters became more contentious. This conflict was tempered by high levels of involvement often reported by divorced mothers and consistently reported by their adolescent offspring. By mid-adolescence, adolescents in divorced families saw their mothers as negative and coercive but also as caring and concerned. Furthermore, adolescents in divorced families viewed their parents as controlling and monitoring their behavior less than those in other family groups. They reported that their parents knew less about where they were, what they were doing, and who they were with than children in any other group. Both adolescents and observers saw divorced mothers as involved but as ineffectual in monitoring and control. However, divorced mothers reported that they were becoming more active in attempting to control and monitor their children's behavior especially their daughters' behaviors. In cross-lagged analyses in the Virginia Longitudinal Study when daughters were younger preadolescents, control and monitoring by divorced mothers did appear to influence their daughter's subsequent behavior which often involved normbreaking, defiance, and early sexual activity. In adolescence, as shown in Figure 9.2, control attempts seem to have been initiated too late and in response to the daughter's ongoing antisocial behavior. It was reactive rather than proactive and preventative.

Parents interacting with their own biological children usually were more involved and expressed both more positive and negative affect than did those interacting with nonbiologically related stepchildren. However, this was related to time in a stepfamily and the complexity of the stepfamily.

We had previously found that in the early stages of a remarriage stepparents reported themselves to be less affectionate with their stepchildren although they spent time with them attempting to establish a relationship (Hetherington, 1993; Hetherington & Clingempeel, 1992). Stepparents

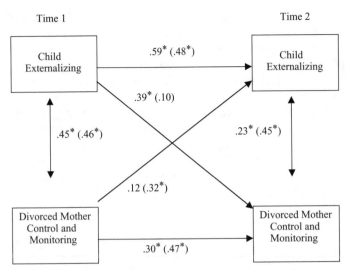

FIGURE 9.2. Cross-lagged regression with divorced mothers control and monitoring and girls externalizing. Coefficients are listed for early to mid-adolescents, second for ages 6 to 10 in brackets. *$p \leq .05$.

expressed less strong positive affect and showed fewer negative, critical responses than did nondivorced or divorced parents. In the initial stage of remarriage they were like polite strangers, self-disclosing, asking questions, sometimes trying to relate the child's experience to their own, often valiantly attempting to establish a relationship or at least a truce in the face of aversive behavior by their stepchildren. Biological parents were freer both in expressing affection and in criticizing their children for poor personal grooming, for not doing their homework, not cleaning up their rooms, or for fighting with their siblings. However, they also reported more rapport and closeness to their children. Initially, stepfathers were far less supportive to stepsons than to stepdaughters, however, with the younger but not the early adolescent children this reversed in longer established remarriages.

Again we found adverse effects of being in a complex stepfamily. Mothers were more negative to their own biological children and stepfathers were more negative to their stepchildren in complex than in simple stepfamilies. In the early stage of a remarriage, stepparents remained relatively pleasant despite the aversive behavior they encountered from their stepchildren, especially from stepdaughters. However, with adolescent children this honeymoon period rapidly passed and stepparents became increasingly impatient. Although stepfathers, especially those in complex stepfamilies, tried to remain disengaged they got into extremely angry and prolonged interchanges with their stepdaughters. This contrasted markedly with the harmonious and warm relationship found between nondivorced fathers and their adolescent daughters. These conflicts tended to focus on issues of parental authority and respect for the mother. Stepdaughters viewed stepparents as hostile, punitive, and unreasonable on matters of discipline. Stepparents made significantly fewer monitoring and control attempts and were less successful in gaining control with both sons and daughters than were nondivorced parents.

Early in a remarriage we had found a pattern for the parenting of stepfathers and stepchildren similar to that just noted with divorced mothers, where the direction of influence over time was from stepchildren's behavior to stepfather's parenting. In the longer established stepfamilies, if stepfathers were able to maintain authoritative parenting characterized by involvement, warmth, and control and monitoring it led to diminished externalizing and increased social responsibility in children. However, for many stepfathers this is no easy task.

Biological relatedness was more salient than the type of family for adolescents' positive responses to parents. There were no differences in positive responses of adolescents to their biologically related mothers in nondivorced, divorced, and remarried families, or to biological fathers in nondivorced families and remarried families. However, adolescents felt less close and responded less positively to stepparents and to noncustodial parents, especially noncustodial fathers.

In negative responses of adolescents to parents, more marked family differences emerged. Adolescents interacting both with divorced biological parents and with stepparents were more noncompliant, resistant, critical, and expressed more negative affect. They were more denying and argumentative. Furthermore, stepdaughters often gave stepparents, especially stepfathers, the slow freeze – withdrawing, ignoring them, and being sullen and contemptuous. In problem-solving interactions, silences were three times longer with stepfathers and stepdaughters than in any other group. As we had found with adolescent daughters and divorced mothers, the behavior of the adolescent often seemed to be driving the later behavior of the stepparent. There were significant pathways between adolescents' rejecting negative behavior and adolescents' externalizing at time 1 and stepparents' negativity toward the child later on. It is difficult for even the best intending stepparent to remain positive in the face of a defiant, rejecting stepchild.

Parental Problem-Solving Style and Spillover Effects in Mothers and Fathers With Sons and Daughters

Patterns of spillover effects from the marital relationship to parenting were similar for nondivorced families and stepfamilies. Clear spillover effects from the marital relationship to parenting were demonstrated for fathers and these were more marked with daughters. Fathers in both nondivorced and remarried families who were confrontational or withdrawn or who had wives who were confrontational or withdrawn in the marital relationship were more irritable and less warm and involved with their children than were those in engaged or avoidant relationships. Furthermore these fathers were more negative in their relationships with daughters, especially with physically unattractive daughters, than with sons.

In contrast, the husband's problem-solving style was not related to the wife's parenting of adolescents. Mothers' parenting was relatively impervious to the behavior of their husbands. However, if a wife was confrontational and hostile in interacting with her husband, she was irritable and coercive with her children and in other social relationships. It was almost as if a hostile confrontational trait underlay the behavior in social relationships of some mothers. Mothers who are antisocial are less skilled and more coercive as partners, parents, and friends.

The relationship of divorced parents and the quality of their parenting of adolescents was less closely associated. With younger children we had found that divorced women who were in a contentious relationship with their ex-spouse were more likely to have mutually coercive hostile relations with their sons. With their adolescent children there were no differences in mothers' parenting related to the quality of their relationship with the ex-spouse. However, noncustodial fathers with a hostile confrontational divorced spouse were less likely to be paying child support and more likely to be seeing their adolescent offspring infrequently. This diminished visitation was greater with daughters than with sons.

Marital Problem-Solving Styles and Adolescent's Adjustment

Next I discuss how the four parental styles of resolving marital conflict were related to differences in child adjustment and in children's behavior with parents, siblings, and peers in different types of families. The same domains of adjustment as are presented in Table 9.1 are included in these analyses. Redundant effects are not discussed.

Surprisingly, the adjustment of adolescents whose parents were hostile confrontational versus hostile withdrawn in their marital conflict resolution styles were fairly similar. Adolescents with parents having either of these hostile conflict resolution styles were higher in externalizing and lower in social responsibility and cognitive agency than those with parents in the engaged or avoidant groups. The only difference between the two hostile styles for adolescent adjustment was that adolescents with parents having a hostile withdrawn style when interacting with their spouse were higher in internalizing than those with a hostile confrontational style. They were angry, noncompliant, anxious, depressed, and insecure children. Neither an interaction between owness and parental conflict resolution style nor an interaction between the sex of child and the sex of parent and parental conflict resolution style was obtained. There was no difference in the impact of biologically related parents' or stepparents' style, with the exception that in divorced families the noncustodial parent's conflict resolution style was not associated with children's adjustment. Nor were there differences in boys' and girls' adjustment attributable to a mother or a father exhibiting the style. We had hypothesized based on identification theory that boys would be more influenced by fathers and girls by mothers and that biologically related parents would be more influential than stepparents, but this was not confirmed.

Problem-Solving Styles and Adolescents' Social Relationships

It was in social interactions and problem-solving behavior with siblings and peers that more differences associated with marital problem solving began to emerge. We had run conflict-resolution sessions for sibling pairs and in the Virginia Longitudinal Study also with a best friend that were similar to those in the marital session. Each person separately identified areas in which they had problems or disagreements with the other, then the dyad was presented with a list of these problems and asked to discuss and resolve them and come to some kind of agreement about how to handle them.

In interactions with siblings and peers, both adolescents with hostile confrontational parents and adolescents with hostile withdrawn parents showed higher negative affect and less reasoning than adolescents with engaged or avoidant parents. However, those with hostile confrontational parents were more aggressive and coercive and more often failed to resolve their conflicts than adolescents in any other group.

It was in these siblings and peer interactions that some of the few differences between adolescents with engaged and avoidant parents began to appear. Adolescents with an engaged parent were more aggressive and showed more failure to agree than those with avoidant parents. In contrast, adolescents with avoidant parents showed more distress, yielding, compromise, and agreement in their conflict resolution sessions with their peers. One of our observational ratings was of "passive acceptance." Passive acceptance involved accepting the other person's position with no effort to counter it or push or elaborate on their own position. An adolescent in his or her own individual session might have said, "I like to go to movies, but George likes to hang out at the mall." When the two were put together, George says, "It's more fun at the mall" and the other teenager passively acquiesces and says, "Yes, I guess it's better to go to the mall." Adolescents with avoidant parents, especially with two avoidant parents, were more likely than those in any other group to passively accept the position of a peer. The problem-solving procedure is one that promotes conflict, and these adolescents were unhappy and agitated in having to deal with conflict, were unable to assert and push their position, collapsed in the face of opposition, and were just generally steam-rollered by their peers. They had not learned how to be assertive especially with aggressive, contentious friends.

Marital Problem-Solving Style and Adolescent Responses to Parents

With preadolescent children in the early stage of stepfamily formation we had found that girls but not boys responded positively to marital distress in parents (Hetherington & Jodl, 1994). The more unhappy the marital relationship, the less negatively the girls behaved toward their remarried mother and especially toward their new stepfather. Girls, who had had a closer relationship than boys with their divorced mothers, resented a satisfying, warm marital relationship and were more hostile and resistant to a stepfather they thought was usurping affection from the biological parent. However, in this study with older children in longer established stepfamilies, adolescents in all groups responded more positively to parents if the couple relationship was avoidant than if it was hostile confrontational or hostile withdrawn. In all family types, adolescent boys and girls were more affectionate and accepting and less contentious with parents when there were few overt conflicts in the marriage or between the divorced spouses.

Combinations of Parental Problem-Solving Styles and Children's Adjustment

Although I have been discussing the effects of the individual marital conflict resolution style of parents, parents obviously do come in pairs. We had hypothesized that adolescents with two parents with hostile-confrontational or hostile-withdrawn styles would have more problems in adjustment than those with one hostile and one engaged or avoidant parent. We expected that having one parent with a constructive marital conflict resolution style could to some extent protect against the adverse effects of a hostile problem solving style in the other parent.

The difficulty in examining all possible combinations of conflict resolution styles was that some of the groups this formed were very small. The hostile styles tended to go together resulting in sullen contemptuous withdrawn couples, intensely argumentative confrontational couples, or pursuer-distancer couples. Similarly, avoidant couples tended to go together. It is difficult for a spouse to remain avoidant in the face of a highly hostile or engaged partner. Engaged partners were sometimes found in combination with hostile confrontational and hostile withdrawn partners and tried to deal with their differences in a rational positive fashion and to moderate conflicts when they became too intense.

Figure 9.3 presents the mean composite externalizing scores for adolescents from parents with different combinations of parenting styles. Mother

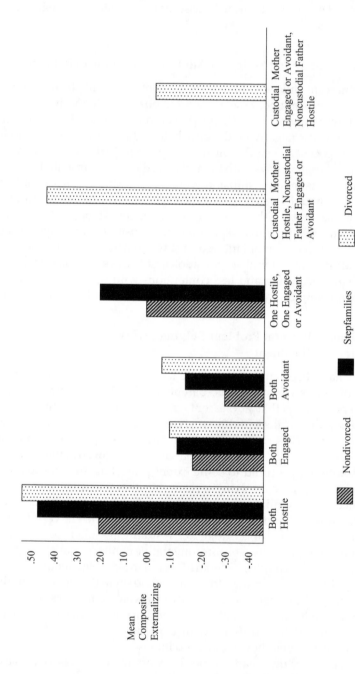

FIGURE 9.3. Adolescents' externalizing in parents with different combinations of problem solving styles in non-divorced, divorced and remarried families.

and father effects are not presented separately for nondivorced and step-families because no gender effects for parents were found, but separate effects for custodial and noncustodial divorced parent combinations are presented. In addition, only the effects when children were in mid-adolescence are presented because the effects were the same in early and mid-adolescence. In this analysis, as in previous analyses, adolescents in divorced and remarried families were higher in externalizing than those in nondivorced families. However, this varies with the parenting combinations. Family type differences emerge when one or both parents are hostile and are not present when both are engaged or avoidant. Hostility promotes family type differences. When both parents have a hostile style, the deleterious effects are greater than when only one does and least when neither does. The exception to this is in divorced families in which a noncustodial parent with a disengaged or avoidant style can do little to counter the effects of a hostile custodial parent who is angry, resentful, coercive, and demeaning in interactions with and in discussions of the ex-spouse. Moreover, stepfamilies and divorced families in which both parents have engaged or avoidant conflict-resolution styles and divorced families in which the custodial mother has an engaged or avoidant style have adolescents with lower levels of externalizing than those in nondivorced families where both have hostile styles. This suggests that in extremely contentious marriages where neither parent has competent problem-solving skills, a marital break-up may be advantageous, if it involves a move to a more harmonious family situation with competent parents who are skilled in conflict resolution.

Linkages Between Family Processes and Changes in Child Adjustment

I turn now to a closer examination of the spillover model presented in Figure 9.1 and examine linkages between the marital relationship, parenting, and child adjustment in different family types. Because of limitations in sample size, we broke our husbands' and wives' problem-solving styles only into destructive problem solving (negative affect, belligerence, transactional conflict, contempt, sarcasm, denial, and withdrawal) and constructive problem solving (positive affect, humor, validation of the partner, explanation and reasoning, and compromise). Parenting was divided into authoritative parenting (high warmth/responsiveness, effective monitoring/control) and coercive/conflictual parenting. Child adjustment variables were externalizing, internalizing, social responsibility, and cognitive agency. In these models we focused on the longitudinal prediction of child adjustment or change in child adjustment, thus child adjustment and family relations in early adolescence were used to predict adjustment at mid-adolescence. Again there were limitations in our modeling because of sample size. Mothers and fathers were analyzed separately and models were run separately for each child adjustment outcome.[1]

We tested our models to address the following questions. Are the family groups (nondivorced, divorced, simple stepfamily, complex stepfamily/ own and complex stepfamily/not own) equivalent with respect to the effects of family processes on child adjustment? Are they equivalent for boys and girls?

The criterion models for mothers are presented in Figures 9.4 and 9.5 and for fathers in Figures 9.6 and 9.7. Only significant pathways are included in the figures to preserve clarity in presentation. Results for internalizing and externalizing and for social responsibility and cognitive agency are presented in the same figures although they were run separately. In Figures 9.4 and 9.6 the results for internalizing and in Figures 9.5 and 9.7 for cognitive agency are presented in brackets. We had expected two processes to be at work in the linkages between marital behavior and child adjustment. First, we expected direct effects of marital problem-solving style on children's adjustment from children modeling their parents' affect, emotional regulation or lack of it, and problem-solving strategies. Second, we expected indirect effects based on the impact of the quality of the marital relationship on husbands' and wives' parenting. However, as can be seen in Figures 9.4 through 9.7, almost all of the impact of the marital relationship on children's adjustment was mediated by the quality of parenting. The only place there was a direct link is between hostile destructive marital behavior and adolescent externalizing. Hostile marital relationships promote more negative conflictual and less authoritative parenting in fathers. These pathways were significantly stronger with girls than with boys. However, the association between marital behavior and fathers' parenting was comparable across nondivorced families and remarried families.

As was suggested by the previous analyses of differences in means related to marital problem-solving style, the quality of the marital relationship had less influence on the parenting of mothers, but a hostile contentious personal style in the mother's relationship with her partner carried over into her relationship with her child. In spite of the difficulties encountered by divorced mothers and stepparents and their children, if they can

---

[1] We used multiple group models to examine group differences in the strength of the paths among the latent constructs. Because of limitations in sample size, latent variables could not be used for all constructs and several alternate models were run. The first set used composites for parenting and latent variables for child outcomes, the second set the reverse. The results were similar. In a series of model comparisons, cross-group equality constraints were imposed to test for family type and gender differences. An attempt was made to minimize method variance by using mother, father, and observer reports to assess the marital relationship and adolescent, teacher and a different observer report to assess child adjustment. The goodness of fit for all models as estimated by GFI and RMSEA was satisfactory.

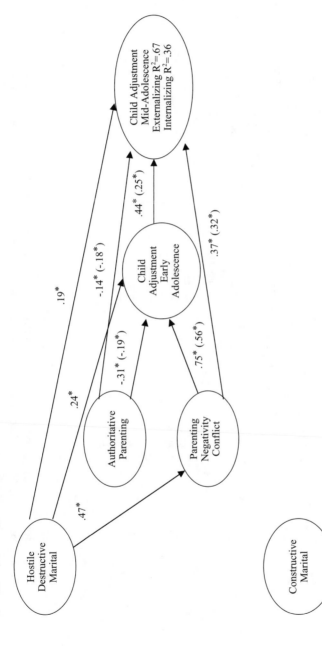

Early Adolescence

Mid-Adolescence

FIGURE 9.4. Adolescent externalizing and internalizing as a function of mothers marital problem-solving behavior and parenting. Standardized parameter estimates for externalizing are presented first. Those in brackets are for internalizing.
* $p \leq .05$.

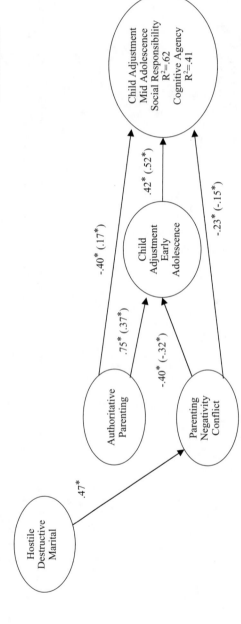

Early Adolescence

Mid-Adolescence

FIGURE 9.5. Adolescent social responsibility and cognitive agency as a function of mother's marital problem-solving behavior and parenting. Standardized parameter estimates for social responsibility are presented first. Those in brackets are for cognitive agency.

* $p \leq .05$.

Early Adolescence

Mid-Adolescence

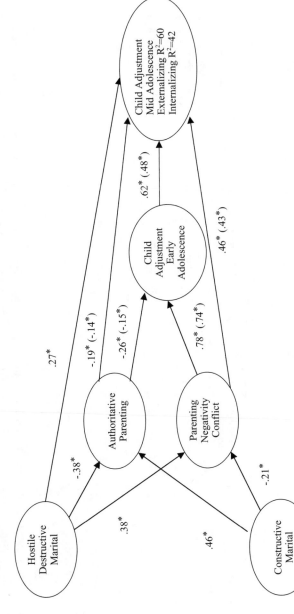

FIGURE 9.6. Adolescent externalizing and internalizing as a function of father's marital problem solving and parenting. Standardized parameter estimates for externalizing are presented first. Those in brackets are for internalizing.
* $p \leq .05$.

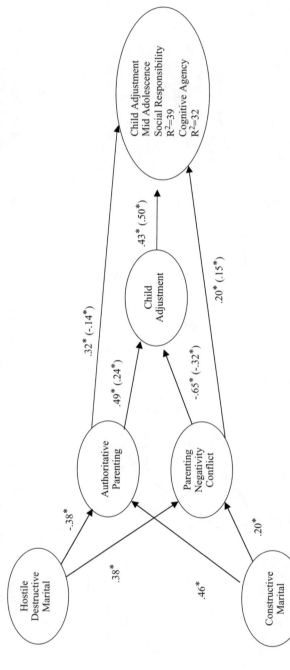

Early Adolescence

Mid-Adolescence

FIGURE 9.7. Adolescent social responsibility and cognitive agency as a function of father's marital problem solving and parenting. Paths for social responsibility are presented first. Those in brackets are for cognitive agency.
* $p \leq .05$.

maintain warm responsive and effective control and monitoring in parenting and not become coercive and contentious it leads to more positive adjustment in their children. For both mothers and fathers in all types of families, authoritative parenting is associated with less psychopathology and increased social responsibility and cognitive agency and the reverse is true for negative conflictual parenting. It also is striking that for the pathological outcomes, negative conflictual parenting is usually more salient than a lack of authoritative parenting. The association between parenting and adjustment is greater within early adolescence than from early to late adolescence, probably because of the bidirectional nature of the parent-child relationship. The most notable finding in the longitudinal analyses is that the strongest pathways are invariably from adolescents' adjustment at early adolescence to adjustment in mid-adolescence. In spite of the many cognitive, social, and emotional changes adolescents go through in this period, there is considerable stability in behavior. Genetic predispositions and earlier life experiences have already laid the foundation for later adjustment.

In our models we have focused on the contributions of family conflict and parenting to child adjustment. We have not included the very important contributing factor of peer relations. In past analyses, we found that about half of the effects of parenting on adolescent adjustment are indirect and are associated with peer relationships. Authoritative parenting protects against adolescents associating with delinquent peers. Hostile, coercive, contentious parent-adolescent relations promote disengagement from the family and involvement with antisocial peers, which in turn is associated with higher externalizing and lower social responsibility in the adolescent (Hetherington, 1999b; Kim, Hetherington, & Reiss, 1999).

SUMMARY AND DISCUSSION

There is great diversity in children's responses to conflict and to their parents' marital transitions. Their responses depend on experiences prior to and following divorce or remarriage, characteristics of the child, family functioning, and risks and resources external to the family that support the child or undermine the child in coping with his or her changing life situation. In this chapter, I examined only a few of the factors that contribute to adolescents' adjustment in nondivorced, divorced, and remarried families – those related to different patterns of marital conflict resolution and parenting.

Hostile patterns of marital problem solving whether confrontational or withdrawn were more deleterious to the adjustment of children than were engaged or avoidant patterns. It would be tempting to conclude that it is the marital hostility rather than the specific problem-solving style that is destructive, and that may be true in regard to characteristics of the child associated with the regulation of behavior – low social responsibility and cognitive agency and high externalizing characterized by noncompliance, norm breaking, impulsivity, and aggression. Adolescents who had parents with either hostile-confrontational or hostile-withdrawn marital problem-solving styles were equally likely to have these attributes. Thus, parental marital hostility may be a key factor underlying unregulated antisocial behavior in adolescents. However, a differential effect between the two destructive marital problem solving styles occurs with adolescent internalizing characterized by elevated anxiety and depressive symptoms. Children whose parents were hostile withdrawn versus those who have a hostile-confrontational problem-solving style were more likely to be disadvantaged. Thus hostility seems to be associated with lack of behavioral control but hostile-withdrawn marital problem solving seems to be associated with lack of emotional regulation. However, it must be emphasized again that in this study most of the effects of conflict and problem solving were mediated by parenting.

Although it has been suggested that different models are needed to predict adjustment in different types of families (Bray, 1999), for the most part, models that predicted the long-term adjustment of adolescents in nondivorced, divorced, and remarried families were similar. Discordant, unsatisfying, hostile marital relations make coercive conflictual parenting more likely and effective authoritative parenting less likely, especially for fathers. Coercive conflictual parenting is a risk factor and authoritative parenting is a protective factor in the development of problems in adolescent adjustment in all types of families.

A persistent finding in all three of our longitudinal studies has been that it is more difficult for parents and children who are biologically unrelated to form involved, close, affectionate ties. However, biology is not destiny. In these long-established divorced and remarried families, disengaged or negative relationships were often found between divorced biologically related noncustodial fathers and children. Moreover, although stepfathers and stepchildren were not biologically related in either simple or complex stepfamilies, closer and more positive parent-child relationships were found in simple stepfamilies. More than three-quarters of our adolescents in these long-established simple stepfamilies described their relationship with their stepparents as "close," or "very close." Both social contexts and biological factors are important in understanding parent child relationships and child adjustment.

FUTURE RESEARCH DIRECTIONS

Almost every recent book on families emphasizes the marked historical changes in the family that have occurred over the past 50 years and the notable diversity that exists in contemporary families. In the early decades of this period the striking changes were in increases in single parenthood, births to teenage mothers, divorce, and the number of working mothers. The past two decades have seen a delay in marriage, an increase in step-families, in adults living alone, and in longevity, demands from gay and lesbian parents for marital rights, and a dramatic rise in the number of people cohabiting as an alternative or precursor to marriage. In conceptualizing and interpreting family research it is important that differences in the functioning of new family forms as opposed to traditional married two-parent families not be viewed as deficits.

In our work on divorce, single-parent households, and stepfamilies we have been impressed by the diversity exhibited in the response to these life situations. Reports solely based on differences in means for family functioning and adjustment in different types of families can be deceiving. Differences associated with conflict and family type are usually modest. More research needs to be done to identify diverse patterns of adjustment and the individual, familial, and extrafamilial resiliency and vulnerability factors that enhance or undermine coping with the challenges associated with family transitions.

Families must be studied longitudinally. Family transitions such as divorce and remarriage cannot be viewed as discrete events but must be seen as an extended process of change in family relationships and life circumstances. The interplay between individual characteristics of parents and children, family relationships, and the social and economic circumstances of families that contribute to adjustment are dynamic and change over time. The response to divorce is influenced by the quality of relations in cohabitation and remarriage and by experiences in a divorced single parent household. Trajectories of family change and adjustment rather than the status of the family at one time needs to be studied. Moreover, family processes and adjustment must be studied before and after a transition occurs. Too often behavior is said to be caused by divorce or remarriage when that behavior antecedes them.

More genetically informed twin, adoption, or sibling studies of marital transitions are essential. We know that there is a genetic contribution to personality characteristics, marital functioning, divorce, parenting, and parent and child adjustment (D'Onofrio, 2004; Jocklin et al., 1996; Neiderhiser, 2004; O'Connor, Caspi, DeFries, & Plomin, 2000). Until we further understand the relative genetic and environmental contributions to these experiences and behaviors and to different domains of child adjustment, the interpretation of the findings of traditional correlational studies of family transitions, parenting, and child adjustment remain questionable.

Additional multi-method studies of marital transitions with representative samples are needed. In the research literature we are confronted with a plethora of survey studies by sociologists and economists based on information from a single informant usually only a mother or child.

Psychological studies often use more sophisticated, multi-method, multi-informant assessments including observations but have small nonrepresentative samples. The correlation between different sources of information is modest. Informants have their biases in describing their own behavior as well as that of other family members. Information from a single informant is best thought of as that person's perception of what is going on. Combined data from multiple informants and methods are more powerful in predicting behavior than data obtained from a single source. Interdisciplinary collaborations will produce more valid and generalizable information about marital transitions.

Finally, much of the intensive, multi-method study of family transitions has been done with white, middle-class American families. More extensive studies in different ethnic and racial groups and cross-national studies are critical. Groups and countries with different standards, values, practices, and social policies associated with families may have different effects on parents and children (e.g., Walper & Beckh, Chapter 10, in this book). How the effects of the dynamics of family relationships, marital transitions and parenting vary in different cultural settings is largely unknown.

POLICY/PRACTICE IMPLICATIONS

Recent social policy in the United States has emphasized the promotion of marriage and an increase in barriers to divorce. However, before initiating a host of new government programs aimed at promoting traditional two-parent families and discouraging divorce, policymakers should take another look at current demographics and research.

Americans are opting to live in a wide array of family forms, and happy, well adjusted children can be found in diverse types of families. There are many kinds of marriages and not all are salutary. Nor are most divorces, single-parent experiences, and stepfamilies associated with lasting distress. It is family process rather than family structure that is critical to the well-being of children, and policies that promote constructive family processes and competent parenting in all types of families should be encouraged.

Destructive conflict in any type of family undermines the well-being of parents and children. Effective therapeutic interventions that decrease conflict and promote positive parenting and adjustment are available but they seem unlikely to be applied as national policy for families. A recent review reports that the most effective approaches are the most comprehensive ones – those that deal with both parents and children, with family dynamics, and with a family's needs for jobs, education, day care, and health care (Cowan, Powell, & Cowan, 1997). Beyond that, which interventions work best seem to vary, depending on people's stage of life, their ethnic group, or the kind of family they are in and the specific challenges before them.

Historically, policymakers have been more reluctant to intervene in marriages than in divorce. A series of policy changes in divorce law have been aimed to diminish conflict, encourage the involvement of noncustodial parents, and provide adequate financial support for parents and children (see Emery, 1999). These include no-fault divorce, joint custody, divorce mediation, recommendations for more equitable division of property and more aggressive mechanisms to ensure compliance with child-support rulings. All of these have, to some extent, been successful in their goals. Although conflict gradually diminishes following divorce, in about 15 percent of divorced couples, high levels of destructive conflict are sustained. For these couples, mandatory joint custody may be deleterious but for most it is associated with continued involvement of the noncustodial parent and payment of child support. There is no "one size fits all" for social policy.

Strengthening and promoting positive family relationships, diminishing conflict, and improving parenting and the many settings in which children develop is a laudable goal. However, policies that constrain or encourage people to remain in hostile destructive marriages or that push uncommitted couples to marry are likely to do more harm than good. The same is true of marriage incentives and rewards designed to create traditional families with the husband as economic provider and the wife as homemaker. If our social policies do not recognize the diversity and varied needs of American families, we easily could end up undermining them.

References

Achenbach, T., & Edelbrock, C. S. (1983). *Manual for the child behavior checklist and revised child behavior Profile*. New York: Queen City Printers.

Amato, P. R. (1999). Children of divorced parents as young adults. In E. M. Hetherington (Ed.), *Coping with divorce, single parenting and remarriage: A risk and resiliency perspective* (pp. 147–164). Mahwah, NJ: Erlbaum Associates.

Amato, P. R. (2001). The consequences of divorce for adults and children. In R. M. Milardo (Ed.), *Understanding families into the new millennium: A decade in review* (pp. 488–506). Minneapolis, MN: National Council on Family Relations.

Amato, P. R., & Booth, A. (1996). A prospective study of divorce and parent-child relationships. *Journal of Marriage and the Family, 58,* 356–365.

Amato, P. R., & Keith, B. (1991a). Parental divorce and the well-being of children: A meta-analysis. *Psychological Bulletin, 110,* 26–46.

Amato, P. R., & Keith, B. (1991b). Parental divorce and adult well-being: A meta-analysis. *Journal of Marriage and the Family, 53,* 43–58.

Anderson, E. R., Greene, S. M., Hetherington, E. M., & Clingempeel, W. G. (1999). The dynamics of parental remarriage: Adolescent, parent and sibling influences. In E. M. Hetherington (Ed.), *Coping with divorce, single parenting and remarriage* (pp. 293–322). Mahwah, NJ: Erlbaum.

Aseltine, R. H. (1996). Pathways linking parental divorce with adolescent depression. *Journal of Health and Social Behavior, 37*, 133–148.

Block, J., Block, J. H., & Gjerde, P. E. (1988). Parental functioning and the home environment in families of divorce: Prospective and concurrent analyses. *Journal of the American Academy of Child and Adolescent Psychiatry, 27*, 207–213.

Bradbury, T. N., & Fincham, F. D. (1990). Attributions in marriage: Review and critique. *Psychological Bulletin, 107*, 3–33.

Bray, J. H. (1999). From marriage to remarriage and beyond: Findings from the Developmental Issues in Stepfamilies Research Project. In E. M. Hetherington (Ed.), *Coping with divorce, single parenting and remarriage: A risk and resiliency perspective* (pp. 253–271). Mahwah, NJ: Erlbaum.

Bray, J. H., & Berger, S. H. (1993). Developmental issues in stepfamilies research project: Family relationships and parent-child interactions. *Journal of Family Psychology, 7*, 1–17.

Buchanan, C. M., & Waezenhofer, R. (2001). The impact of interparental conflict on adolescent children: Considerations of family systems and family structure. In A. Booth, A. C. Crouter, & M. Clements (Eds.), *Couples in conflict* (pp. 149–160). Mahwah, N.J.: Erlbaum.

Capaldi, D. M., & Patterson, G. R. (1991). Relation of parental transitions to boys' adjustment problems: I. A linear hypothesis. II. Mothers at risk for transitions and unskilled parenting. *Developmental Psychology, 27*, 489–504.

Cherlin, A. J., & Furstenberg, F. F. (1994). Stepfamilies in the United States. *Review of Sociology, 20*, 359–381.

Cherlin, A. J., Furstenberg, F. F., Chase-Lansdale, P., Kiernan, K. E., Robins, P. K., Morrison, D. R., & Tietler, J. O. (1991). Longitudinal studies of the effects of divorce on children in Great Britain and the United States. *Science, 252*, 1386–1389.

Cowan, C. P., & Cowan, P. A. (1992). *When partners become parents. The big life changes for couples*. New York: Basic Books.

Cowan, P. A., Powell, D., & Cowan, C. P. (1997). Parenting interventions: A family systems perspective. In I. E. Sigel & K. A. Renninger (Eds.), *Handbook of child psychology* (5th ed., pp. 3–72). Vol. 4: Child psychology in practice. New York: Wiley.

Cummings, M. E., Goeke-Morey, M. C., & Rapp, L. M. (2001). Couple conflict, children and families: It's not just you and me, Babe. In A. Booth, A. C. Crouter, & M. Clements (Eds.), *Couples in conflict* (pp. 117–148). Mahwah, NJ: Erlbaum.

D'Onofrio, B. M. (2004). *Causation versus selection: A genetically informed study of marital instability and its consequences for young-adult offspring*. Unpublished doctoral dissertation, University of Virginia, Charlottesville.

Davies, L., Avison, W. R., & McAlpine, D. D. (1997). Significant life experiences and depression among single and married mothers. *Journal of Marriage and the Family, 59*, 294–308.

Doherty, W. J., & Needle, R. H. (1991). Psychological adjustment and substance use among adolescents before and after a parental divorce. *Child Development, 62*, 328–337.

Emery, R. E. (1999). *Marriage, divorce and children's adjustment*. Thousand Oaks, CA: Sage.

Fincham, F. D., Bradbury, T. N., & Scott, C. K. (1990). Cognition in marriage. In F. D. Finchman & T. N. Bradbury (Eds.), *The psychology of marriage* (pp. 118–149). New York: Guilford.

Gottman, J. M. (1993). The roles of conflict engagement, escalation and avoidance in marital interaction: A longitudinal view of five types of couples. *Journal of Consulting and Clinical Psychology, 61*, 6–15.

Gottman, J. M. (1994). *What predicts divorce?* Hillsdale, NJ: Erlbaum.

Gottman, J. M., & Levenson, R. W. (1992). Marital processes predictive of later dissolution: Behavior, physiology, and health. *Journal of Personality and Social Psychology, 63*, 221–223.

Gottman, J. M., & Notarius, C. T. (2001). Decade review: Observing marital interaction. In R. M. Milardo (Ed.), *Understanding families into the new millennium: A decade in review* (pp. 146–166). Minneapolis, MN: National Council on Family Relations.

Hetherington, E. M. (1987). Family relations six years after divorce. In K. Pasley & M. Ihinger-Tallman (Eds.), *Remarriage and stepparenting: Current research and theory* (pp. 125–156). New York: Guilford.

Hetherington, E. M. (1991a). The role of individual differences and family relationships in children's coping with divorce and remarriage. In P. Cowan & E. M. Hetherington (Eds.), *Advances in family research: Vol. 2. Family transitions* (pp. 165–194). Hillsdale, NJ: Erlbaum.

Hetherington, E. M. (1991b). Families, lies, and videotapes. *Journal of Research on Adolescence, 1*, 323–348.

Hetherington, E. M. (1993). An overview of the Virginia Longitudinal Study of Divorce and Remarriage with a focus on early adolescence. *Journal of Family Psychology, 7*, 39–56.

Hetherington, E. M. (1999a). Social capital and the development of youth from nondivorced, divorced, and remarried families. In A. Collins (Ed.), *Relationships as developmental contexts: The 29th Minnesota Symposium on Child Psychology* (pp. 170–210). Hillsdale, NJ: Erlbaum.

Hetherington, E. M. (1999b). Should we stay together for the sake of the children? In E. M. Hetherington (Ed.), *Coping with divorce, single parenting and remarriage: A risk and resiliency perspective* (pp. 93–116). Mahwah, NJ: Erlbaum.

Hetherington, E. M. (2003). Intimate pathways: Changing patterns in close personal relationships across time. *Family Relations, 52*, 318–331.

Hetherington, E. M., Bridges, M., & Insabella, G. (1998). Five perspectives on the association between marriage and children's adjustment. *American Psychologist, 53*, 167–183.

Hetherington, E. M., & Clingempeel, W. G. (1992). Coping with marital transitions: A family systems perspective. *Monographs of the Society for Child Development, 57* (Serial No. 227, Nos. 2–3).

Hetherington, E. M., Cox, M., & Cox, R. (1985). Long-term effects of divorce and remarriage on the adjustment of children. *Journal of the American Academy of Child Psychiatry, 24*, 518–530.

Hetherington, E. M., Henderson, S. H., & Reiss, D. (1999). Adolescent siblings in stepfamilies: Family functioning and adolescent adjustment. *Monographs for the Society for Research in Child Development, 64* (4, Serial No. 222).

Hetherington, E. M., & Jodl, K. (1994). Stepfamilies as settings for development. In A. Booth and J. Dunn (Eds.), *Stepfamilies* (pp. 55–80). Cambridge, MA: Harvard University.

Hetherington, E. M., & Stanley-Hagan, M. M. (2000). Diversity among stepfamilies. In D. H. Demo, M. A. Fine, & K. R. Allen (Eds.), *Handbook of family diversity* (pp. 173–176). New York: Oxford University.

Hetherington, E. M., & Stanley-Hagan, M. M. (2002). Parenting in divorced and remarried families. In M. Bornstein (Ed.), *Handbook of parenting: Being and becoming a parent* (pp. 287–316). Mahwah, NJ: Erlbaum.

Hetherington, E. M., & Stanley-Hagan, M. M. (2003). Diversity among stepfamilies. In D. H. Demo, M. A. Fine, & K. R. Allen (Eds.), *Handbook of family diversity* (pp. 173–176). New York: Oxford University.

Hetherington, E. M., & Kelly, J. (2002). *For better or for worse: Divorce reconsidered.* New York: Norton.

Hope, S., Power, C., & Rodgers, B. (1999). Does financial hardship account for elevated psychological distress in lone mothers? *Social Science and Medicine, 29,* 381–389.

Jocklin, V., McGue, M., & Lykken, D. T. (1996). Personality and divorce: A genetic analysis. *Journal of Personality and Social Psychology, 71,* 288–299.

Kanoy, K., Ulku-Steiner, B., Cox, M., & Burchinal, M. (1993). Marital relationship and individual psychological characteristics that predict physical punishment of children. *Journal of Family Psychology, 17,* 20–28.

Katz, F. S., & Woodin, E. M. (2002). Hostility, hostile detachment, and conflict engagement in marriages: Effects on child and family functioning. *Child Development, 73,* 636–652.

Kim, J. E., Hetherington, E. M., & Reiss, D. (1999). Relations between family, peers and adolescents' externalizing behaviors: Gender and family type differences. *Child Development, 70,* 1209–1230.

Kitson, G. C. (1992). *Portrait of divorce: Adjustment to marital breakdown.* New York: Guilford.

Kurdek, L. A. (1990). Divorce history and self-reported psychological distress in husbands and wives. *Journal of Marriage and the Family, 52,* 701–708.

Matthews, L. S., Wickrama, K. A. S., & Conger, R. D. (1996). Predicting marital instability from spouse and observer reports of marital interaction. *Journal of Marriage and the Family, 58,* 641–655.

McGue, M., & Lykken, D. T. (1992). Genetic influence on risk of divorce. *Psychological Science, 6,* 368–373.

McHale, J. P. (1997). Overt and covert co-parenting processes in the family. *Family Process, 36,* 183–201.

McLanahan, S. (1999). Father absence and the welfare of children. In E. M. Hetherington (Ed.), *Coping with divorce, single parenting and remarriage: A risk and resiliency perspective* (pp. 117–146). Mahwah, NJ: Erlbaum.

Neiderhiser, J. M. (2004). Genetic and environmental influences on mothering of adolescents: A comparison of two samples. *Developmental Psychology, 40,* 335–351.

O'Connor, T. G., Hetherington, E. M., & Reiss, D. (1998). Family systems and adolescent development: Shared and nonshared risk and protective factors in nondivorced and remarried families. *Development and Psychopathology 10*, 353–375.

O'Connor, T. G., Caspi, A., DeFries, J. C., & Plomin, R. (2000). Are associations between parental divorce and children's adjustment genetically mediated? An adoption study. *Developmental Psychology, 36*, 429–437.

O'Connor, T. G., Dunn, J., Jenkins, J. M., Pickering, K., & Rasbash, J. (2001). Family settings and children's adjustment: Differential adjustment within and across families. *British Journal of Psychiatry, 179*, 110–115.

Papernow, P. L. (1984). The step-family cycle: An experiential model of stepfamily development. *Family Relations, 33*, 355–363.

Reiss, D., Neiderhiser, J., Hetherington, E. M., & Plomin, R. (2000). *The relationship code: Genetic and social analysis of adolescent adjustment.* Cambridge, MA: Harvard University Press.

Rutter, M. (1987). Psychosocial resilience and protective mechanisms. *American Journal of Orthopsychiatry, 5*, 315–331.

Sun, Y. (2001). Family environment and adolescents' well being before and after parents' marital disruption: A longitudinal analysis. *Journal of Marriage and the Family, 63*, 697–713.

Weiss, R. S. (1979). Growing up a little faster: The experience of growing up in a single-parent household. *Journal of Social Issues, 35*, 97–111.

10

Adolescents' Development in High-Conflict and Separated Families

Evidence from a German Longitudinal Study

Sabine Walper and Katharina Beckh

As in many other Western countries, divorce rates have steadily increased in Germany during the past century (Engstler & Menning, 2003; Walper & Schwarz, 1999). At present, 37 percent of all marriages in Germany are estimated to end in court, placing Germany at an average level of risk for divorce when compared with other European countries. Not surprisingly, the rise in divorce rates was accompanied by an increase in the number of children growing up in single-parent families. Since 1975, the number of single-parent households grew by about 50 percent. In 2000, 15.4 percent of all children below age 18 lived with a single parent (Engstler & Menning, 2003). An additional 5.5 percent had a stepparent in their household, either married to or cohabitating with their biological parent (Teubner, 2002).

Although much public concern has focused on the risks of marital break-up and single parenting for children's development, the consequences of parental separation and remarriage for children and adolescents have only recently been addressed by systematic research in Germany (Walper & Schwarz, 1999). The largest body of evidence concerning the development of children from divorced and separated homes still comes from the United States (see Amato, Chapter 8 and Hetherington, Chapter 9 in this book) and guides educators and counselors, as well as policy making in other countries. In this chapter, we present findings from a longitudinal study conducted in Germany to investigate adolescents' development in nuclear and separated families, the latter including single mother and stepfather families. Findings from this study complement those from American studies and inform us about differences and similarities in processes involved in parental separation and new partnerships.

Divorce rates are lower in Germany than in the United States, where about 40 percent of all children experience parental divorce before reaching adulthood (cf. Amato, 2000). Remarriage rates, too, are lower. Given lower maternal employment rates in Germany (cf. Walper & Galambos, 1997), however, the economic risks of divorce are higher in Germany than in the

United States. Comparative data from the 1980s showed that every third woman in the former West Germany experienced a 50 percent drop in income following divorce, whereas "only" 22 percent of divorced women in the United States did so (Burkhauser, Duncan, Hauser, & Berntsen, 1991). In addition, lower divorce rates may indicate a higher reluctance among German parents to expose children to marital transitions. A reconsideration of the decision to divorce is built into German divorce law, which requires a one-year separation before filing for divorce. Accordingly, the divorce process takes longer. As suggested by some findings, even three years after parental separation only half of the former couples got legally divorced (Schmidt-Denter & Schmitz, 1999). Thus, our study is not restricted to divorced families, but includes families with still married, but separated parents.

In this chapter, we first address effects of parental separation and stepfamily formation on adolescents' psychosocial development. Given that the majority of children who experience parental separation do so in their early and preschool years (Schneider, Krüger, Lasch, Limmer et al., 2001), many adolescents in divorced or separated homes have lived with only one biological parent for several years. Some of these are confronted with further family transitions and see new partners of their custodial parent move in and out, while others grow up in stable stepfamilies. Accordingly, adolescence is particularly well suited to investigate the long-term consequences of parental separation, which may point to chronic stress related to single parenting or stepfamily life or to the salience of acute stress involved in more recent family transitions. A large array of outcomes regarding adolescents' development will be considered in the empirical analyses, including well-being, problem behavior, social, competence, academic competence, individuation in parent-child relations, and adolescents' romantic relationships.

However, the significance of parental separation and family structure per se is far from clear or widely accepted among researchers (Amato, 2000; Lamb, 1999). The quality of family relationships has been found to play a key role in children's post-divorce adaptation (Buchanan, Maccoby, & Dornbusch, 1996; Butz & Boehnke, 1999; Forehand et al., 1991; Hetherington & Clingempeel et al., 1992; Schmidt-Denter, 2001; Simons, 1996). We consider the role of interparental conflict in nuclear and separated families with respect to parent-adolescent relationships.

PARENTAL DIVORCE AND INTERPARENTAL CONFLICT AS RISK FACTORS FOR CHILDREN'S DEVELOPMENT

Parental Divorce As Stressor

As suggested by numerous studies, parental divorce and remarriage challenge children's and adolescents' well-being, behavioral adaptation, and academic performance (Amato, 1994, 2000; Coleman, Ganong, & Fine, 2000; Hetherington, 1993; Hetherington & Jodl, 1994; McLanahan, 1999; Pryor & Rodgers, 2001). Although responses are certainly not uniform, the risks for detrimental effects have frequently been pointed out and do not seem to have decreased within the United States across the past decade (Amato, 2001). Studies conducted in Germany show a somewhat mixed picture. In the Children's Panel Study conducted by the German Youth Institute, 5- to 6-year olds and 8- to 9-year olds growing up with a single parent or in a stepfamily showed some problems, but no subgroup showed pervasive problems across several domains of development, and effect sizes were small (Walper & Wendt, 2005). Children from recently separated families showed acute post-separation stress in various indicators of well-being and problem behavior, but such disadvantages were no longer significant three years later (Schmidt-Denter, 2000). In later childhood and adolescence, a longitudinal study from the former East Germany found that teachers rated children from divorced homes as more restless, less emotionally stable, and less compliant than their age mates in nuclear families at age 10 (Reis & Meyer-Probst, 1999). However, neither the reports of mothers nor children's self reports indicated higher adjustment problems for children from divorced families. Only later at age 14, the young adolescents with divorced parents saw themselves as more aggressive and emotionally unstable when compared with youth from nuclear families. According to cross-sectional and longitudinal data from a school-based study in Berlin, eighth to tenth graders' problem behavior was higher among youth from single parent and stepfamilies when compared with nuclear families, but differences in emotional well-being were not found (Butz & Boehnke, 1999). Another longitudinal study using a representative sample did not find differences in social functioning and parent-child relations among youth from nuclear and divorced families (Fend, 1998).

Adolescence is a period of particular significance, because adolescents' social resources within the family are at risk (Amato, 2000; Hetherington, 1993; McLanahan, 1999; Pryor & Rodgers, 2001), increasing the odds of a lack of support, affection, and guidance that are still needed during this developmental period. The relationship with the noncustodial father is particularly likely to suffer (Coiro & Emery, 1998). Financial hardship (more common in single-parent households, see Andreß & Lohmann, 2000; Burkhauser et al., 1991) not only limits options for leisure time activities and investments in education, but also often brings about strains in the family system that undermine parenting (Brooks-Gunn, Duncan, & Mariato, 1997; Conger, Conger, & Elder, 1997). Such family problems may contribute to adolescents' striving for autonomy and separateness. Indeed, findings from studies on divorce suggest that separated families are more likely to foster early – perhaps premature – development of autonomy (e.g., Dornbusch, Carlsmith, Bushwall, Ritter et al., 1985; Smetana, 1993), which can be explained by increased risk for family discord, lack of parental support, and higher demands on children's self reliance (Sessa & Steinberg, 1991).

Although remarriage provides an additional adult as a resource for family management and child support, parental monitoring is reported to be lower in single-parent and stepfamilies than in nuclear families (Kerns, Aspelmeier, Gentzler, & Grabill, 2001). Most research shows that children in stepfamilies are not better off than their age-mates in single-mother families and that parent-child relationships are suggestive of early detachment from the family (Amato, 1994; Hetherington & Clingempeel, 1992).

Nonetheless, past research on stress and coping and particularly research on divorce demonstrates that children show considerable resilience in the face of stress and may successfully cope with initially demanding life circumstances such as parental separation (Emery & Forehand, 1994; Hetherington, 1993; Schmidt-Denter, 2000). However, evidence is mixed, and some findings suggest even more marked differences between nuclear and divorced families across time reaching into young adulthood (Chase-Lansdale, Cherlin, & Kiernan, 1995; Cherlin, Chase-Landsdale, & McRae, 1998). As Chase-Lansdale, Cherlin and Kiernan (1995, p. 163) pointed out: "It seems that the developmental challenges of adolescence and young adulthood may have reinvoked certain vulnerabilities for the divorced group, evidenced by stronger deleterious effects of the aftermath of divorce in their early 20s."

One of the major developmental tasks of adolescence and early adulthood is to cope with the challenges of romantic relationships. Having experienced instability in their parents' marriage, individuals from divorced families may enter their romantic relationships with stronger needs for affection and support, but more negative expectations and lower interpersonal skills than their peers from nuclear families. Indeed, several findings suggest that adolescents with divorced parents are more frequently involved in heterosexual activities (Sinclair & Nelson, 1998), but show more negative communication in their partnership relations (Herzog & Cooney, 2002), and later on, when married, have a higher risk of divorce (Diekmann & Engelhardt, 1999; see Amato, Chapter 8 in this book).

To explore these issues for a German sample, we first investigate whether youth from long-term separated families report increased problems across time when compared to adolescents from nuclear families. Alternatively, problems in adolescents' development may be restricted to families currently undergoing a transition to single parenting or step-parenting. Because stepfamilies have repeatedly been pointed out as a distinct context for child development with particular demands in adolescence (Bray & Berger, 1993; Coleman et al., 2000; see Hetherington, Chapter 9 in this book), stepfamilies are considered separately and compared with single-mother families. These questions are addressed using longitudinal data for several age groups from late childhood to middle/late adolescence following them across a 6-year time span.

Effects of Interparental Conflict

In explaining detrimental effects of parental divorce, conflict and antagonism between biological parents play a key role (Amato, 1993; Emery, 1988; Fincham, 1998; Hetherington, Bridges, & Insabella, 1998). Interparental conflict is a frequent concomitant of parental divorce, but problems between parents are not restricted to divorcing couples. As shown by research on nuclear families, frequent, intense, and unresolved disputes between married parents are a substantial stressor for children and adolescents, contributing to reduced well-being, higher internalizing and more externalizing problem behavior (Buehler & Gerard, 2002; Davies, Harold, Goeke-Morey, & Cummings, 2002; Fincham, 1998; Harold & Conger, 1997). Some negative effects even seem to be carried over into adulthood (see Amato, Chapter 8 in this book). Parents' conflicted, unhappy marriage is likely to contribute to more negative communication behavior and conflict styles in offspring's own partnerships (Herzog & Cooney, 2002; Martin, 1990).

To what extent are children's adjustment problems after divorce brought on by the conflicted relationship between parents before and following separation? A number of findings support this hypothesis, for the United States as well as for Germany. First, children from nuclear families characterized by considerable spousal conflict show adjustment problems similar to those of children from divorced homes (Jenkins & Smith, 1993; Peterson & Zill, 1986; Reis & Meyer-Probst, 1999). Second, the differences in adjustment problems between children with married and divorced parents are reduced or even disappear when the detrimental effects of conflict between parents are taken into account (e.g., Schick, 2002).

Interparental conflict may directly affect children, undermining their emotional security in the family (Davies et al., 2002). At the same time, there is considerable evidence for a spillover of interparental conflict into parent-child interactions (Erel & Burman, 1995; Krishnakumar & Buehler, 2000). The tensions between parents appear be carried into the parent-child relationship and contribute to increased negativity and lower levels of parental support provided to children. Such increased hostility and negativity in parent-adolescent interaction provide a strong explanation for detrimental effects of interparental conflict on children's and adolescents' functioning (Buehler & Gerard, 2002; Harold & Conger, 1997; Harold, Fincham, Osborne, & Conger, 1997).

Does interparental conflict have a different impact on children in nuclear and in separated families? Given that interaction between both ex-partners is reduced in divorced families, we might assume that their children are less frequently exposed to antagonism between parents than children in nuclear families whose parents have a conflicted relationship. Furthermore, parental separation may help to cut the link between subsystems and remove the parent-child relationship from the negative impact of stress between both ex-partners. Finally, living with a single parent may make it easier for children to escape loyalty conflicts by siding with the custodial parent. These processes may be summarized as the *"exposure hypothesis,"* which assumes that the negative impact of interparental conflict on children should be weaker in separated than in nuclear families. However, some findings suggest that negative effects of interparental conflict are accentuated in divorced families (Forehand, McCombs, Long, Brody et al., 1988). Such increased vulnerability could result from children's experiences during the course of parental separation which may undermine their coping resources. Furthermore, the likely long-term experience of unresolved conflict which even extends beyond separation may be particularly stressful. Finally, if the custodial parent's involvement with the child suffers from the stressful relationship with the ex-spouse, the non-residential parent may not be available to compensate for this lack of affection and support. Such processes may be seen as a *"double dose"* of stressors because of separation and conflict piling up to a level that is particularly difficult to cope with. So far, findings are mixed, and data from another study suggest rather similar correlations between various aspects of interparental conflict and adolescents' problem behavior (Hetherington 1999).

In this chapter, we present findings on this issue, looking at a wide range of outcomes for adolescents across time.

THE LONGITUDINAL STUDY: FAMILY DEVELOPMENT AFTER PARENTAL SEPARATION

The German longitudinal study "Family Development after Parental Separation" was designed to compare the development of adolescents growing up in different family types and to address five key questions:

(1) Do problems in well-being, competence, and behavior decrease or increase among adolescents from single-mother and/or stepfather families? How does their adaptation across time compare with that of youth from nuclear families? Are any differences in this respect related to adolescents' age and gender?

(2) Does interparental conflict affect adolescents' development in nuclear and separated families differently? Are effects more pronounced in separated families (where conflict and separation may function as a "double dose") or in nuclear families (where adolescents' exposure to interparental conflict is likely to be higher)?

(3) How do parental separation and interparental conflict jointly influence adolescents' relationships with mother and father across time?

Are the relationships of adolescents with their mothers similarly affected by interparental conflict and separation as their relationship with their fathers or does the mother-child relationship prove to be more "immune"?

(4) If adolescents' adaptation is compromised by parental separation and/or interparental conflict, can this be explained by more distance or insecurity in their relationship with their mother?

(5) Are problems in partnerships transmitted from parents to adolescents? Do adolescents' romantic relationships suffer from parental separation and/or interparental conflict? If so, are these effects brought on by increased problems in adolescents' relationship to their mother?

Equal numbers of youth from nuclear, single-mother, and stepfather families were recruited through a school-based screening of 6,000 students in five different cities in the former East and West Germany. Students from grades 5 to 10 from all school tracks were included. Among these, 749 children and adolescents were selected for the longitudinal interviews, which started in 1996, $n = 292$ living in nuclear families, $n = 251$ being raised by a single mother, and $n = 202$ and living in stepfather families. Family type was defined by household composition, not by marital status because many stepfamilies are unmarried coresiding couples (as discussed earlier). Families in which the child's biological father had died were not included. To address specific research questions, an additional small sample of nuclear families with high interparental conflict was recruited and interviewed (see Walper, 1998).

When the study began, adolescents were between 9 and 19 years old, half were boys and half were girls. Age and the proportion of boys and girls were comparable in different family types. The adolescents were interviewed three times, in 1996, 1997, and 2002 (referred to as t1, t2 and t3). In the majority of cases their mothers and, in fewer cases, their fathers or stepfathers participated, too. Of the 749 children and adolescents interviewed at the first assessment in 1996, 63.7 percent could be contacted again in 1997 and 59.3 percent in 2002. Because of the high drop-out rate from wave 1 to wave 2, particularly in the former East Germany, where regional mobility was very high, 49 new participants were recruited in the East in wave 2. Data for all three waves are available for a total of 437 children and adolescents.

Defining Family Type

Family type was identified from mothers' reports or, if not available, from adolescents' reports during oral interviews. For our analyses addressing the first question, household composition and stability across time were taken into account, distinguishing stable nuclear families (with both bio-logical parents), single-mother families (no partner living in the household between 1996 and 2002), stable stepfather families (married or unmarried), and families in transition (with entry or exit of a stepparent during the course of the study). Thirty-six percent of the adolescents and young adults had left the parental household by 2002, but were categorized accord-ing to their primary parents' household composition. Of the remaining 401 adolescents, 138 grew up in nuclear families (with both biological parents), 99 lived with a single mother who remained single, 73 came from a stable stepfather family, and 91 of the participants went through at least one family transition during the assessment period (parental sep-aration, separation of mother and stepfather, or entry of a new steppar-ent). When the study began, adolescents were 14 years old, on average, with 44.6 percent of the sample being male. Age and proportions of boys and girls did not differ across family types. Among separated families, average time since parental separation was 9 years at t1, with no differ-ences emerging between single mother and stepfather families. Stepfathers had entered the household about 5 years prior to the first interviews, on average.

Measuring Interparental Conflict

In 1996 and 1997, adolescents' perception of *interparental conflict* was assessed by means of a three-item scale on the frequency of conflicts between parents. In order to identify high conflict families, scores for t1 and t2 were dichotomized at a level of 2.65, which distinguishes average answers of "never" and "rarely" from answers ranging from "sometimes" to "very frequently." Because some adolescents provided data on inter-parental conflict for only t1 or t2, but not both, the high conflict group was defined in terms of high scores for either t1 or t2.

Analyses involving effects of interparental conflict are restricted to nuclear families and those separated families in which biological parents had contact with each other in the initial phase of the study so adoles-cents could identify conflict level. The additional subsample of nuclear families with high interparental conflict was also included. This increased the group size for high-conflict nuclear families. Of the adolescents, 202 were identified as living in a low-conflict family (102 nuclear and 100 separated families); 112 lived in a high-conflict family (63 nuclear and 49 separated families). The 149 separated families included all families that were either separated at the onset of the study or separated later dur-ing the course of the study. High- and low-conflict families did not dif-fer by adolescents' gender, but they did differ by age. Youth from high-conflict families were slightly older than adolescents from low-conflict families.

Measuring Adolescents' Well Being, Competence, and Problem Behavior

Self-esteem was assessed using a German version of the Rosenberg scale (Rosenberg, 1965). Depressive symptoms were indicated by a German short version of the CES-D scale (Hautzinger & Bailer, 1993). *Somatic complaints* were indicated by 13 items taken from the most recent version of the *Gießener Beschwerdebogen* (Brähler, 1992). This scale assesses the frequency of diverse symptoms such as headache, stomach pain, and allergies during the past two months. *Social competence* was indicated by two scales reflecting peer integration and peer rejection derived from the "Revised Class Play" method of peer assessment (RCP; Masten, Morison, & Pellegrini, 1985). The items were reworded for assessing adolescents' self reports (e.g., "I have many friends." "Others are mean to me"). Perceived *academic competence* was indicated by a five-item scale on academic self concept developed by Alsaker (1989), example item: "I am able to solve tasks at school quite well." Finally, two scales were chosen to indicate *problem behavior*. The first is a 21-item delinquency scale that is frequently used in German research (Lösel, Averbeck, & Bliesener, 1997). These self-reports of delinquency were assessed only for participants above age 12. For each item (e.g., "Did you ever steal anything in a store or shop?"), life time prevalence and incidence during the past year were reported. The indicator used here summarizes frequencies for the past year across items. The second scale indicates *explosiveness* (Heitmeyer et al., 1996) and comprises five items (e.g., "When others provoke me, I get angry quickly.").

Measuring Adolescents' Relationship With Mother, Father, and Romantic Partner

Adolescents' perceived attachment and individuation in relation to both parents as well as any romantic partner were assessed using the Munich Individuation Test of Adolescence (MITA; see Walper, 1997; 1998), which was developed based on the Separation-Individuation Test of Adolescence (Levine, Green, & Millon, 1986; Levine & Saintonge, 1993). Among the six scales of the MITA, four were selected for the present analyses. *Successful individuation* indicates the balance of relatedness and individuality in a given relationship (e.g., "Even if I don't like everything my mother does, I try to understand her"). *Nurturance seeking* indicates a strong desire for closeness and support (e.g., "When she is near me, I have the feeling that nothing bad can happen to me"). *Fear of love withdrawal* addresses adolescents' fear of losing their parents' (or partner's) love and affection if not meeting their expectations (e.g., "If I disappointed my mother, I am anxious that she does not like me any more"). *Ambivalence* indicates an insecure relationship in which adolescents feel higher emotional involvement as they perceive it on the parent's or partner's side (e.g., I would like to do more things with her but I am anxious about being a nuisance"). For testing effects on adolescents' romantic relationships, only two scales were considered here: Fear of love withdrawal and ambivalence. All indicators were reliable.

ADOLESCENTS' DEVELOPMENT BY FAMILY TYPE

The first question addresses differences between family types regarding adolescents' development across time. Using multivariate analyses of covariance with repeated measures of outcomes in 1996, 1997, and 2002, we compared four family types: stable nuclear families, stable single mother families, stable stepfather families, and families that experienced changes in composition related to parents' exit or entry. Outcomes were self-esteem, depression, somatic complaints, peer integration, peer rejection, and academic self. Delinquency and explosiveness were analyzed separately because they were only assessed at t2 and t3. In all analyses, effects of age and gender were tested, too, but are only reported here if they affect findings for family type.

Significant main effects of *family type* were found for only three of the eight outcomes considered. Adolescents from stable mother families showed less peer integration than their age-mates from stable stepfather families and adolescents from nuclear families reported lower levels of explosiveness as well as less delinquency than youth from unstable families. Interestingly, no differences emerged between adolescents from nuclear families and those from stable single-mother or stepfather families.

Further, differences in development across time depending on adolescents' family type (as indicated by a significant interaction effect between *family type* and *time*) proved to be significant for self-esteem, depressive symptoms, and marginally for somatic complaints. With regard to self-esteem, Figure 10.1 shows that adolescents from all family types started off comparatively similar in 1996. Across time, however, they got increasingly different, with growing advantage for youth from nuclear families, while adolescents from changing families fared the worst. The latter exhibited the lowest self-esteem in 2002, followed by youth from stepfather families and those from single-mother families, who showed a similar trend as their age-mates from nuclear families and showed marginal advantages over youth from changing families in 2002. While adolescents and young adults from stepfather families did not differ from the other subgroups at t3, those from nuclear families ended up having the highest self-esteem.

Similarly, Figure 10.2 depicts the course of depressive symptoms across time, pointing to an increased differentiation between the different family groups. Family type was not a significant predictor of depressive

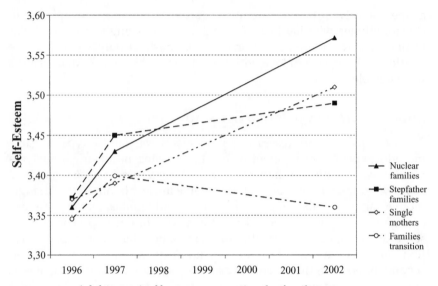

FIGURE 10.1. Adolescents' self-esteem across time by family type.

symptoms at the first two waves; however, in 2002, the advantage of youth from nuclear families compared with those who experienced a transition in family composition was highly significant. Again, youth from nuclear families fared best, indicating the least depressive symptoms in 2002, while adolescents from families in transition reported the highest number of depressive symptoms.

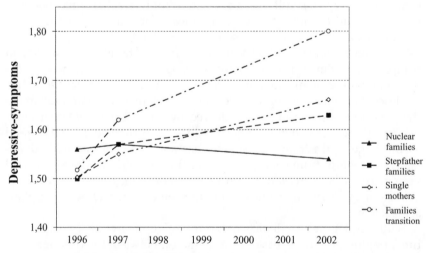

FIGURE 10.2. Adolescents' depressive symptoms across time by family type.

Overall, these findings suggest that youth from separated families that remained stable across time do not suffer from more psycho-social problems than adolescents from nuclear families. However, adolescents who experienced family transitions during the time period studied here, decreased in well-being and fared significantly worse in the last wave than those from nuclear families. Note that these transitions include only a minority of primary family breakups between biological parents (16.5 percent); the larger share involves a separation between mother and stepfather or the entry of a new stepfather (both 41.8 percent). Accordingly, these latter transitions do not seem to be of minor importance for adolescents' well-being.

Effects of Age, Gender and Time Since Separation

To determine whether effects of family type differ for certain age groups, our analyses included age at t1 as an additional factor, comparing 9- to 12-year-old preadolescent (30.4 percent of the sample), 13- to 14-year-old early adolescents (36.2 percent) and 15- to 19-year-old adolescents and young adults (33.4 percent). Only one significant interaction of family type and age group was found. With respect to academic self, adolescents undergoing a family transition during the course of the study rated themselves lower than those from other family types, but this was restricted to the subgroup of early adolescents. This might suggest that early to mid-adolescents' school performance is especially vulnerable to the negative effects of a familial transition. Although this seems plausible given that school motivation usually tends to drop during early adolescence, this effect stands alone and, more importantly, is not mirrored in a different trend across time for adolescents from families in transition. Furthermore, it is not in line with findings reported by Amato (Chapter 8 in this book) who found most negative outcomes for educational attainment when parental separation occurred early in children's lives. Hence, it should not be overestimated.

Developmental trends for adolescents' somatic complaints did not differ substantially by family type for the younger and older group, however for the middle age group (age 13–14 at t1), in contrast, several marginally to highly significant effects of family type were found (see Figure 10.3). At t1, youth from stepfather families indicated marginally higher somatic complaints than youth from single mother families, and this disadvantage became more pronounced at t2, although it disappeared by 2002, when these adolescents were about 19 to 20 years old. In 2002, there was a marked difference between the young adults from nuclear families and those who experienced a family transition, with the lowest somatic complaints among the former and the highest somatic complaints among the latter. Their age-mates from single mother and stepfather families fell between these two groups. Interestingly, this diverging pattern for early adolescence matches

Age Group 1: 9-13 years at t1

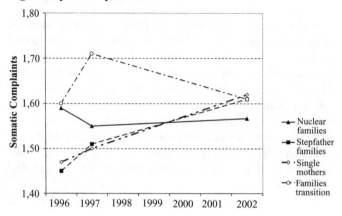

Age Group 2: 14-15 years at t1

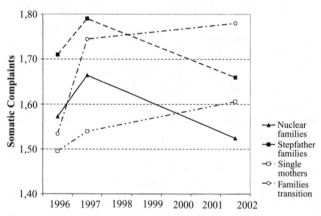

Age Group 3: 16-19 years at t1

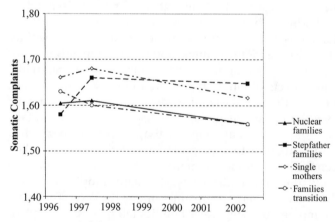

FIGURE 10.3. Adolescents' somatic complaints across time by family type and age group.

our findings for indicators of psychological well-being as observed in the overall sample. The psychological stresses of experiencing family transitions may translate more readily into somatic problems after puberty. At the same time, the older age group may not be affected because with young adulthood there is the option to leave the parental home and thus escape unfavorable, unstable circumstances.

Finally, findings for delinquency also indicate that effects of family type were not uniform across age groups and measurement points. Family type mattered for delinquency only for the younger two age groups, not for older adolescents as they entered young adulthood, and even the two younger groups were not affected at the same point in time. There is, however, considerable consistency regarding the age at which adolescents appear to be most at risk for delinquent behavior when facing family transitions. In 2002, when the youngest group reached age 15 to 18 years, these adolescents indicated higher delinquency if living in an unstable as compared to a nuclear family. For the middle age group, however, it was in 1997 (when these adolescents reached age 14 to 15) that experiencing family transitions predicted more delinquency than indicated by age-mates from nuclear families. In both cases, middle adolescence seemed to be the period when increased problem behavior was most likely triggered by family instability.

In summary, youth from separated families in general were not more delinquent than youth from nuclear families. Changes in family structure seem to be more important than structure per se, contributing to stresses that translate into delinquency if such problem behavior is developmentally "at stake" (see Dodge et al., Chapter 5 in this book). The lack of similar effects among older adolescents may be due to age-related differences in coping styles. While younger and middle adolescents have been shown to be quite susceptible to deviant behavior as a response to stress (Seiffge-Krenke, 1995), the older group may have largely "grown out" of such problem behavior in response to stress.

To assess *gender differences* with respect to the effects of family type, interaction effects of family type and gender were tested. Out of 16 possible effects, only self-esteem showed a marginally significant interaction effect of family, gender, and time. This suggests that effects of family type do not differ for boys and girls, a finding that is in line with those reported by Hetherington (Chapter 9 in this book) and Amato results (Chapter 8 in this book) for psychological well-being, social support, and educational attainment.

Given that recency of family transitions has been pointed out to be an important factor (e.g., Hetherington, 1993), we also investigated time since separation as a likely candidate for distinguishing adolescents' well-being within separated families. However, time since parental separation was not significant in any of these analyses, most probably because of the low number of youth from recently separated families in the original sample.

Effects of Parental Separation and Interparental Conflict on Adolescent Outcomes in 1997 and 2002

The second question was whether interparental conflict differed in its effects on adolescent outcomes in families in which parents had separated or stayed together. The analyses included all nuclear families, but separated families were only considered if biological parents were still in touch at the beginning of the study. Again, the same indicators for adolescent adjustment were used as in the first analyses (excluding delinquency since it would have limited the available sample to youth aged 13 and older). Our multivariate analyses of covariance with repeated measurement compared outcomes across time (1997–2002) with respect to effects of parental separation and interparental conflict (high versus low). Age and gender were controlled.

Effects of Parental Separation

With respect to parental separation, analysis revealed only one significant main effect: adolescents from stable nuclear families reported being less explosive than those whose parents had separated. Significant interactions of parental separation and time were found for depressive symptoms and marginally for self-esteem. Depressive symptoms increased considerably across time among youth from separated families, but were quite stable and even slightly reduced for adolescents from nuclear families. A similar, although less marked gap opened for self-esteem. While self-esteem was largely stable in separated families, it increased in nuclear families. In both cases, stable nuclear families appeared to provide a more facilitative context for positive development across time. While these findings largely reflect those reported in our first analyses, they are not redundant, given that adolescents whose separated parents lost contact with each other were not included. The increasing disadvantage in well-being among youth from separated families was, we infer, largely brought on by increased family instability during and subsequent to parental separation.

Effects of Interparental Conflict

Although parental separation had no marked overall effect, interparental conflict proved highly significant for all outcome variables except for academic self. The effect of interparental conflict was most pronounced for depressive symptoms, followed by explosiveness, peer integration, and peer rejection, while effects on self-esteem and somatic complaints were slightly weaker, but still significant. As can be seen in Figure 10.4, youth

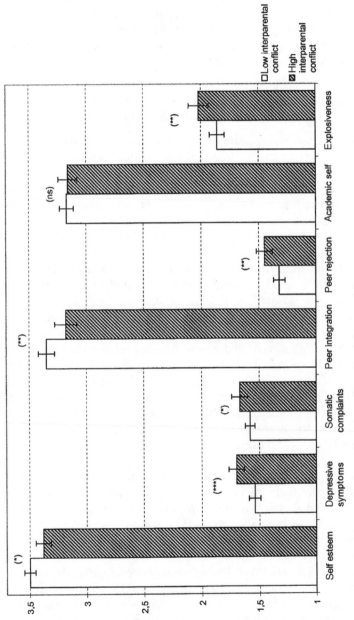

FIGURE 10.4. Effects of interparental conflict on adolescents' outcomes.
* $p < .05$. ** $p < .01$. *** $p < .001$.

from high-conflict families fared consistently worse than their age-mates from low-conflict families. These effects were similar across time. Further, no significant interaction with parental separation was found, suggesting a homogeneous negative impact of interparental conflict in nuclear as well as in separated families. It appears that neither increased exposure to inter-parental conflict in nuclear families nor the double dose of separation and enduring conflict leads to especially negative outcomes for adolescents.

Effects of Parental Separation and Interparental Conflict on Adolescents' Individuation in Relation to Mother and Father

Next, we address the question of whether parental separation and/or interparental conflict affect adolescents' individuation as reflected in their perceived relationship with mother and father. The same design for mul-tivariate analyses of covariance was used as in Question 2. Dependent variables are the four MITA scales. Analyses were conducted separately for mother-adolescent- and father-adolescent-relationships. In the latter case, only data for continuing father-child relations were used.

Individuation in Relation to Mother. Findings for individuation in rela-tion to mother revealed no effect of *parental separation*, but highly signifi-cant effects of *interparental conflict*. All indicators of adolescents' perceived relationship with mother were affected, with most pronounced effects for successful individuation and ambivalence. Figure 10.5 shows that youth in high-conflict families indicated more impaired relationships with mother as reflected in less successful individuation, higher ambivalence, and lower nurturance-seeking than reported by adolescents from low-conflict fami-lies. There was no evidence for interaction effects between parental separa-tion and parental conflict, or conflict and time, suggesting that the spillover of interparental conflict in the mother-child relationship was homogeneous across family types and time.

Individuation in Relation to Father. Adolescents' relationships with their biological fathers were affected by *parental separation*. As can be seen in Figures 10.6 and 10.7, adolescents from separated families reported less nurturance seeking in relation to their father, but also less fear of father's love-withdrawal than youth from nuclear families. Reduced nurturance-seeking in relation to the nonresidental father is in line with other research indicating less close relationships between nonresidential fathers and their offspring (see also Amato, Chapter 8 in this book). Considered in this con-text, adolescents' low fear of nonresidential father's disapproval and rejec-tion does not seem to indicate a particularly reliable, secure relationship, but is more likely to reflect reduced interdependence. Given that youth from separated families indicate similar levels of successful individuation

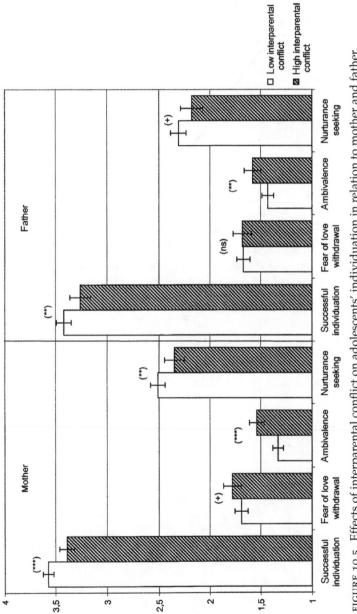

FIGURE 10.5. Effects of interparental conflict on adolescents' individuation in relation to mother and father.
*$p < .05.$ **$p < .01.$ ***$p < .001.$

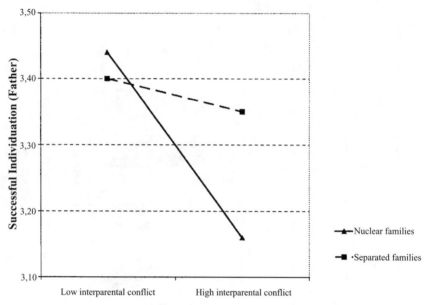

FIGURE 10.6. Successful individuation and nurturance seeking in relation to father by interparental conflict and parental separation.

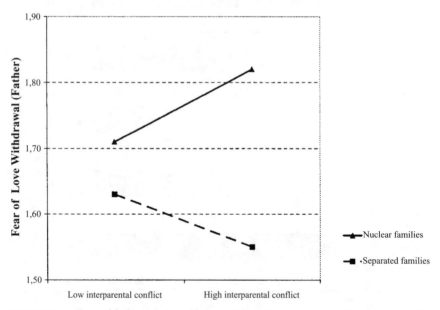

FIGURE 10.7. Fear of father's love withdrawal by interparental conflict and parental separation.

in relation to their fathers as adolescents from nuclear families, adolescents' feelings about their nonresidential fathers do not reflect a dismissing attitude, but rather correspond to a pattern of peaceful detachment.

This process of an earlier individuation from father among youth from separated families was also reflected in the interaction of *parental separation* and *time* for successful individuation and – marginally – for nurturance seeking. Adolescents from separated families reported particularly high successful individuation at t2, exceeding scores of youth from nuclear families, but successful individuation decreased at t3 while adolescents from nuclear families reported somewhat higher scores at t3 than at t2 (although these trends are not significant). In 2002, groups did not differ. With respect to nurturance seeking, no differences between nuclear and separated families were found in 1997, but while nurturance seeking in relation to father remained high for adolescents from nuclear families, a considerable decrease was found for adolescents from separated families in 2002.

Regarding the effects of *interparental conflict*, findings for individuation in relation to father were very similar to those reported for adolescents' relations to mother. As shown in Figure 10.5, youth from high-conflict families reported less successful individuation, higher ambivalence, and somewhat lower nurturance seeking in relation to their biological fathers than those from families with low interparental conflict. Effects of interparental conflict proved consistent across time, as was the case for mother-child relationships.

Finally, interactions between *parental separation* and *interparental conflict* were found for successful individuation, fear of love withdrawal, and nurturance seeking, effects that were not evident for adolescents' relationships with mothers. Negative effects of interparental conflict on adolescents' successful individuation and nurturance seeking in relation to father were restricted to nuclear families (see Figure 10.6). In separated families, neither successful individuation nor nurturance seeking were affected by interparental conflict. While successful individuation was not undermined by high postseparation conflict between parents, nurturance seeking was similarly low in relation to nonresidential fathers, no matter how both parents related to each other. Further, effects of interparental conflict on adolescents' fear of father's love withdrawal diverged slightly by family type, yielding significant differences between nuclear and separated families if interparental conflict was high. Taken together, these findings support the exposure hypothesis. Contrary to the "double dose" hypothesis, it is not separated families but nuclear families that show more negative impacts of conflicts between parents.

These findings are in line with those reported by Hetherington (Chapter 9 in this book) suggesting that spillover of interparental conflict is stronger in nuclear than in separated families. However, while Hetherington found such differential spillover to be restricted to mothers, we observed such differences with respect to the father-child relationship only. These findings are not necessarily at odds as our focus is on adolescents' perception of the parent-child relationship while Hetherington analyzed parenting behaviors. Parental separation may allow mothers to remove their parenting behavior from the stresses of a conflicted relationship with the ex-partner, while at the same time, adolescents' relationships with their nonresidential fathers may become more distant and independent simply because of less frequent contact. Furthermore, at this age, adolescents' relationship with the noncustodial father may have become established independently from maternal attitudes towards the ex-spouse.

LINKS BETWEEN INTERPARENTAL CONFLICT, PARENT-CHILD RELATIONS AND ADOLESCENT OUTCOMES

Next, we turn to the question of whether strain in adolescents' relationships with their mothers explains the effects of interparental conflict on adolescents' well being. Given that we found evidence for a spillover of interparental conflict into parent-adolescent relationships, and given that parent-adolescent relationships have frequently been shown to play a major role in adolescents'well-being, competence, and problem behavior (Steinberg, 2001), it seemed quite possible that compromised parent-child relationships provide the link between interparental conflict and adolescent outcomes. Because the father-child relationship was less contingent on parental conflict in separated families than in nuclear families, we focus on adolescents' relationships with their mothers. In these analyses we also controlled for ambivalence and successful individuation in relation to mother. These two aspects of the mother-adolescent-relationship were selected because they were most strongly affected by interparental conflict. Age and gender were controlled, also.

Ambivalence, in the adolescent-mother relationship was related to all the outcome measures except peer-integration, with highly significant links to self-esteem, depressive symptoms, somatic complaints, and peer-rejection. In all cases, higher ambivalence was related to un favorable outcomes. Successful individuation had significant independent effects on three of the seven outcome indicators, contributing to higher self-esteem, lower peer rejection, and higher academic self.

After controlling for the impact of successful individuation and ambivalence in mother-adolescent relationships, the links betwen interparental conflict and self-esteem, somatic complaints and peer-rejection were no longer significant. All other effects of interparental conflict were reduced, too, even though they remained significant or marginally significant. These findings provide support for the mediation hypothesis suggesting that it is the spill-over of interparental problems into the parent-child relationship that explains most of their detrimental links with adolescents' psychosocial development.

Effects of Parental Separation and Interparental Conflict on Adolescents' Romantic Relationships

Finally, we address the question of whether parental separation and interparental conflict as assessed in 1996 and 1997 affected adolescents' and young adults' romantic relationships in 2002, and if so, whether these effects were due to adolescents' felt insecurity in relation to mother, as indicated by their ambivalence in relation to their mothers and their fear of maternal love-withdrawal. The sample for these analyses was restricted to those adolescents and young adults who reported having a partner in 2002 (50 percent of the participants at t3). The likelihood of having a romantic partner did not vary by parental separation or by interparental conflict. But while only 33.1 percent of the boys indicated a current romantic relationship, 64.5 percent of the girls did so. The duration of the partnership was two years, on average.

In the first step of our analysis, parental separation and interparental conflict as well as age and gender were included as predictors of insecure attachment to partner. Indeed, parental separation as well as interparental conflict contributed to increased insecurity in adolescents' romantic relationships independently. In the second step of our analysis, insecure attachment to mother (estimated from ambivalence and fear of maternal love withdrawal) was included in order to explain these effects. As was evident in an earlier analysis, antagonism between parents led to increased insecurity in relation to mother, while parental separation proved insignificant regarding insecurity in mother-adolescent relationships. In line with the continuity hypothesis assuming links in insecure attachment across attachment figures, insecurity in relation to mother was significantly related to insecurity in romantic relationships (see Figure 10.8). Effects of parental separation, however, cannot be explained by adolescents' insecure attachment to mother. Parental separation still has a significant negative impact on adolescents' romantic relationships contributing to higher insecurity even when the quality of mother-adolescent relationship is included.

These results are well in line with our hypothesis that insecurity in parent-child relationships is key to the negative impact of interparental conflict on the quality of adolescents' romantic relationships. This suggests that the intergenerational transmission of relationship qualities occurs largely through experiences in those relationships that adolescents are directly involved in and not only through observation of interparental relationships. Furthermore, the findings support the notion that parental separation negatively affects the partner relationships of offspring. As evident

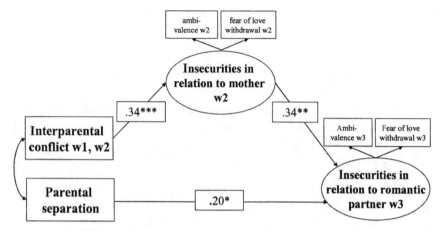

FIGURE 10.8. Effects of interparental conflict and parental separation on adolescents' and young adults' romantic relationships.
$^* p < .05.$ $^{**} p < .01.$ $^{***} p < .001.$

from these analyses, parental separation triggers increased insecurity in romantic relationships even at an early point in adolescents' lives.

DISCUSSION

Our focus was not only on family composition, comparing nuclear, single mother, and stepfather families, but also on stability and change in families, and last but not least, on the quality of the interparental relationship. Furthermore, we investigated the role of parent-child relationships as providing a link between parent-related instability of the family system and interparental strains on the one hand, and adolescent outcomes on the other hand. Covering a time span of 6 years, we were able to trace children ranging from late childhood to late adolescence at the onset of the study through their middle adolescence to young adult years. Finally, the evidence presented here comes from Germany, a country that had just united the Western and Eastern parts when the study began. Since both regions were formerly ruled by quite different political systems and traditions of family policy, the sample provides considerable heterogeneity. Accordingly, our findings are of particular interest when compared to studies conducted in the United States or United Kingdom. In the following, we first summarize the findings and then turn to their practical implications for counseling and intervention.

Family Instability Matters More than Parental Separation

First, contrary to many other studies, we did not find any disadvantages among youth from separated families per se when compared to nuclear families. On average, adolescents who grew up in stable single-mother or stable step father-families did not show lower levels of well-being, reduced social or academic competencies, or elevated problem behavior; they did just as well as their age mates in biologically intact families. In explaining these similarities, it is important to keep in mind that the majority of these families had experienced parental separation and in the case of stepfamilies the entrance of the stepfather many years earlier. Accordingly, these families seemed well-established in their new structure when our study began and they remained so during the subsequent 6 years. These findings are not entirely surprising, because other studies conducted in Germany and the United States, too, suggest considerable post-separation adaptation among children across the first 2 to 3 years after the breakup of their parents' relationship (Schmidt-Denter, 2000). The capacity for successful coping and even developmental gains by escaping detrimental family dynamics must not be ignored.

At this point, it would be clearly overstretching the evidence if we concluded from our findings that adolescents in Germany are better prepared to cope with parental separation than their age mates from other countries where there is more evidence of negative long-term effects. However, it seems worthwhile to aim at more rigorous crossnational comparisons as well as the role of institutions such as schools and health care systems in the families' struggle to cope with internal problems while trying to prepare their children for a better future.

In our comparison of family types, only one group stands out: youth from families that experienced a transition brought on by the exit or entry of a parent figure during the course of our study. In line with the "divorce stress and coping perspective" – which might be complemented by a similar perspective on stepfamily formation and dissolution – these adolescents showed increasing emotional distress and behavior problems that rendered them at a significant disadvantage in the last assessment as compared with youth from nuclear families. Given that only a small minority of these transitions involved the separation of biological parents, these findings highlight the importance of family stability in general for adolescents' well-being. Having to adapt to a new stepparent or having to face another break-up during the demanding years of adolescence seems to be a substantial stressor, at least in the short run.

The fact that these adolescents did not differ from the other groups at earlier assessments speaks against the selection perspective (Amato, 2000). This view focuses on individual and family characteristics that increase the risk for divorce, as a likely third factor explaining maladaptation among individuals from divorced families. Evidence from prospective studies has contributed to this view indicating that children from families undergoing parental divorce show problems even years before their parents separate (Block, Block, & Gjerde, 1986; Cherlin et al., 1991). In our study, we did not find any earlier problems or disadvantages of youth from families in transition that might have preceded later changes in family structure. However, given the low number of families in which biological parents separated during the course of this study, we cannot rule out such previously elevated levels of distress in this particular subgroup.

Experiencing Interparental Conflict: A Stressor in Nuclear and Separated Families

On the interplay of parental separation and conflict between parents, our findings are quite straightforward: Unlike parental separation, interparental conflict was a significant stressor to adolescents' mental health and social relationships, affecting almost all domains of development studied here. In line with findings reported by Hetherington (1999), the effects of a conflict-ridden relationship between parents did not differ for nuclear and separated families. Hence, there is no support for either the exposure hypothesis (expecting stronger effects of interparental conflict in nuclear families) or the double dose hypothesis (expecting stronger effects in separated families).

Separated families as a group showed only weak disadvantages, restricted to a few indicators of adolescents' adjustment. There is some indication that nuclear and separated families diverged across time, a pattern similar to findings reported by Chase-Lansdale et al. (1995). Taken alone, this might have suggested that parental separation brings about new challenges in later adolescence and early adulthood, undermining adaptation more strongly in these later phases. However, our initial analyses caution against this interpretation. Given that such increased distress was restricted to families in transition, which represent a substantial share of separated families, we may conclude that it is rather the greater likelihood of instability in family structure triggered by parental separation than living in a separated family per se that contributes to increasing problems among youth from separated families.

Evidence for differential effects of interparental conflict moderated by parental separation was found in only one domain: the father-child relationship. These findings support the exposure hypothesis, indicating a stronger disadvantage of youth experiencing high-conflict between parents when conflict occurs in nuclear families. Further, it was only the father-child relationship, not the mother-child relationship, that was negatively affected by parental separation per se. These results echo other findings suggesting that the father-child relationship is at higher risk than the mother-child relationship when parents separate (Coiro & Emery, 1998). However, we also found considerable negative effects of frequent arguments between parents on mother-adolescent relationships. Adolescents who reported high levels of conflict between their parents indicated a more distant and less secure relationship with their mothers. Given that inter-parental conflict affected the father-adolescent relationship in the same way but at a less marked level, we are led to conclude that the father-adolescent relationship may be less vulnerable in separated than in nuclear families when parents encounter problems in their relationship – at least in some respects.

Our findings for the mother-adolescent relationship in particular support the notion that a conflict-ridden relationship between parents undermines children's emotional security in the family (Davies et al., 2002) and shows that adolescents are not immune to these processes. Although these analyses did not focus on the quality of parenting, other findings from the present study suggest that impaired parenting explains much of the negative outcomes of interparental conflict for adolescents' relationship to their mother (Walper, Kruse, Noack, & Schwarz, in press; Walper & Schwarz, 2001). A lack of sensitive support and increased restrictive parenting undermine successful individuation and trigger feelings of insecurity in relation to mothers. In addition, however, maternal pressure on adolescents to side with them, and adolescents' feelings of being caught between parents, provide another link between interparental conflict and increased insecurity in relation to mother.

Impaired Parent-Adolescent Relationships as a Link Between Interparental Conflict and Adolescent Outcomes

Our assumption that impaired parent-adolescent relationships carry most of the negative impact of interparental conflict on adolescents' adjustment was well supported. In line with many other findings (Krishnakumar & Buehler, 2000), negativity in the relationship between parents seems to spill over into parent-child relationships which in turn undermine adolescents' well-being and competencies. Interestingly, it was particularly adolescents' felt insecurity in relation to their mothers that proved important. This finding, too, matches the emotional security hypothesis. Parents' destructive conflict behavior does not so much act as a model for children's behavior, but rather compromises well-being and competence brought on by children's increased emotional insecurity when confronted with intense, threatening emotional family climates (Davies, Harold, Goeke-Morey, & Cummings, 2002). Because our analyses focused on the mother-adolescent relationship, it should be noted that findings are highly similar when father-adolescent relationships are investigated as a potential link to adolescents' adjustment. Hence, we should not underestimate the importance of fathers for adolescents' development.

Our final analyses showed that such insecurity in relation to mother not only undermines well-being, but also extends beyond the family and reaches into adolescents' romantic relationships. These, too, are characterized by high insecurity if the mother-adolescent relationship is ambivalent and fearful. In fact, increased insecurity in the mother-child relationship explains why adolescents from families with high discord between parents felt less secure with their own partners. They appeared to develop a more generalized fearful and ambivalent attitude in close relationships. This notion also finds some support in longitudinal studies that reach further back into childhood and link early attachment to mother to later romantic relationships (Collins & Madsen, 2002).

IMPLICATIONS FOR PRACTICE

What do these findings suggest for parents and practitioners? First, given that family transitions emerged as a stressor that compromises adolescents' development, it is important to focus more on such transitions following parental separation. Stepfamily formation has been pointed out to be particularly challenging when coinciding with adolescents' quest for autonomy and their growing ties to peers and other adults outside the family (Bray & Berger, 1993). Parents' sensitivity to adolescents' needs is strongly demanded at those points of family development, and step-parents may have to show substantial tolerance of frustration if their efforts to establish a closer relationship to their stepchildren do not prove welcome (Ganong, Coleman, Fine, & Martin, 1999). Providing guidance and support through these phases may not only help parents to cooperate successfully in their new partnership, but could also prevent adolescents' increased stress, loyalty conflicts between nonresidential and stepparent, and premature distancing from the family (Visher & Visher, 1991). At the same time, disruptions of new partnerships deserve more attention. Much effort has focused on strengthening the bond between biological parents. However, the stable availability of a caring "merely" social parent may prove of real importance.

Second, the strong focus of public attention on children and adolescents from divorced families may distract from the needs of others who are raised in troubled nuclear families. Although conflict per se is not harmful, frequent, intense, and unresolved antagonisms between parents provide a considerable stressor challenging children's and adolescents' emotional competencies to cope. Preventive approaches strengthening young couples' competencies to cooperate and communicate successfully may well reduce divorce rates and secure high quality marriages – something children would clearly profit from. However, more innovative approaches are needed for later phases of family development to help parents deal with their problems in ways that do not undermine children's development. Given that most parents care strongly about their children's well-being, focusing on children may be a promising way to improve interparental dynamics.

Finally, it should be emphasized that families do not lose their importance as developmental contexts in adolescence and young adulthood. The secure base for exploration, the acceptance, support, and demands for competence experienced in the family contribute to adolescents' well-being and competence and, thus, should be a target for intervention. Most intervention programs, however, address families with young children because positive outcomes are more likely than for older groups when problems have often stabilized (Layzer, Goodson, Bernstein, & Price, 2001). Given that parents frequently struggle with their relationship to adolescent children (Steinberg, 2001), approaches that help to build or maintain positive, reliable relationships while fostering successful individuation would seem promising. Although our findings have focused more on family risk factors for adolescents' development than on resources, they clearly underscore the importance of the quality of relationships over and above structural features of the family system.

FUTURE RESEARCH DIRECTIONS

Insecurity in romantic relationships proved to be one of the few aspects of adolescents' development that pointed to significant and direct effects of parental separation in our study. Although many studies have shown that marriages of adult offspring from divorced homes are more problematic and less stable (see Amato, Chapter 8 in this book), few studies have linked parental separation with adolescents' romantic relationships (Amato & Booth, 1997). In general, adolescents' romantic relationships have been neglected, most likely because they were not considered "serious" relationships worthy of study (Collins, 2003). Our findings, however, suggest that later problems in adulthood may be better understood if early precursors are not neglected.

References

Alsaker, F. D. (1989). School achievement, perceived academic competence, and global self-esteem. *School Psychology International, 10,* 147–158.

Amato, P. R. (1993). Children's adjustment to divorce: Theories, hypotheses, and empirical support. *Journal of Marriage and the Family, 55,* 23–38.

Amato, P. R. (1994). The implications of research findings on children in stepfamilies. In A. Booth & J. Dunn (Eds.), *Stepfamilies: Who benefits? Who does not?* (pp. 81–87). Hillsdale, NJ: Erlbaum.

Amato, P. R. (2000). The consequences of divorce for adults and children. *Journal of Marriage and the Family, 62,* 1269–1287.

Amato, P. R. (2001). Children of divorce in the 1990s: An update of the Amato and Keith (1991) meta-analysis. *Journal of Family Psychology, 15*(3), 355–370.

Amato, P. R., & Booth, A. (1997). *A generation at risk. Growing up in an era of family upheaval.* Cambridge, MA: Harvard University Press.

Andreß, H.-J., & Lohmann, H. (2000). *Die wirtschaftlichen Folgen von Trennung und Scheidung*: Vol. 180. Stuttgart: Kohlhammer.

Arbuckle, J. L. (1997). *Amos user's guide. (Version 3.6)*. [Computer Software]Chicago, IL: Small Waters Corporation.

Block, J. H., Block, J., & Gjerde, P. F. (1986). The personality of children prior to divorce: A prospective study. *Child Development, 57*, 827–840.

Brähler, E. (1992). *Gießener Beschwerdebogen für Kinder und Jugendliche (GBB-KJ)*. Bern: Huber.

Bray, J. H., & Berger, S. H. (1993). Developmental issues in stepfamilies research project: Family relationships and parent-child interactions. *Journal of Family Psychology, 7*(1), 76–90.

Brooks-Gunn, J., Duncan, G. J., & Mariato, N. (1997). Poor families, poor outcomes: The well-being of children and youth. In G. J. Duncan & J. Brooks-Gunn (Eds.), *Consequences of growing up poor* (pp. 1–17). New York: Russell Sage Foundation.

Buchanan, C. M., Maccoby, E. E., & Dornbusch, S. M. (1996). *Adolescents after divorce*. Cambridge, MA: Harvard University Press.

Buehler, C., & Gerard, J. M. (2002). Marital conflict, ineffective parenting and children's and adolescents' maladjustment. *Journal of Marriage and Family, 64*, 78–92.

Burkhauser, R. V., Duncan, G. J., Hauser, R., & Berntsen, R. (1991). Wife or Frau, women do worse: A comparison of men and women in the United States and Germany after marital dissolution. *Demography, 28*(3), 353–360.

Butz, P., & Boehnke, K. (1999). Problemverhalten im Kontext familiärer Veränderungen durch Trennung und neue Partnerschaft der Eltern. In S. Walper & B. Schwarz (Eds.), *Was wird aus den Kindern? Chancen und Risiken für die Entwicklung von Kindern aus Trennungs und Stieffamilien* (pp. 171–189). Weinheim: Juventa.

Chase-Lansdale, P. L., Cherlin, A. J., & Kiernan, K. E. (1995). The long-term effects of parental divorce on the mental health of young adults: A developmental perspective. *Child Development, 66*, 1614–1634.

Cherlin, A. J., Chase-Landsdale, P. L., & McRae, C. (1998). Effects of parental divorce on mental health throughout the life course. *American Sociological Review, 63*, 239–249.

Cherlin, A. J., Furstenberg, F. F., Jr., Chase-Lansdale, P. L., Kiernan, K. E., Robins, P. K., Morrison, D. R., & Teitler, J., O. (1991). Longitudinal studies of effects of divorce on children in Great Britain and the United States. *Science, 252*, 1386–1389.

Coiro, M. J., & Emery, R. E. (1998). Do marriage problems affect fathering more than mothering? A quantitative and qualitative review. *Clinical Child and Family Psychology Review, 1*(1), 23–40.

Coleman, M., Ganong, L., & Fine, M. (2000). Reinvestigating remarriage: Another decade of progress. *Journal of Marriage and the Family, 62*, 1288–1307.

Collins, W. A. (2003). More than myth: The developmental significance of romantic relationships during adolescence. *Journal of Research on Adolescence, 13*(1), 1–24.

Collins, W. A., Henninghausen, K. C., Schmit, D. T., & Sroufe, L. A. (1997). Developmental precursors of romantic relationship: A longitudinal analysis. In W. Damon, S. Schulman, & W. A. Collins (Eds.), *Romantic realtionships in adolescence: Developmental perspectives* (pp. 69–84). San Francisco: Jossey-Bass.

Conger, R. D., Conger, K. J., & Elder, G. H. J. (1997). Family economic hardship and adolescent adjustment: Mediating and moderating processes. In G. J. Duncan & J. Brooks-Gunn (Eds.), *Consequences of growing up poor* (pp. 288–310). New York: Russell Sage Foundation.

Davies, P. T., Harold, G. T., Goeke-Morey, M. C., & Cummings, E. M. (2002). Child emotional security and interparental conflict. *Monographs of the Society for Research in Child Development, 67* (3, Serial No. 270).

Diekmann, A., & Engelhardt, H.(1999). The social inheritence of divorce: Effects of parent's family type in postwar Germany. *American Sociological Review, 64,* 783–793.

Dornbusch, S. M., Carlsmith, J. M., Bushwall, S. J., Ritter, P. L., Leiderman, P. H., Hastorf, A. H., & Gross, R. T.(1985). Single parents, extended households, and the control of adolescents. *Child Development, 56,* 326–341.

Emery, R. E. (1988). *Marriage, divorce, and children's adjustment.* Newbury Park, CA: Sage.

Emery, R. E., & Forehand, R. (1994). Parental divorce and children's well-being: A focus on resilience. In R. J. Haggerty & L. R. Sherrod & N. Garmezy & M. Rutter (Eds.), *Stress, risk, and resilience in children and adolescents* (pp. 64–99). Cambridge: Cambridge University Press.

Engstler, H., & Menning, S. (2003). *Die Familie im Spiegel der amtlichen Statistik.* Berlin: Bundesministerium für Familie, Senioren, Frauen und Jugend.

Erel, O., & Burman, B.(1995). Interrelatedness of marital relations and parent-child-relations: a meta-analytic review. *Psychological Bulletin, 118,* 108–132.

Fend, H. (1998). Eltern und Freunde. Soziale Entwicklung im Jugendalter, *Entwicklungspsychologie der Adoleszenz in der Moderne (Band 5).* Bern: Huber.

Fincham, F. D. (1998). Child development and marital relations. *Child Development, 69,* 543–574.

Forehand, R., McCombs, A., Long, N., Brody, G. H., & Fauber, R. L. (1988). Early adolescent adjustment to recent parental divorce: The role of interparental conflict and adolescent sex as mediating variables. *Journal of Consulting and Clinical Psychology, 56,* 624–627.

Forehand, R., Wierson, M., McCombs Thomas, A., Faubner, R., Armistead, L., Kemptom, T., & Long, N. (1991). A short-term longitudinal examination of young adolescent functioning following divorce: The role of family factors. *Journal of Abnormal Child Psychology, 19,* 97–111.

Ganong, L., Coleman, M., Fine, M., & Martin, P. (1999). Stepparents' affinity-seeking and affinity-maintaining strategies with stepchildren. *Journal of Family Issues, 20,* 299–327.

Harold, G. T., & Conger, R. D. (1997). Marital conflict and adolescent distress: The role of adolescent awareness. *Child Development, 68,* 333–350.

Harold, G. T., Fincham, F. D., Osborne, L. N., & Conger, R. D. (1997). Mom and Dad are at it again: Adolescent perceptions of marital conflict and adolescent psychological distress. *Developmental Psychology, 3,* 333–350.

Hautzinger, M., & Bailer, M. (1993). *Allgemeine Depressionsskala (ADS). Deutsche Form der Center of Epidemiologic Studies Scale (CES-D).* Weinheim: Beltz Test.

Heitmeyer, W., Collmann, B., Conrads, J., Matuschek, I., Kraul, D., Kühnel, W., Möller, R., & Ulbrich-Hermann, N. (1996). *Gewalt. Schattenseiten der Individualisierung bei Jugendlichen aus unterschiedlichen Milieus* (2nd. ed.). Weinheim: Juventa.

Herzog, M. J., & Cooney, T. M.(2002). Parental divorce and perceptions of past interparental conflict: influences on communication of young adults. *Journal of Divorce and Remarriage, 36*(3/4), 89–109.

Hetherington, E. M. (1993). An overview of the Virginia longitudinal study of divorce and remarriage with a focus an early adolescence. *Journal of Family Psychology, 7,* 39–56.

Hetherington, E. M. (1999). Should we stay together for the sake of the children? In E. M. Hetherington (Ed.), *Coping with divorce, single parenting, and remarriage. A risk and resilience perspective* (pp. 93–116). Mahwah, NJ: Erlbaum.

Hetherington, E. M., Bridges, M., & Insabella, G. M. (1998). What matters? What does not? Five perspectives on the association between marital transitions and children's adjustment. *American Psychologist, 53,* 167–184.

Hetherington, E. M., & Clingempeel, W. G. (1992). Coping with marital transitions: A family systems perspective. *Monographs of the Society for Research in Child Development, No. 227, 57*(2–3).

Hetherington, E. M., & Jodl, K. M. (1994). Stepfamilies as settings for child development. In A. Booth & J. Dunn (Eds.), *Stepfamilies. Who benefits? Who does not?* (pp. 55–79). Hillsdale, NJ: Erlbaum.

Jenkins, J. M., & Smith, M. A. (1993). A prospective study of behavioral disturbance in children who subsequently experience parental divorce: A research note. *Journal of Divorce and Remarriage, 19*(1/2), 143–160.

Kerns, K. A., Aspelmeier, J. E., Gentzler, A. L., & Grabill, C. M. (2001). Parent-child attachment and monitoring in middle childhood. *Journal of Family Psychology, 15,* 69–81.

Krishnakumar, A., & Buehler, C. (2000). Interparental conflict and parenting behaviors. A meta-analytic review. *Family Relations, 49,* 25–44.

Lamb, M. E. (1999). Parental behavior, family processes, and child dvelopment in nontraditional and traditionally understudied families. In M. E. Lamb (Ed.), *Parenting and child development in "nontraditional" families* (pp. 1–14). Mahwah, NJ: Erlbaum.

Layzer, J. I., Goodson, B. D., Bernstein, L., & Price, C. (2001). *National evaluation of family support programs: Vol. A. The meta-analysis.* Cambridge, MA: Abt Associates.

Levine, J. B., Green, C. J., & Millon, T. (1986). The Separation-Individuation Test of Adolescence. *Journal of Personality Assessment, 50,* 123–137.

Levine, J. B., & Saintonge, S. (1993). Psychometric properties of the Separation-Individuation Test of Adolescence within a clinical population. *Journal of Clinical Psychology, 49,* 492–507.

Lösel, F., Averbeck, M., & Bliesener, T. (1997). Gewalt zwischen Schülern der Sekundarstufe: Eine Untersuchung zur Prävalenz und Beziehung zu allgemeiner Aggressivität und Delinquenz. *Zeitschrift für empirische Pädagogik, Themenheft Gewalt in der Schule, 11*(3), 327–351.

Martin, B. (1990). The transmission of relationship difficulties from one generation to the next. *Journal of Youth and Adolescence, 19,* 181–220.

Masten, A. S., Morison, P., & Pellegrini, D. S. (1985). A revised class play method of peer assessment. *Developmental Psychology, 21,* 523–533.

McLanahan, S. (1999). Father absence and the welfare of children. In E. M. Hetherington (Ed.), *Coping with divorce, single parenting, and remarriage. A risk and resilience perspective* (pp. 117–146). Mahwah, NJ: Erlbaum.

Peterson, J. L., & Zill, N. (1986). Marital disruption, parent-child relationships, and behavior problems in children. *Journal of Marriage and the Family, 48*, 295–307.

Pryor, J., & Rodgers, B. (2001). *Children in changing families. Life after parental separation.* Oxford: Blackwell.

Reis, O., & Meyer-Probst, B. (1999). Scheidung der Eltern und Entwicklung der Kinder: Befunde der Rostocker Längsschnittstudie. In S. Walper & B. Schwarz (Eds.), *Was wird aus den Kindern? Chancen und Risiken für die Entwicklung von Kindern aus Trennungs- und Stieffamilien* (pp. 49–72). Weinheim: Juventa.

Rosenberg, M. (1965). *Society and the adolescent self-image.* Princeton: Princeton University Press.

Schafer, J. L. (1999). *NORM: Multiple imputation of incomplete multivariate data under a normal model (Version 2)* Computer Software for Windows 95/98/NT, available from http://www.stat.psu.edu/jls/misoftwa.html.

Schick, A. (2002). Behavioral and emotional differences between children of divorce and children from intact famlies: Clinical significance and mediating processes. *Swiss Journal of Psychology, 61*, 5–14.

Schmidt-Denter, U. (2000). Entwicklung von Trennungs- und Scheidungsfamilien: Die Kölner Längsschnittstudie. In K. A. Schneewind (Ed.), *Familienpsychologie im Aufwind. Brückenschläge zwischen Forschung und Praxis* (pp. 203–221). Göttingen: Hogrefe.

Schmidt-Denter, U. (2001). Differentielle Entwicklungsverläufe von Scheidungskindern. In S. Walper & R. Pekrun (Eds.), *Familie und Entwicklung. Aktuelle Perspektiven der Familienpsychologie* (pp. 292–313). Göttingen: Hogrefe.

Schmidt-Denter, U., & Schmitz, H. (1999). Familiäre Beziehungen und Stukturen sechs Jahre nach der elterlichen Trennung. In S. Walper & B. Schwarz (Eds.), *Was wird aus den Kindern? Chancen und Risiken für die Entwicklung von Kindern aus Trennungs- und Stieffamilien* (pp. 73–90). Weinheim: Juventa.

Schneider, N. F., Krüger, D., Lasch, V., Limmer, R., & Matthias-Bleck, H. (2001). *Alleinerziehen. Vielfalt und Dynamik einer Lebensform.* Weinheim: Juventa.

Seiffge-Krenke, I. (1995). *Stress, coping and relationships.* Hillsdale, NJ: Erlbaum.

Sessa, F. M., & Steinberg, L. (1991). Family structure and the development of autonomy during adolescence. *Journal of Early Adolescence, 11*, 38–55.

Simons, R. L. (1996). *Understanding differences between divorced and intact families. Stress, interaction, and child outcome.* Thousand Oaks, CA: Sage.

Sinclair, S. L., & Nelson, E. S. (1998). The impact of parental divorce on college students' intimate relationships and relationship beliefs. *Journal of Divorce and Remarriage, 29* (1/2), 103–129.

Smetana, J. G. (1993). Conceptions of parental authority in divorced and married mothers and their adolescents. *Journal of Research on Adolesence, 3*, 19–39.

Steinberg, L. (2001). We know some things: parent-adolecent relationships in retrospect and prospect. *Journal of Research on Adolesence, 11*, 1–19.

Teubner, M. (2002). Wie viele Stieffamilien gibt es in Deutschland? In W. Bien & A. Hartl & M. Teubner (Eds.), *Stieffamilien in Deutschland. Eltern und Kinder zwischen Normalität und Konflikt.* Opladen: Leske + Budrich.

Visher, E. B., & Visher, J. S. (1991). *How to win as a stepfamily* (2 ed.). New York: Brunner/Mazel.

Walper, S. (1997). Individuation im Jugendalter – Skalenanalyse zum Münchner Individuationstest. *Berichte aus der Arbeitsgruppe "Familienentwicklung nach der Trennung" #23/1996*.

Walper, S. (1998). Die Individuation in Beziehung zu beiden Eltern bei Kindern und Jugendlichen aus konfliktbelasteten Kernfamilien und Trennungsfamilien. *Zeitschrift für Soziologie der Erziehung und Sozialisation, 18*(2), 134–151.

Walper, S., & Galambos, N. L. (1997). Employed mothers in Germany. In J. Frankel (Ed.), *Families of employed mothers. An international perspective* (pp. 35–66). New York: Garland.

Walper, S., Kruse, J., Noack, P., & Schwarz, B.(in press). Links Between Parental Separation and Adolescents' Felt Insecurity in Relation to Mother: Effects of Financial Hardship, Interparental Conflict, and Maternal Parenting in East and West Germany. *Marriage and Family Review*.

Walper, S., & Schwarz, B. (1999). *Was wird aus den Kindern? Chancen und Risiken fuer die Entwicklung von Kindern aus Trennungs- und Stieffamilien*. Weinheim: Juventa.

Walper, S., & Schwarz, B. (2001). Adolescents' individuation in East and West Germany: Effects of family structure, financial hardship, and family processes. *American Behavioral Scientist, 44*, 1937–1954.

Walper, S., & Wendt, E.V.(2005). Nicht mit beiden Eltern aufwachsen - ein Risiko? Kinder von Alleinerziehenden und Stieffamilien. In C. Alt (Ed.), *Kinder-Leben. Aufwachsen zwischen Familie, Freunden und Institutionen. Band 1: Aufwachsen in Familien* (pp. 187–216). Wiesbaden: VS Verlag für SozialWissenschaften.

PART FIVE

NEW AND EXTENDED FAMILY FORMS

11

New Family Forms

Susan Golombok

In July 2004, Louise Brown, the first "test-tube" baby celebrated her 25th birthday. In the years since her birth, in vitro fertilization (IVF) has made the transition from the realm of science fiction to a commonly accepted treatment for infertility. The 1970s was also a time when another new and controversial family type, lesbian-mother families, came to the fore, and when families headed by single heterosexual mothers began to cast off the stigma associated with illegitimacy and divorce. Today, there exists a variety of new family forms made possible through advances in assisted reproduction technology. An example is the small but growing number of lesbian and single heterosexual women who are actively choosing assisted reproduction, particularly donor insemination, as a means of conceiving a child without the involvement of a male partner. In this chapter, I examine research on the psychological outcomes for parents and children in assisted reproduction families, with particular attention to the concerns and policy issues that have been raised by creating families in this way. The chapter is structured according to four major types of assisted reproduction: (1) Those involving "high-tech" procedures such as in vitro fertilization (IVF) and intracytoplasmic sperm injection (ICSI), (2) those involving gamete donation such as donor insemination (DI) and egg donation, (3) those resulting in nontraditional families such as single mother- and lesbian-mother families, and (4) those involving surrogate mothers. Although the four categories are not mutually exclusive, each raises a specific set of concerns regarding family functioning.

IVF involves the fertilization of an egg with sperm in the laboratory and the transfer of the resulting embryo to the mother's womb (Steptoe & Edwards 1978). When the mother's egg and the father's sperm are used, both parents are genetically related to the child. With ICSI, a single sperm is injected directly into the egg to create an embryo. Donor insemination involves the insemination of a woman with the sperm of a man who is not her husband or partner, and the child is genetically related to the mother but not the father. Egg donation is like donor insemination in that the child is genetically related to only one parent, but in this case it is a mother with whom the child lacks a genetic link. Egg donation is a much more complex and intrusive procedure than donor insemination and involves IVF techniques. When both egg and sperm are donated, sometimes referred to as embryo adoption, the child is genetically unrelated to both parents, a situation that is like adoption except that the parents experience the pregnancy and the child's birth. With surrogacy, one woman bears a child for another woman. There are two types of surrogacy; partial (genetic) surrogacy where conception occurs using the commissioning father's sperm and the surrogate mother's egg, and full (nongenetic) surrogacy where both the egg and sperm are those of the commissioning parents. As Einwohner (1989) has pointed out, it is now possible for a child to have five parents: an egg donor, a sperm donor, a surrogate mother who hosts the pregnancy, and the two social parents whom the child knows as mother and father. In the case of lesbian-mother families, the two social parents are both mothers, and in solo-mother families, the father is often an anonymous sperm donor whom the child will never meet.

"HIGH-TECH" FAMILIES

IVF Families

Concerns about IVF Families. Although it may seem that the only difference between IVF and natural conception is the conception itself, there are a number of reasons that having a child by IVF may result in a rather different experience for parents. One very important difference is the higher incidence of multiple births, preterm births, and low-birthweight infants following IVF (e.g., Olivennes et al., 2002; Vayena, Rowe, & Griffin, 2002). Whereas only 1 percent of natural births involve twins, triplets, or more (Bergh, Ericson, Hillensjo, Bygren & Wennerholm, 1999), this is true of more than one quarter of births resulting from IVF (Nygren & Andersen, 2002; Nyboe Andersen, Gianaroli, & Nygren, 2004). The problem is greatest in developing and newly industrialized regions, such as Latin America, where the multiple birth rate for assisted reproduction pregnancies in 2000 was 50 percent, with more than 13.5 percent of IVF and ICSI births involving triplets or quadruplets (Zegers-Hochschild, 2002). Parents who have multiple births not only have to cope with two or more infants born at once but also with infants who may have greater needs as a result of prematurity and low birth weight (Botting, MacFarlane, & Price, 1990; Vayena, Rowe, & Griffin, 2002). As the children grow older, twins have consistently been found to show delayed language development and to obtain lower scores on verbal intelligence and reading tests (Lytton & Gallagher, 2002; Rutter, Thorpe, Greenwood, Northstone, & Golding, 2003). Although little is known about higher order births, a small study of language development found triplets to show greater impairment than twins (McMahon & Dodd, 1997). The impact of these factors on parenting and child development must be considered separately from the impact of IVF per se. Most of the empirical investigations described below have focused on families with a singleton child born as a result of IVF to avoid the confounding effect of a multiple birth.

It has also been suggested that the stress of infertility and its treatment may result in parenting difficulties when a long-awaited baby is eventually born. Burns (1990) argued that parents who had difficulty in conceiving might become emotionally over-invested in their long-awaited child, and other authors have suggested that those who become parents after a period of infertility may be overprotective of their children, or may have unrealistic expectations of them or of themselves as parents (Hahn & DiPietro, 2001; McMahon, Ungerer, Beaurepaire, Tennant et al., 1995; Mushin, Spensley, & Barreda-Hanson, 1985; van Balen, 1998). Additionally, it has been predicted that the stress of infertility and its treatment may lead to psychological disorder and marital dysfunction for those who become parents following IVF (McMahon et al., 1995).

Research on Parenting in IVF Families. Investigations of parenting in IVF families have focused on three areas of functioning: the psychological well being of parents, the quality of parent-child relationships, and security in the parental role. Studies of IVF families with infants and toddlers have been conducted in Australia (Gibson, Ungerer, Leslie, Saunders et al., 1999; Gibson, Ungerer, Tennant, & Saunders, 2000; McMahon, Ungerer, Tennant, & Saunders, 1997; McMahon, Gibson, Leslie, Cohen et al., 2003), the Netherlands (Colpin, Demyttenaere, Vandemeulebroecke, 1995; van Balen, 1996), France (Raoul-Duval, Bertrand-Servais, Letur-Konirsch, & Frydman, 1994), and the United Kingdom (Weaver, Clifford, Gordon, Hay et al., 1993). These investigations have generally found no evidence of psychological problems among IVF parents. However, in the only study to include fathers, fathers of 12-month-old IVF babies reported lower marital satisfaction than fathers whose babies had been naturally conceived (Gibson, Ungerer, Tennant & Saunders, 2000). The authors suggested that IVF mothers may have been more preoccupied with their baby and may have excluded the father more than natural conception mothers, thereby contributing to the fathers' lower marital satisfaction. With respect to parent-child relationships, the few differences that have been identified between IVF and natural conception families reflect more positive feelings toward the baby but also a tendency to view the baby as more vulnerable (Gibson et al., 2000; van Balen, 1996; Weaver et al., 1993). IVF mothers of infants were also found by Gibson et al., (2000) to consider themselves less competent as parents than natural conception mothers, which the authors attributed to the IVF mothers' judging themselves too harshly. In contrast, van Balen (1996) found that IVF mothers of 2- to 4-year-olds reported greater parental competence than mothers with no history of infertility. This discrepancy may well reflect differences between the two studies in the ages of the children. It is conceivable that the lack of confidence reported by IVF mothers of infants diminishes over time.

IVF families with preschool and early school-aged children were the focus of the European Study of Assisted Reproduction Families conducted in the United Kingdom, the Netherlands, Spain, and Italy (Golombok, Cook, Bish & Murray, 1995; Golombok et al., 1996). We found that IVF mothers showed greater warmth to their children, were more emotionally involved, interacted more and reported less stress associated with parenting than natural-conception mothers. In addition, IVF fathers were reported by mothers to interact with their child more than natural-conception fathers, and the fathers themselves reported less parenting stress. In the first study to be conducted in a non-Western culture, Hahn and DiPietro (2001) examined IVF families with preschool and early school-aged children in Taiwan. The quality of parenting was generally found to be good, although IVF mothers showed greater protectiveness of their children. The children's teachers, who were unaware of the nature of the children's conception, rated the IVF mothers as more affectionate toward their children but not more protective or intrusive in their parenting behavior, compared with the natural-conception parents.

When we followed up on the families in the European study as the children approached adolescence, we generally found that the IVF parents had good relationships with their children, characterized by a combination of affection and appropriate control (Golombok, MacCallum & Goodman, 2001; Golombok, Brewaeys, Cook, Giavazzi et al., 2002a). The few differences identified between the IVF families and the other family types reflected more positive functioning among the IVF families, with the possible exception of the over-involvement with their children of a small proportion of IVF parents.

Research on Children in IVF Families

Cognitive Development. The early studies of the cognitive development of IVF children found no evidence that IVF resulted in impaired cognitive ability. However, these studies did not use comparison groups and looked only at small samples of IVF children (Cederblad, Friberg, Ploman, Sjoberg et al., 1996; Mushin, Spensley, & Barreda-Hanson, 1985, Mushin, Barreda-Hanson, & Spensley, 1986; Yovich, Parry, French, & Grauaug, 1986). A number of controlled studies have now been reported. For example, the Bayley Scale scores of 65 IVF infants were compared with a matched control group of 62 naturally conceived infants at age 12 months, and no significant differences were found (Gibson, Ungerer, Leslie, Saunders, & Tennant, 1998). Other studies with large samples of IVF infants and matched comparison groups have reported similar findings using the Bayley Scales (Brandes, Scher, Itzkovits, Thaler et al., 1992; Morin, Wirth, Johnson et al., 1989), the Brunet-Lezine test (Raoul-Duval, Bertrand-Servais, & Frydman, 1993), and the General Cognitive Index (Ron-El, Lahat, Golan et al., 1994).

With respect to school-age children, the cognitive development of a sample of IVF children in Israel did not differ from that of naturally conceived children as assessed by the Wechsler Intelligence Scale for Children (Levy-Shiff, Vakil, Dimitrovsky, Abramovitz et al., 1998). Similarly, in France, educational attainment among children conceived by IVF was found to be within the normal range (Olivennes, Kerbrat, Rufat, Blanchet et al., 1997).

Socioemotional Development. In McMahon et al.'s (1997) study, IVF mothers rated their infants as more temperamentally difficult at 4 months than did natural-conception mothers and the IVF infants showed more negative behaviors in response to stress. Although at the age of one, no differences between the two groups of infants were found for either social development or test-taking behavior (Gibson et al., 1998), the IVF mothers rated their infants as having more behavioral difficulties and more difficult temperaments than the control group. The authors suggested that these findings may be related to IVF mothers' greater anxiety about their infants' well being. The security of infant-mother attachment was assessed at 12 months of age using the Strange Situation procedure (Gibson, Ungerer, McMahon, Leslie et al., 2000). The IVF infants showed predominantly secure attachment relationships, and there was no difference between groups in the proportion classified as insecurely attached.

With respect to toddlers, no differences in the behavior of 24- to 30-month-old IVF and naturally conceived children as rated during an interaction task with the mother were found by Colpin et al. (1995). Similarly, two studies that used the Achenbach Child Behavior Checklist found no indication of raised levels of psychological problems in children conceived by IVF compared to the general population (Cederblad et al., 1996; Montgomery, Aiello, Adelman, Wasylyshyn et al., 1999). In van Balen's (1996) study, IVF mothers, but not fathers, rated their 2- to 4-year-old children as more social and less obstinate than did the other mothers as assessed by a self-report questionnaire. The European Study of Assisted Reproduction Families assessed the socioemotional development of 4- to 8-year-old IVF children using standardized questionnaires of behavioral and emotional problems completed by mothers and teachers (Golombok et al., 1996). In addition, the children were administered tests of self-esteem and of feelings toward their parents. We found that the IVF children did not differ from their adoptive or naturally conceived counterparts with respect to these measures. In the United Kingdom, an assessment was also made of the children's security of attachment to their parents using the Separation Anxiety Test. In addition, interview transcripts relating to children's psychological functioning were rated by a child psychiatrist who was "blind" to the child's family type. We found no group differences for either security of attachment or the incidence of psychological disorders (Golombok et al., 1995). When followed up at age 12, the IVF children were continuing to function well (Golombok, MacCallum & Goodman, 2001; Golombok et al., 2002a). One study from Israel has reported a higher incidence of emotional problems among IVF children of middle-school age (Levy-Shiff et al., 1998). In comparison with naturally conceived children, the IVF children showed poorer adjustment to school as rated by teachers and reported themselves to be more aggressive, more anxious, and more depressed. However, this finding may be explained by the older age of the IVF parents.

ICSI Families

Concerns about ICSI Families. The introduction of IVF has paved the way for increasingly high tech reproductive procedures such as ICSI. Specific concerns have been raised in relation to ICSI, including the use of abnormal sperm, the bypassing of the usual process of natural selection of sperm, and the potential for physical damage to the egg or embryo, all of which may produce changes in genetic material (Bowen, Gibson, Leslie, & Saunders, 1998; te Velde, van Baar, & van Kooij, 1998) and may thus have implications for children's psychological development. As with IVF, multiple births are a common feature of ICSI (Van Steirteghem, Bonduelle, Devroey, & Liebaers, 2002).

Research on Parenting in ICSI Families. A five-center study conducted in Belgium, Denmark, Sweden, Greece, and the United Kingdom compared 440 ICSI families with 541 IVF and 542 naturally conceived families. The family types did not differ on measures of parental psychological well being, parenting stress, or quality of the marital relationship. However, ICSI and IVF mothers reported greater commitment to their role as a parent and were less negative about their children (Barnes et al., 2004). Similarly, a study of a Belgian sample found no differences between ICSI, IVF, and natural-conception parents in anxiety, depression, marital satisfaction, or parenting stress (Place & Englert, 2002). In contrast, an Australian investigation reported raised levels of marital distress in mothers and fathers of ICSI children (Cohen, McMahon, Gibson, Leslie, & Saunders, 2001).

Research on Children in ICSI Families

Cognitive Development. The Bayley Scales were administered to 201 ICSI children at 2 years of age in Belgium (Bonduelle, Joris, Hofmans, Liebaers et al., 1998) and no evidence was found of delayed mental development. A comparison between 439 ICSI children and 207 IVF children by the same research team found no difference in Bayley Scale scores (Bonduelle et al., 2003). Similar findings were reported in the United Kingdom from the administration of the Griffiths Scales to a representative sample of 1- to 2-year-old singleton ICSI children and a matched group of naturally conceived children (Sutcliffe, Taylor, Li, Thornton et al., 1999; Sutcliffe et al., 2001) and in a small study of Greek infants using the Bayley Scales (Papaligoura, Panopoulou-Maratou, Solman, Arvaniti et al., 2004). In contrast, significantly lower Bayley Scale scores were found among 89, 1-year-old ICSI children when compared with 84 IVF and 80 naturally conceived children in Australia, particularly boys (Bowen et al., 1998). Seventeen percent of the ICSI children experienced mildly or significantly delayed development (MDI < 85) compared with 2 percent of the IVF and 1 percent of the natural conception children. However, when these children were followed up at age 5 and the sample size increased, there were no differences in IQ scores between the ICSI children and the control groups, and no differences identified in the proportion of children who showed delayed development (Leslie et al., 2002). The five-center study of ICSI, IVF, and natural conception children at age 5 found no group differences for verbal or performance IQ scores (Ponjaert-Kristoffersen, 2003).

Socioemotional Development. Again in the five-center study, Barnes et al. (2004) found no differences in emotional or behavioral problems between ICSI children and either IVF or natural conception children as assessed by the Achenbach Child Behavior Checklist at age 5. In an investigation using the Strengths and Difficulties Questionnaire (Goodman, 1994) completed by parents and teachers, Place and Englert (2002) similarly found no evidence of raised levels of emotional or behavioral problems in ICSI children compared with IVF and naturally conceived comparison groups.

GAMETE DONATION FAMILIES

Donor Insemination Families

Concerns about Donor Insemination Families. In recent years, there has been growing unease about the secrecy that surrounds families created by DI. Although donor insemination has been practiced for more than a century to enable couples with an infertile male partner to have children, the majority of adults and children conceived in this way remain unaware that the person they know as their father is not their genetic parent. It has been argued that secrecy will have an insidious and damaging effect on family relationships and, consequently, on the child.

Findings suggestive of an association between secrecy and negative outcomes for children have come from two major sources: adoption research, and the family therapy literature. It is now generally accepted that adopted children benefit from knowledge about their biological parents, and that children who are not given such information may become confused about their identity and at risk for emotional problems (Brodzinsky, Smith, & Brodzinsky, 1998; Grotevant & McRoy, 1998). Parallels have been drawn to the DI situation, and it has been suggested that lack of information about the donor may be harmful for the child (Baran & Pannor, 1993; Daniels & Taylor, 1993; Snowden, Mitchell, & Snowden, 1983; Snowden, 1990). Family therapists have argued that secrecy can jeopardize communication between family members and result in a distancing of some members of the family from others (Bok, 1982; Karpel, 1980; Papp, 1993). In relation to donor insemination, Clamar (1989) has suggested that keeping the circumstances of conception secret will separate those who know the secret (the parents) from those who do not (the child). A further concern is that parents may feel or behave less positively toward a nongenetic child and that the child may not be fully accepted as part of the family, which may have an undermining effect on the child's identity and psychological development. Fathers, in particular, have been predicted to be more distant from their child (Baran & Pannor, 1993).

Research on Parenting in Donor Insemination Families. The majority of parents of children conceived by gamete donation have not told their children about the nature of their conception. In a review of studies of parents' disclosure of donor insemination published between 1980 and 1995, Brewaeys (1996) found that few parents (fewer than 20 percent) intended to tell their child about his or her genetic origins, and in the majority of studies, fewer than 10 percent of parents intended to tell. In spite of their decision to opt for nondisclosure, almost half of the parents had told at least one other person that they had conceived as a result of DI treatment, thus creating a risk that the child would find out through someone else. After their child had been born, many parents regretted their earlier openness (Amuzu, Laxova, & Shapiro, 1990; Back & Snowden, 1988; Klock & Maier, 1991). Although it might be expected that a higher proportion of parents in the more recent studies would be open with their children, this was not the case, a finding replicated by van Berkel et al. (1999) in a comparison between recipients of donor insemination in 1980 and 1996. In the European Study of Assisted Reproduction Families (Golombok et al., 1996; Golombok et al. 2002b), which included a representative sample of more than 100 donor insemination families in Italy, Spain,

The Netherlands, and the United Kingdom, we found that not one set of parents had told their child by early school age, and only 8.6 percent of parents had told their child by early adolescence. Recent studies in the United States have produced similar findings (Leiblum & Aviv, 1997; Nachtigall, Becker, Szkupinski Quigora, & Tschann, 1998).

There are, however, some exceptions to this pattern. In New Zealand, the importance of knowledge about genetic origins to Maori culture has resulted in greater openness about donor conception (Daniels & Lewis, 1996). In a study of a representative sample of 181 families, 30 percent of parents of children aged up to 8 years old had talked to them about the donor insemination, and 77 percent of the remaining parents intended to do so (Rumball & Adair, 1999). In the United States, the Sperm Bank of California has instituted an identity-release program whereby donor offspring may obtain the identity of their donor on reaching age 18. Almost all of the parents who opted for identifiable donors informed their child about their donor conception (Scheib, Riordan, & Rubin, 2003). The most recent information on the disclosure of donor insemination in the United Kingdom comes from a representative sample of 50 sets of DI parents with babies born between 1999 and 2001 in the United Kingdom, of whom 46 percent reported that they intended to be open with their child (Golombok et al., 2004). These figures suggest a marked rise in the proportion of parents who plan to tell their child about the donor conception. Nevertheless, the babies were only 1 year old at the time of study, and longitudinal research suggests that some parents who consider disclosure when their child is young change their mind as the child grows up (Golombok et al., 2002b). Even in Sweden, where legislation gives individuals the right to obtain information about the donor and his identity, a recent survey found that only 11 percent of parents had informed their child about the donor insemination, although a further 41 percent intended to tell (Lindblad, Gottlieb, & Lalos, 2000; Gottlieb, Lalos, & Lindblad, 2000). Parents who are most concerned about keeping the child's genetic origins secret are least likely to participate in research and thus the figures relating to the proportion of parents who intend to be open with their children represent an overestimate.

A number of studies have examined donor insemination parents' reasons for their decision not to tell their child (Snowden, Mitchell, & Snowden, 1983; Cook, Golomboks, Bish, & Murray, 1995; Nachtigall, Pitcher, Tschann, Becker et al., 1997). The predominant reason is parents' concern that disclosure would distress their child and have an adverse effect on the parent-child relationship. In particular, they fear that the child may feel less love for, or possibly reject, the father. Other considerations that are taken into account in parents' decision not to tell include a desire to protect the father from the stigma of infertility, concern about a negative reaction from paternal grandparents who may not accept the child as their grandchild, uncertainty about the best time and method of telling the child, and lack of information to give the child about the donor. In addition, some parents, emphasizing the greater importance of social than biological aspects of parenting for children's psychological adjustment, believe that there is simply no need to tell.

Brewaeys (1996, 2001) also reviewed studies of the characteristics of DI parents. In the large majority of cases, DI was felt by parents to be a positive choice and, with few exceptions, fathers reported that DI did not influence their relationship with their child and that they felt themselves to be "real" fathers. With respect to psychological adjustment and marital satisfaction, there was little indication of disorder in couples who opted for DI (Humphrey & Humphrey, 1987; Klock & Maier, 1991; Klock, Jacob, & Maier, 1994; Owens, Edelman, & Humphrey, 1993; Reading, Sledmere, & Cox, 1982; Schover, Collins, & Richards, 1992).

Regarding parent-child relationships, we found the outcomes for donor insemination families with 4- to 8-year-old children in the European Study of Assisted Reproduction Families to be just as positive as for the IVF families, suggesting that genetic ties are less important for family functioning than a strong desire for parenthood (Golombok et al., 1996). When the families were followed up at adolescence, the findings pointed to stable and satisfying marriages, psychologically healthy parents, and a high level of warmth between parents and their children accompanied by an appropriate level of discipline and control (Golombok et al., 2002a; Golombok et al. 2002b). No differences were identified between the DI and the IVF families for any of the variables relating to the quality of relationships between parents and the child. Similar findings have been found with a new cohort of DI children born 15 years later than those in the original study (Golombok et al., 2004).

Research on Children in Donor Insemination Families

Cognitive Development. A small number of uncontrolled studies, reviewed by Brewaeys (1996), have examined the cognitive development of children conceived by DI in comparison with general population norms. The results showed that DI children were more advanced than their same-age peers with respect to intellectual, psychomotor, and language development (Amuzu, Laxova, & Shapiro, 1990; Clayton & Kovacs, 1982; Izuka, Yoshiaki, Nobuhiro, & Michie, 1968; Leeton & Blackwell, 1982; Milson & Bergman, 1982). One controlled study in France also found 3- to 36-month-old DI children to be more advanced in psychomotor and language development than a comparison group of naturally conceived children (Manuel et al., 1990).

Socioemotional Development. The early studies found no evidence of emotional or behavioral problems in children conceived by DI (Clayton

& Kovacs, 1982; Leeton & Blackwell, 1982). One study did find a higher incidence of psychological problems among DI than naturally conceived children as assessed in an interview with parents (Manuel, Facy, Choquet, Grandjean et al., 1990), but other controlled studies that used standardized measures showed no evidence of raised levels of psychological disorder among children conceived by DI. For example, DI children aged 6 to 8 years old were studied in comparison with matched groups of adopted and naturally conceived children in Australia (Kovacs, Mushin, Kane, & Bak, 1993). Also, we compared 4- to 8-year-old DI children with adopted, IVF, and naturally conceived children in the United Kingdom (Golombok et al., 1995) and Europe (Golombok et al., 1996), and followed them up at age 11 to 12 (Golombok et al., 2002a; Golombok et al., 2002b). The children did not seem to experience negative consequences arising from the absence of a genetic link with their father or from the secrecy surrounding the circumstances of their conception.

Little is known about children who are aware of their conception by donor insemination, largely because the majority of children conceived in this way have not been told about their genetic origins. Rumball and Adair (1999) reported that the majority of young children in their sample who had been told about their donor conception responded with interest, others appeared neutral or uninterested, and a small minority responded with disbelief. There are also qualitative studies of adults who are aware of their conception by DI, although the number of individuals for whom there are systematic data remains very small. Whereas some report good relationships with their parents (Snowden, Mitchell, & Snowden, 1983), others report more negative feelings, including hostility, distance, and mistrust (Cordray, 1999; Donor Conception Support Group of Australia, 1997; Turner & Coyle, 2000). For example, the adults interviewed by Turner and Coyle (2000) expressed feelings of loss, abandonment, and grief in relation to their lack of knowledge of their genetic origins, a need to find out about their donor father, and, if possible, to have some kind of relationship with him to achieve a sense of genetic continuity. Some had felt that something was wrong since childhood and now attributed their poor relationship with their father to their DI origins. However, these adults were recruited from support groups and it is not known how representative they are of the entire population of DI adults who are aware of their genetic origins.

Egg Donation Families

Concerns about Egg Donation Families. Although the use of donor sperm to enable couples with an infertile male partner to have children has been practiced for many years, it is only since 1983, following advances in IVF, that infertile women have been able to conceive a child using a donated egg (Lutjen et al., 1984; Trounson, Leeton, Besanka, Wood et al., 1983). The concerns that have been expressed about egg donation are similar to those raised by DI. It is the absence of a genetic bond between the mother and the child and the effect of secrecy about the child's conception that have been the topics of greatest debate. Unlike DI, in which the donor is usually anonymous, egg donors are more often relatives or friends of the parents and may remain in contact with the family as the child grows up. Contact with the genetic mother has been viewed by some as a positive experience for children in that they have the opportunity to develop a clearer understanding of their origins. However, it is not known what the impact of this contact will be on a child's social, emotional and identity development through childhood and into adult life, or how contact between the genetic mother and the child will affect the social mother's security as a parent and her relationship with her child.

Research on Parenting in Egg Donation Families. The first study of parenting in families with a child conceived by egg donation was conducted in France (Raoul-Duval et al., 1994). The authors reported on twelve egg donation families assessed at 9 months and 18 months, and nine of these families at 36 months. It was reported that all of the mother-infant relationships were excellent. However, no details were given of the way in which an "excellent" mother-infant relationship had been defined. In a controlled study of families with 3- to 8-year-old children in the United Kingdom, we contrasted egg donation families, in which the child was genetically related to the father but not the mother, and DI families, in which the child was genetically related to the mother but not the father (Golombok, Murray, Brinsden & Abdalla, 1999). The only difference to emerge was that mothers and fathers of children conceived by egg donation reported lower levels of stress associated with parenting than parents of DI children. The egg donation families, like the DI families, were functioning well. Interestingly, only one of the 21 sets of egg donation parents had told their child about his genetic origins. The reasons for not telling are similar to those given by donor insemination parents: a desire not to jeopardize the child's psychological well-being or the relationship between the parents and the child, and the view that there is no need to tell (Murray & Golombok, 2003). Similarly, a study conducted in Finland of 49 families with an egg donation child aged between 6 months and 4 years found that none of the parents had told their child about the donor conception (Soderstrom-Anttila, Sajaniemi, Tiitinen, & Hovatta, 1998). However, 38 percent of these parents intended to do so, a higher proportion than is generally reported for DI parents. As with the DI parents, many (73 percent) had told someone other than the child. In a recent study of egg donation babies born in the United Kingdom between 1999 and 2001, 56 percent of parents intended to be open with their child, a higher proportion than that found for DI parents (Golombok et al., 2004).

Research on Children in Egg Donation Families

Cognitive Development. Data from Raoul-Duval et al.'s (1994) study of 12 egg-donation children showed no evidence of psychomotor retardation for any of the children investigated.

Socioemotional Development. Soderstrom-Anttila et al. (1998) compared 59 egg-donation children to 126 IVF children, all aged between 6 months and 4 years. There were no group differences in the proportion of children with eating or sleeping difficulties, and the egg-donation parents were less likely than the IVF parents to express concern about their child's behavior. In the study of 3- to 8-year-old egg-donation children, we made assessments of the presence of emotional and behavioral problems by parental questionnaire and the children were administered a standardized assessment of self-esteem (Golombok et al., 1999). There was no evidence of psychological difficulties among the egg-donation children.

NON-TRADITIONAL FAMILIES

Lesbian- and Solo-Mother Donor Insemination Families

Concerns about Lesbian- and Solo-Mother DI Families. There has been a great deal of controversy in recent years about whether lesbian couples and single heterosexual women should have access to assisted reproduction. With respect to lesbian-mother families, there have been two main concerns: First, that the children of lesbian mothers would be teased and ostracized by peers because of the social stigma still associated with homosexuality and would develop emotional and behavioral problems as a result; and second, that the lack of a father figure alongside the presence of one or two mothers who are not following conventional gender-typed roles would affect children's gender development (i.e., that boys would be less masculine and girls less feminine than their counterparts from heterosexual families). Although there is no evidence for either of these assumptions (see Golombok, 1999 and Patterson, 1992, for reviews), the early body of research focused on families in which the child had been born into a heterosexual family and then made the transition into a lesbian family after the parents' separation or divorce.

With respect to solo mothers, the concerns center around the effects of growing up in a fatherless family and are based on research showing negative outcomes in terms of cognitive, social, and emotional development for children raised by single mothers following parental separation or divorce (Amato, 1993; Chase-Lansdale & Hetherington, 1990; Hetherington & Stanley-Hagan, 1995; McLanahan & Sandefur, 1994; Weinraub, Horvath, & Gringlas, 2002). However, factors such as economic hardship and the experience of parental conflict have been shown to play a major part in children's adjustment difficulties in single-mother families. These outcomes cannot necessarily be generalized to children born to single mothers following assisted reproduction since these children have not experienced parental separation and generally are raised without financial hardship. It is possible, however, that other pressures on solo mothers, such as social stigma and lack of social support, may interfere with parenting and leave their children vulnerable to emotional and behavioral problems.

Research on Parenting in Lesbian Mother and Solo Mother DI Families. In recent years, a number of controlled studies of lesbian couples with a child conceived by DI have been reported. In the United States, Flaks et al. (1995) compared 15 lesbian DI families with 15 heterosexual DI families, and Chan et al. (1998) studied 55 DI families headed by lesbian parents in comparison with 25 DI families headed by heterosexual parents. The sexual orientation of the parents was found to be unrelated to parental adjustment, parental self-esteem, or relationship satisfaction. In the United Kingdom, Golombok, Tasker, and Murray (1997) compared 30 lesbian DI families with 41 heterosexual two-parent DI families and 42 families headed by a single heterosexual mother. We found the lesbian-mother families to be functioning well in terms of maternal warmth and mother-child interaction. Similarly, in Belgium, Brewaeys et al. (1997) studied 30 lesbian-mother families with a 4- to 8-year-old child in comparison with 38 heterosexual families with a DI child and 30 heterosexual families with a naturally conceived child. No major differences were found between the lesbian couples and the other family types with respect to quality of parenting or the quality of the couples' relationship. The most striking finding to emerge from these investigations was that co-mothers in two-parent lesbian families were more involved with their children than were fathers in two-parent heterosexual homes. In the Belgian study, information was obtained from parents regarding the decision-making process about whether or not to tell the child about the method of their conception. All the lesbian mothers intended to tell their children that they had been conceived by DI, and 56 percent would have opted for an identifiable donor had that been possible (Brewaeys et al., 1995). Comparable findings regarding the openness of lesbian mothers have been reported in the United States (Leiblum, Palmer, & Spector, 1995; Wendland, Byrn, & Hill, 1996; Jacob, Klock, & Maier, 1999). The attitude of lesbian mothers toward this issue is in striking contrast to that of heterosexual parents who prefer not to tell.

Little research has yet been carried out on the quality of parenting of single women who opt for DI as a means of having a child. These mothers are referred to as "solo" mothers to distinguish them from mothers who become single following separation or divorce (Weinraub, Horvath,

& Gringlas, 2002). A small, uncontrolled study of ten such women requesting DI (cited by Fidell & Marik, 1989) found that an important reason for choosing this procedure was to avoid using a man to produce a child without his knowledge or consent. Donor insemination also meant that they did not have to share the rights and responsibilities for the child with a man to whom they were not emotionally committed. Similarly, in our investigation of 27 solo mothers of 1-year-old DI children, the main reason for opting for DI was to avoid the need to have casual sex in order to become pregnant (Murray & Golombok, in press). There was a strong sense that time was running out to fulfill the lifelong dream of having a child and that there was no choice but to have a child in this way because of the lack of a partner. Solo DI mothers appeared to be more open toward disclosing the donor conception to the child than were a comparison group of married DI mothers; 93 percent of solo mothers reported that they planned to tell their child compared with 46 percent of the married DI mothers. With respect to parent-child relationships, we found that solo DI mothers showed similar levels of warmth and bonding towards their infant as married DI mothers. However, solo mothers showed lower levels of interaction and sensitivity. A possible explanation for this finding is that the presence of a partner allowed married DI mothers more time with their child.

Research on Children in Lesbian- and Solo-Mother DI Families. The evidence so far suggests that the DI children of lesbian mothers do not differ from their peers in terms of gender development (Brewaeys, Ponjaert-Kristoffersen, Van Hall, & Golombok, 1997). Neither is there any indication of raised levels of emotional and behavioral problems as rated by mothers and teachers at age 4 to 8 years (Brewaeys et al., 1997; Chan, Raboy, & Patterson, 1998; Flaks, Ficher, Masterpasqua, & Joseph, 1995; Golombok, Tasker, & Murray, 1997). In addition, the children of lesbian mothers consider themselves to be just as accepted by peers as children of heterosexual parents (Golombok, Tasker, & Murray, 1997). In a follow-up of the children studied by Brewaeys et al. (1997) when they were aged between 7 and 17 years, 27 percent reported that they would like to know the identity of their donor, 19 percent wished to have nonidentifying information about his appearance and personality, and the remaining 54 percent did not wish to have any information about him (Vanfraussen, Ponjaert-Kristoffersen, & Brewaeys, 2001). No detailed investigations have yet been conducted of the psychological adjustment of children born to single heterosexual mothers by donor insemination. However, we found that DI infants born to single mothers were no more likely to experience eating or sleeping difficulties than DI children born to married mothers (Murray and Golombok, in press).

Surrogacy Families

Concerns about Surrogacy Families. The practice of surrogacy remains highly controversial. As with known egg donors, surrogate mothers are often relatives or friends of the commissioning couple, and even when the surrogate mother was not known to the commissioning couple prior to the surrogacy arrangement, contact may continue after the child's birth. It is not known how this will affect the child's psychological and identity development and the feelings and parenting behavior of the commissioning mother, particularly when the surrogate mother is also the genetic mother of the child. Neither is it known how children will feel when they discover that their gestational mother had conceived them with the specific intention of relinquishing them to the commissioning parents.

Research on Parenting in Surrogacy Families. In interviews with twenty commissioning couples, Blyth (1995) found that all believed that the child should be told the full truth about their origins. However, it is not known whether the parents followed through this intention. Similarly, MacCallum et al. (2003) reported that 100 percent of a sample of 42 commissioning parents of 1-year-olds intended to be open with their child in the future. In the latter study, we found the commissioning parents to show higher levels of warmth and involvement with their child than a comparison group of natural conception parents (Golombok et al., 2004). Interestingly, 95 percent of the surrogacy families had kept in touch with the surrogate mother to some extent and the large majority reported that they maintained a good relationship with her.

Research on Children in Surrogacy Families. In a study of cognitive development, no evidence of speech or motor impairment was found in singleton children born after IVF surrogacy (Serafini, 2001). Assessments of children's temperament using the Infant Characteristics Questionnaire (Bates Freeland, & Lounsbury, 1979) found no differences between children born through a surrogacy arrangement and either egg donation children or natural conception children for fussiness of mood, adaptability to new situations, general activity level or predictability of reaction (Golombok et al., 2004).

CONCLUSIONS

Creating families by means of assisted reproduction has raised a number of concerns about potentially adverse consequences for parenting and child development. It seems, however, from the evidence available so far, that such concerns are unfounded. Parents of children conceived by assisted reproduction generally appear to have good relationships with their children, even in families where one parent lacks a genetic or gestational link with the child. With respect to the children themselves, children born at full term as a result of IVF or ICSI procedures do not exhibit cognitive impairment, although research on ICSI children is still ongoing. The reports of superior cognitive functioning among DI children have not been supported by large-scale controlled studies but could conceivably result from the use of highly educated donors. In relation to socioemotional development, assisted-reproduction children appear to be functioning well. The greater difficulties of IVF infants are based on maternal reports and probably result from the higher anxiety levels of IVF mothers. Studies during the preschool and school-age years do not indicate a higher incidence of emotional or behavioral problems among assisted reproduction children. Thus new family forms do not appear to constitute a risk factor for children (see Chapters 1 and 2 in this book). Just because children are conceived in unusual ways or live in unusual family circumstances does not mean that they are more likely to grow up psychologically disturbed. Instead, the findings presented in this chapter suggest that family structure, in itself, makes little difference to children's psychological development. Instead, what seems to matter is the quality of family life.

Nevertheless, few studies have included children at adolescence or beyond, and little is known about the consequences of conception by assisted-reproduction from the perspective of the individuals concerned. Moreover, the existing studies are of variable quality. Some investigations have been conducted with methodological rigor, for example, by matching the assisted reproduction families to the comparison groups with respect to the potentially confounding factors of maternal age, socioeconomic status (SES) and number of children in the family. However, research in this area is hampered by small, unrepresentative, and poorly defined samples, the absence of appropriate control groups, and unreliable and poorly validated measures. In addition, there are some types of assisted reproduction family, such as families created through embryo donation, about whom little is known at all (MacCallum, 2004).

POLICY IMPLICATIONS

As a result of growing concern about the escalating multiple birth rate arising from the increasing use of assisted reproduction procedures, a major policy issue in recent years has been the number of embryos that should be used in an IVF/ICSI cycle, and whether regulation should be introduced to limit the number of embryos that may be transferred. As the ESHRE Task Force (2003) has pointed out, the decision about the number of embryos to be transferred in IVF or ICSI cycles can lead to conflict between the professional autonomy of the physician who has a responsibility toward the well-being of the prospective mother and her future children, and the reproductive autonomy of the prospective parents who may request the transfer of a high number of embryos because of a strong desire for a child, the inability to pay for repeated IVF/ICSI cycles, and lack of information on the consequences of multiple births. A recent study in the United States has shown that the rate of multiple pregnancies following IVF has decreased as a result of fewer embryos being transferred (Jain, Missmer, & Hornstein, 2004). However, this decrease reflects a reduction in the number of triplet and higher-order births rather than a decrease in the number of twins.

The other major policy issue at the present time is whether or not donor anonymity should be removed to allow offspring access to identifying information about their donor. The Ethics Committee of the American Society for Reproductive Medicine has recently come out in support of disclosure to offspring about the use of donor gametes, and the U.K. government has recently announced a change in the law, whereby children conceived by gamete donation from 2005 onwards will have access to identifying information about their donor on reaching age 18. Donor identification would allow offspring who so wish, providing they are aware of their donor conception, to find out about, and possibly have contact with, their genetic parent(s). They may also have the opportunity to meet half-siblings, and full siblings in the case of embryo donation. The psychological consequences of donor identification for offspring, parents, donors, and their families are currently unknown. Light will be shed on this issue when offspring conceived with identifiable donors reach the age at which they become eligible for donor identification. At the Sperm Bank of California, the first children to have been conceived through an identity-release program have just turned 18 and have begun to obtain the identity of their donor (Scheib, Riordan, & Rubin, 2003). The impact on everyone concerned will be followed closely in the years to come.

FUTURE RESEARCH DIRECTIONS

Although existing knowledge about new family forms does not give undue cause for concern, there are many questions that warrant further investigation. For example, "What are the long-term consequences of assisted reproduction, particularly of secrecy about the child's genetic origins?"; "What is the effect on children conceived by gamete donation of finding out that one or both parents is genetically unrelated to them?" For children conceived through egg donation or surrogacy, "What is the effect of ongoing contact with the egg donor or surrogate mother?" And with respect to lesbian- or single-mother families created through donor insemination, "How will children respond as they grow up to the knowledge that their father is an anonymous sperm donor whom they will never meet?" These are just some of the questions that should be looked at more closely. Instead of uninformed opinion, systematic controlled studies of representative samples are needed so that the outcomes for both parents and children can be fully understood.

References

Amato, P. R. (1993). Children's adjustment to divorce: Theories, hypotheses and empirical support. *Journal of Marriage and the Family, 55,* 23–38.

Amuzu, B., Laxova, R., & Shapiro, S. (1990). Pregnancy outcome, health of children and family adjustment of children after DI. *Obstetrics and Gynecology, 75,* 899–905.

Back, K., & Snowden, R. (1988). The anonymity of the gamete donor. *Journal of Psychosomatic Obstetrics and Gynaecology, 9,* 191–198.

Baran, A., & Pannor, R. (1993). *Lethal Secrets.* New York: Amistad.

Barnes, J., Sutcliffe, A., Kristoffersen, I., Loft, A., Wennerholm, U., Tarlatzis, V. et al. (2004). The influence of assisted reproduction on family functioning and children's socio-emotional development: Results from a European study. *Human Reproduction, 19,* 1480–1487.

Bates, J., Freeland, C., & Lounsbury, M. (1979). Measurement of infant difficultness. *Child Development, 50,* 794–803.

Bergh, T., Ericson, A., Hillensjo, T., Bygren, K. G., & Wennerholm. U. B. (1999). Deliveries and children born after *in vitro* fertilization in Sweden 1982–5: A retrospective cohort study. *Lancet, 354,* 1579–1585.

Blyth, E. (1995). "Not a primrose path": Commissioning parents' experiences of surrogacy arrangements in Britain. *Journal of Reproductive and Infant Psychology, 13,* 185–196.

Bok, S. (1982). *Secrets.* New York: Pantheon.

Bonduelle, M., Joris, H., Hofmans, K., Liebaers, I., & Van Steirteghem, A. (1998). Mental development of 201 ICSI children at 2 years of age. *Lancet, 351,* 1553.

Bonduelle, M., Ponjaert, I., Steirteghem, A. V., Derde, M. P., Devroey, P., & Liebaers, I. (2003). Developmental outcome at 2 years of age for children born after ICSI compared with children born after IVF. *Human Reproduction, 18,* 342–350.

Botting, B. J., MacFarlane, A. J., & Price, F. V. (1990). *Three, four and more. A study of triplet and higher order births.* London: HMSO.

Bowen, J. R., Gibson, F. L., Leslie, G. I., & Saunders, D. M. (1998). Medical and developmental outcome at 1 year for children conceived by intracytoplasmic sperm injection. *Lancet, 351,* 1529–1534.

Brandes, J. M., Scher, A., Itzkovits, J., Thaler, I., Sarid, M., & Gershoni-Baruch, R. (1992). Growth and development of children conceived by in vitro fertilization. *Pediatrics, 90,* 424–429.

Brewaeys, A. (2001). Review: Parent-child relationships and child development in donor insemination families. *Human Reproduction Update, 17,* 38–46.

Brewaeys, A. (1996). DI, the impact on family and child development. *Journal of Psychosomatic Obstetrics and Gynaecology, 17,* 1–13.

Brewaeys, A., Ponjaert-Kristoffersen, I., Van Hall, E. V., & Golombok, S. (1997). DI: Child development and family functioning in lesbian-mother families. *Human Reproduction 12,* 1349–1359.

Brewaeys, A., Ponjaert-Kristoffersen, I., van Hall, E. V., Helmerhorst, F. M., & Devroey, P. (1995). *Lesbian mothers who conceived after DI: A follow-up study. Human Reproduction, 10,* 2731–2735.

Brodzinsky, D. M., Smith, D. W., & Brodzinsky, A. B. (1998). *Children's adjustment to adoption. Developmental and clinical issues.* London: Sage Publications.

Burns, L. H. (1990). An exploratory study of perceptions of parenting after infertility. *Family Systems Medicine, 8,* 177–189.

Cederblad, M., Friberg, B., Ploman, F., Sjoberg, N. O., Stjernqvist, K., & Zackrisson, E. (1996). Intelligence and behavior in children born after in-vitro fertilization treatment. *Human Reproduction, 11,* 2052–2057.

Chan, R. W., Raboy, B., & Patterson, C. J. (1998). Psychosocial adjustment among children conceived via DI by lesbian and heterosexual mothers. *Child Development, 69,* 443–457.

Chase-Lansdale, P. L., & Hetherington, E. M. (1990). The impact of divorce on life-span development: Short and long-term effects. In P. B. Baltes, D. L. Featherman and R. M. Lerner (Eds.). *Life-span development and behavior.* Hillsdale, NJ: Erlbaum.

Clamar, A. (1989). Psychological implications of the anonymous pregnancy. In J. Offerman-Zuckerberg (Ed.), *Gender in transition: A new frontier.* New York and London: Plenum.

Clayton, C., & Kovacs, G. (1982). AID offspring: initial follow up study of 50 couples. *Medical Journal of Australia, 1,* 338–339.

Cohen, J., McMahon, F., Gibson, F., Leslie, G., & Saunders, D. (2001). *Marital adjustment in ICSI families: A controlled comparison.* Paper presented at the 17th World Congress on Fertility and Sterility, Melbourne, Australia.

Colpin, H., Demyttenaere, K., & Vandemeulebroecke, L. (1995). New reproductive technology and the family: The parent-child relationship following *in vitro* fertilization. *Journal of Child Psychology and Psychiatry, 36,* 1429–1441.

Cook, R., Golombok, S., Bish, A., & Murray, C. (1995). Keeping secrets: A study of parental attitudes toward telling about donor insemination. *American Journal of Orthopsychiatry, 65,* 549–559.

Cordray, B. (1999). *Speaking for ourselves: Quotes from men and women created by DI/remote father conception.* 11th World Congress on In Vitro Fertilization and Human Reproductive Genetics, Sydney, Australia.

Daniels, K., & Lewis, G. M. (1996). Openness of information in the use of donor gametes: Developments in New Zealand. *Journal of Reproductive and Infant Psychology, 14,* 57–68.

Daniels, K., & Taylor, K. (1993). Secrecy and openness in DI. *Politics and Life Sciences. 12,* 155–170.

Donor Conception Support Group of Australia (1997). *Let the offspring speak: Discussions on donor conception.* New South Wales: Georges Hall.

Einwohner, J. (1989). Who becomes a surrogate: Personality characteristics. In J. Offerman-Zuckerberg (Ed.), *Gender in transition: A new frontier* (123–149). New York: Plenum.

ESHRE Task Force (2003). *Ethical issues related to multiple pregnancies in medically assisted procreation.* Brussels: European Society of Human Reproduction and Embryology.

Fidell, L., & Marik, J. (1989). Paternity by proxy: Artificial insemination by donor sperm. In J. Offerman-Zuckerberg (Ed.), *Gender in Transition: A new frontier.* New York: Plenum.

Flaks, D. K., Ficher, I., Masterpasqua, F., & Joseph, G. (1995). Lesbians choosing motherhood: A comparative study of lesbian and heterosexual parents and their children. *Developmental Psychology, 31,* 105–114.

Gibson, F. L., Ungerer, J. A., Leslie, G. I., Saunders, D. M., & Tennant, C. C. (1998). Development, behavior and temperament: A prospective study of infants conceived through in-vitro fertilization. *Human Reproduction, 13,* 1727–1732.

Gibson, F. L., Ungerer, J. A., Leslie, G. I., Saunders, D. M., & Tennant, C. C. (1999). Maternal attitudes to parenting and mother-child relationship and interaction in IVF families: A prospective study. *Human Reproduction, 14,* 131–132.

Gibson, F., Ungerer, J., McMahon, C., Leslie, G., & Saunders, D. (2000). The mother-child relationship following in vitro fertilization (IVF): Infant attachment, responsivity, and maternal sensitivity. *Journal of Child Psychology and Psychiatry, 41,* 1015–1023.

Gibson, F. L., Ungerer, J. A., Tennant, C. C., & Saunders, D. M. (2000). Parental adjustment and attitudes to parenting after in vitro fertilization. *Fertility and Sterility, 73,* 565–574.

Golombok, S. (1999). Lesbian mother families. In A. Bainham, S. Sclater & M. Richards (Eds.), *What is a parent? A socio-legal analysis.* Oxford: Hart.

Golombok, S., Brewaeys, A., Cook, R., Giavazzi, M. T., Guerra, D., Mantovanni, A., Van Hall, E., Crosignano, P. G., & Dexeus, S. (1996). The European Study of Assisted Reproduction Families. *Human Reproduction, 11,* 2324–2331.

Golombok, S., Brewaeys, A., Giavazzi, M. T., Guerra, D., MacCallum, F., & Rust, J. (2002a). The European Study of Assisted Reproduction Families: The transition to adolescence. *Human Reproduction, 17,* 830–840.

Golombok, S., Cook, R., Bish, A., & Murray, C. (1995). Families created by the New Reproductive Technologies: Quality of parenting and social and emotional development of the children. *Child Development, 66,* 285–298.

Golombok, S., Lycett, E., MacCallum, F., Jadva, V., Murray, C., Rust, J., Abdalla, H., Jenkins, J., & Margara, R. (2004). Parenting infants conceived by gamete donation. *Journal of Family Psychology, 18,* 443–452.

Golombok, S., MacCallum, F., & Goodman, E. (2001). The 'test-tube' generation: parent-child relationships and the psychological well-being of IVF children at adolescence. *Child Development, 72,* 599–608.

Golombok, S., MacCallum, F., Goodman, E., & Rutter, M. (2002b). Families with children conceived by DI: A follow-up at age 12. *Child Development, 73,* 952–968.

Golombok, S., Murray, C., Brinsden, P., & Abdalla, H. (1999). Social versus biological parenting: Family functioning and the socioemotional development of children conceived by egg or sperm donation. *Journal of Child Psychology and Psychiatry, 40,* 519–527.

Golombok, S., Tasker, F., & Murray, C. (1997). Children raised in fatherless families from infancy: Family relationships and the socioemotional development of children of lesbian and single heterosexual mothers. *Journal of Child Psychology and Psychiatry, 38,* 783–792.

Goodman, R. (1994). A modified version of the Rutter parent questionnaire including extra items on children's strengths: A research note. *Journal of Child Psychiatry and Psychology, 35*, 1483–1494.

Gottlieb, C., Lalos, O., & Lindblad, F. (2000). Disclosure of donor insemination to the child: The impact of Swedish legislation on couples' attitudes. *Human Reproduction, 15*, 2052–2056.

Grotevant, M. D., & McRoy, R. G. (1998). *Openness in adoption: Exploring family connections*. New York: Sage.

Hahn, C., & DiPietro, J. A. (2001). In vitro fertilization and the family: Quality of parenting, family functioning, and child psychosocial adjustment. *Developmental Psychology, 37*, 37–48.

Hetherington, E. M., & Stanley-Hagan, M. M. (1995). Parenting in divorced and remarried families. In M. Bornstein (Ed.), *Handbook of Parenting:* Vol. 3. (pp. 233–254). Hove, U.K.: Erlbaum.

Humphrey, M., & Humphrey, H. (1987). Marital relationships in couples seeking DI. *Journal of Biosocial Science, 19*, 209–219.

Izuka, R., Yoshiaki, S., Nobuhiro, N., & Michie, O. (1968). The physical and mental development of children born following artificial insemination. *International Journal of Fertility, 13*, 24–32.

Jacob, M., Klock, S., & Maier, D. (1999). Lesbian mothers as therapeutic donor insemination recipients: Do they differ from other patients? *Journal of Psychosomatic Obstetrics and Gynecology, 20*, 203–215.

Jain, T., Missmer, S., & Hornstein, M. (2004). Trends in embryo-transfer practice and in outcomes of the use of assisted reproductive technology in the United States. *New England Journal of Medicine, 350*, 1639–1645.

Karpel, M. A. (1980). Family secrets: I. Conceptual and ethical issues in the relational context. II. Ethical and practical considerations in therapeutic management." *Family Process, 19*, 295–306.

Klock, S., Jacob, M., & Maier, D. (1994). A prospective study of DI recipients: Secrecy, privacy and disclosure. *Fertility and Sterility, 62*, 477–484.

Klock, S., & Maier, D. (1991). Psychological factors related to DI. *Fertility and Sterility, 56*, 549–559.

Kovacs, G. T., Mushin, D., Kane, H., & Baker, H. W. G. (1993). A controlled study of the psycho-social development of children conceived following insemination with donor semen. *Human Reproduction, 8*, 788–790.

Leeton, J., & Blackwell, J. (1982). A preliminary psychosocial follow-up of parents and their children conceived by artificial insemination by donor (AID). *Clinical Reproduction and Fertility, 1*, 307–310.

Leiblum, S., & Aviv, A. (1997). Disclosure issues and decisions of couples who conceived via donor insemination. *Journal of Psychosomatic Obstetrics and Gynecology, 18*, 292–300.

Leiblum, S., Palmer, M., & Spector, I. (1995). Non-traditional mothers: Single heterosexual/lesbian women and lesbian couples electing motherhood via donor insemination. *Journal of Psychosomatic Obstetrics and Gynecology, 16*, 11–20.

Leslie, G. I., Cohen, J., Gibson, F. L., McMahon, C., Maddison, V., Saunders, D., & Tennant, C. (2002, 1–3 July). *ICSI children have normal development at school age.*

Paper presented at the 18th Annual Meeting of the European Society of Human Reproduction and Embryology, Vienna.

Levy-Shiff, R., Vakil, E., Dimitrovsky, L., Abramovitz, M., Shahar, N., Har-Even, D., Gross, S., Lerman, M., Levy, I., Sirota, L., & Fish, B. (1998). Medical, cognitive, emotional, and behavioral outcomes in school-age children conceived by in-vitro fertilization. *Journal of Clinical Child Psychology, 27,* 320–329.

Lindblad, F., Gottlieb, C., & Lalos, O. (2000). To tell or not to tell – what parents think about telling their children that they were born following DI. *Journal of Psychosomatic Obstetrics and Gynecology, 21,* 193–203.

Lutjen, P., Trounson, A., Leeton, J., Findlay, J., Wood, C., & Renou, P. (1984). The establishment and maintenance of pregnancy using in vitro fertilization and embryo donation in a patient with primary ovarian failure. *Nature, 307,* 174.

Lytton, H., & Gallagher, L. (2002). Parenting twins and the genetics of parenting. In M. Bornstein (Ed.), *Handbook of Parenting,* (2nd ed., Vol. 1, pp. 227–253). Mahwah, NJ: Lawrence Erlbaum Associates.

MacCallum, F. (2004). *Embryo donation families: Parenting and child development.* Paper presented at 20th Annual meeting of the European Society of Human Reproduction and Embryology, Berlin.

MacCallum, F., Lycett, E., Murray, C., Jadva, V., & Golombok, S. (2003). Surrogacy: The experience of commissioning couples. *Human Reproduction, 18,* 1334–1342.

Manuel, C., Facy, F., Choquet, M., Grandjean, H., & Czyba, J. C. (1990). Les risques psychologiques de la conception par IAD pour l'enfant. [The psychological risks of conception by IAD for the child.] *Neuropsychiatrie de l'enfance, 38,* 642–58.

McLanahan, S., & Sandefur, G. (1994). *Growing up with a single parent: What hurts, what helps.* Cambridge, MA., Harvard University Press.

McMahon, C., Gibson, F., Leslie, G., Cohen, J., & Tennant, C. (2003). Parents of 5-year-old in vitro fertlization children: Psychological adjustment, parenting stress, and the influence of subsequent in vitro fertilization treatment. *Journal of Family Psychology, 17,* 361–369.

McMahon, C., Ungerer, J., Beaurepaire, J., Tennant, C., & Saunders, D. (1995). Psychosocial outcomes for parents and children after in vitro fertilization: a review. *Journal of Reproductive and Infant Psychology, 13,* 1–16.

McMahon, C. A., Ungerer, J. A., Tennant, C., & Saunders, D. (1997). Psychosocial adjustment and the quality of the mother-child relationship at four months postpartum after conception by in vitro fertilization. *Fertility and Sterility, 68,* 492–500.

McMahon, S., & Dodd, B. (1997). A comparison of the expressive communication skills of triplet, twin and singleton children. *European Journal of Disorders of Communication, 32,* 328–345.

Milson, I., & Bergman, P. (1982). A study of parental attitudes after DI. *Acta Obstetricia et Gynecologica Scandinavica, 61,* 125–128.

Montgomery, T. R., Aiello, F., Adelman, R. D., Wasylyshyn, N., Andrews, M. C., Brazelton, T. B., Jones, G. S., & Jones, H. W. (1999). The psychological status at school age of children conceived by in-vitro fertilization. *Human Reproduction, 14,* 2162–2165.

Morin, N. C., Wirth, F. H., Johnson, D. H., Frank, L. M., Presburg, H. J., Van de Water, V. L., et al. (1989). Congenital malformations and psychosocial development in children conceived by in vitro fertilization. *Journal of Pediatrics, 115*, 222–227.

Murray, C., & Golombok, S. (in press). Going it alone: Solo mothers and their infants conceived by donor insemination. *American Journal of Orthopsychiatry.*

Murray, C., & Golombok, S. (2003). To tell or not to tell: The decision-making process of egg donation parents. *Human Fertility, 6*, 89–95.

Mushin, D., Spensley, J., & Barreda-Hanson, M. (1985). Children of IVF. *Clinical Obstetrics and Gynecology, 12*, 865–875.

Mushin, D. N., Barreda-Hanson, M. C., & Spensley, J. C. (1986). In vitro fertilization children: Early psychosocial development. *Journal of In Vitro Fertilization and Embryo Transfer, 3*, 247–252.

Nachtigall, R., Becker, G., Szkupinski Quigora, S., & Tschann, J. (1998). The disclosure decision: Concerns and issues of parents and children conceived through donor insemination. *American Journal of Obstetrics & Gynecology, 176*, 1165–1170.

Nachtigall, R. D., Pitcher, L., Tschann, J. M., Becker, G., & Szkupinski Quiroga, S. (1997). Stigma, disclosure and family functioning among parents of children conceived through DI. *Fertility and Sterility, 68*, 83–89.

Nyboe Andersen, A., Gianaroli, L., & Nygren, K. (2004). Assisted reproductive technology in Europe, 2000: Results generated from European registers by ESHRE. *Human Reproduction, 19*, 490–503.

Nygren, K. G., & Andersen, A. N. (2002). Assisted reproductive technology in Europe, 1999: Results generated from European registers by ESHRE. *Human Reproduction, 17*, 3260–3274.

Olivennes, F., Fanchin, R., Ledee, N., Righini, C., Kadoch, I. J., & Frydman, R. (2002). Perinatal outcome and developmental studies on children born after IVF. *Human Reproduction Update, 8*, 117–128.

Olivennes, F., Kerbrat, V., Rufat, P., Blanchet, V., Franchin, R., & Frydman, R. (1997). Follow-up of a cohort of 422 children aged 6–13 years conceived by in vitro fertilization. *Fertility and Sterility, 67*, 284–289.

Owens, D., Edelman, R., & Humphrey, M. (1993). Male infertility and DI: Couples decisions, reactions, and counselling needs. *Human Reproduction, 8*, 880–885.

Papaligoura, Z., Panopoulou-Maratou, O., Solman, M., Arvaniti, K., & Sarafidou, J. (2004). Cognitive development of 12-month-old Greek infants conceived after ICSI and the effects of the method on their parents. *Human Reproduction, 19*, 1488–1493.

Papp, P. (1993). The worm in the bud: Secrets between parents and children. In E. Imber-Black (Ed.), *Secrets in families and family therapy* (pp. 66–85). New York: Norton.

Patterson, C. J. (1992). Children of lesbian and gay parents. *Child Development, 63*, 1025–1042.

Place, I., & Englert, Y. (2002). *The emotional and behavioral development of ICSI children. How are the ICSI families coping in comparison with IVF and run-of-the-mill families?* Paper presented at the 18th Annual Meeting of the European Society for Human Reproduction and Embryology, Vienna.

Ponjaert-Kristoffersen, I. (2003). *Follow-up of ICSI Children: Cognitive and neurodevelopmental outcome.* Paper presented at the 19th Annual Meeting of the European Society of Human Reproduction and Embryology, Madrid, 29 June–2 July.

Raoul-Duval, A., Bertrand-Servais, M., & Frydman, R. (1993). Comparative prospective study of the psychological development of children born by in vitro fertilization and their mothers. *Journal of Psychosomatic Obstetrics and Gynecology, 14,* 117–126.

Raoul-Duval, A., Bertrand-Servais, M., Letur-Konirsch, H., & Frydman, R. (1994). Psychological follow-up of children born after in-vitro fertilization. *Human Reproduction, 9,* 1097–1101.

Reading, A., Sledmere, C., & Cox, D. (1982). A survey of patient attitudes towards artificial insemination by donor. *Journal of Psychosomatic Research, 26,* 429–433.

Ron-El, R., Lahat, E., Golan, A., Lerman, M., Bukovsky, I., & Herman, A. (1994). Development of children born after ovarian superovulation induced by long-acting gonadatrophin-releasing hormone antagonists and menotrophins, and by in vitro fertilization. *Journal of Pediatrics, 125,* 734–737.

Rumball, A., & Adair, V. (1999). Telling the story: Parents' scripts for donor offspring. *Human Reproduction, 14,* 1392–1399.

Rutter, M., Thorpe, K., Greenwood, R., Northstone, K., & Golding. J. (2003). Twins as a natural experiment to study the causes of mild language delay: Vol 1. Design; twin-singleton differences in language, and obstetric risks. *Journal of Child Psychology and Psychiatry, 44,* 326–341.

Schover, L. R., Collins, R. L., & Richards, S. (1992). Psychological aspects of DI: evaluation and follow up of recipient couples. *Fertility and Sterility, 57,* 583–590.

Scheib, J., Riordan, M., & Rubin, S. (2003). Choosing identity-release sperm donors: The parents' perspective 13–18 years later. *Human Reproduction, 18,* 1115–1127.

Serafini, P. (2001). Outcome and follow-up of children born after in vitro fertilization surrogacy (IVF surrogacy). *Human Reproduction Update, 17,* 23–27.

Snowden, R. (1990). The family and artificial reproduction. In E. A. Bromham (Ed.), *Philosophical Ethics in Reproductive Medicine.* Manchester: Manchester University Press.

Snowden, R., Mitchell, G. D., & Snowden, E. M. (1983). *Artificial reproduction: A social investigation.* London: George Allen & Unwin.

Soderstrom-Anttila, V., Sajaniemi, N., Tiitinen, A., & Hovatta, O. (1998). Health and development of children born after oocyte donation compared with that of those born after in-vitro fertilization, and parents' attitudes regarding secrecy. *Human Reproduction, 13,* 2009–2015.

Steptoe, P. C., & Edwards, R. G. (1978). Birth after reimplantation of a human embryo. *Lancet, 2,* 366.

Sutcliffe, A. G., Taylor, B., Li, J., Thornton, S., Grudzinskas, J. G., & Lieberman, B. A. (1999). Children born after intracytoplasmic sperm injection: A population control study. *British Medical Journal, 318,* 704–705.

Sutcliffe, A. G., Taylor, B., Saunders, K., Thornton, S., Lieberman, B. A., & Grudzinskas, J. G. (2001). Outcome in the second year of life after in-vitro fertilization by intracytoplasmic sperm injection: UK case-control study. *Lancet, 357,* 2080–2084.

te Velde, E. R., van Baar, A. L., & van Kooij, R. J. (1998). Concerns about assisted reproduction. *Lancet, 351,* 1524–1525.

Trounson, A., Leeton, J., Besanka, M., Wood, C., & Conti, A. (1983). Pregnancy established in an infertile patient after transfer of a donated embryo fertilized in vitro. *British Medical Journal, 286,* 835–838.

Turner, A., & Coyle, A. (2000). What does it mean to be a donor offspring? The identity experiences of adults conceived by donor insemination and the implications for counselling and therapy. *Human Reproduction, 15,* 2041–2051.

van Balen, F. (1996). Child-rearing following in vitro fertilization. *Journal of Child Psychology and Psychiatry, 37,* 687–693.

van Balen, F. (1998). Development of IVF children. *Developmental Review, 18,* 30–46.

van Berkel, D., van der Veen, L., Kimmel, I., & te Velde, E. R. (1999). Differences in the attitudes of couples whose children were conceived through artificial insemination by donor in 1980 and in 1996. *Fertility and Sterility, 71,* 226–231.

Van Steirteghem, A., Bonduelle, M., Devroey, P., & Liebaers, I. (2002). Follow-up of children born after ICSI. *Human Reproduction Update, 8,* 1–8.

Vanfraussen, K., Ponjaert-Kristoffersen, I., Brewaeys, A. (2001). An attempt to reconstruct children's donor concept: A comparison between children's and lesbian parents' attitudes towards donor anonymity. *Human Reproduction, 16,* 2019–2025.

Vayena, E., Rowe, P. J., & Griffin, P. D. (Eds.) (2002). *Current practices and controversies in assisted reproduction.* Report of a meeting on medical, ethical and social aspects of assisted reproduction. Geneva: World Health Organization.

Weaver, S. M., Clifford, E., Gordon, A. G., Hay, D. M., & Robinson, J. (1993). A follow-up study of 'successful' IVF/GIFT couples: Social-emotional well-being and adjustment to parenthood. *Journal of Psychosomatic Obstetrics and Gynecology, 14,* 5–16.

Weinraub, M., Horvath, D. L. & Gringlas, M. B. (2002). Single parenthood. In M. H. Bornstein (Ed.), *Handbook of Parenting*: Vol. 3. (pp. 109–139). Hillsdale, NJ: Lawrence Erlbaum Associates.

Wendland, C., Byrn, F., & Hill, C. (1996). Donor insemination: A comparison of lesbian couples, heterosexual couples and single women. *Fertility and Sterility, 65,* 764–770.

Yovich, J., Parry, T., French, N., & Grauaug, A. (1986). Developmental assessment of 20 in vitro fertilization (I.V.F.) infants at their first birthday. *Journal of In Vitro Fertilization and Embryo Transfer, 3,* 225–237.

Zegers-Hochschild, F. (2002). The Latin American Registry of Assisted Reproduction. In E. Vayena, P. J. Rowe, & P. D. Griffin (Eds.) *Current practices and controversies in assisted reproduction: Report of a meeting on medical, ethical and social aspects of assisted reproduction.* Geneva: World Health Organization.

12

Grandparents, Grandchildren, and Family Change in Contemporary Britain

Judy Dunn, Emma Fergusson, and Barbara Maughan

The recent demographic changes in family life – increases in parental separation, single parenthood, the formation of stepfamilies, and the striking increase in the employment of mothers with young children over the past two decades have been widely documented for countries in Europe and North America. The evidence that each of these can be associated with problems for parents and children has contributed to current anxiety about the "decline of the family." The notion that there has been a breakdown in American families has for instance had wide currency (Popenoe, 1993; Wilson, 2002), especially in relation to the idea that youth are currently a generation "at risk" (Amato & Booth, 1997).

A more optimistic account of family change in the United State was given in a longitudinal study of intergenerational relationships, in which Bengtson and his colleagues (Bengtson, Biblarz, & Roberts, 2002) studied four generations of the same families in Southern California. The study was based on youth born in the 1970s and 1980s, who were children of individuals born in the 1940s and 1950s, who had been studied in 1971 (together with their parents and grandparents). The researchers emphasize that their findings show that in terms of their aspirations, values, self-esteem, and family relations, these young persons born in the 1970s were doing "quite a bit better" than their elders as young persons, despite the striking social changes of the last 30 years. They argue that the evidence from their study challenges the idea that families are declining in function and influence or that nontraditional or alternative family structures spell the downfall of American youth. In a thoughtful discussion of how and why families still matter, they set out a number of propositions that summarize their major findings and provide an agenda for future research to test with larger and nationally representative samples. It is the first of these propositions that we consider here: that families are adapting to the new stresses and changes in part by expanding support across generations; that there is increasing interdependence and exchange across several generations of family members; and that this expansion has protected and enhanced the well-being of new generations of children. Bengtson and colleagues note in particular that an important direction for future research is to investigate the concept of the importance of "extending kin" to the family and individual changes following divorce.

To what extent does recent evidence from the United Kingdom support such a proposition? There is now a large and growing literature on grandparents and their significance in family life from research in the United States, and this literature has highlighted a number of key principles (which apply in fact not only to patterns of intergenerational relationships, but to all family relations). Five of these are of particular importance and will be considered here, as they relate to families in the United Kingdom. The first principle is the importance of recognizing that relationships between family members need to be considered within the framework – the network – of other family relationships. The second principle is that the pattern of relations across generations will differ across cultural/ethnic groups. The third principle is that rural/urban social ecologies structure the relations between grandparent-grandchild relationships. The fourth, is that a life-course perspective can be illuminating – that childhood experiences with grandparents, for instance, can influence current experiences with grandchildren. And the fifth, is that patterns of relationships change over time with the age and development of the individuals and that there can be considerable diversity in the relationships a grandparent can have with various grandchildren.

A convincing case has been made from the U.S. research for framing our considerations about current family processes involving grandparents in terms of these principles. But how relevant are they to the lives of children and their families in the United Kingdom? And how good is the case for considering the grandparent generation as a key part of families currently in Britain? We consider first the recent evidence on patterns of grandparental contact and involvement in the United Kingdom, in relation to the principles set out above. Second, we focus on two aspects of grandparental family support relating to recent changes in families – the provision of child care and patterns of grandparent-grandchild involvement following separation of parents.

PATTERNS OF CONTACT AND INVOLVEMENT: GRANDPARENTS IN THE UNITED KINGDOM

Information on intergenerational patterns of support and involvement of family members "beyond the household" in the United Kingdom has until recently been relatively sparse. However, recent studies of nationally representative data sets in Britain have begun to fill this gap in our

understanding of family matters. The Omnibus Survey (interviews collected each month in Great Britain, focussed on socioeconomic and demographic characteristics of a randomly-selected representative population)
in 1999 included a special module on kin, including questions on the existence and demographic characteristics of, proximity to, and contact with
specified close relatives (Grundy, Murphy, & Shelton, 1999). The findings
show that nearly all people in contemporary Britain have either a living
parent or a child and many have both (Figure 12.1). Close to three-quarters
of people were members of three-generational families, and especially
among those aged 80 or older, substantial minorities were members of
four-generation families. The demographic changes have led to what has
been described as "beanpole families." On the one hand, life expectancy is
increasing, on the other hand, fertility is decreasing – women have fewer
children and start their families later. There are fewer relatives in each
generation, while the increase in divorce and parental separation, and the
formation of stepfamilies increases the complexity of kin networks.

Contact between the generations in the Omnibus Survey was
documented: A third of grandmothers and a quarter of grandfathers aged
70 to 79 saw their eldest grandchild at least once a week. In the 1998 British
Social Attitudes Survey, information on three-generational families (based
on 2000 families) also highlights the "bean-pole" effect – showing that more
than half the British population are now grandparents by the age of 54, that
two-thirds of grandparents are currently not the senior generation in their
families (people are living longer), and that women are having fewer children (Dench & Ogg, 2002). Frequency of contact was affected by the age
of the grandchild, with nearly half of the grandparents with a grandchild

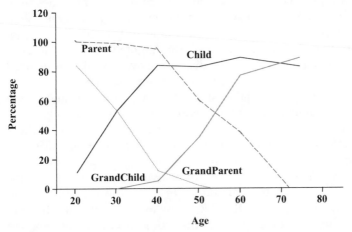

FIGURE 12.1. Proportions of respondents with different types of kin by age, from
the Omnibus Survey, 1999.

under 6 seeing him or her several times a week, and 76 percent of those with a grandchild under 6 reporting that they felt "very close" to their grandchild. In the Millenium Cohort Study – a study of a representative cohort of babies born in the millennium and their parents, which included data on grandparents – almost two-thirds of the mothers saw their own mother at least once a week when the babies were 9 months old; almost one-quarter saw them every day (Dex & Joshi, 2003).

Intergenerational exchanges of help were common and largely reciprocal according to the Omnibus Survey and the British Social Attitudes Survey data, with those providing help being more likely to receive it, and vice versa. Eighty percent of mothers with one child in the Omnibus Survey were helped by their own mothers, and 79 percent of those with a child under 5 received such help. Proximity to kin who are not coresident was related to contact, but close to half of the respondents lived within half an hour's journey to their mother, father, and eldest child. The support given by grandparents and by grandchildren is described in detail in the British Social Attitudes Survey, where even the youngest grandchildren are reported by their parents to be doing things to help their grandparents (with one in five of the under-sixes helping their grandparent around the house (Dench, Ogg, & Thomson, 1999). As Dench and his colleagues point out, the notion of reciprocity in these extended family relationships is planted early in life.

A Framework of Interlocking Relationships

Perhaps the most striking evidence for the significance of the connections between the various relationships within the family network comes from the information on how the contact and involvement of grandparents with their grandchildren is affected by the relationship between the mother and father of the children – dramatically highlighted by what happens following parental separation, as we discuss below. It is also influenced by the parent generation, who can hinder or facilitate the grandparent-grandchild relationship. The relationship between grandparent and parent has been shown to have significant positive effects on contact and closeness between grandparents and children in the U.S. research (e.g., Cherlin & Furstenberg, 1986; King & Elder, 1997; King, Russell, & Elder, 1998; Mueller & Elder, 2003; Rossi & Rossi, 1991; Thompson & Walker, 1987).

A second line of evidence comes from investigations of life-course associations. Thus in longitudinal studies of rural Iowan families, King and Elder (1997) showed that the degree to which grandparents were involved with their grandchildren and the type of involvement they had with them was influenced by their childhood relationships with their own grandparents. Experiences with grandparents that had often occurred 50 to 60 years before were apparently linked (albeit modestly) to current grandparental relationships. (For remarkable evidence for intergenerational links over three generations in the sequelae of divorce and marital conflict, see Amato & Cheadle, in press). In the United Kingdom, Fergusson, Maughan and Golding (2003) report that in the Avon Longitudinal Study of Parents and Children (ALSPAC), a longitudinal study of a representative community sample of around 10,000 families in the West of England, the quality of mothers' childhood relationships with their own mothers was significantly associated with the care and involvement of the grandmothers in their grandchildren.

The mechanisms underlying these connections remain to be ascertained: it could be that mothers who recalled positive experiences with their mothers were happy for them to take care of their own children, and it could also be that the grandmothers who enjoyed and valued their roles as mothers were especially eager to take part in "mothering" their grandchildren. Genetics may also play a part, influencing individual differences in both grandparent and parental generations. While the processes underlying the connection remain to be clarified, the general principle – that each relationship within a family needs to be considered within the framework of other close relationships and in the context of the history of these relationships– is one that we know applies not only to parents and children who live together, but to nonresident parents and their children (e.g., Dunn, Cheng, O'Connor, & Bridges, 2004).

Ethnic and Cultural Group Differences

Generalizations about grandparent-grandchild involvement and relationships across ethnic and cultural groups should be made with great caution, however. This is evident in the U.S. studies, including extensive studies of African-American families (e.g., Burton & Bengtson, 1985; Burton & Dilworth-Anderson, 1991; Chase-Lansdale, Brooks-Gunn, & Zamsky, 1994), and it is now beginning to be documented for the various British ethnic groups. For instance in the Millenium Cohort Study (Dex & Joshi, 2003), differences between families from ethnic minorities (Pakistani, Bangladeshi, Indian, Black, and Mixed) and the white majority were evident in many aspects of the three-generational patterns (Collishaw & Maughan, 2003, op. cit.). Differences were marked, for example, in the likelihood that the parents' own parents would be alive, with parents from all the minority groups less likely to have their own parents alive, compared with white parents. There were also ethnic differences in the likelihood that the parents of the mother's partner were coresident in the household (paternal grandparents from the three South Asian groups were much more likely to be living with the family than were white grandparents). There were large ethnic group variations in amount of contact with grandparents when the babies were 9 months old. The norm for white mothers was contact at least once a week (true for more than 75 percent); in contrast, almost half the black and mixed-race respondents had contact with a grandparent less than once a month. At the other extreme, Pakistani mothers were the most likely to see their own mothers every day. Only 3 percent of white mothers were likely to see their mother less than once a year. In comparison, the percentage of mothers from ethnic minorities who reported seeing their mothers less than once a year was much higher (29–37 percent), a figure that may indicate that minority ethnic parents were more likely to have their own parents living outside the United Kingdom.

There were marked differences in financial support from grandparents. While most white families received some financial support from the children's grandparents (90 percent), nearly half of black mothers (49 percent) and Bangladeshi mothers (46 percent) reported no financial support. This in part at least may reflect the relatively disadvantaged economic situation of these groups in the United Kingdom. Clearly, we should not make generalizations about the role and significance of grandparent relations across these widely differing ethnic groups.

Changes with Age

A consistent pattern of changes in the contact and closeness between children and grandparents with age (of both the children and the grandparents) is reported in the large-scale surveys. Thus the British Social Attitudes Survey found that an infant grandchild had a powerful emotional pull, and the frequency of contact was highest after a grandchild was born and gradually tailed off as the children grew up (Dench et al., 1999). Three quarters of grandparents felt "very close" to their grandchild under 6, and this fell to 58 percent among those with a grandchild aged 16 or older.

The simple pattern of decreasing contact between child and grandparent with child's age becomes more complex when the type of interaction between the two is taken into account. While activities such as visiting playgrounds, playing games at home, watching television, or shopping, decrease after the preschool years, other activities such as giving advice, going away on holiday, or staying overnight together without parents, peak when the grandchild is between 6 and 15 years. The age of grandparents is important in their satisfaction with their role, and involvement peaks among grandparents aged under 60 (for detailed consideration of grandparental age see Dench & Ogg, 2002).

Context Differences

The U.S. research on grandparents emphasizes the importance of the social ecology of the family and community as an influence on grandparenting. Thus, the differences of rural and urban ecologies have been highlighted, in relation to lifecourse patterns and historical time and place (King et al., 1998). We have little equivalent information on rural versus urban comparisons in the United Kingdom. Other context differences such as the coresidence of grandparents, emphasized in U.S. research (e.g., Vandell, McCartney, Owen, Booth et al., 2003), are clearly important in the United Kingdom, but are confounded with ethnic minority differences (see Dex & Joshi, 2003). But the key factors of mothers' age and employment, marital situation and support systems, highlighted in the U.S. research on grandparent childcare, for example, are evidently linked to intergenerational relations here too, as the research on child care and on parental separation, considered next, makes clear.

How Has Contact and Support Between the Grandparent and Parent Generations Changed Over the Last Decades? Does the picture from the British Social Attitudes Surveys carried out in 1986 and 1995 give a different picture from that revealed in the U.S. study by Bengtson and colleagues (Bengtson et al., 2002), for families with dependent children (McGlone, Park, & Smith, 1998)? In the United Kingdom, overall levels of contact with relatives had fallen over this decade. Thus, weekly contact with grandmothers for children had fallen by 9 percentage points, from 59 percent in 1986 to 50 percent in 1995. This fall in contact was apparently partly attributable to increasing geographical distance between families (there was a rise of 12 percent in the number of nonmanual workers who lived more than an hour's journey time from their parents); it was particularly clear among nonmanual workers with dependent children. Among manual workers, there were no significant changes in maternal or paternal contact.

The survey data also showed that relatives, and particularly grandparents, were still a crucial source of aid and assistance in the lives of young parents. In 1995, a series of positive and negative statements about the family were included in the Survey and people were asked how much they agreed or disagreed with each. These questions had not been asked in the 1986 survey so a direct comparison over time could not be made; however the findings showed that the majority of the adult population was in 1995 very family-centered. Older people did have a more family-centered outlook than younger ones. However, among those with dependent children there was very little variation – men and women were very similar in their views, as were those from nonmanual and manual occupations, and those from one-parent and two-parent families, and single-earner and dual-earner families. The respondents – whatever their age – overwhelmingly believed that the family was more important than friends. It is not clear, however, whether the implication of the age-related pattern is that as the younger generation age, and replace the present older generation, the attitudes toward the family in the United Kingdom will substantially change.

In summary, the picture from the U.K. research in terms of the principles emphasized by Bengtson et al. (2002), is that the significance of the network of family relationships (including intergenerational links) is certainly important, as are ethnic variations; on the rural urban differences, we have no relevant information, but the emphasis on the significance of lifecourse experiences is supported. Finally, evidence for the diversity of grandparent-grandchild relationships is also accumulating. While in some respects the account of intergenerational contact and involvement provides a less optimistic picture than that outlined for the families studied by Bengtson and colleagues, attitudes toward the family in the United Kingdom are still overwhelmingly positive. We turn next to consider two particular aspects of grandparental involvement within families, as they relate to two of the most striking changes in family life in recent decades–first, working mothers and the provision of childcare in early childhood, and second, the involvement of grandparents following parental separation and family change.

GRANDPARENTAL SUPPORT IN THE UNITED KINGDOM

Provision of Childcare

The striking increase in the proportion of mothers who return to full- or part-time work before their babies are a year old – from 20 percent in 1981 to 36 percent in 1990 (Gregg & Wadsworth, 2000) and by 1999 to 49 percent in the United Kingdom. (Office for National Statistics, 2000) has been well documented. These changes in maternal employment have meant that patterns of early child care have changed dramatically in recent years. What part do grandparents play in this great increase in nonmaternal care? The General Household survey (Office for National Statistics 1991, 1994) reported that about one-quarter of children were cared for by their grandparents, and the British Social Attitudes Survey indicated that grandparents were involved in caring for their grandchildren in between 20 and 40 percent of families, with grandparent care especially important in families in which the mother worked part time. The ALSPAC study provides the opportunity to explore the part played by grandparents in some detail, in the context of the investigation of influences on children's and parents' health and development. With ALSPAC data collected from 8,752 families between 32 weeks antenatally and 21 months postnatally, Fergusson, Maughan, and Golding (2003), focused on nonmaternal care at 8, 15, and 18 months, and report that around 45 percent of children were regularly cared for by their grandparents at all three time points. Most children were involved in a complex care system involving formal and informal networks, but grandparents formed a crucial strand of such care. The mean level of grandparent involvement was 10 hours a week, but this average value masked a skewed distribution, with modal grandparent involvement for 2.5 hours and a small group of children cared for by their grandparents full time. (Only 1.3 percent of families had a grandparent living with the family – the great majority of grandparents were not coresident).

Grandparent care varied systematically with a range of demographic indicators. Frequency of grandparent care varied with access to other types of care, with grandparents less involved in families who had access to paid help. Families with financial problems received more grandparental involvement, and firstborn children and those born to single mothers, or with unstable marital status were more likely to be cared for by grandparents.

Mothers' age, educational level, and extent of work outside the home were all key variables (for findings from the United State that in some respects parallel these, see Vandell et al., 2003). Young mothers were much more likely to receive help from grandparents than older mothers – an association that was not explained by higher levels of coresidence with grandparents, and which remained significant when the effects of education and marital status were controlled. Among teenage mothers, only 12 percent reported no grandparent care, and more than 53 percent had grandparental involvement at each of the three time points. Comparable figures for the mothers aged 35 years and older were 58 percent and 16 percent. Grandparents may view younger mothers as more in need of help, or grandparents of older mothers may themselves be older and less able to help. In terms of future patterns, this is important, given the evidence that the age at which women have their children is increasing. The link between higher levels of maternal education and lower levels of grandparent involvement in child care (an association that was independent of employment status and age) could reflect geographical distance from grandparents. Mothers who did not work outside the home were less likely to receive grandparental help than those who worked part time. A similar pattern was found in the British Social Attitudes Survey in 1999.

Of particular interest was the finding that among the 6,306 families in which there was no paid child care, mothers' perceptions of the care they had received from their own mothers in childhood were related to grandparents' involvement. Higher levels of grandparental involvement were found in those families in which the mothers themselves reported positively on their own childhood experiences. When the independent contribution of these different variables were examined with a series of logistic regression analyses, this childhood experience variable and most of the demographic indicators remained as significant independent predictors of grandparental involvement.

In summary, this study of a representative population of white British families shows that grandparent care was important in the lives of a substantial proportion of parents and children – especially for younger, less well-educated mothers who were working part time (as also found in the United States by Vandell et al., 2003). The point made by Vandell and colleagues that grandparent care during the first 3 years is heterogeneous and may occur in response to different family circumstances is also supported by the U.K. data. The intergenerational associations in the quality of relationships and the key role grandparents played in supporting women working outside the home, shows grandparents' involvement was an important feature of changing family patterns for these families. This general point was particularly clear when we consider the second feature of current family experiences – parental separation and remarriage.

Grandchild-Grandparent Involvement following Parental Separation

As extensively discussed in this book, increases in parental separation and the formation of new partnerships, single parenthood, and stepfamily formation have dramatically changed patterns of family experiences. In the United Kingdom, by the age of 16, one in eight children have experienced parental separation or divorce and are living with a step-parent as a result of remarriage or cohabitation (Haskey, 1994; 1998; Office for National Statistics, 1998). More than 20 percent of children are currently growing up with a single parent. Parental separation frequently forms part of an ongoing process of changes in family relationships (Pryor & Rodgers, 2001); for most children the separation of their parents involves multiple subsequent family changes, including changes in contact and involvement with grandparents. These changes begin early: most of the children (72 percent) of the children identified as living in stepfamilies in the ONS analyses started to do so before they were 10 years old. Children who have experienced these changes show higher rates of adjustment difficulties (behavior problems, emotional difficulties, and problems at school). However these average effects are small and individual differences in children's responses to family transitions are marked – even within the same family (Amato, 2001; Amato & Keith, 1991; O'Connor, Dunn, Jenkins, Pickering et al., 2001). A key question is, therefore, what factors in the children's lives act to protect them or to increase their risk of problems? Here we consider in particular what role the relationship between child and grandparent may play in contributing to these individual differences.

Reports on the influence of grandparents on the outcomes for children of single or teenage mothers began to document the positive effects of grandparent support in the 1970s (Furstenberg, 1976; Kellam, Ensminger, & Turner, 1977), and a body of research has grown in the last two decades on patterns of grandparent-child relationships in families experiencing parental separation, and stepfamily formation (Johnson, 1988; Szinovacz, 1998). Among the many changes that follow parental separation, a common theme is the accentuation of the matrifocal bias in kinship patterns:

custody of children is in the majority of cases awarded to the mother (Johnson, 1999), and grandparental ties following separation are frequently stronger for maternal parents than paternal parents. In North American research this is reported for frequency of contact (Anspach, 1976; Kruk, 1995; Smith, 1991), level of involvement (Gladstone, 1988; Johnson & Barer, 1987; Sprey & Matthews, 1982), and feelings of closeness between grandparents and grandchildren (Smith, 1991).

In the United Kingdom, the British Social Attitudes survey findings unequivocally reinforce this matrifocal picture. Grandparents' links with grandchildren are much more likely to be negatively affected by parental separation when the link is through a son than through a daughter (Dench et al., 1999). The findings also show that grandparents may become more or less involved in their grandchildren's lives depending on how close they were to the custodial parent before the separation. The nature of their relationship may also change: A grandparent whose relationship with her grandchild was one of companionship and shared play may suddenly find herself in the role of surrogate parent (Lavers & Sonuga-Barke, 1997).

These changes in grandparents' involvement and family roles following changes in family structure have led to concern among many grandparents whose children have separated, and to the formation of grandparents' rights groups (Dench & Ogg, 2002; Dench et al., 1999; Drew & Smith, 1999; Thompson, Tinsley, Scalora, & Parke, 1989). These expressions of concern make very clear how important the grandparent-grandchild relationship is to many grandparents, and the poignancy for grandparents (especially paternal grandparents) of the changing patterns of contact following parental separation and repartnering (Dench & Ogg, 2002; Thompson et al., 1989). The consequences of loss of contact with grandchildren can be devastating. In Canada (Kruk, 1995) and in England (Drew, 2000; Drew & Smith, 1999, 2002), studies reported symptoms of chronic grief, bereavement, negative effects on physical and emotional health, including clinical depression following loss of conflict.

The perceptions of the young children who experience family change concerning their relations with their grandparents have been less extensively explored. We have relatively little information from children, especially younger children, on the quality of their relationships with grandparents in different family settings. How do children view their relations with grandparents as they experience family transitions?

Children's Views on Grandparents, in Relation to Family Problems and Changes

The importance of understanding children's perspectives on their lives following family transitions is increasingly stressed by those concerned with the care of children and with family policies (Dowling & Gorrell Barnes,

2000). As part of a program of longitudinal research into family transitions, we have included a focus on children's perspectives on their experiences and family relationships, including their relationships with their grandparents (Lussier, Deater-Deckard, Dunn, & Davies, 2002). The research is framed within the ALSPAC longitudinal study: In an intensive study, the Avon Brothers and Sisters Study (ABSS: Dunn et al., 1998) we recruited 192 families participating in ALSPAC, each with at least two children, from four family types – 50 nonstep families, 48 single mother families, 49 stepfather families, and 45 stepmother/complex stepfamilies in which each parent had brought children from a previous relationship. In terms of parental education, weekly family income, and children's adjustment, the families within each family type in ABSS did not differ from those in these family types within the main ALSPAC sample. With the children aged 7 and older, we used informal interviews and more structured questionnaires. With the younger children aged between 5 and 7 we used family "maps" and drawings (Dunn & Deater-Deckard, 2001).

In relation to the significance for the children of their relationships with their grandparents, we consider here three questions: First, what was the role of grandparents in children's confiding and communication about family problems? Second, how did individual differences in contact and closeness to grandparents vary with family setting and with patterns of biological relatedness? Third, how did closeness to grandparents relate to the children's adjustment?

Confiding and Communication about Problems
following Parental Separation

It is broadly assumed that it is helpful to children undergoing potentially stressful transitions to have opportunities to talk about what is happening, or has happened in their families (Gorell Barnes, Thompson, Daniel, & Burchardt, 1998). Clinical work with children suggests that they often need help and explanations of what has happened and will happen, to enable them to come to terms with family change (Dowling & Gorrell Barnes, 2000). Confiding and disclosure have been extensively studied in adults undergoing stressful experiences and found to be important (e.g., Brown & Harris, 1978). And research with adults who have lived through family transitions in their childhoods has highlighted that they recall *lack of communication* as a key feature of the stress that they experienced (Gorell Barnes et al., 1998; Walczack & Burns, 1984). To whom did the children in our study turn to talk about the changes in their family lives in the first weeks following parental separation?

We focused on the children who had experienced a family change; 94 children were able to recall details of the early weeks after the separation. The key people to whom children talked immediately following the separation were their grandparents, and in the weeks following, grandparents were the most frequent source of intimate confiding, followed by the children's friends (Dunn, Davies, O'Connor, & Sturgess, 2000). Mothers were the next most frequent source. Fathers and siblings were rarely confided in intimately, and very few children confided in counselors or teachers. So contact and closeness to grandparents take on particular significance for children faced with family transitions. It is noteworthy that in a very different sample – rural Midwestern families – the majority of children reported confiding in grandparents about family worries, and children who had a close relationship with at least one grandparent were less likely to be classified as vulnerable (King, Elder, & Conger, 2000).

Contact and Closeness to Grandparents and Family Setting

Children were asked about the kind and frequency of contact they had with their grandparents, how close they felt to each grandparent, and how important this relationship was to them. Parents also reported on these issues. In terms of contact, in this relatively stable community, contact between grandparents and children was frequent, according to both children and parents. Most children reported that they had had phone contact or seen their grandparents in the last week, and notably all of the children with stepgrandparents reported at least weekly contact with them.

However, these patterns varied across the various family settings. Contact was greater with maternal than with paternal grandparents and with grandmothers than with grandfathers – a pattern of responding that was consistent across different family types, except that children living with a stepmother and biological father reported less contact with maternal than paternal grandparents. These children in stepmother families reported higher rates of contact with their stepmaternal grandparents than with their biological mothers' parents. The significance of *who you live with* was also apparent in the comparison of this contact between child and stepmaternal grandparents, and the contact between children and their nonresident stepmothers' parents (that is, the parents of the partner of their nonresident fathers). Contact was greater in the former case than in the latter.

The children's accounts of contact then parallel the reports from large-scale surveys of adults in terms of frequency and the matrilineal pattern (Dench & Ogg, 2002). The findings on closeness showed children reported greater closeness to maternal grandparents than paternal grandparents, and those living with a stepmother were closer to the stepmother's parents than were children with a nonresident stepmother. The lowest levels of closeness were with nonresident-parent grandparents – again paralleling the adult reports from large-scale surveys (Dench & Ogg, 2002; Drew & Smith, 1999). The importance of including children's reports, as well as the accounts of adults however, is evident in two sets of findings: first, there was little agreement between parents and children about the children's emotional closeness to grandparents, complementing the studies showing generational differences in appraisal of family relationship quality. Second, the children's reports of closeness showed important associations with their adjustment.

Closeness to Grandparents and Children's Adjustment

Children's accounts of the closeness of their relationships with their grandparents were systematically linked to their parents' and teachers' reports on their adjustment and well-being. Children who reported feeling close to their maternal grandparents were described as having fewer internalizing and externalizing problems (see Figure 12.2). For children growing up with a stepfather, it was notable that there was a stronger association between adjustment and closeness to the step-paternal grandparents than between adjustment and the biological (nonresident) paternal grandparents. Children who felt close to their stepfather's parents were relatively unlikely to have externalizing problems.

Although these correlations indicate there were consistent associations between the emotional closeness that the children felt toward their grandparents and their adjustment, we know that a number of other family factors are linked to the children's emotional well-being – the quality of

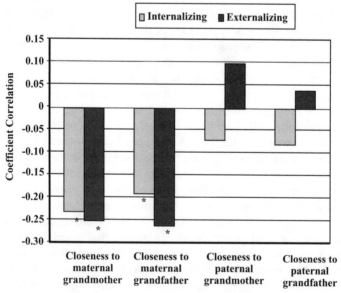

FIGURE 12.2. Relations between closeness to grandparents and adjustment: Avon Brothers and Sisters Study. * $p < .05$.

parent-child relationships, parental mental health, events earlier in their parents' lives, and multiple transitions in their parents' adult relationships. Did closeness to grandparents contribute to the wide variation in children's adjustment beyond these current family factors and earlier adversities?

A regression approach was used to assess the independent contribution of the child-grandparent relationship to children's adjustment (Lussier et al., 2002). The results showed that closeness to maternal grandmothers, and also to maternal grandfathers, accounted for variation in internalizing problems, beyond the variation explained by other family factors. Closeness to paternal grandparents did not however explain additional variance in internalizing problems. Similarly, closeness to maternal grandparents explained additional variance in externalizing problems, but closeness to paternal grandparents did not explain additional variance.

Of course it must be noted that, in these findings, the direction of effects is not clear. It could be that grandparents feel more warm and affectionate toward their grandchildren when these children are not difficult or disturbed – that is, the closeness of the relationship is in part a consequence of the children's adjustment. Alternatively, or in addition, a close relationship between grandparent and child could exert a protective effect on children who are having to cope with family difficulties. The relatively small size of this sample and its restriction to white families should be noted. In spite of these limitations, the findings draw attention to the importance of including grandparents in studies of children's response to family change, as well as the importance of including the views of children themselves, even in early childhood.

POLICY AND PRACTICE IMPLICATIONS

First, on the issue of child care, it is clear that there is likely to be continuing and growing pressure on grandparents to provide part-time child care (Presser, 1989). In the United Kingdom, government interest in supporting grandparental care is increasing (Supporting Family, Home Office). But to develop policies that are sensitive to the needs of all family members, we must recognize that grandparent child care is related to a complex set of factors: ethnicity, mothers' age, grandmother's age, and the work schedules of both generations. It will be important to understand these more fully, and to obtain information on parents' and grandparents' reasons for using different sorts of care and their satisfaction with such arrangements, in developing policies on child care.

Second, on the issue of parental separation and grandparent contact, the access and visitation rights of grandparents with grandchildren of noncustodial parent families is an important topic (Thompson et al., 1989). Statutes granting legal rights had been passed in all 50 states in the United States, however these have more recently been rescinded because of parental challenges to the laws. A recent landmark decision in the U.S. Supreme Court struck down the law in Washington State that gave grandparents rights to contact with grandchildren; the decision leans toward the rights of parents over the rights of children (see Smith & Drew, 2002 for details and for discussion of the complex U.K. situation). The problems of using legal measures to solve these family problems are considerable, with difficulties within the family likely to be exacerbated (Kornhaber, 1996). Grandparents often stress the importance of attempting nonlegal means to resolve conflicts over access (Smith & Drew, 2002).Generally, there is a need to focus on the experiences and needs of all three generations, in formulating policy.

FUTURE RESEARCH DIRECTIONS

The growing body of literature on grandparents has raised a number of issues on which we clearly need further research. In terms of our understanding of family relationships, the diversity and individual differences in grandparent-grandchild relationships deserve further study; relationships between a grandparent and his or her different grandchildren are likely to differ (Mueller & Elder, 2003), and the methods developed for studying within-family differences could usefully be applied to studying these differences (see O'Connor et al., 2001).

A second relationship issue that deserved comment is the matter of asymmetry between grandparents and grandchildren in their interest and involvement in the relationship. The greater interest and satisfaction of the grandparent in the relationship than that of the grandchild has been highlighted in the British Social Attitudes Survey (Dench & Ogg, 2002). It has also been emphasized in research on the sequelae of parental separation (Douglas & Fergusson, 2003). However, this asymmetry does not diminish the developmental significance of the relationship (as is sometimes implied) – it should be acknowledged that asymmetry characterizes parent-child relationships, many sibling relationships, and indeed many adult partnerships. It is a feature of relationships that deserves our research attention – not one that indicates the relationship is unimportant.

Further gaps in our information on grandparent-grandchild relationships include the following: First, research on grandparents and lesbian mothers and other "new" family forms (see Golombok, Chapter 11 in this book; also Patterson, Hurt, & Mason, 1998). Second, studies of stepgrandparenthood: Here the information from the British Social Attitudes (Dench & Ogg, 2002) and from the ABSS (Lussier et al., 2002) indicate the importance of these step ties; these are inevitably based on small samples, but this is a form of relationship that is multiplying and likely to become a significant dimension of extended family life.

CONCLUSIONS

To return to the original proposition by Bengtson and his colleagues concerning the role of grandparents in relation to the new stresses and changes faced by families, the evidence from the recent U.K. research indicates that although patterns of contact have decreased in frequency for some sections of the population, they remain very high for others. Relationships with family members including grandparents and grandchildren remain of major importance to most individuals.

In terms of the two current family issues considered here – nonmaternal care in relation to the increase in maternal employment and support to families following parental separation – the research has highlighted the significant role of grandparents. Although we do not yet have the over-time data to investigate whether the "increasing interdependence and exchange" suggested by Bengtson and colleagues is occurring in the United Kingdom, it is clear that maternal grandparents, at least, are potentially central figures in the arrangements women make for child care and a central source of confiding and communication to children facing family change.

References

Amato, P. R. (2001). Children of divorce in the 1990s: An update of the Amato and Keith (1991) meta-analysis. *Journal of Family Psychology, 15,* 355–370.

Amato, P. R., & Booth, A. (1997). *A generation at risk: Growing up in an era of family upheaval.* Cambridge, MA: Harvard University Press.

Amato, P. R., & Cheadle, J. (2003, August) The legacy of divorce: Tracking the implications of marital dissolution across three generations. *Paper Presented at European Developmental Psychological Association, Milan, Italy.*

Amato, P. R., & Keith, B. (1991). Parental divorce and the well-being of children: A meta-analysis. *Psychological Bulletin, 110,* 26–46.

Anspach, D. (1976). Kinship and divorce. *Journal of Marriage and the Family, 38,* 343–350.

Bengtson, V. L., Biblarz, T. J., & Roberts, R. E. L. (2002). *How families still matter: A longitudinal study of youth in two generations.* Cambridge: Cambridge University Press.

Brown, G. W., & Harris, T. (1978). *Social origins of depression: A study of psychiatric disorder in women.* London: Tavistock Press.

Burton, L. M., & Bengtson, V. L. (1985). Black grandmothers: Issues of timing and continuity of roles. In V. L. Bengtson & J. F. Robertson (Eds.), *Grandparenthood* (pp. 61–77). Beverley Hills, CA: Sage.

Burton, L. M., & Dilworth-Anderson, P. (1991). The intergenerational family roles of aged Black Americans. In S. K. Pelfer & M. B. Sussman (Eds.), *Families: Intergenerational and generational connections* (pp. 311–330). Binghamton, NY: Haworth.

Chase-Lansdale, P. L., Brooks-Gunn, J., & Zamsky, E. S. (1994). Young African-american multigenerational families in poverty: Quality of mothering and grandmothering. *Child Development, 65,* 373–393.

Cherlin, A. J., & Furstenberg, F. F. (1986). *The new American grandparent.* New York: Basic Books.

Collishaw, S., & Maughan, B. (2003). Contribution to Dex, B., & Joshi, H (op. cit).

Dench, G., & Ogg, J. (2002). *Grandparenting in Britain: A baseline study.* London: Institute of Community Studies.

Dench, G., Ogg, J., & Thomson, K. (1999). The role of grandparents. In R. Jowell, J. Curtice, A. Park, & K. Thomson (Eds.), *British Social Attitudes, the 16th report.* Aldershot: Ashgate.

Dex, S., & Joshi, H. (2003). *Milleenium Cohort Study First Survey: Descriptive Report.* Institute of Education, University of London: Center for Longitudinal Studies.

Douglas, G., & Fergusson, N. (2003). The role of grandparents in divorced families. *International Journal of Law, Policy and the Family, 17*, 41–67.

Dowling, E., & Gorrell Barnes, G. (2000). *Working with children and parents through separation and divorce.* London: Macmillan.

Drew, L. M. (2000). *What are the implications for grandparents when they lose contact with their grandchildren?* Unpublished doctoral dissertation Goldsmiths' College, University of London.

Drew, L. A., & Smith, P. K. (1999). The impact of parental separation/divorce on grandparent-grandchild relationships. *International Journal of Aging and Human Development, 48*, 191–216.

Drew, L. M., & Smith, P. K. (2002). Implications for grandparents when they lost contact with their grandchildren: Divorce, family feud, and geographical separation. *Journal of Mental Health and Aging, 8*, 95–119.

Dunn, J., Cheng, H., O'Connor, T. G., & Bridges, L. (2004). Children's perspectives on their relationships with their non-resident fathers: influences, outcomes and implications. *Journal of Child Psychology and Psychiatry, 45*, 553–566.

Dunn, J., Davies, L., O'Connor, T., & Sturgess, W. (2000). Parents' and partners' life course and family experiences: Links with parent-child relationships in different family settings. *Journal of Child Psychology and Psychiatry, 41*, 955–968.

Dunn, J., & Deater-Deckard, K. (2001). *Children's views of their changing families.* York: Joseph Rowntree Foundation.

Dunn, J., Deater-Deckard, K., Pickering, K., O'Connor, T., Golding, J., & the ALSPAC Study Team. (1998). Children's adjustment and pro-social behavior in step- single and non-step family settings: Findings from a community study. *Journal of Child Psychology and Psychiatry, 39*, 1083–1095.

Fergusson, E., Maughan, B., & Golding, J. Intergenerational care in a large longitudinal sample. Manuscript submitted for publication.

Furstenberg, F. (1976). *Unplanned parenthood: The social consequences of teenage childbearing.* New York: Free Press.

Gladstone, J. W. (1988). Perceived changes in grandmother-grandchild relations following a child's separation or divorce. *The Gerontologist, 28*, 66–72.

Gorell Barnes, G., Thompson, P., Daniel, G., & Burchardt, N. (1998). Growing up in stepfamilies. Oxford: Clarendon Press.

Gregg, P. & Wadsworth J. (eds.). (2000) *The state of working Britain.* Manchester: Manchester University Press.

Grundy, E., Murphy, M., & Shelton, N. (1999). Looking beyond the household: intergenerational perspectives on living kin and contacts with kin in Great Britain. *Population Trends, 97*, 19–27.

Haskey, J. (1994). Stepfamilies and stepchildren in Great Britain. *Population Trends, 76,* 17–27.

Haskey, J. (1998). One-parent families and their dependent children in Great Britain. *Population Trends, 91,* 5–14.

Johnson, C. H. (1988). *Ex familia: Grandparents, parents and children adjust to divorce.* New Brunswick, NJ: Rutgers University Press.

Johnson, C. H. (1999). Effects of adult children's divorce on grandparenthood. In M. Szinovacz (Ed.), *Handbook on grandparenthood* (pp. 184–199). Westport, CT: Greenwood Press.

Johnson, C. H., & Barer, B. M. (1987). Marital instability and the changing kinship networks of grandparents. *The Gerontologist, 27,* 330–335.

Kellam, S. G., Ensminger, M. E., & Turner, R. J. (1977). Family structure and the mental health of children: Concurrent and longitudinal community wide studies. *Archives of General Psychiatry, 34,* 1012–1022.

King, V., & Elder, G. H. (1997). The legacy of grandparenting: Childhood experiences with grandparents and current involvement with grandchildren. *Journal of Marriage and the Family, 59,* 848–859.

King, V., Elder, G. H., & Conger, R. D. (2000). Wisdom of the ages. In G. H. Elder & R. D. Conger (Eds.), *Children of the land: Adversity and success in rural America* (pp. 127–150). Chicago: University of Chicago Press.

King, V., Russell, S. T., & Elder, G. H. (1998). Grandparenting in family systems: An ecological perspective. In M. E. Szinovacz (Ed.), *Handbook on grandparenting* (pp. 53–69). Westport, CT: Greenwood Press.

Kornhaber, A. (1996). *Contemporary grandparenting.* Newbury Park, CA: Sage.

Kruk, E. (1995). Grandparent-grandchild contact loss: Findings from a study of "grandparent rights" members. *Canadian Journal on Aging, 14,* 737–754.

Lavers, C. A., & Sonuga-Barke, J. S. (1997). Annotation: On the grandmother's role in the adjustment and maladjustment of grandchildren. *Journal of Child Psychology and Psychiatry, 38,* 747–753.

Lussier, G., Deater-Deckard, K., Dunn, J., & Davies, L. (2002). Support across two generations: Children's closeness to grandparents following parental divorce and remarriage. *Journal of Family Psychology, 16,* 363–376.

McGlone, F., Park, A., & Smith, K. (1998). Families and kinship. York: Joseph Rowntree Foundation.

Mueller, M. M., & Elder, G. H. (2003). Family contingencies across the generations: Grandparent-grandchild relationships in holistic perspective. *Journal of Marriage and the Family, 65,* 404–417.

O'Connor, T., Dunn, J., Jenkins, J., Pickering, K., & Rasbash, J. (2001). Family settings and children's adjustment: Differential adjustment within and across families. *British Journal of Psychiatry, 179,* 110–115.

Office for National Statistics. (1991, 1994). *General Household Survey.* London: The Stationery Office.

Office for National Statistics. (1998). *Marriage and divorce statistics 1995:* Series FM2, no 23, Table 4.4a. London: The Stationery Office.

Office For National Statistics (2002). *Social trends, 32.* London: The Stationery Office.

Patterson, C. J., Hurt, S., & Mason, C. D. (1998). Families of the lesbian baby boom: Children's contact with grandparents and other adults. *American Journal of Orthopsychiatry, 68,* 390–399.

Popenoe, D. (1993). American family decline, 1960–90: A review and appraisal. *Journal of Marriage and the Family, 55,* 527–556.

Presser, H. B. (1989). Some economic complexities of child care provided by grandmothers. *Journal of Marriage and the Family, 51,* 581–591.

Pryor, J., & Rodgers, B. (2001). *Children in changing families: Life after parental separation.* Oxford: Blackwell Publishers.

Rossi, A. S., & Rossi, P. H. (1991). *Of human bonding: Parent-child relations across the life-course.* New York: Aldine de Gruyter.

Smith, M. S. (1991). An evolutionary perspective on grandparent-grandchild relationships. In P. K. Smith (Ed.), *The psychology of granparenthood: An international perspective.* London: Routlage.

Smith, P. K., & Drew, L. M. (2002). Grandparenthood. In M. Bornstein (Ed.), *Handbook of parenting* (Vol. 3, pp. 141–172). Mahwah, NJ: Lawrence Erlbaum Associates.

Sprey, J., & Matthews, S. H. (1982). Contemporary grandparenthood: A systematic transition. *The Annals of the American Academy of Political and Social Science, 464,* 91–103.

Szinovacz, M. E. (1998). Grandparent research: Past present, and future. In M. E. Szinovacz (Ed.), *Handbook on grandparenthood* (pp. 1–20). Westport, CT: Greenwood Press.

Thompson, L., & Walker, A. J. (1987). Mothers as mediators of intimacy between grandmothers and their young adult granddaughters. *Family Relations, 36,* 72–77.

Thompson, R. A., Tinsley, B. R., Scalora, M. J., & Parke, R. D. (1989). Grandparents' visitation rights: Legalising the ties that bind. *American Psychologist, 9,* 1217–1222.

Vandell, D. L., McCartney, K., Owen, M. T., Booth, C., & Clarke-Stewart, A. (2003). Variations in child care by grandparents during the first three years. *Journal of Marriage and the Family, 65,* 375–381.

Walczack, Y., & Burns, S. (1984). *Divorce: The children's point of view.* London: Harper & Row.

Wilson, J. Q. (2002). *The marriage problem: How our culture has weakened families.* New York: Harper Collins.

PART SIX

CONCLUSIONS AND COMMENTARIES

13

What Have We Learned

Proof That Families Matter, Policies for Families and Children, Prospects for Future Research

Alison Clarke-Stewart

The chapters in this volume address a common question: How do families matter in young people's development? During recent years there have been strong claims suggesting that how parents rear their children is of little consequence, on the grounds that most of the supposed environmental effects are actually genetically mediated, or that the important environmental effects derive from the peer group rather than the family. In addition, there have been claims that many of the associations between parents' behavior and children's development represent children's effects on their parents rather than the effects of socialization experiences. The purpose of this volume was to consider how far this rejection of environmentally mediated family influences is warranted and what can be concluded about such influences in relation to different aspects of children's psychosocial development.

The book brings together the latest research findings on key aspects of families' influence on their children, specifically, the ways in which families function as sources of risk and adversity or as sources of strength and protection; the ways in which parents act as brokers of resources or mediators of risks; the links between families and peers in causing problems or promoting positive outcomes; the connections between parents' work lives and children's family lives; the continuing influence of parents even when contact is limited by the children's attendance in child care; the impacts of divorce and parental separation on children's immediate and long-term adjustment; the significance of grandparents for children's emotional well-being; and the consequences of new family forms such as lesbian- and surrogate-mother families.

In this summary and commentary, I highlight four topics that seem of particular importance in this extraordinary compilation of research on family influences. First, I draw attention to some of the noteworthy empirical findings embedded in the extensive literature on families and children presented by the authors. Second, I collate the proof that families matter from each of the chapters. Third, I discuss some of the implications of this proof for policies to promote children's healthy development and well-being. And fourth, I summarize the authors' suggestions about the prospects for future research on family influence. The chapters themselves contain many details, nuances, complexities, and subtleties that I do not discuss, of course. This commentary merely touches the edges of a very large and rich mother lode of information. Two other commentaries are provided: In Chapter 14, Jacqueline Goodnow discusses models of development and alerts us to some of the practical and political complexities of making and implementing research-based policies for children and families, and, in Chapter 15, Robert Hinde offers valuable counsel regarding directions for policy and research in the future. The unique views of these two commentators demonstrate wisdom found only in the melding of scholarly minds with political hearts.

NOTEWORTHY FINDINGS

Contained in all these chapters are many important and interesting empirical findings about families and children. Among the specific findings the following seem to me to have particular significance for understanding the influence families have on their children and thinking about research-based policies to improve children's plight:

- It is not poverty, per se, that presents a risk for children's development; it is the number of risks to which the child is exposed.
- It is not the influence of peers alone that leads youngsters to use drugs, but the influence of parents as well.
- Even if children from risky environments are adopted into well-functioning families, they are unlikely to experience complete recovery.
- The longer children spend in an adverse environment, the less recovery is observed.
- The nature of parents' employment is more important than simply whether or not the parent works outside the home.
- Fathers' work is as important as mothers'.
- Family factors predict child outcomes no matter how many hours a child is in out-of-home child care.
- Remarriage doesn't mend children's broken hearts.
- It is worse for children's psychological well-being when battling parents stay together than when they get divorced.
- Negative effects of divorce on children persist into adulthood.
- Children's well-being is not related to the manner of their conception.

These findings, which may not be common knowledge for every man- and woman-in-the-street, illustrate the scope and significance of the research presented in these chapters.

PROOF THAT FAMILIES MATTER

The research presented in these chapters also offers ample evidence that families have direct and indirect effects on their children's development. Perusing these chapters, thoughtful readers cannot be left wondering whether families matter beyond providing genes, beyond peer-picking, and beyond child effects. In five separate domains, the authors have presented evidence that families "count."

Risk and Resilience

In the section of the book dealing with risk and resilience, the authors consider the role of families in generating risk conditions on the one hand and in protecting children from risks to development on the other. In Chapter 1, Ann Masten and Anne Schaffer use the risk-and-resilience framework to overview ways in which families matter. They describe how families can be sources of risk and adversity or sources of support and strength. Parents influence children in both passive ways (e.g., by neglect) and active ways (e.g., by punishment). They provide resources within the family (food, shelter, clothing, and books) and access to resources outside the home (art lessons, sports teams, religious activities, and neighborhoods with good schools). They act as mediators and moderators of external risks; as mediators, they bring home stresses they experience in the workplace; as moderators, their behavior determines the extent to which their children are affected by living in a poor neighborhood. Thus, in direct and indirect and always-complicated ways, parents influence children's development, and their influence extends across multiple domains, affecting children's reactions to threat, explorations of the environment, regulation of arousal, adaptation to trauma, formation of social and cultural identities, and development of psychological disorders.

In Chapter 2, Michael Rutter further marshals evidence that families are a source of both risk and protection for children's development. The direct risks in the family described in his chapter include mothers' mental illness and low education, fathers' employability and criminal inclinations, and parents' neglect and abuse. In agreement with Masten and Schaffer, he too points out that families mediate risks present in the larger society, such as war or poverty, and, conversely, that families promote young people's resilience and offer protection against other risks. For example, children in bad neighborhoods benefit from high parental control but in good neighborhoods high parental control has the opposite effect – overprotection.

According to Arnold Sameroff, in Chapter 3, it is not a single risk in the family or the outside world, even a major risk like poverty or single parenting, that leads to problems for children, but the accumulation of many risks. It is not a single promotive factor that leads to increased competence in the child, but being exposed to many promotive factors. The number of risks (or promotive factors), his research demonstrates, is even more powerful than the personal characteristics of the child in predicting later psychological outcomes.

The most compelling evidence that families matter presented in this section on risk and resilience comes from two kinds of research: longitudinal, multivariate studies and adoption studies. Both research designs go beyond simply showing statistical associations between parents' and children's behavior; they demonstrate that changes in parenting lead to changes in child outcomes. When children are removed from high risk environments and provided with better rearing environments through adoption, their development improves; when children in longitudinal investigations continue to live in high-risk families, their development deteriorates over time.

Peers and Parents

The two chapters in the section on peers and parents address the issue of the relative importance of parents and peers for children's development. The authors provide a balanced view, showing that both sets of socialization agents are important. In Chapter 4, Andrew Collins and Glen Roisman review research from a wide variety of approaches indicating that even though children are affected by their peers, family still matters: Experimental training studies demonstrate that how parents discipline their children affects the children's antisocial behavior and school adjustment, because when parents are trained to be less coercive, children's behavior improves. Longitudinal studies show that significant associations between parents' treatment of children and children's later competence remain even after researchers control for earlier child characteristics and peer factors. Adoption studies indicate that normal parenting buffers adopted children against bad genes inherited from their biological parents, for example, genes for schizophrenia or criminality. Correlational studies provide evidence that good relationships with parents predict children's positive romantic relationships and moral maturity in adolescence. And finally, multivariate studies indicate that parents moderate and mediate the effects of other social influences and that the joint contribution of peers and parents is greater than either factor alone. Taken together, the results of all these types of research offer convincing support for the suggestion that families count for fostering children's competence and peer relationships.

In Chapter 5, Ken Dodge and his colleagues describe a single longitudinal study that documents the joint contributions of peers and parents to a specific outcome in adolescence – early drug use. The multi-step study shows that the likelihood that an adolescent will use drugs by age 12 is increased by a sequence of factors: being born into a high-risk family (with a poor, single, or teen mother) increases the probability of harsh and abusive parenting in childhood, which increases the probability that the child will have conduct problems when he or she enters school and will therefore be rejected by peers, which then increases the probability of conflict with parents in adolescence, who then give up their socialization and supervisory efforts, which, finally, increases the probability that the child will gravitate to deviant peers and begin using drugs. This example of one carefully constructed longitudinal investigation offers further strong evidence that families count, by illustrating a multidimensional path from parents to problems.

Work and Family

The two chapters in the section of the book on work and family show how families matter because they connect children to the outside world. In Chapter 6, Ann Crouter describes how parents bring the outside world into their homes as a result of their experiences at work. Parents with poor working conditions – long hours, overtime work, nonstandard shifts, stressful work, and lack of autonomy on the job – withdraw from parenting and, in the long run, become irritable and provide home environments of lower quality. Their children exhibit more behavior problems, lowered academic competence, and inferior well-being in adolescence. Research described in this chapter goes beyond simple associations by controlling for confounding factors and by showing that parents who change their work schedules or change jobs change in their parenting practices as well.

Another way in which families connect their children to the outside world is through the use of nonparental child care. In Chapter 7, Kathleen McCartney describes how parents choose the type, quality, and hours of child care for their children. She compiles research to show that even when children are in child care – regardless of type or quality or hours – family factors continue to predict children's development. In fact, family characteristics predict children's behaviors and abilities four times more strongly than child-care characteristics, regardless of hours and kind of care. Parents also moderate the effect of child care on children: children profit more from high quality care when they come from at-risk (low income, minority) families than when their families provide middle-class advantages. Although these results by themselves do not prove that families influence children's development, they offer indirect support for that argument.

Discord and Divorce

In the chapters on discord and divorce (Chapters 8, 9, and 10), Paul Amato, Mavis Hetherington, and Sabine Walper and Katharina Beckh make a compelling case that parental conflict and separation lead to negative consequences for children. Amato's chapter highlights the long-term fallout of discord and divorce when the children in such families are adolescents and even young adults. He finds that both discord and divorce lead to emotional adjustment problems, and that divorce, in addition, predicts damaged relations with the father, unstable romantic or marital relationships, and low levels of education in adulthood. The only time that divorce has a positive consequence is when it terminates intense conflict between the parents. Under these circumstances, ending the marriage can improve children's emotional well-being and the stability of their relationships (although the problem of less education and a distant dad remain).

Hetherington and Walper and Beckh also document how conflict between parents is linked to poor outcomes for children – specifically adolescents' poor mental health, insecure social relationships, and unregulated antisocial behavior. Problems are particularly acute if the parents' conflict is intense, prolonged, and hostile: Parents who fight with each other express their hostility with their children and their children, in turn, are hostile toward their siblings and peers. Remarriage also can have negative consequences for adolescents, especially in the early stages of the stepfamily formation, if the new family includes children from two previous marriages, and when the stepfamily itself breaks up. The studies on which these three chapters are based are longitudinal, following children of divorce into adolescence and adulthood, and they control for a myriad of other confounding factors, including parents' socioeconomic status (SES) antisocial behavior, religiosity, attitudes toward divorce, and alcohol use, as well as children's behavior before the discord or separation. Thus, they provide strong empirical evidence that families – in this case, the stability and harmony of families – matter for the well-being of children and youth.

New and Extended Family Forms

Finally, in the last section of the book, the authors discuss ways in which families matter by examining research in two new areas of investigation, new and extended family forms. In Chapter 11, Susan Golombok reviews research in the brave new world of high-tech fertilization, donated gametes, solo mothers, lesbian mothers, and surrogate mothers. Studies of these atypical families suggest that children turn out much the same regardless of the nature of their conception. The form of the family may differ, but as long as there is an involved and nurturing adult, children flourish. It is the quality of the parent-child relationship rather than the biological link, sexual orientation, or mode of conception that matters for children's development.

In Chapter 12, Judy Dunn and her colleagues show that the essence of family is not restricted to children and their parents; grandparents also have an influential role. Grandparents offer children an opportunity to share intimate confidences with adults who are not their parents (particularly when children are young or after their parents have separated). They give mothers assistance with child care (especially young mothers with less education who work part time). Children who develop close relationships with their grandparents are better adjusted psychologically. This chapter underscores the necessity of broadening our view of the agents that are important members of the family system.

The research on new and extended family forms is in its infancy compared with the other domains discussed in this book, and although confounding factors such as the quality of parent-child relations were statistically controlled, clear causal links between child adjustment and grandparent involvement or manner of conception have not yet been established. Further research is necessary to prove unequivocally that families count in these ways too.

Proof Positive

Proof of family influence, as the authors of this volume show, comes in many guises, but together the evidence is compelling that families do indeed matter for the development of children and youth and they matter in a variety of ways. The studies reviewed here reveal a plethora of complex pathways and processes linking parents' behavior and circumstances with children's competence, well-being, and ultimate life success.

POLICIES FOR FAMILIES AND CHILDREN

This body of research on family influence does not lead to a single unified or unifying family policy. It is clear that different families have different needs and different studies expose different risks that call for different policies. But to what extent are we ready to translate the research findings compiled in this volume into specific policies? Can we propose or support particular policies that we are reasonably certain will benefit some children and do no harm to others, or at least policies in which the benefits clearly outweigh the risks and the costs? Thinking about the policy implications of the results of research on family influence raises challenging pragmatic and ethical questions:

- If working long hours at a job with limited autonomy makes parents irritable and inattentive to their children, are there workplace policies that will reduce this problem?
- If having children in good quality child care improves the quality of their parents' care, should governments provide more support and regulation of child care?
- If being exposed to a large number of environmental risks is detrimental for children's development, how can we reduce the number of risks?

- If children are affected by circumstances outside the family – for example, health care, social services, the education system – should we focus our efforts on these factors rather than within the family?
- If parent training programs improve the quality of parenting and reduce children's negative behavior, should these programs be mandated (and for whom)?
- If divorce leads to negative outcomes for some children, how can policies be targeted to those children who are most at risk?
- If parental separation has negative effects on children, should we support a policy that makes it harder for couples to split up?
- If divorce is worse for younger children than for adolescents, should we support a policy that requires couples to wait until their children are older (or dead) before they separate?
- If having grandparents involved in children's lives is good for them and their mothers, should we advocate a policy that protects grandparents' legal rights to such involvement?

The contributors to this volume were asked to think about the policy implications of research results in their particular areas. Although they were surprisingly cautious about advocating specific policies, they did come up with many creative and thought-provoking ideas about policies for families and children. It would have been interesting to challenge this group of experts to come to a consensus and recommend a single practical policy that could be implemented in a single community with the maximum positive payoff for children. The authors were not given this challenge, however. As a consequence, the chapters contain a variety of different policy ideas related to different domains of family influence. Some ideas are quite general; they would receive wide if not universal agreement, in principle, but the question is how to turn them into implementable policies. Other ideas were more specific, but they need to be tested empirically before turning them into policies to be implemented in the real world.

The broadest ideas about policy came from the research on risk and resilience. The authors in this section of the book, in fact, suggested that the most important policy implication to be drawn from their research is that we need to broaden our views of how children's resilience can be fostered. They suggested that to promote children's resilience, policies should be in place even before children encounter adverse experiences. The goals of these policies would be two fold: (1) to foster protective qualities in the children themselves, such as high intelligence, scholastic achievement, secure relationships with caregivers, a sense of self-efficacy, a range of social problem solving skills, a positive social interactional style, and a flexible adaptive approach to new situations; and (2) to give children opportunities to cope successfully with challenges and stresses, exercise responsibility and judgment, and succeed in a range of experiences across a range of settings at home, in school, and with the peer group. Policies should also support children at the time of the adverse experience – for example, by providing alternative sources of support if a parent is depressed or mentally ill – or following the adverse experience. If the family environment is pervasively stressful and adversity cannot be reduced to a reasonable level, a total change of environment that brings about a combination of positive experiences and new opportunities for the child may be necessary. Thus the research on risk and resilience provides a basis for policies focused directly on children. The research also provides support for policies focused on parents, policies providing interventions to alter parenting as a mediator of developmental risk factors such as divorce and poverty.

The underlying message from the researchers on risk and resilience is to think big, to envision policies leading to changes in the child, the family, the school, and the community. They do not advocate intervening separately in each of these arenas, but rather, looking for policies that have a broad impact. They do not advocate intervening narrowly by teaching children specific coping skills in a classroom, but rather, offering them real-life experiences that will bring them success, foster their self-efficacy, and encourage alternative methods of coping. They recommend creating interventions that produce everyday competence in all children rather than targeting select groups of children or single factors in the family, the school, or the community. When resources are limited, however, they suggest that policies should target those young people who are greatest risk because they are exposed to multiple risk factors.

Research on risk and resilience suggests that policies to change children's early circumstances are more efficient than those that intervene later in life, because some early experiences have neurological consequences that are difficult to reverse. Even in adulthood, life experiences that break the chain of disadvantage and open up new opportunities can provide beneficial turning points that counter earlier adversity. However, if resources are limited, policies should focus on interventions in childhood and aim for prevention of problems rather than remediation.

The authors reviewing research on peers and parents use this body of evidence as well to support intervening early in children's lives. Rather than waiting until children have developed problems such as drug use and juvenile delinquency, they recommend initiating policies to interrupt these negative developmental trajectories and prevent initiation of problem behavior in the first place. Specifically, these authors endorse providing economic and social support to families during the children's early years, when the families have the greatest economic need. One such policy would be to allow families to borrow against their future earnings in the same way that college loans provide a needed economic crutch for students. Intervention programs to change parenting styles in the early years were also endorsed as a way to improve both child behavior and parent-child relationships.

The authors discussing the research on peers and parents did see a place for classroom skill-building programs, specifically to prevent drug abuse in adolescence. However, even with this specific aim, they suggested that programs should begin early, before the problem behavior began, and be broadly conceived, focusing on children's social-cognitive skills, social competence, and positive interactions with peers, rather than restricted to drug-use prevention programs per se.

In the section of the book describing research in the domain of work and family, the authors presented several other policy ideas. They described "family friendly policies" in the workplace, such as parental leaves, flexible work schedules, opportunities for part-time employment and job sharing, and employer-supported child care; these would potentially enhance the well-being of employed parents and their children. They described stress management and health promotion programs in the workplace that might enhance employee functioning and strengthen parenting and family dynamics. And they alluded to the possibility that improving the quality of child care might improve the quality of parenting and that providing information and education about child care might encourage parents to pressure child-care producers to improve their services. These policy ideas are intriguing, but, as the authors acknowledge, require further empirical test.

Policies related to divorce and discord have been the subject of discussion and debate for as long as people have been unhappily married. Over the years, policy makers have embraced many different divorce reforms as they have tried to reduce the frequency of divorce, diminish post-separation conflict, encourage the continued involvement of both parents, and provide adequate financial support for children. The reforms they have supported include no-fault divorce, joint custody, divorce mediation, guidelines for equitable division of property, and mechanisms to ensure compliance with child support rulings. All of these reforms have been successful to some extent. However, even with these policies in place, parental separation continues to have negative effects on some children. The problem according to these authors is that there is no "one size fits all" divorce policy. Joint custody is associated with continued involvement of the non-custodial parent and payment of child support for most couples, but there are divorced couples who cannot get along and for whom mandatory joint custody is deleterious. Divorce increases the probability of negative outcomes for most children, but if parents are in an intractable high-conflict marriage, it may be better for parents to separate than to stay together.

There are a number of ways in which the recommendations of the authors reviewing research on discord and divorce echo those of the authors reviewing research on risk and resilience. They, too, suggest that policies should be comprehensive – dealing with parents and children, family dynamics, and families' needs for jobs, education, child care, and health care. These authors, too, recommend policies that would promote constructive family processes and competent parenting in *all* types of families rather than focusing on specific types of families. They, too, support prevention policies, in this case, programs to strengthen young couples' competencies to cooperate and communicate before conflict and incompatibilities become issues. And finally, these authors, too, emphasize the importance of policies that would protect children in the early years. Because of the negative effects of parental separation on young children, they suggest that policies should encourage parents whose unions are marked by mutual disengagement rather than dysfunctional discord to attempt to strengthen their relationship through counseling and postpone separation until their children are older. By late adolescence, children's educational trajectories and relationships with fathers are less vulnerable to the stress of family disruption. However, these authors, too, agree that if adversity cannot be avoided – in this case, the adversity brought on by parental divorce – intervention programs can benefit older children as well as younger ones. In terms of specific interventions, they point to two periods of particular need, the transitions of parental separation and parental remarriage, during which guidance and support could enhance parents' abilities to cooperate and could reduce children's stress, loyalty conflicts, and premature distancing from the family.

Finally, in the last section of the book, which focuses on new and extended family forms, the authors describe three specific policies: (1) regulations to limit the number of embryos transferred in IVF or ICSI cycles, thereby reducing the number of multiple births; (2) disclosure of the identity of gamete donors to allow offspring to find out about, and possibly have contact with, their genetic parents and siblings; and (3) policies to protect the access and visitation rights of grandparents with grandchildren of noncustodial parent families. All of these policies, they point out, have risks as well as possible benefits and need to be tested. In addition to describing these specific policies, these authors, like the others in the book, underscore the need for a broad view of policy, as they recommend that policy makers focus on the experiences and needs of all three generations in formulating policies related to grandparent rights and focus on the experiences and needs of both children and donors in formulating policies related to assisted reproduction.

In sum, the common suggestions about policy made by the authors in this book are that a broadly conceived universal approach should be given high priority in policy deliberations, that prevention should be the front line of attack, and that policies should focus on early intervention as often as possible. As research progresses, we can modify our policy ideas, but for now, it is clear that we have solid information to serve as a reliable guide for policy discussions.

PROSPECTS FOR FUTURE RESEARCH

Although the chapters in this volume provide a rich buffet of evidence that families matter for children's well-being and development and offer intriguing ideas for policies to support and enhance families' influence, this is not the end of the story. There are still lingering questions and uncertainties for researchers to investigate in the future. The authors of this volume also laid out some guidelines for these researchers to follow if they are to gather more useful information about how families matter and are to test the limits of families' influence. They do not suggest a single, simple next-step study or even a finite number of such studies, except in the area of new family forms, where there are still many unanswered descriptive questions, such as, "What are the long-term consequences of assisted reproduction?" For the most part, the authors in this book offer suggestions about general research strategies that will move us to the next level of understanding about family influences on children's development.

Complex Models. Foremost among these research strategies is a focus on more complex models of family influence. Life for researchers was simpler when "family" meant "mother" and "influence" meant "is correlated with." We now know that researchers in the future must deal with interconnections, systems, multiple pathways, and multiple variables as they navigate the seas of research. They will need to devise and test models that reflect the complexity of the real world and multiple sources of influence – mothers and fathers, parents and peers, work and child care. They will need to include in their models controls for a plethora of potentially confounding factors.

Longitudinal Designs. It is also important for future researchers that these complex models be tested longitudinally. Family effects are not only complex but transactional in nature and need to be tested with longitudinal panel studies that follow children and their families over time. These longitudinal studies should continue as long as necessary, extending from the early years of childhood into adolescence and adulthood. Although the period from infancy to adulthood is a long one, this timeframe is necessary if we want to follow children's individual developmental trajectories through significant life turning points and determine whether the same factors influence development in the same ways at each stage of life. Studies need to include trajectories of family change rather than focussing on the status of the family at one point in time, and transitions in the family, such as divorce and remarriage, must be studied as extended processes of change in family relationships and life circumstances, not as discrete events.

Interactions and Moderators. These complex, longitudinal models will allow future researchers to explore statistical interactions among the different dimensions of children's life experiences. For example, it will be possible to explore the significance of ethnicity, religion, and neighborhood as moderating contexts for parents' behavior. They will also allow researchers to investigate how child characteristics such as gender and temperament moderate children's responses to identical experiences.

Broader Samples. However, in order to investigate the significance of these background contexts and child characteristics, it will be necessary for future researchers to be more inclusive in their sampling. In the past, most researchers have focused on white, middle-class, professional families. Extending samples to a broader range of subpopulations including families of color and low-income families is important for future researchers. Broader sampling will make it possible to determine the significance of background contexts such as SES and to see the extent to which family effects vary across different subpopulations. It is important to investigate the effects of family factors – childrearing practices, child care use, child abuse, parental conflict, marital transitions – in family groups as diverse as lesbian moms, step grandparents, co-habiters, inner-city residents, and parents from all ethnic groups. Another reason to broaden future research samples is that increasingly large numbers of children are growing up in working-poor and low-income families and research on these groups in particular is necessary to inform social policy. Ideally, in the future, researchers in psychology as well as those in sociology will put greater emphasis on recruiting research samples that are representative of the population they wish to study.

Cross-National Comparisons. It will also benefit researchers to broaden their samples beyond particular populations within a country and conduct investigations across different cultures. We know little about how the effects of family factors vary in different cultural settings. We know little about whether different standards, values, practices, and policies associated with families in different countries have different effects on parents and children. The cross-national comparison of marital conflict and separation in Germany and the United States represented in this volume (Chapters 8, 9, and 10) illustrates the value of this type of work. Cross-cultural work would be helpful to inform policymakers about the potential benefits and costs of child care subsidies, employment regulations, post divorce programs, and grandparent rights legislation – to name a few.

Larger Studies. Studying complex models and using longitudinal designs also means that researchers will need to recruit much larger samples than are found in the typical study of development today. Larger samples will permit more sophisticated methods of analysis such as HLM and SEM, which allow researchers to study multiple variables over time and to explore within- as well as between-family effects on children. (Of course, as Hinde reminds us in Chapter 15, there will still be issues in the future that lend themselves to small-scale, targeted studies to probe specific processes of family influence.) Large studies may also require larger groups of investigators.

Expanded and Improved Measures. Another suggestion for future researchers is to expand the repertoire of assessments beyond typical family inputs – parental income, education, employment, discipline – and traditional child outcomes – depression, anxiety, school grades, and drug use. Researchers need more and better measures of inputs. For example, they need assessments of the overall extent of risk exposure. They need assessments that dip beneath the demographic surface to tap the psychology of parents' behavior; for example, in addition to counting how many hours parents work, they should find out *why* they work these hours and schedules. Future researchers also need more and better measures of outcomes – for example, positive competencies like cooperation, happiness, harmonious relationships, moral maturity and more subtle and probing assessments than standardized tests and inventories. Qualitative research methods may be needed to adequately evaluate the personal meanings of experiences that affect children or adolescents in different ways. Researchers should also expand their sources of information; combining data from multiple informants (mothers, fathers, teachers, employers, grandparents, and especially, children themselves) is more powerful than simply collecting data from a single source.

Combined Methods. To advance future research, researchers should also combine different methods within a program of research. Combining quantitative and qualitative research approaches will provide deeper understanding of family influences, illuminating why and how particular experiences are risky or protective, and why and how there are so many individual variations in children's responses to these experiences. Combining psychosocial methods with biological approaches such as molecular genetics, functional brain imaging, and neurotransmitter analyses will also be enlightening.

Process, Process, Process. In any future research, the focus should be on discovering and describing processes of family influence, not just obtaining statistical associations. For example, researchers should study the causal processes underlying individual and gender differences in susceptibility to family factors. Children are not passive organisms; they process their experiences and think about what they mean. As a result, some children are resilient to some types of family risk more than others, at some ages more than others. Researchers should concentrate on the processes underlying these individual differences in response to family factors. All family influences need to be considered in terms of interactions between children and their environments.

Genetically Sensitive Designs. The questions of how and when families influence children's development must ultimately be answered with genetically sensitive research designs. We know that genetics and environment are both important for children's development and that family processes can mediate genetic influences, but to disentangle the two and determine how the genetic-environment interactional model plays out across development, we must include both in any study. Examples of genetically sensitive research designs include cross-fostering designs with nonhuman primates, sibling designs, prospective adoption designs, molecular genetic studies, twin studies, and studies of donor families.

Direct Causal Tests. In addition to studying family processes "naturalistically," even in genetically sensitive deigns, it is recommended that future researchers test family influences directly using experimental designs. The advantage of experimental research is that, over time, parents serve as their own controls and researchers can see whether a particular factor is related to changes in parents' behavior and, in turn, to changes in children's psychosocial functioning and development. Experiments using animal models can be informative, and natural experiments continue to be a useful strategy for evaluating direction of causality. However, intervention studies provide the "gold standard" for testing causal hypotheses. Intervention and prevention efforts such as Fast Track have provided evidence that the quality of experience can alter children's adjustment. In the future, there should be more such efforts. These intervention efforts are not only important as strategies for improving the lives of families and children but provide opportunities to evaluate the soundness of our theories of family functioning. Intervention experiments afford both the scientific control to tease apart factors in child development and prototypes for broader implementation. Moreover, smaller-scale supplemental, experimental studies offer the chance to assess the relative importance of different theoretical components or processes that are assumed to be important in achieving changes in child functioning. A wide range of family factors can be studied experimentally. One such factor is family income; studies in which income levels are raised would aid in clarifying the pathways by which money helps and the cases in which more money makes no difference. Another factor that can be studied experimentally is parents' employment conditions, such as flexible work hours, parental leaves, or increased overtime work. Yet other factors include premarital education to improve the quality and stability of marriages, training programs to improve parents' monitoring of adolescents' activities, information to improve parents' child care choices, and regulations to guide access to information about parentage for children conceived through assisted reproductive technology. In fact, all the policies and practices suggested by the authors of this volume could and should be tested by intervention experiments before adoption on a wide scale. In evaluating the effects of these interventions, it will be crucial to go beyond documenting "success" to determine exactly how the intervention works, so that researchers can create more efficient and effective interventions with each iteration.

If researchers follow the research guidelines provided by the authors in this volume, the future will be, as Masten and Schaffer (in Chapter 1 in this book) predicted, "a new era, in which dynamic, multilevel models about family processes in development, spanning genes to culture, will be put to the test in elegant, longitudinal studies," and, I would add, in incisive intervention experiments, as well.

14

Research and Policy

Second Looks at Views of Development, Families, and
Communities, and at Translations into Practice

Jacqueline J. Goodnow

Cutting across the several chapters in this book and marking many current articles about development is an interest in translating what we know about development into actions that will benefit children, youth, and families. Of particular interest are actions in the form of policies, regulations or guidelines – actions that affect the demands, difficulties, opportunities, or resources encountered by both individuals and groups.

This kind of interest raises questions about what we know – about the way families function and how they influence development. These questions have been a major part of the earlier chapters in this book, taking us well beyond any need to demonstrate further that families do matter.

Questions are raised also about the models brought to bear on possible actions. Do we see development, for example, as a steady progression from a pattern established in early childhood or as marked more by fits and starts, digressions and time-outs, recoveries, second chances, and changes in path? Do we regard families as a world apart from what happens "outside" ("havens in a heartless world," to use one description), or as more interwoven with that "outside world"? Do we see families as functioning well only if there is a conventional structure and total harmony or as containing ample room for varied forms and changing relationships?

My emphasis in this chapter will be on models. Models shape the way we view development, the research questions we ask, and the kinds of advice we offer to policy makers. They influence decisions about timing (e.g., the timing of intervention or evaluation) and of target (e.g., the choice of goals or of circumstances and people to influence). The models to be considered are by no means all that might be covered. Instead, the "second looks" are restricted to some areas where I see a particular relevance to questions about families and some particular possibilities for considering some alternative positions and their implications. They have to do with the course of development, the interconnection of influences known as "family" and "community," and the flow between research and policy.

These three areas prompt the division of the chapter into sections. The first section focuses on ways of looking at the course of development. An emphasis on families and their influence is often seen as inevitably calling for a focus on "the early years," accompanied by phrases such as "as the twig is bent." The chapters on adolescence in the present volume (Collins & Roisman, Chapter 4 in this book; and by Dodge et al., Chapter 5 in this book) make it clear that the preschool years are not all that matter. The chapters by Rutter (Chapter 2 in this book) and by Sameroff (Chapter 3 in this book) make it clear that we also need to consider carefully just what may be carried forward from one time to another and how we can determine any continuing effects. There is benefit also, I propose, in looking at models that view the course of development in terms of pathways (and perhaps in looking toward alternate metaphors: e.g., "trees grow toward the light" or "where there is room to grow"). For examples, I turn to some developmental approaches to the occurrence of acts against the law. This field often offers a different perspective on how various ways of acting rise and fall over time, as well as a reminder that policies need to consider not only prevention but also the ways in which we can provide exits, recovery routes, alternate paths, and maintenance as well as the initial establishment of particular ways of acting.

The second section – the longest of the three – focuses on ways of bringing together the contexts usually known as "family" and "community" or "neighborhood." At this point, the developmental literature acknowledges both as sources of influence. That acknowledgment, however, prompts three sets of questions. One of these asks about productive ways of viewing "family" and "community." Finding productive ways to view families has been a major concern within this volume, with particular attention to changes in the wake of technical possibilities such as in-vitro fertilization (Golombok, Chapter 11 in this book), both families being in the paid workforce and grandmothers playing a changed part in family life (Dunn et al., Chapter 12 in this book), and a rising frequency of divorce (Amato, Chapter 8 in this book; Hetherington, Chapter 9 in this book; Walper & Beckh, Chapter 10 in this book). I wish to add some further ways of describing families and to combine these with ways of specifying communities, with a particular interest in the possibility of using similar dimensions to describe both. A second set of questions has to do with how the two sources of influence – families and communities – are related to one another. Within the present volume, an interest in interconnections is exemplified especially by analyses of interconnections between families and places of paid work (Crouter, Chapter 6 in this book) and between families and child care settings (McCartney, Chapter 7 in this book). It is also part of the interest in how the influences of parents and of peers are interwoven (Collins &

Roisman, Chapter 4 in this book; Dodge et al., Chapter 5 in this book). My aim is to add additional ways of considering interconnections, drawing examples again from developmental approaches to acts against the law. The third set of questions has to do with "processes," – ways of considering how and when various effects occur.

The last section looks at links between research and policy. Interests in prevention and intervention are not new. They underlie, for example, a variety of past policy actions, from orphanages to kindergartens and compulsory schooling. How far they take new forms or reflect different kinds of input from developmental science are more open questions. Open also are the underlying images people hold about how influence occurs in practice. We may, for example, hold large-scale and abstract models, perhaps in the form of seeing "data" and "proofs" as becoming transformed into "shared understanding" of where a problem lies and of what should now be done. In practice, the links appear to be more often at the level of specific people, each with some particular interests. Coming to understand those links, and to act within their constraints, becomes one of the special tasks that we face if we wish to influence policies.

WAYS OF VIEWING THE COURSE OF DEVELOPMENT

A tempting and popular model combines a focus on the child's first years with a view of development as following a fixed path thereafter. In some contemporary versions of this model, the first 3 years are when most brain development occurs and when the brain becomes "sculpted." After that, change does not occur or is relatively minor.

This kind of model is easily associated with a heavy emphasis on the significance of family influence. Community conditions then tend to be ignored or to be seen as influencing children only by way of an impact on the nature of parenting. In the worst-case policy scenario, all one needs to do is to support early parenting. All one needs to do, it has been said, is to "believe in magic" (Brooks-Gunn, 2003).

There are, however, other ways of viewing the course of development, ways that alter the direction of both research and policy. One of these takes the form of life-span perspectives on development. These perspectives encourage the recognition that over the course of time, new relationships, new tasks, or new skills emerge and that life may take a spiral form, with some earlier dilemmas or challenges reappearing and possibly being worked through more effectively on the second or third time round. Life-span perspectives also prompt a view of the life-course as marked by loops, recoveries, and moves in and out of states such as depression, involvement in paid work, marriage, or parenting.

Another alternative to fixed-course models takes the form of regarding development as marked by various trajectories or pathways. To take some summary phrases from two lines of research, we need to recognize and study both "straight and devious paths from childhood to adulthood" (Robins & Rutter, 1994), both moves in and out of crime (e.g., Loeber, 1996). From the same starting point, this position emphasizes, people may fan out in different directions. From different starting points, they may also converge toward a common end point.

Pathways perspectives carry several implications for research and for actions aimed at prevention or intervention. For research, one implication is that we need to explore the likelihood that one action will lead to another. A second implication is that we need to trace progressions and ask about the circumstances that influence the nature of the path. A provocative example traces, for actions against the law, both the usual courses followed and departures from them (cf. Loeber & LeBlanc, 1990; Loeber 1996). In these longitudinal studies, the usual ladder of progression for crimes against property and crimes against people is from minor forms of involvement to more major ones. Progression up the one ladder is not usually accompanied by progression up the other. The usual progression, however, is not ironclad. People may sometimes become involved in both kinds of crime, but this tends to be toward the top end of the ladder (e.g., an interrupted crime against property shifts into a first but major crime against a person). Alternatively, starting at the top end of the ladder either form of crime may occur with little previous involvement in less serious acts. An adolescent's first involvement might suddenly be at a serious level, prompted by a new neighborhood (e.g., one that offers easier access to weapons), or by new friends who have already moved up the ladder of involvement in illegal acts (Loeber, 1996; Wikström & Loeber, 2000).

The implications for policy are related both to forms of intervention and to questions of timing. For the former, recommendations for movement out of a path provide some first examples. Movement out of a path that involves acts against the law, Braithwaite (1989) argues, calls for intervention actions that block one route and open another. Movement out of a path is also seen as calling for a sense of having something to lose if one continues. One may lose, for example, a relationship that matters, the good opinion of others or, as Hughes (1998) points out, the possibility of staying alive a little longer. Studies of movement on to a new academic path point to some further circumstances as likely to be influential. To encourage students to consider going to college – students who normally would not do so – intervention actions need both to supply information about the routes that could be followed and to encourage the perception of following those routes as one of the students' "possible selves" (Cooper, Dominquez, & Rosas, in press). New directions apparently need to be known about, seen as worth taking, and seen as in keeping with a person's sense of current or possible identity.

Those implications have to do with the forms that intervention may take. Pathways perspectives also carry implications for the timing of intervention or advice. The time of greatest effectiveness appears to be shortly before a transition or a choice is made (cf. Developmental Crime Prevention Consortium, 1999; Ruble & Seidman, 1996). What happens shortly after a step has been taken is less clear cut. Arguing for least effectiveness at this point are social-cognitive studies of what has been called "the Rubicon effect." Arguing for continued openness is the possibility that although a first step has been taken, a position may not yet be entrenched. In family system terms, an initial state of affairs may have become destabilized, but a new state of affairs may not yet be consolidated. Both possibilities, however, suggest that when we come to ask about the effect of conditions at various points in development, we consider the openness of individuals or families to change at that point and the several directions that change may take (Goodnow, 2002b).

FAMILIES AND COMMUNITIES

Developmentalists are sometimes a little slow to consider neighborhood or community effects. There is by now, however, a sizeable set of studies documenting those effects (for two reviews, see Leventhal & Brooks-Gunn, 2000, 2003). Some of the studies are correlational, linking features of neighborhoods to various aspects of development. A few are experimental, covering the effects of moving families from one neighborhood to another. (In the United States, these are the studies known as the Movement to Opportunity study and the Gautraux study; cf. Katz, Kling & Liebman, 2001; Rubinowitz & Rosenbaum, 2000).

Emerging now is the recognition that paying attention to community factors may change our concepts of what parenting involves. We have for some time looked at families (parents especially) in terms of the skills they bring to life within the house, to the management of children, or of a household. When we start adding communities, we begin to see that an important feature may also consist of skill in the management of what a community offers: skill in the form of being alert to any resources available, taking advantage of opportunities, and negotiating alternatives to the usual constraints (Furstenberg, Eccles, Elder, Cook et al., 1999). Now what we seek to measure and what we see as possibly mediating various outcomes change.

Recognizing community influences, however, brings with it several new challenges. I break these into three parts, dealing respectively with ways of defining family or community, ways of viewing the interconnections between them, and ways of considering how effects from either or both come about.

Specifying Family or Community

Asking how any two sources are linked calls first for reasonable descriptions of each source, preferably descriptions that facilitate the making of links between them. One way of doing this consists of breaking each into

components, with questions then raised about how these are interconnected and how various outcomes are influenced not only by each component but also by the links among them.

To take a familiar example from the description of families, developmentalists have come to regard families as containing a web of relationships:
relationships between parent and child, between parents, among siblings,
across generations, among various relatives (e.g., Dunn et al. Chapter 12
in this book; Hinde & Stevenson-Hinde, 1988). Likely to be less familiar is
an example from analyses of family income (Hartmann, 1981). Knowing
the total amount only, Hartmann argues, is not sufficient. Who earns it?
Receives it? Spends it? Decides on its disposal? How far is one of these
involvements linked to others? How are competing interests negotiated?
Each form of involvement and their inter-connections (e.g., a sense of discrepancy between what I earn and what I get to spend) can alter satisfaction
or the allocation of resources: for example, the translation of money into
benefits for children. In effect, describing the components and their interconnections becomes the first task to be faced.

The same kind of shift is occurring within analyses of social contexts.
"Culture," for example, is increasingly seen as exhibiting "plurality and
contest – a mix of people with various interests and values, taking various
stances toward each other, and actively competing, negotiating, or forming alliances with one another (e.g., D'Andrade & Strauss, 1992; Goodnow,
2002a). The same kind of change is to be found in analyses of neighborhoods, increasingly seen as needing to be described in terms of interconnections among several parts. Those parts may be described in terms of
spatial areas. Between these there may then be spillover effects (e.g., crimes
against property are often by people from other areas; a low-resource area
benefits by having a high-resource one next to it). Between them there
may also be tensions, for example, between moves toward "takeover" and
toward resistance or flight.

These interconnections are between physical spaces. Neighborhoods,
it has been proposed, may also be specified in terms of interconnections
among people. That specification may be by features such as neighborhood ties, mutual trust, or social control (e.g., by way of supervision by
others). The two kinds of descriptions may be combined in the form of
considering the paths that link people's routine activities, the way some
physical features of a neighborhood (e.g., the location of homes, schools,
bars, shopping malls, and transport routes) "are relevant to organizing how
and when children come into contact with peers, adults, and nonresident
activity" (Sampson, Morenoff, & Gannon-Rowley, 2002, p. 458).

The comments just made are about "neighborhoods" rather than "communities." How far are these terms the same as one another? In the analysis
of social contexts and in relation to family influences, analysts may in fact
use both terms in ways that seem interchangeable. A review article by

Sampson et al. (2002), for example, uses the term neighborhoods. A chapter by Wikström and Sampson (in press) uses the term community. Both are concerned with the same outcome: the involvement of young people in acts against the law.

There is at the moment no consensus on how to define either term. The most active discussion probably has to do with how to define neighborhoods and to measure their features, with efforts directed toward covering both physical and social features (e.g., Sampson et al., 2002). The term community, however, is also under review for its definition, a problem heightened by an interest in using the term to cover both physical and electronic interconnections among people. Here, for example, is one definition of community that assigns it several specific features, with none of these having to do with physical space: "communities can be defined as groups of people who have some common and continuing organization, values, understanding, history and practices.... A community involves people trying to accomplish some things together, with some stability of involvement and attention to the ways they relate to one another.... their relations may be comfortable or conflictual and oppressive.... Their relations involve personal connections and procedures for resolving inevitable conflicts.... Even after leaving, participants in a community often continue to regard their involvement as central to their lives, whether this is expressed as affection and loyalty ... or resentment or efforts to avoid community ways.... A community involves generations that move through it, with customary ways of handling the transitions of generations" (Rogoff, 2003, pp. 80–81).

Neighborhoods may or may not have some of these features of communities. Definitions aside, however, the general point remains. Both family and social context (with social context seen in terms of neighborhood, community, or culture) are emerging as productively seen in terms of internally interconnected parts rather than being monolithic units, with questions then arising of how to think about and specify those internal interconnections.

Linking Sources of Change

Developmental psychology in general is marked by moves away from single sources and toward seeing sources as linked (cf. Collins, Maccoby, Steinberg, Hetherington et al., 2000). We no longer see the need, for example, to decide between nature and nurture, between child characteristics and family characteristics, between family influences and neighborhood or cultural influences. Instead, we ask about bi-directional or transactional effects, about co-construction or co-constitution. We also ask whether sources are linked in interactive, additive, or chain-style fashion with one event prompting another (e.g., aggressive behavior attracts a social label and the label maintains or escalates the behavior). In short, the nature of interconnections among influences becomes the salient issue.

For the particular case of families and communities, I see two further steps as useful. One considers what has happened to some particular models. The changes in these provide a kind of summary picture of the challenges that combining these sources of influence represents. The other asks: Can we use the same dimensions or features for both sources? We now speak, for example, of "family contexts" and "social contexts." Can we use the same models for each, or at least the same dimensions for each?

Changes Within Some Particular Models of Interconnection. Bronfenbrenner's (1979) "social ecological model" provides an example from developmental psychology. It has often been quoted and its diagram form has become very popular. This is the "nested circles" diagram: the individual surrounded by family, the family by neighborhood, and so on. Less widely recognised have been several expansions on the original model. These expansions go beyond social contexts appearing as simply "surrounds" for the family and for segments within the ecological context. Added, for example, has been a closer attention to the ways in which the circumstances in one context affect the nature and the impact of circumstances in another. Effects in the form of "spillover" are a prominent example (e.g., Bronfenbrenner & Crouter, 1983). Further expansions propose the need to think always in terms of: (1) person-process-context, (2) the person as an active and selective agent, (3) context as covering people, objects and symbols, and (4) both individuals and contexts as continually changing (Bronfenbrenner 1995).

Even with these changes, concerns remain about the need to add still further "dynamics" to the model. One addition proposed consists of asking about the ways in which children and parents perceive possible interconnections (e.g., paths from home to school or from school to paid work), and about the nature of "outreach" by people in various circles (e.g., the nature of parents' search for information about a school, and of schools' invitations to children or parents) (Cooper et al., in press). One change proposed consists of abandoning the "nested circles" metaphor, asking instead about access, exclusion, opportunities, pressure, or negotiation, and drawing attention to the way contexts such as neighborhoods influence children directly rather than always through an influence on parenting (Goodnow, 1995, in press). More broadly still, the separation into parts (framing the issue as one of the effects of context *on* development) has been seen as denying the intrinsically cultural nature of development; the two cannot be placed in separate boxes (Rogoff, 2003).

An example from criminology provides a second picture of changes to some attractively simple models of interconnections among influences. By and large, analyses of acts against the law have traditionally contained a stronger emphasis on neighborhood than on family influences. In a reverse of the shift among developmentalists, a close concern with how families have effects is the more recent interest. One way to accommodate both has been to turn to a long-held distinction between "propensity" and "opportunity," neatly aligning families with propensity and neighborhoods with opportunity (Weatherburn & Lind, 2001). Specifically, families provide children who are "susceptible"; and neighborhoods provide peers or adults who encourage, teach, or facilitate acts against the law. The "susceptibles" and the "facilitators" still have to be brought together. The probability of that is regarded as increased as the number of people in each group increases, but the specific ways in which contact occurs are largely left open.

Wikström and Sampson (in press) take several steps away from this one-to-one picture and help fill in how interactions and changes in involvement come about. First, the general notion of "propensity" is broken into two components: (1) "motivation," referring to the way people see various acts as options with perceived costs and benefits, and (2) "morality," referring to the perception of an act as not an option even if there is the opportunity to act with little material cost.

In a second step, communities are seen as offering more than easy opportunities or peers who lead one astray. A distinction is first drawn between community-built environment (e.g., the arrangement of buildings and spaces and the activities related to them) and community-social environment (e.g., the social activities and social relationships in an area). These two features may influence one another. The built environment and the activities it fosters or facilitates, for example, may facilitate or constrain the development of social ties.

A third step proposes "behavior settings" as a central concept. These are the settings in which various actions can occur. Attached to each are what Wikström (1998, p. 284) has called "the three R's": resources, rules, and routines. It is the behavior settings that promote the development of morality, the perception of options, and the encouragement or facilitation of acts against the law.

In a fourth and final step, both community and family are regarded as contributing to all components. The emphasis is on community contributions. Community features influence the way families function and the way individuals perceive costs, benefits, and nonoptions. Community features (community routines especially) are also the major contributor to the presence and shape of the behavior settings in which actions of various kinds may occur. Families, however, also contribute to the behavior settings that children encounter, with a major source of influence being by way of the supervision they provide or the activities they encourage.

In short, attractively simple models of links among various influences on development seem inevitably to move away from their original forms. We clearly need to work with the complexity, even though it may make more difficult both the nature of research questions and any translations into recommendations for policy.

Locating Comparable Descriptions in Various Contexts. One of the difficulties in linking the several conditions that influence development consists of shifting dimensions. Take, for example, descriptions of families and descriptions of neighborhoods. Traditionally, descriptions of families have been in terms such as family structure (e.g., the presence of one or two parents), family harmony (e.g., the presence of conflict), and methods of discipline or control (e.g., authoritarian or authoritative parenting). Traditionally, descriptions of neighborhoods have been in terms of features such as the range of incomes, the ethnic mix, or the presence of physical "disorder" (e.g., the presence of "broken windows"). It is very difficult to bring together such descriptions of families and neighborhoods, let alone combine them with a further set of terms used to describe the characteristics of individuals and of the ways in which they change. The same kind of difficulty applies, I suggest, when we try to bring together settings such as family, paid work, or child care. We seem to shift dimensions when we move from one social setting to the other, making it difficult to compare one with another, to ask about interconnections among them, or to borrow concepts from, say, the analysis of family and child care centers for the analysis of families and paid work settings.

Is it possible to use the same concepts or dimensions to describe both family and social contexts? One way to do so is to *regard families and communities as one and the same unit.* In some sociological positions, for example, "the family" is simply a "microcosm" of the larger society: a "locus," for instance, of a more general "gender, class and political struggle" (Hartmann, 1981, p. 366). The same set of features then apply. Moreover, it makes sense to work toward social change within a particular "locus" such as "the family," because here is "society." That collapsing of what we usually see as two contexts may seem at first strange. It is, however, a welcome change from thinking about the two as opposites of each other, the kind of opposition implied, for example, by descriptions of the family as "a haven in a heartless world" or as a "private" place into which "public" policies should not intrude.

A second way is to *use the same analytic frame for family contexts, social contexts, and the links between them.* From family systems theory, for example, we might take the argument that when one family member becomes less available – through death, divorce, or illness – the system restabilizes by developing new divisions of labor or new coalitions. We can also regard "family" and "state" as forming a single system, with "the state" or "the community" stepping in when "the family" is seen as unable to continue its previous efforts or to meet its expected functions. The state steps in, for example – sometimes reluctantly, sometimes with zeal, sometimes in welcomed and sometimes in resented fashion – by providing schools, child care, medical care, or places of detention and correction for children seen as "out of control." This merger of family and community into a single system with alliances and replacements may not be a familiar move to developmentalists. It is part, however, of the history of state support for public schooling (e.g., Rogoff, 2003), and of analyses of "substitution hierarchies" in areas such as the provision of care for parents in need of assistance (e.g., Qureshi & Simons, 1987).

A third way to avoid discrepant descriptions is to *define family and social contexts in similar terms*. Some possible ways of doing so are as follows:

• We may view contexts as containing opportunities and resources, varying in kind and in access. Differences in kind refer to variations in opportunities for schooling or paid work, for new definitions of "possible selves" or possible social positions. Differences in access refer to features such as the presence of open and closed doors or the availability of recovery routes. The match is then with a view of parents as effective managers of opportunities and resources (Furstenberg et al., 1999), as knowledgeable about "how the system works" (Bourdieu & Passeron's, 1977, "cultural capital"), and probably as encouraging their children to be alert to opportunities, to resist assigned positions, or to develop negotiating skills.

• We may view contexts as containing activities of various kinds and parents as encouraging and providing ways to learn various forms of participation. Family activities may differ from neighborhood activities. In both cases, however, descriptions can focus on the nature of the activities, who participates in them, the kinds of participation expected or possible, and the kinds of arrangements made for people to learn how to participate. This kind of approach addresses a major problem: how can we bring together features of families, features of communities, and aspects of development? If we consider development in terms of changing forms of participation or changing skills in either participation or non-participation, the same kind of descriptive concept – the nature of participation in various activities – can be used to specify social contexts, parental actions, and developmental changes. That degree of conceptual economy, together with the presence of some specific ways of measuring each aspect, is one of the attractive features of analyses of contexts and development that emphasize shifts in activities and in the nature of participation (e.g., Rogoff, 2003). It is also one of the reasons for my giving particular attention to the kinds of analyses of involvement in crime that Wikström and Sampson (in press) offer. There is at the moment little attention within these models to the development of the personality characteristics that developmentalists often attend to (e.g., the ability to regulate emotion, or resilience), but they are extremely attractive ways of considering how various kinds of action are influenced by physical spaces, routine paths, promoted activities and – internally, at least – the perception of various actions in terms of their costs and their benefits.

- We may regard contexts as containing a variety of "attractive hazards," of provocations and temptations that make it difficult to "stay on track" or to work for a distant goal, and parents as promoting activities and routes that lower exposure or increase resistance. Parents may, for example, guide children toward places with fewer hazards or with peers "of the right kind." They may also encourage a sense of obligation to parents or family, of there being "something to lose" if children wander off track, or of it always being possible to recover or rebound from unproductive or false steps.

- We may regard contexts as made up of competing groups, with varying "stances" toward one another (from tolerance to indifference, hostility or denigration) and parents as "cocooning" or pre-arming their children (Goodnow, 1997). Parents may, for example, prepare children for encounters with ethnic or racial prejudice by way of promoting pride in one's own history, discounting statements by negative others, or coaching in specific forms of reply.

- We may regard contexts as containing various levels of unpredictability, disorder, chaos, or loss (e.g., in their worst forms, occasions of war, flood, fire, famine), and parents as able to provide some daily routines and to offer interpretations, with the aim of promoting some sense of safety, order and predictability or with the aim of facilitating recovery from "destabilization."

In effect, there are several possible ways of aligning descriptions of social contexts with descriptions of what parents contribute. We can use these descriptions as ways of beginning to specify the particular kinds of circumstances that children or parents encounter and the particular strengths or supports that parents may need in the face of these circumstances. We can also ask whether parents' existing or enhanced skills in meeting particular challenges give rise to positive developmental outcomes.

There is, however, a major caveat to the list offered. I have phrased those interconnections in the form of parents' possession of various skills and parents' taking active roles: locating, selecting, facilitating, encouraging, cushioning, interpreting, providing road-maps or a useful level of routine and order. Parents, however, are not the only ones who might take such active steps or be the target of intervention actions. Such steps could also be taken by various others within families or outside the family. Schools, for example, can reach out to families, making clear and feasible the opportunities available and the routes to follow. Parents need not be put in the position of everything depending on their skills and energy when it comes to searching out what is possible. In similar fashion, a variety of people and agencies can provide safety, structure or order. A set of recommendations for actions related to child abuse (from an English National Commission, 1996) provides an example. The positive steps advocated are "systemic" in the sense that they range through the action of family members, school staff, physicians, police, courts, and law-makers. The particular steps taken at each level may differ from one another but all are designed to have the common quality of moving toward the creation of a world that is "child-friendly," "child-protective," or "growth-facilitating."

Research on effects also need not be limited to the actions that parents take. It makes sense to ask, for instance, whether parents in various situations are aware of and responsive to the difficulties and challenges their children encounter or are likely to encounter, and whether the children of parents who are alert and responsive come to display particular strengths. On a larger scale, we can observe the nature and the effects of changes in laws regulating divorce, child custody, the mandatory reporting of signs of child abuse, or the position of children as witnesses in court. In both cases, however, it would seem wise to ask if the same dimensions and the same concepts can be used to consider the two kinds of circumstances and their influences.

Specifying Effects and Processes

Phrases such as a "child-friendly world" provide an indication of both the kinds of outcome we might hope to achieve and the measures we might aim at developing. So also do references to participation or nonparticipation. They are, however, far from any direct answers to the question: What effects should we consider or aim for when it comes to recommending intervention or changes in policy? They are also far from answering questions about the processes by which any effects may come about.

The Choice of Effects. When it comes to targeting particular changes in children, the life of criminologists may seem simpler than that of developmentalists. Criminologists usually focus on actions against the law. They do engage in some distinctions within those actions. They distinguish, for example, between acts against property and acts against people. They also distinguish between acts such as shoplifting and acts of serious or violent crime. Some analyses of neighborhood effects cover a wider range. They cover, for example, several forms of "high-risk" behaviors (early sexual activity, early pregnancy, school leaving, substance abuse, and acts against the law; e.g., Brooks-Gunn, Duncan, & Aber, 1997). Nonetheless, the range is still narrower than what might be covered by a term such as "the health and well-being" of children and youth, a term that could cover everything from physical illness to mood, the quality of attachment, school performance, friendship patterns, and a variety of coping strategies.

Once the range widens, we inevitably face questions about how various effects are related to one another: questions, for example, about "comorbidity" or about one effect leading to another. We also need to ask about the bases for choice. On what grounds could we, for example, single out some particular targets for research or for intervention? A major charity in Australia, for example (The Smith Family) has recently decided to target "education" as its priority, on the grounds that education is the most probable route out of disadvantage. "Resilience" is another quality that has been singled out: one with the advantage that it could apply to a variety of forms of adversity. On what grounds can we argue for various other possibilities?

That question quickly comes up whenever the issue arises of choosing some kinds of behavior to target for change or to use as an indicator of whether "serious" change has occurred. It is a question for which I have at the moment no sense of surety or even comfort. The bases for choice seem to range from the likelihood of opening the way to a chain of other events (a basis likely to be associated with a focus on child abuse or, more positively, on education or resilience) to concerns with our moral responsibilities to children and to others in dire straits and with fewer resources than we have (a basis emphasized, at least in Australia, in debates over actions toward children in detention centers), and issues of social or financial cost (a basis often mentioned in relation to crime prevention).

In fact, the question I wish to raise may complicate the issue still further. This has to do with asking whether any effect is likely to be specific or to generalize. Within studies of cognitive development, for example, there has been a move away from thinking about change in terms of shifts in some general capacity or some general logical structure that cuts across a variety of tasks. The alternative is a view of change in the form of acquiring varying levels of competence in particular tasks. In similar fashion, we may move toward asking whether the interpersonal skills or difficulties displayed at home are the same as those that occur in school, whether the friendship patterns displayed with peers at school are the same as those displayed with peers outside school, whether a sense of efficacy or confidence acquired in one situation is limited to that kind of situation or is more general.

Does this kind of move present a problem in the analysis of interventions and outcomes? On the one hand, thinking in situated terms may seem to offer little that is positive. (Ideally, we would like to see positive effects that spread). At the least, it would seem to make research questions about effects (questions about measurement and carryover, especially) even more complex than usual. It is also possible, however, that the notion of situated development holds out a hopeful way of looking at the negative effects of previous experiences. Instead of any inevitable repeat of a pattern established in one setting, or any ready carryover from one relationship to another, effects may be limited by people not perceiving two settings or two situations as like one another. That could, alas, also be true for the effects of intervention actions. Either way, analyses of effects seem to call for closer attention to the features of family life, community life, or intervention experiences that encourage compartmentalization or spread.

Processes. How might we view the steps by which the characteristics of family, of neighborhood, or of their interconnection as leading to any particular outcomes? For an example of some different points of view, I turn again to some developmental analyses of acts against the law, beginning with some proposals by Sampson and his colleagues (Sampson et al., 2002). They single out four moves as especially promising approaches to the question of *how* neighborhood characteristics exert an effect on outcomes such as the incidence of crime or of depression. All four are regarded as aspects of "social process."

The first of these is generally referred to as *social capital* (the presence of social ties, social interaction, and patterns of neighboring). The second is often referred to as *collective efficacy*, covering especially the presence of mutual trust, a shared willingness to intervene for the public good, and informal social control. The third focuses on *resources*, usually referring to the quality, quantity, and diversity of institutions that address the needs of parents and children. The fourth looks to *routine activities*: the ways in which the location of places (schools, bars, shopping malls, and street corners), and the flow of movement from one to another, promote contact and facilitate action of various kinds.

Those forms of "social process," however, do not immediately lay out the steps that developmentalists might look for when it comes to effects on individuals rather than on the general incidence of various problems. They say little about what one group of researchers has called "psychological mediators" (Shumow, Vandell, & Posner, 1998). There are, however, some studies of that kind and it is interesting to note how they overlap with some emphases in psychology. There is, for example, at least one study that emphasizes not only the presence of organisations that could function as resources but also family members' participation in them (e.g., Veysey & Messner, 1999). There is also a sizeable set of studies that emphasize the way neighborhood features are perceived. These studies cover perceived supports, perceived disorder, or perceived dangers, with these perceptions sometimes separated into those perceived by the child and by the parent (e.g., Shumow et al., 1998, on perceived dangers, with the child's perceptions associated with distress and the parents' perceptions associated with explanations for the child's misconduct). In some studies also there is an additional interest in the way some circumstances prompt particular emotions (e.g., an association of perceived disorder with a sense of powerlessness that then is associated with fear and distress, with these inhibiting resourceful action; Ross, Reynolds, & Geis, 2000). If those feelings are shared by others, or if the neighborhood contains no ways of countering the sense of powerlessness, it is argued, positive action seems all the more unlikely.

Such variations in position remind us that there is more than one way of viewing how effects come about from various contexts. They also raise the question: What prompts attention to some kinds of processes or mediators rather than others? The mediators one might look to when accounting for depression, for example, might well be different from those one moves toward if the challenge is to account for acts against the law or levels of school achievement.

There seem as well to be some general preferences that mark various fields. Psychologists, in my perception, move readily toward regarding processes in terms of the meanings that individuals give to events or actions. Anthropologists appear to move more readily toward asking how far those meanings are shared with others (forming "cultural models"). Both anthropologists and sociologists seem to move more readily toward considering what people routinely do (their "routines," their "cultural practices"). Over time, I have come to think more in terms of the extent to which meanings and routines are shared and in terms of the way this kind of quality influences the extent to which a way of acting or interpreting events is regarded as right, natural, or not open to question (Goodnow, Miller, & Kessel, 1995). I still feel, however, that there is room for considerable thought when it comes to asking why we might look for some ways of viewing processes rather than others, especially when it comes to asking how the characteristics of families and communities – singly or combined – give rise to various effects.

SCIENCE AND SOCIAL POLICY

This is the last kind of interconnection I consider. It is again by no means a review of what is now emerging as a strong concern for developmentalists (for some overviews, see Shonkoff & Meisels, 2000; Shonkoff & Phillips, 2000). I instead limit my comments to one historical question and to some features of links that have stood out for me. Those features have to do with differentiating within the groups of people involved and within aspects of relationships among groups.

The historical question takes the form: What makes the current expressions of interest in action, by researchers and by politicians, any different from those expressed at earlier times? On the research side, there have always been links between the views social scientists hold about development and the intervention actions taken or funded by informal or official groups. There have also, perhaps always, been distinctions between "pure" and "applied" social science. There do, however, now appear to be shifts in the extent to which developmental psychologists consider conditions such as child care, forms of paid work, the legal provisions for divorce or child custody, or whether neighborhoods are "toxic" or "child-friendly." Changes also appear to exist in the extent to which social scientists ask about the effects of changes and variations in environmental conditions, either as they occur naturally or as they are deliberately introduced. On the policy-making side, there appear as well to be changes in the extent to which children and youth are regarded as the responsibility only of parents, and in the extent to which policy-making bodies are asking for advice or evidence, or are ready to fund research in policy-related areas. The sources of change on both the research and the policy sides seem worthy of a closer look, especially with an eye to whether the same patterns and sources of change apply to the two directions of change.

I treat less briefly some aspects of the links between researchers and policy-makers. The aspects I single out stem less from theory and more from my own involvement in some intervention actions. That involvement is limited compared with that of many other developmentalists. Part of it has been at the level of teaching. I started some time ago to organize graduate seminars on intervention actions such as Head Start, broadening out to consider issues of theory and action in relation to topics such as day care, child abuse, and the position of children in the law. The book written with Ailsa Burns on children and families in Australia (Burns & Goodnow, 1979; 1985), and some related papers on child care stem from those seminars. I have learned a great deal also from the direct involvement of several graduate students in the development and implementation of policies related to day care, preschools, and child abuse.

Over the last 6 years, however, I have come into more direct contact with policy makers (bureaucrats and politicians). That has partly been by way of being on the advisory committees for several forms of policy making or policy implementation. It has also been by way of being part of a consortium group that produced a report on developmental approaches to crime prevention (written at the request of the Attorney-General's Department: Developmental Crime Prevention Consortium, 1999). Those involvements have made me more aware of how action comes about and of conditions that affect the fate of advice, either to parents or to representatives of government (e.g., Goodnow, 2002b).

That awareness is undoubtedly shaped by a set of particular experiences. It would be useful to know how far these correspond to others' experiences and perceptions. For the moment, however, I draw from my own direct experience. I also divide my comments into two parts: one related to coming to differentiate within the units to be linked, the other to observations on the kinds of links that may occur.

Differentiations Within Policy-Making Groups

Neither of the groups I consider – those that produce concepts and evidence related to action, and those that endorse or fund intervention actions – is monolithic. That social scientists vary among themselves is, of course, no surprise to social scientists. It has been interesting for me, however, to begin noting how policy makers (bureaucrats and politicians especially) vary.

One line of differentiation has to do with variations in interests and in jurisdiction. Areas of jurisdiction are critical. At the moment, for example, Australia has a Federal Minister for Children and Families (a new unit). He has broad interests. He cannot, however, alter conditions in schools or for children "in care." These are under state jurisdiction. He can also do little about children in detention centers. These are centers for people classed as "illegal immigrants" and under review for "true refugee status," sometimes for 1 to 3 years. These centers are under the control of the Minister for Immigration (Federal, but a different Department and a different minister).

A second line of differentiation has to do with variations in what are regarded as appealing grounds for action. For Australia's current Federal government, for example, appeals on the basis of the "rights of children" have a negative impact. The needs of society, and the financial costs and benefits of action or inaction, have more appeal.

A third line of differentiation has to do variations in the departmental interests that people represent and seek to protect or enhance. As an example, some tension has existed between advocates of a "zero to three" emphasis and advocates of longer-term approaches. The "zero to three" emphasis, together with a push for "parent education" as the key intervention, tends to come most strongly from people in fields such as pediatrics and the early years of schooling. It is also very appealing to many policy makers, to a point where the view may be taken that this is all one has to do. At this point, however, the interests of other departments often come into play. There is the risk that finances, staff, and support will be pulled away from departments whose main concerns are with older children and with changes in both within-family and outside-family conditions. People from those departments (departments concerned with juvenile crime, and with drug and alcohol abuse, for example) emerge as finding the notion of variable paths, recovery routes, and assistance close to times of transition more attractive than the notion of fixed paths or "rocket-launch" views of development. In related fashion, but often within departments or within services, a strong emphasis on "prevention" can prompt concerns that few resources will be left for helping those whose difficulties have not been prevented: the bulk of the clientele for most existing services.

Do such differences have implications for developmentalists? One implication has to do with persuasiveness. If we wish to be persuasive, we need to recognize the multiplicity of interests and try to estimate the appeal of our proposals accordingly. High on my list of features that appeal to government bodies, for example, would be features such as meeting multiple goals, being electorally attractive, being easy to announce and implement, and having some degree of fit with popular views of how "good behaviors" – at home, school, or in the streets – are achieved and what governments should do.

As an example, I offer the ready adoption in Australia of the policy of random breath taking (the stopping of cars in order to check on the driver's level of alcohol intake). It was in the interest of several groups: those who might be hurt by dangerous drivers and the drivers themselves. It had a base in evidence already available: alcohol was implicated in many road fatalities. It was easy to announce, easy to implement (a police force and the minimal equipment were already at hand), easy to evaluate (fatalities could be shown to have dropped within 6 months of the announcement), and easy to describe as successful (a drop in road fatalities is easy to announce and readily grasped by all). The policy ran into some objections on the grounds of being an invasion of privacy, but it also fit with popular assumptions about the role of governments. Australian governments are expected to make regulatory laws. They have, for example, moved without a great deal of public fuss toward compulsory seat-belts for everyone and compulsory baby-seats for infants (even in a taxi, these must be requested and used). At the same time, regulations are expected to be reasonable. The usual alcohol limit, for example, has stayed at 0.5. Dropping to the Norwegian limit of 0.2 has been introduced only for drivers who are in the first years of using a driver's license and are required to attach L or P plates to the cars they drive (L for Learner, P for Provisional License, to be displayed for the first 12 months of holding a license). These drivers are mostly in the 18 to 21-year age group, and one state has now introduced zero alcohol limits for them. Several in this age group have expressed themselves as not happy with a lower or a zero limit, but there has been little objection from the bulk of the voting public. All told, if we could find, for the area of children or youth, policies that have similar features, our recommendations might meet with a similarly positive political response.

Links Between Groups: The Flow of Information and Areas of Tension

It has been said that there are now "three cultures in search of a shared mission" (Shonkoff, 2000, p. 181). The three are the cultures of science, policy, and practice, seen as different in what they regard as evidence, in their values, and in the tasks they see as needing to be faced. Cashmore (2003) has used that description of cultures as a base for asking how to build bridges across cultures, and how research in particular may change to make bridges more likely. Those changes include, for example, a closer look at designs aimed at "control groups," making values more explicit, and recognizing that policy-makers and practitioners have a particular interest in what is feasible and affordable.

I focus on two aspects of links across groups. The first has to do with the flow of information across groups, the second with some particular areas of tension or difference.

The Flow of Information. As social scientists, we may start with the expectation that ideas can flow easily from developmental sources to policy makers. I would suggest that we ask what flows most easily and that we consider the flow as being in both directions.

On the first of those suggestions, my sense is that specific evidence, unless it is in a very straightforward form, flows less easily than some general ways of framing development. "It takes a village to raise a child"; "Well-begun is half-done"; "Life is not a simple straight line"; "We need to close some doors and open others"; "Spend $1 now and save $7 later"; "Make your move shortly before children do." These framing concepts seem to flow easily. As Collins et al. (2000) have advised, we need to learn how to frame our complex views in ways that are readily translatable into everyday words.

On the second score, we need to recognize, as we have done with parents and children and with families and neighborhoods, that influences are bi-directional. There is no single flow from evidence producers to policy makers. Government funding agencies can and do set priorities for research. And social scientists can, with the interests of children and the nature of social action in mind, moderate their comments. I have, for example, long held several conceptual reservations about Bronfenbrenner's (1979) nested-circles model, especially in its diagram form. It is, however, a model that many policy makers find attractive and it does alert them – and developmentalists – to the presence of conditions that include but also extend beyond the nature of parenting. I am sure that reservations and restricted comments applied also to the early proposals for mother-infant bonding theory. The data may have been flawed and the concepts one-sided. The proposals did, however, alter some very negative hospital procedures and alerted people in many areas to the significance of separations. In effect, until one has an alternative that serves the same purposes, and does so more effectively, there is little to be gained by focusing only on the conceptual limitations of proposals that are producing positive changes.

Areas of Tension. I offer again the beginnings of "a little list" that others could undoubtedly extend. One of these has to do with whether actions should take the form of local, state-wide or nation-wide programs. Local variations allow for differences in circumstances and for local involvement. State-wide programs, implemented identically in many areas, tend to have the more immediate appeal to state-level politicians. Another has to do with the nature of evaluation. That is a tendentious issue even among specialists in evaluation, one in which there are changing interests in impact at the population level, effect sizes, and cost-benefit estimates. Evaluation is also an area of tension in practice. Some state departments in Australia, for example, require that a certain percentage of any funding be set aside for evaluation by an independent person or group. Who makes the evaluation, however, is less tightly regulated and program directors may make recommendations. Needless to say, no group – government departments included – welcomes negative evaluations. Nor do practitioners welcome the intrusion of unsympathetic or careless evaluators into an often delicate pattern of working relationships between program staff and the clients they serve. What starts out as a research ideal then often changes in the course of its translation into practice.

In short, there is much to learn, much to explore, and much to effectively utilize when it comes to moving back and forth between research and policy or intervention.

A FINAL COMMENT

My aim has been to suggest alternatives to models that have for some time dominated developmental thinking and that are often still dominant outside developmental psychology. The emphasis throughout has been on ways of thinking about a variety of interconnections, with families and communities used not only as an area of interconnection that we need to know more about but also as a springboard for questions and suggestions, likely to apply to the analysis of other contributions to development. I am painfully aware of several limitations to the comments offered. My hope, however, is that the limitations will serve as one further base for the lively and productive discussions this volume will prompt.

ACKNOWLEDGMENTS

I am indebted to several colleagues with whom I have worked on a variety of issues. I thank Judy Cashmore, Alan Hayes, Ross Homel, and Jeanette Lawrence. They have extended my understanding of neighborhoods (Ross Homel deserves special thanks in this regard, and for persuading me to join a consortium to consider developmental approaches to crime prevention), of pathways (Jeanette Lawrence especially in this regard), and of translations into policy (Judy Cashmore and Alan Hayes especially in this regard).

References

Bourdieu, P., & Passeron. J-C. (1977). *Reproduction in education, society, and culture.* Beverly Hills, CA: Sage.

Braithwaite, J. (1989). *Crime, shame, and reintegration.* Cambridge: Cambridge University Press.

Bronfenbrenner, U. (1979). *The ecology of human development: Experiments by nature and design.* Cambridge, MA: Harvard University Press.

Bronfenbrenner, U. (1995). Developmental ecology through space and time: A future perspective. In P. Moen, G. H. Elder Jr., & K. Lüscher (Eds), *Examining lives in context: Perspectives on the ecology of human development* (pp. 619–648). Washington DC: American Psychological Association.

Bronfenbrenner, U., & Crouter, A. (1983). The evolution of environmental models in developmental research. In P. H. Mussen (Ed.), *Handbook of child psychology.* Vol. 1, (pp. 357–414). New York: Wiley.

Brooks-Gunn, J. (2003). Do you believe in magic? What we can expect from early childhood intervention programs. *Social Policy Report, 17*(1), 3–14.

Brooks-Gunn, J., Duncan, G. J., & Aber, L. (1997). *Neighborhood poverty: Vol. 1. Context and consequences for children.* New York: Russell Sage Foundation.

Burns, A., & Goodnow, J. J. (1979, 1985). *Children and families in Australia: Contemporary issues and problems.* Sydney: Allen & Unwin.

Cashmore, J. (June 2003). *Linking research, policy, and practice: Including children's input.* Paper presented at Children's Issues Center Conference, Dunedin, New Zealand.

Collins, W. A., Maccoby, E., Steinberg, L., Hetherington, M. H., & Bornstein, M. (2000). Contemporary research on parenting: The case for nature *and* nurture. *American Psychologist, 53,* 218–232.

Cooper, C. R., Dominquez, E., & Rosas, S. (in press). *Soledad's dream: Diversity, children's worlds, and pathways to college in democracies.* In C. R. Cooper, C. García Coll, T. Bartko, H. Davis, & C. Chatman, (Eds.), *Hills of gold: Rethinking diversity and contexts as resources for children's developmental pathways.* Mahwah, NJ: Erlbaum.

D'Andrade, R. G., & Strauss, C. (Eds.) (1992). *Human motives and cultural models.* Cambridge: Cambridge University Press.

Developmental Crime Prevention Consortium (1999). *Pathways to prevention: Developmental and early intervention approaches to crime.* Canberra, Australia: Attorney-General's Department.

Furstenberg, F. F. Jr., Cook, T. D., Eccles, J., Elder, G. H. Jr., & Sameroff, A. (1999). *Managing to make it: Urban families and adolescent success.* Chicago: University of Chicago Press.

Goodnow, J. J. (1995). Differentiating among social contexts: By spatial features, forms of interaction, and social contracts. In P. Moen, G. H. Elder, & K. Lüscher (Eds.), *Examining lives in context: Perspectives on the ecology of human development* (pp. 269–302). Washington, DC: American Psychological Association.

Goodnow, J. J. (1997). Parenting and the "transmission" and "internalization" of values: From social-cultural perspectives to within-family analyses. In J. E. Grusec & L. Kuczynski (Eds.), *Handbook of parenting and the transmission of values* (pp. 333–361). New York: Wiley.

Goodnow, J. J. (2002a). Adding culture to studies of human development: Changes in procedure and theory. *Human Development, 45*, 237–245.

Goodnow, J. J. (2002b). Parents' knowledge and expectations: Using what we know. In M. Bornstein (Ed.), *Handbook of Parenting* (2nd. ed., Vol. 3, pp. 439–460). Mahwah, NJ: Erlbaum.

Goodnow, J. J. (in press). Contexts, diversity, pathways: Linking and extending with a view to theory and practice. In C. R. Cooper, C. García Coll, T. Bartko, H. Davis, & C. Chatman, (Eds.), *Hills of gold: Rethinking diversity and contexts as resources for children's developmental pathways*. Mahwah, NJ: Erlbaum.

Goodnow, J. J., Miller, P. J., & Kessel, F. (Eds.) (1995). *Cultural practices as contexts for development*. San Francisco: Jossey-Bass.

Hartmann, H. (1981). The family as the locus of gender, class and political struggle. *Signs, 6*, 366–394.

Hinde, R. A., & Stevenson-Hinde, J. (Eds.) (1988). *Relationships within families: Mutual influences*. Oxford: Oxford University Press.

Hughes, M. (1998). Turning points in the lives of young inner-city men foregoing destructive criminal behaviors: A qualitative study. *Social Work Research, 22*, 143–151.

Katz, L. F., Kling, J., & Liebman, J. B. (2001). Moving To Opportunity in Boston: Early results of a randomized mobility experiment. *Quarterly Journal of Economics, 116*, 607–654.

Leventhal, T., & Brooks-Gunn, J. (2000). The neighborhoods they live in: The effects of neighborhood residence upon child and adolescent outcomes. *Psychological Bulletin, 126*, 309–337.

Leventhal, T., & Brooks-Gunn, J. (2003). Children and youth in neighborhood contexts. *Current Directions in Psychological Science, 12*, 27–31.

Loeber, R. (1996). Developmental continuity, change, and pathways in male juvenile problem behaviors and delinquency. In D. Hawkins (Ed.), *Delinquency and crime: Current theories*. Cambridge: Cambridge University Press.

Loeber, R., & LeBlanc, M. (1990). Toward a developmental criminology. *Crime and Justice – A Review of Research, 12*, 375–473.

National Commission of Inquiry into the Prevention of Child Abuse (1996). *Childhood matters*. Stationery Office: London.

Qureshi, H., & Simons, K. (1987). *Resources within families: Caring for elderly people*. London: Allen & Unwin.

Robins, L., & Rutter, M. (Eds.) (1994). *Straight and devious paths from childhood to adulthood*. Chichester, England: Wiley.

Rogoff, B. (2003). *The cultural nature of human development*. New York: Oxford University Press.

Ross, C. E., Reynolds, J. R., & Geis, K. J. (2000). The contingent meaning of neighborhood stability for residents' psychological well-being. *American Sociological Review, 65*, 581–597.

Rubinowitz, L. D., & Rosenbaum, J. E. (2000). *Crossing the class and color lines: From public housing to white suburbia*. Chicago: University of Chicago Press.

Ruble, D. N., & Seidman, E. (1996). Social transitions: Windows into social psychological processes. In E. T. Higgins & A. Kruglanski (Eds.), *Handbook of social processes*. New York: Guilford.

Sampson, R. J., Morenoff, J. D., & Gannon-Rowley, T. (2002). Assessing "neighborhood effects": Social processes and new directions in research. *Annual Review of Sociology, 28,* 443–478.

Shonkoff, J. P. (2000). Science, policy and practice: Three cultures in search of a shared mission. *Child Development, 71,* 181–187.

Shonkoff, J. P., & Meisels, S. J. (Eds.) (2000). *Handbook of early childhood intervention* (2nd Ed.). New York: Cambridge University Press.

Shonkoff, J. P., & Phillips, D. A. E. (2000). *From neurons to neighborhoods: The science of early childhood development.* Washington, DC: National Academy Press.

Shumow, L., Vandell, D. L., & Posner, J. (1998). Perceptions of danger: A psychological mediator of neighborhood demographic characteristics. *American Journal of Orthopsychiatry, 68,* 468–478.

Veysey, B. M., & Messner, S. F. (1999). Further testing of social disorganization theory: An elaboration of Sampson and Groves' "community structure and crime." *Journal of Research on Delinquency, 36,* 156–174.

Weatherburn, D., & Lind, B. (2001). *Delinquent-prone communities.* Cambridge: Cambridge University Press.

Wikström, P-O. H. (1998). Communities and crime. In M. Tonry (Ed.), *The Handbook of crime and punishment* (pp. 269–301). New York: Oxford University Press.

Wikström, P-O. H., & Loeber, R. (2000). Do disadvantaged neighborhoods cause well-adjusted children to become delinquent adolescents? A study of male juvenile serious offending, individual risk and protective factors, and neighborhood context. *Criminology, 38,* 1109–1142.

Wikström, P-O. H., & Sampson, R. J. (in press). Social mechanisms of community influence on crime and pathways in criminality. In B. B. Lahey, T. R. Moffitt, & A. Caspi (Eds.), *The causes of disorder and serious juvenile delinquency.* New York: Guilford.

15

Prognosis

Policy and Process

Robert A. Hinde

To provide a commentary at the end of a volume with such exceptional contributions, a volume that will certainly be a landmark in the field, is a formidable assignment. Rather than commenting on the obvious elegance and excellence of the chapters, I shall try to comment on the volume as a whole from three perspectives – contributions to policy, to intervention, and to prevention.

Impact on Policy

The chapters have two goals, one aimed toward policy makers with the aim of guiding interventions and the other, the understanding of process to benefit clinicians. So far as policy is concerned, I suggest that these chapters may mark a high point, after which further work of this sort will bring decreasing returns in the form of policy changes. Longitudinal studies will continue to be essential for revealing sleeper and steeling effects, for consequential models, and for assessing resilience. New situations and new problems will arise, and there will be need for new studies in the future. But, given the nature of the variables used in these large-scale studies, the main conclusions are already laid out, and practically every study implies *complexity*.

All the chapters deal with an extremely complex network of inter-related mutual influences, and an important characteristic of the volume as a whole is that it recognizes complexity more clearly than much of the earlier work. There is nothing more boring than to say that life is complicated, but the fact is that any study of this sort must isolate a small set of interacting influences and proceed by ignoring the others. And it is as well to be aware of what is being omitted. Individuals are not just mothers, fathers, or children, they have their own personalities, and how individuals interact within relationships depends both on their personalities and on the relationship in which their interactions are embedded. In turn every interaction influences the

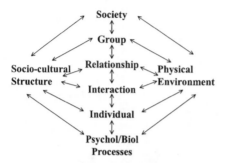

FIGURE 15.1. A simplified view of levels of social complexity.

relationship, and relationships influence, and are influenced by, the group
and society. And each of these – personalities, interactions, relationships,
groups, and societies – are influenced by, and influence, the physical environment, and the socio-cultural structure of beliefs, values, morals, and so
on (Figure 15.1). All the influences may be direct or indirect, are two-way,
and operate with different time courses. For instance, on the one hand a
single interaction can change the quality of a relationship almost instan-
taneously, and a change in the quality of a relationship brings a change
in subsequent interactions. But, on the other hand, the dialectic between
cultural values and behavior is likely to change more slowly: over the last
few decades, as divorce has become more frequent, it has become more
morally acceptable, and as it has become more acceptable, it has become
more frequent. Furthermore, the climate of values enters into every interaction, influencing, for instance, how a child of divorced parents is perceived
by the peer group and by the peers' parents. It is important to remember
that the culture and its values are not just givens, but may be reaffirmed or
changed by the dialectical and diachronic relations between what people
do and what they are supposed to do (Hinde, 1997, 2002).

Models such as that developed by Dodge et al. (Chapter 5 in this book),
quite apart from the understanding of process that they provide, are likely
to be of value in planning intervention as they indicate what is needed
and when. But there is a limit to which policy can cope with complexity.
This is neither a comment on the inherent limitations in work of the type
discussed (McCartney, Chapter 7 in this book), nor on deficiencies in the
policy makers, though, as Goodnow (Chapter 14 in this book) points out,
they may have idiosyncratic criteria for distributing funds. But how can
they formulate policies to cope with, for instance, differences in world-
views between communities and subcommunities; ethnic differences in
traditions, practices and values; the multiple influences of relationships on
relationships, and the fascinating diversity of individual differences, not
to mention the diversity of risk factors emphasized by Sameroff (Chapter 3
in this book). Sameroff emphasizes that "there are no universal treatments

applicable to all children." So one may ask: Are we not getting near to knowing enough for framing policies that will permit interventions where they are most needed and ameliorate the most urgent issues, and indeed for framing any policy that is likely to be implemented? We know that families matter, we know that it is not only the early years that are important, and we have a good appreciation of what teenagers need. To attempt to shape policies that would cope with every eventuality would require extensive legislation and an army of civil servants that would consume all available resources and leave nothing for implementation. Further studies of this type may help to convince governments that money spent on the individual development of its citizens is likely to be a profitable investment, but are they necessary to show them precisely how their resources should be invested?

Process (or Mechanism)

I suggest, therefore, that the importance of this volume lies in the pointers it provides for "lower-level" studies of process. Several papers stress the importance of marrying the present studies to analyses of mechanism or process, and some actually do so. But understanding process to an extent that will be useful in planning intervention requires more detail and more refined variables than those used in most of these studies. For instance, is resilience a unitary factor, effective against all risks? What exactly is entailed in "family support"? How does "moving home" produce its effects? What is meant by a "romantic relationship"? And what are the most useful intervening variables (e.g., self-concept, self-esteem, security)? In picking out a few of the issues that seem worth emphasizing in this way, I may be unduly influenced by my own interests, but here are some examples. They may require smaller scale studies, perhaps linked to ones of the type discussed in this volume, but using more refined variables.

Individual Differences. Several authors imply that the individual characteristics of parents and children are important: Hetherington (Chapter 9 in this book), for instance, cites evidence that an antisocial personality trait may underlie both contentious marital relations and coercive parenting, and McCartney (Chapter 7 in this book) emphasizes the importance of family values in choice of child care. Rutter (Chapter 2 in this book) cites data showing that individual differences in resilience may be brought on by genetic differences or social experience or both. He makes the important point that the influence of social experience could stem from differential parental treatment, itself the result of differences in either parents or children. But on the whole, individual differences are by-passed in these studies of large samples – inevitably so, for logistical reasons. But they constitute a clearly crucial matter for the study of process.

Gender Differences. The assessment of gender as a variable poses much less of a problem. But, although it is likely to be an important variable, it is seldom mentioned in these papers. This is surprising because we know from a wide variety of studies that close relationships are more important to girls and women than to boys and men. Young boys tend to play in groups, girls form one-to-one relationships; boys' worries center on their achievement and autonomy, girls on their relationships; women tend to want more closeness in marriage or heterosexual partnerships, men more autonomy; femininity in both partners is conducive to marital satisfaction, and so on (cf. Hinde, 1997, 2002; Amato, Chapter 8 in this book).

Some of the chapters do mention gender differences. For instance, Hetherington (Chapter 9 in this book) discussed the difference in responses to conflict and divorce in male and female partners and in the adjustment of the children; Amato (Chapter 8 in this book) showed that the father-daughter relationship was more vulnerable than the father-son; and Dunn, Fergusson, and Maughan (Chapter 12 in this book) commented on the greater closeness of children to the maternal than the paternal grandparents. Walper and Beckh (Chapter 10 in this book) found that the father-child relationship was more at risk than the mother-child after separation. Dodge et al. (Chapter 5 in this book), however, cite data showing rather small gender differences in alcohol use.

One wonders why gender was not more of a central issue. In many chapters the effects of parental discord, or of extrafamilial relationships, refer only to "children" without specifying gender, although some found the effects stronger for girls. Of course, it may be that there were no gender differences in addition to those noted, but if so, such a remarkable fact would be worth comment.

To cite one example of particular interest, Rutter (Chapter 2 in this book) reports a study showing that the risk effect from a poor parental marriage was negligible in the case of children who had a very good close relationship with an adult, and vice versa. Was this equally true for girls and boys? One is prompted to ask by the general finding, noted above, that relationships are in general more important to girls and women than to boys and men. Other studies indicate a possible mechanism. Walper and Beckh's data (Chapter 10 in this book) show that the effect of parental conflict is mediated by the felt insecurity in the parent-child relationship. And a study of 14-, 18- and 23-year-olds found that high self-esteem was associated with the ability to relate positively to others in females, but in males the sense of identity was related to their ability to control social anxiety and to function effectively (Block & Robins, 1993). So perhaps the effects of a poor parental marriage may be mediated by an effect on self-esteem, and would be larger in girls. This, of course, is speculation, and many other factors, including the age of the child, may be involved.

Properties of Interactions and of Relationships. The importance of parental discord shows clearly that the quality of the marital relationship has an impact on the children. For example, Amato (Chapter 8 in this book) found that discord as well as parental separation was an important predictor of negative effects on the child and that parental separation with little conflict could produce more negative effects than separation preceded by conflict. Walper and Beckh (Chapter 10 in this book) showed that conflict had a major effect mediated by felt insecurity in the child-parent relationship. Hetherington (Chapter 9 in this book) stressed that discordant disagreement may be much more damaging than disagreement with mutual respect and that experience of conflict may produce a positive "steeling" effect, rendering the child more capable of coping with risk factors in the future. And the quality of the environment external to the family may have vital effects on family functioning (Crouter, Chapter 6 in this book; McCartney, Chapter 7 in this book).

Collins and Roisman (Chapter 4 in this book) stress the importance of the quality of relationships in a number of contexts. Of special interest is a study that they cite showing that the perceived quality of adolescents' relationships with their parents was related to their imitation of parents' substance abuse. This could be paralleled by a study in a quite different area. Granqvist (in press) has shown in a Swedish sample that when parent and child have a secure attachment relationship, the child's religiosity is likely to resemble that of the parent, with any change being a gradual process, whereas children with an insecure relationship have no tendency to resemble their parents' religiosity, and any change is likely to be sudden.

Such studies, involving disparate areas of functioning, show that studies of the type discussed in this volume could profitably be extended to include assessments of the qualities of the relationships in question (Hinde, 1997). And it raises questions about other data reported in these papers. For instance, Dodge et al. (Chapter 5 in this book) report that parental substance abuse predicts substance use by age 12. One wonders if this was independent of the quality of the parent-child relationship?

Of course, assessing the properties of interactions and relationships, like individual characteristics, poses logistical problems with large samples. But it is clear that the quality of interaction may be more important than the total amount (e.g., Ainsworth, 1979). And the prejudice that attempts to assess quality inevitably means descent into mushy subjectivism are falsified by the data already available.

In general, the properties of both interactions and relationships may be important. The quality of interactions may be assessed in terms of intensity (Did they whisper or shout?), the verbal content and nonverbal concomitants, and the relation between the behavior of the partners ("meshing"), and so on. Of special importance among the properties of relationships are the relative proportions of different types of interactions (a facet of authoritative versus authoritarian versus indulgent parenting); the similarity versus difference between the behavior of the participants; the incidence and intensity of conflict and the power relations; the degree of self-disclosure; the accuracy and depth of interpersonal perception; the extent of the partners' commitment; and their satisfaction with the relationship. Assessing such qualities may not be feasible in large samples, but methods are available, and they are critical for a full understanding of process (for a review, Hinde 1997). Conflict, self-disclosure, commitment, and satisfaction are of special importance in marital relationships; interpersonal perception (sensitivity and understanding), in some aspects of the parent-child relationship. Perhaps most important in all relationships is trust (Goodnow, Chapter 14 in this book).

Dialectical Relations Within and Between Relationships. Extending the last point, several of these chapters point out that dyadic relationships between individuals, and relations between relationships and between contexts, are _mutual and bidirectional,_ and may be synchronic, as in Dunn et al.'s (Chapter 12 in this book) study of grandmothers, or diachronic (e.g., that of parents on peer relationships). As emphasized earlier, such mutual influences within relationships lead to complex problems, as the properties of a relationship are affected by the personalities of both partners as well as their influences on each other – not to mention extradyadic influences. This complexity is enhanced still further by influences between relationships, crucial in virtually all these chapters, and by the effects of the physical and social environments. The latter is clearly brought out in McCartney's chapter (Chapter 7 in this book) on child-care arrangements, and in Crouter's chapter (Chapter 6 in this book) on the reciprocal influences between home and work, and Goodnow (Chapter 14 in this book) implies that interactions at all levels may affect the development of individuals. The same issue appears in many other contributions. For instance, the behavior of adolescents may affect the behavior of step-parents (Hetherington, Chapter 9 in this book; Rutter, Chapter 2 in this book), and bidirectional processes are important in adolescents' relationships (Collins & Roisman, Chapter 4 in this book) and peer groups (Dodge et al., Chapter 5 in this book). Perhaps the clearest example is given by Hetherington's data (Chapter 9 in this book) on the consequences of different combinations of parental problem-solving strategies on child development. In addition, the mass of evidence provided by family systems theorists shows that relationships within families affect each other, and are also affected by extra-familial relationships.

But that is the essence of all relationships: Each party affects the other, and the properties of the relationship are a consequence of their influences on each other and of other relationships in which the individuals are involved. However, among these studies, only those by Amato (Chapter 8 in this book) and by Walper and Beckh (Chapter 10 in this book) explore the ways in which parental conflict affects children. This suggests further profitable extensions for such studies.

Perception. What matters in interpersonal relationships is not so much what the two participants are like or do, but how they perceive each other and the situation. This is mentioned by Collins and Roisman (Chapter 4 in this book), Dunn et al. (Chapter 12 in this book), Goodnow (Chapter 14 in this book), Amato (Chapter 8 in this book), Walper (Chapter 10 in this book), and, to me surprisingly, especially by Rutter (Chapter 2 in this book; perhaps age mellows!).

Though not discussed in these chapters, perception of the situation may have an important methodological effect in studies that depend on the reports of some of the subjects of the study. That maternal perceptions influence their ratings of children is well known. For example, infant temperament ratings were influenced by maternal social status, anxiety levels, and mental health status (Sameroff, Seifer & Elias, 1982). And mothers of insecurely attached preschoolers underreported their children's fearfulness in a temperament questionnaire, and overreported their security in an attachment Q-sort, as compared with direct observations of behavior (Stevenson-Hinde & Shouldice, 1995). In the latter case the maternal perceptions may be seen as reflecting the insensitivity of mothers with insecurely attached children (DeWolff & van IJzendoorn, 1997).

Are the Measures Relevant? In all these studies, fundamental decisions about the variables to be used had to be made. Several studies used IQ, but Dodge et al. (Chapter 5 in this book) found that social adjustment was a better predictor of later drug use than academic performance. And Tizard and Hodges (1978) demonstrated the importance of distinguishing between sociability and the ability to form relationships.

Morality and Values. These are issues too often regarded as outside the province of developmentalists. But their importance is clearly implied in some of the studies. The very term "deviant peer group" implies not a group without values, but one with a value system differing from that of the society as a whole. Religious affiliation and religiosity are mentioned, but neither are entirely satisfactory for understanding the dynamics of family relationships in a heterogeneous population, and a more direct approach to values is needed. For instance, parenting is influenced by both the parent's values and their perceptions of the values of the society in which they expect their child to grow up. The concept of an "ideal family" is dismissed by the heterogeneity of the relationships studied here, but the relation between family values and those of the society at large is important for the developing child. And, as stressed earlier, values change.

Nothing in the preceding paragraphs is intended to be critical of the highly sophisticated and elegant studies reported in this volume. The point being made is that large samples inevitably constrain the subtlety of the variables assessed. For intervention to be economic and effective, finer grained measures are needed, and this may mean linking large-scale studies to ones of smaller scale. Furthermore, economy may be achieved with procedures that assess fairly global properties of relationships, such as assessment of the attachment parent-child relationship (Main, 1995, in press).

Prevention

Most of the preceding discussion refers to interventions where things have already gone wrong, or where there is a high element of risk. But it would clearly be better if the causes of malfunction could be eliminated or at least reduced in the society as a whole. Perhaps the most startling things in these chapters are the data cited by Sameroff (Chapter 3 in this book) for the incidence of diagnosable disorders, suicide attempts, aggression, and academic underperformance. Although the figures for the United States may be at the high end for western countries, many others are in a similar situation.

Surely these figures mean that we live in societies that are really *sick*? Something must be radically wrong with our cultures. Given that this is the case, as well as intervening with vulnerable groups, should we not give thought to how we can make more fundamental changes? Sameroff's demonstration that the number of risk factors is a vital matter can be interpreted as pointing to the need for a more global approach. Now I am well aware that it is dangerous for a nonspecialist to start pontificating here, but change will not come from silence. While there are some things that policy cannot affect, it would seem that improved educational programs and the combination of a more equitable distribution of wealth coupled with some other societal adjustments, would go a long way. As Rutter (Chapter 2 in this book) pointed out, enormous improvements in physical health have been brought about by changes in society not aimed at specific diseases. The two issues proposed might be the equivalent for psychological well-being.

Improved education, especially education for women, is likely to ameliorate a considerable number of risk factors – for instance large family size, young motherhood, and aspects of family processes involving especially parental attitudinal rigidity and a lack of positive mother-child interaction. Perhaps an even more important influence of educational changes might be an influence on moral norms, including greater sensitivity to and intolerance of violent acts.

Evidence from both agricultural and industrial societies shows that the incidence of interpersonal violence is strongly linked to unequal distribution of wealth, the inequality probably being as important as poverty itself. Reduction in inequalities thus requires more drastic changes than the mere alleviation of poverty. Quite a number of other risk factors might well be ameliorated at the same time – for instance, paternal criminality and the problems associated with low parental occupational status and with minority status.

To put that in the context of the scheme I used earlier, wealth differentials affect the peer group and the parent-child relationship, the two latter affecting and being affected by the child's behavior and developing personality. Cultural values affect and are affected by wealth differentials and, in the longer term, parent-child relationships and children's behavior. Education could affect cultural values, parent-child relationships, and child behavior.

Other factors associated with interpersonal violence are institutionalized state violence (e.g., capital punishment and militarism), and the availability of firearms. In addition, certain societal features are conducive to low levels of violence: informal control with highly consensual norms; networks of mutual interdependence and mutual obligations; and institutions that cut across ascribed groupings (Gartner, 1997). In this context, the recent emphasis on the importance of "social capital" should be noted (e.g., Coleman, 1990). There is a need to manage the community as well as the family.

All of these are societal issues requiring not just interventions in situations of vulnerability, but more radical changes in society which might be slower to enact but more effective in the long run. Of note, both educational deficiencies and wealth differentials are implicated in the nexus of factors that make war more likely (Hinde & Rotblat, 2003).

References

Ainsworth, M. D. S. (1979). Attachment as related to mother-infant interaction. *Advances in the Study of Behavior, 9*, 2–52.

Block, J., & Robins, R. W. (1993). A longitudinal study of consistency and change in self-esteem from early adolescence to early adulthood. *Child Development, 64*, 903–23.

Coleman, J. S. (1990). *Foundations of social theory.* Cambridge, MA: Harvard University Press.

DeWolff, M. S., & van IJzendoorn, M. H. (1997). Sensitivity and attachment: A meta-analysis on parental antecedents of infant attachment. *Child Development, 68*, 571–91.

Gartner, R. (1997). Cross-cultural aspects of violence. In Grisolia et al. (Eds.) *Violence: From biology to society,* (pp. 171–80). Amsterdam: Elsevier.

Granqvist, P. (in press). Attachment theory and religious conversions: A review, and a resolution of the classic and contemporary paradigm chasm. *Review of Religious Research.*

Hinde, R. A. (1997). *Relationships: A dialectical perspective*. Hove: Psychology Press.

Hinde, R. A. (2002). *Why good is good*. London: Routledge.

Hinde R. A., & Rotblat, J. (2003). *War no more*. London: Pluto.

Main, M. (1995). Recent studies in attachment: overview, with implications for clinical work. In S. Goldberg, R. Muir & J. Kerr (eds.) *Attachment theory: Social developmental and clinical perspectives*. Hillsdale, NJ: Academic Press.

Main, M. (in press). The adult attachment interview: Fear, attention, safety and discourse processes. *Journal of the American Psychoanalytic Association*.

Sameroff, A. J., Seifer, R., & Elias, P. K. (1982). Sociocultural variability in infant temperament ratings. *Child Development, 53*, 164–75.

Stevenson-Hinde, J., & Shouldice, A. (1995). Maternal interactions and self-reports related to attachment classifications at 4.5 years. *Child Development, 66*, 583–96.

Tizard, B., & Hodges. J. (1978). The effect of early institutional rearing on the development of 8-year-old children. *Journal of Child Psychology and Psychiatry, 19*, 99–118.

Index